# Messianism, Apocalypse and Redemption in 20th Century German Thought

Edited by

Wayne Cristaudo

and

Wendy Baker

ATF Press
Adelaide

First published 2006

National Library of Australia
Cataloguing-in-Publication data

Messianism, apocalypse and redemption in twentieth century German thought.

Includes index.
ISBN 1 920691 40 5

1. Philosophy, German – 20th century. 2. Theology – Germany. 3 Messianism – Germany. 4 Redemption. I. Cristaudo, Wayne, 1954- . II. Baker, Wendy, 1951- .

193

Published by
ATF Press
An imprint of the Australasian Theological Forum
P O Box 504
Hindmarsh
SA 5007
www.atfpress.com

Cover design by Openbook Print, Adelaide, Australia

# Acknowledgments

With thanks to all those who have participated and helped along the way, especially to Mike Pietsch, Lutheran chaplain at the University of Adelaide, who has been with the project all the way through. Thanks also to the University of Adelaide. We have been encouraged and gratefully supported by Hilary Regan from ATF Press.

# Contents

# Introduction

Shortly before his death, one of France's most influential political writers, André Malraux made the prophecy that the twentieth century would be 'religious or it will not be at all'. The phrase resonated with Kierkegaard's observation of 1848 that 'what looks like politics and imagines itself to be politics, one day will show itself to be a religious movement'. When Malraux made his remark the French intellectual scene was driven by psychoanalysis, structuralism and post-structuralism. And like the dominant strand of existentialism that had ruled the mid-century, they seemed to have more in common with the overtly atheistic movements of surrealism, fascism and communism. However, by the end of the century, with the rise to prominence of Levinas's religious ethic and Derrida's later thought taking an increasingly theological concern, Malraux's insight seemed highly apposite. What Malraux saw from the perspective of France was even more true of Germany. For in Germany, at least up until World War II, philosophy was as steeped in theology as theology was in philosophy. It is no overstatement to say that it is impossible to grasp twentieth century German thought without addressing the theological elements which gave it its peculiar complex of concerns and solutions.

In the early part of the twentieth century France's intellectual tradition had been largely shaped by a polarisation between anti-clerical (the majority) and Catholic (the minority) intellectuals; so much so that even its brand of fascism had Catholic nationalist tributaries that bore little relationship to the intellectual currents that flowed into National Socialism. In England, the empiricist spirit quietly took its hold upon philosophy in such a way that the 'Death of God' seemed a very quiet affair indeed, at least after the initial ructions caused by Darwin's scandalous application of principles of naturalism, that had long since eliminated anything special about human beings in the field of physics, to biology. Perhaps nothing so remarkably demonstrates the difference between England and Germany than the comparison between Darwin and Nietzsche. Darwin quietly sloughs off his religious faith like some old garment as he sees the continuity between life forms contributing to a greater natural harmony. In Darwin there is the potentially socially enflaming idea of the turbulent struggle of nature as well as the disturbing social engineer's belief that certain people should not be allowed to breed. But the delivery is so matter of fact that, in comparison with the racially motivated theories of Gobineau in France and anti-Semitic movements in Germany, it is rather innocuous. Nietzsche, on the other hand, calls himself the most terrible human being who has ever lived, announces God's death, screeches his hatred of Christianity, calls for the surgical excision of the weak so that the strong can become supermen, and writes in his notebook that one must have the strength to accept that millions must perish so that the new dawn may come. Concomitantly, Nietzsche sees Darwin's theory as completely in keeping with the survival of the weakest, who are the most numerous and who hunt down and destroy the strong.

It is of great significance to twentieth century German thought that it was the home for the two most revolutionary and inflammatory thinkers of the nineteenth century. And as opposed as Marx and Nietzsche are politically, both are eschatological thinkers who have weighed the incipient bourgeois world in the scales of their respective visions of the future and found it worthy of damnation. While German theology pottered with lives of Jesus, Marx and Nietzsche cried to the living of subsequent generations to redeem the world from its tyranny of the few over the many (Marx), of the many over the few (Nietzsche).

For the young Marx, the dissolution of religion into philosophy provided the basis for the identification of the social and political solution, which was to be actualised by the triumphant proletariat.[1] Marx's redemptive reading of history (until now, he says in the Preface to a *Contribution to a Critique of Political Economy*, there has only been pre-history but with communism history proper—where all the capacities of our species-being can be collectively developed—will begin) can be seen as a transposition of Judaic-Christian messianism into the here and now with the collectivity of the proletariat taking on the role of the singular Christ as the universal redeemer, and the defeated bourgeoisie taking the role of the demonic impediment of God's love. The break down of capitalism, due to the falling rate of profit and the periodic crisis embedded in the contradiction between

1.  In a letter to Arnold Ruge, September 1843, Marx writes: 'Like Feuerbach's critique of religion, our whole aim can only be to translate religious and political problems into their self-conscious human form.' Karl Marx, *Early Writings*, introduction Lucio Colletti, translated by Rodney Livingstone and Gregor Benton (London: Penguin, 1975), 209.

the real source of value (labour power) and the drive to increase labour displacing technology (relative surplus value) leads to the inevitable apocalypse and last judgment that is the proletariat revolution. Perhaps, surprisingly, it is the Jewish Karl Marx, as opposed to the son of the Lutheran pastor, Nietzsche, whose messianic tale bears the hallmarks of the Christian understanding of the Messiah as providential (historically necessary).

Nietzsche's eschatology breaks with the Christian sense of historical continuity and providential inevitability, making the moment of salvation an unexpected possibility that may come at any time. But it would be a gross oversimplification to read Nietzsche's elitist eschatology as either Christian or Jewish. His desire to scout out all residues of the Platonic/ Christian God (which he rather dubiously equates) is bound up with his resuscitation of the pagan god, Dionysus. Twentieth century North Americans readings of Nietzsche have largely underscored Nietzsche's opposition to German pan-nationalism and his hostility to anti-Semitism in order to accentuate the distance between him and National Socialism, while French readings continued in the surrealist appropriations of Nietzsche which found in him a source of inspiration in their attack upon their own rationalistic and scientistic traditions which they held responsible for World War I. But he was also a source of the totalising (pseudo-) scientistic doctrines of race behind Nazism and the administrative capacities that facilitated the death camps. The German reading of Nietzsche, on the other hand (including National Socialist enthusiasts like Rosenberg and Bäumler) has mainly, until relatively recently, emphasised the continuity between Nietzschean neo-paganism and Nazism—something that is evident, for example, in Habermas' reluctance to embrace Nietzsche with the enthusiasm of his French contemporaries.

If Marx and Nietzsche are the two great currents of the nineteenth century feeding into German twentieth century thought, World War I (as in France) is the event that forces a re-configuration of all Germany's past intellectual resources. What at first seems most strange is the revival of theological interest in a generation who heard the voices of Nietzsche and Marx, but who no longer accepted the liberal rationalism of the German Enlightenment which had dominated nineteenth century German theology. Many sought to tap deeper into the religious potencies of the past, whether pagan, Judaic or Christian. Indeed it is this peculiar configuration of post-Nietzscheanism, pagan and Judaic and/ or Christian currents and Marxism (though not playing a role in some circles) that gives German thought its peculiar character in the first part of the twentieth century. Even in a figure like Heidegger—who joined the National Socialists and who turned wholeheartedly against Christianity (not to mention, in spite of his unconvincing protestations to the contrary, compromising so easily with the anti-Semites) and who was firmly anti-Marxist—we see a thinker who, prior to *Being and Time*, steeps himself in St. Augustine, becomes a major influence upon Christian theology (largely through Rudolph Bultmann) and finds himself appropriated by Marxists (such as Herbert Marcuse and the Yugoslav praxis school). Heidegger, Nietzsche and Marx then become the triumvirate forming the template for French post-structuralist/ postmodernist thought of the 1960s and 70s.

Heidegger's apocalyptic strain in *Being and Time* is, as his own subsequent historical resolve demonstrated all too clearly, linked to the messianic hope that had been so widely swelling within Germany after World War I. As Karl Jaspers lamented, and as Heidegger's posthumously published interview of 1966 with *Der Spiegel* showed, Heidegger remained convinced that our liberal democratic and economic structures, which were themselves but further metaphysical triumphs of beings over Being and had given the West its terrible fatality, could only be overturned by an apocalyptic event. We were, said Heidegger, living in a time of waiting for the new god—and only a new god, could save us now.

If Heidegger's tones were apocalyptic and messianic, they were so in the Nietzschean sense of a longing for 'redemption from the redeemer', redem-ption from that hybrid of Christianity/ Platonism which had shaped the West. The same cry, albeit expressed in far less philosophical nuances and conceptual fineness, could also be heard coming from the populist vitalistic philosophy of the now almost forgotten Ludwig Klages. Like Heidegger and Nietzsche, he saw humanity as having a great fall due to the imposition of a rational culture. The details differed: Klages saw the fall as having occurred far earlier. It is not just the pre-Socratics, but the Minoans and Pelasgians of the Neolithic and Bronze ages who Klages sees as having truly and vitally lived. His ideal of a humanity unburdened by labour and consciousness, a people whose freedom of soul has not been handicapped by the weight of *Geist* (mind and spirit) and the commands of technology, like Nietzsche's, was based upon an unimpeded immersion in the eternal flow and flux of the instinctual life.

A very different response to the times, yet no less symptomatic, was the conscious reappropriation of Judaism. Here was a messianism that was unencumbered by Christian and pagan perversions: the former which was corrupted by the idolatrous belief that the Messiah had already come once and the latter corrupted by a kind of pseudo-redemption which really never leaves the plane of creation and is blind and deaf to revelation and hence fails to fathom redemption. This was the stance taken by Franz Rosenzweig whose voice was to spread in Germany to Scholem, Benjamin and Leo Strauss (most paradoxically in terms of his own teaching), and in France to Levinas and Derrida. Rosenzweig's initial Hegelianism was challenged by his teacher and friend, Eugen Rosenstock. That challenge resulted to the philosophical attack upon totalism, which is possibly the defining philosophical gesture of the twentieth century. Rosenzweig's attack upon the metaphysical arc that spans from Parmenides to Hegel has parallels in the Frankfurt school, post-structuralism and the ethics of Levinas. In Rozenweig's case, the totalism against which he reacts has its socio-religious correlation in the universalism of Christianity—a universalism that simultaneously brings the world into ever greater union via its being a religion of conversion governed by the (Jewish) commandment of neighbourly love and perpetual hatred of the Jew. He provided a philosophical clearing for German liberal Jews to re-embrace their heritage, as he simultaneously demonstrated the limits and dead ends of philosophy as a practice.

As well as taking his methodological direction from Rosenstock's insight that speech is the true wellspring of our being, Rosenzweig also drew inspiration from another of his teachers, Hermann Cohen, the father of Marburg neo-Kantianism. Late in life, Cohen became increasingly attuned to the ethical and religious truth he found in his Jewish heritage and he sought to marry philosophy and Judaism. Rosenzweig's friend and collaborator on the translation of the Jewish Bible into German, Martin Buber, also emphasised the dialogical basis of truth and the dialogical roots of the Jewish religious experience and its redemptive, revelatory and messianic dimensions which could not adequately be refuted by, nor absorbed in, secular forms. Neither the Zionist, Buber, nor, the non-Zionist, Rosenzweig, accepted that the essentially pagan form of the state (and hence politics) could provide the salvation that was so deeply desired in the human heart. To this extent, they stood in much greater proximity to theologians, even Christian ones, than to Jewish Marxists such as Adorno and Benjamin.

Adorno and Benjamin saw that the attempt to return liberal Jews to their faith and unify them in their tradition was not really the issue at hand. Both saw in the method of historical materialism the true key to understanding their contemporary social circumstance. Both also saw that Marxism continued in the tradition of the great refusal to compromise with a world steeped in barbarousness and its bloody history. Marxism, rather than orthodox Judaism, had become the historical conduit of the messianic. But neither abandoned the Judaic hope in a better world to come, which would be free of those conditions which routinise and justify the oppression of one's neighbour. In Adorno's case that affirmation of the possible and the negative, over the murderousness of the real, carries the spectre of a Kantian moralism. That moralism, however, is divested from its formalism and invested with a content socially adumbrated by Marx. To be worthy of entrance to the kingdom, though, human beings must be freed from the mind-numbing rhythms, visual patternings and empty verbiage that are the product of the culture industry and bourgeois society.

In Benjamin's case, an emphasis is placed upon the redemption of those victims crushed by 'historical progress'. Benjamin harkens to the wails of the dead who demand to have justice on judgment day. Neither Benjamin nor Adorno can be classified as completely orthodox in their Marxism and certainly they, quite consciously, bequeath to Marxism a religious spirit and depth of philosophical nuance that make Marx's own musings on philosophy and religion look shallow by comparison.

More orthodox (that is, more frequently overtly Stalinist) in his Marxism, though definitely no less theologically charged, is Ernst Bloch. For him, humankind has permanently lived in the space of possibility. In spite of the constant defeats and the resistance of the real, our true humanity lies in this very longing for the beyond that is the future that we strive and hope for here on earth: that is 'the spirit of utopia'. To this end Bloch takes his readers on an excursus through 'the cries to heaven' of political activists, like Thomas Müntzer, whose social emancipatory struggles are articulated through the religious symbols he has inherited. Bloch understood, again much more so than Marx or Engels (who also admired Müntzer), that humanity's deepest needs cannot be so swiftly severed from the symbolic forms which are used to express them. Bloch searches the past for its symbols of hope in his attempt to reintegrate humanity as a whole, albeit from the perspective of one cleansed and redeemed from those who stop it being what it is entitled to be.

If the tropes of messianism, apocalypse and redemption find themselves continually reworked in early twentieth century German thought, there were also those who saw that this messianic longing was a dangerous matter. Krackauer, for example, was as suspicious of Rosenzweig's project as he was of any deployment of such archaic tropes for political action. Eric Voegelin, the Austrian political scientist who fled to America after the *Anschluss*, argued that the transposition of religious symbols onto the mundane has been an enormous disaster of the West. What had facilitated, in Christianity and Platonism, our fathoming of historical and social order through the accen-tuation of 'the in-between-ness' of the human circumstance—as opposed to what belonged in the beyond—has become a justification of mass murder when deployed as a form of historical 'gnosis'. For Voegelin, National Socialism and communism (as well as reformist liberalism) were essentially religious deformations and the marriage of philosophy and theology within Germany was largely a disaster. Like Voegelin, Leo Strauss is hostile to the entreatment of heaven that characterise those like Bloch, Adorno and Benjamin, even going as far as to insist that Plato's *Republic* is fundamentally misread if interpreted as a utopian work. It would not be going too far to say that Strauss' defence of the truth and the classical tradition of political philosophy is directed at all false messianic movements which cannot but have (humanly created) apocalyptic consequences.

The extent of the messianic longing in Germany—that is, of the German refusal to accept a purely secular range of symbols and tropes—is also conspicuous in artistic movements of the time. Perhaps the most outlandish is the George circle in which Stefan George had made of himself the new messiah. For George and his followers art itself was the redeemer. His circle could be transported, through their participation in the ceremonies which George, as divinely inspired artist, conducted into the ecstatic states of the divine. George represents a degenerate form of Romanticism in an age longing for redemption, and to later generations the whole affair looks as silly and childish as the Dadaist claims that they would build the world anew by their unruly behaviour in theatres and galleries. His messianic reign was necessarily short lived in an age which failed to find satiety in art and which demanded that the messiah be a man of political action who, in the act of saving culture, will demand the elimination of artists who do not conform to the nation's political will. (Of course this was equally true of the communists who applauded Stalin's show trials and his aesthetic tyranny.)

Also short lived, but equally significant for its day, was the attempt to integrate Christian symbols in painting and drama by that group of German artists ascribing to the tenets of expressionism. In his 'Two Pictures' the painter Franz Marc had discerned that a new religion was rising in Germany and the new art was to be its spearhead. Christian redemptive and apocalyptic symbols were also deployed by the new artists not always as a joke or object of mockery (as was the case in French surrealism), but as, in say Max Beckman's 'Descent from the Cross', as the expression of the shared suffering of a people hoping for redemption. Expressionist drama also worked with heavy-handed Christian symbolism before both dramatists and public grew weary of the symbols which, having vitalised art throughout Christendom for so long, had been increasingly severed from the institutions which had infused them with significance. Perhaps the most enduring artist of this period is Franz Kafka whose very name has come to symbolise the alienating experiences of exile and modernity. He uses the tradition of the Kabbalah, more than its actual symbolism, to render within the catastrophe of creation a waiting, a kind of hope and possible redemption.

If the first half of the twentieth century in Germany had demonstrated the resilience of religious tropes and symbols for philosopher and artists, it is equally true to say that there was a growing awareness that the traditional version of the Church may have been spent. The sociologist, and sometimes theologian, Eugen Rosenstock—whose corpus is devoted to demonstrating the existential truth and ongoing historical relevance embedded in Christian rituals and institutions—saw Christianity as something that had to be practiced 'incognito'. Dietrich Bonhoeffer spoke of a future religion-less Christianity, and Karl Rahner of 'anonymous Christianity'. Such formulations would (in spite of Rahner's Catholicism) seem to be but the final step in the path opened by the Reformation: not atheism as such (which is one of the modern's possible paths) but the absorption of the religious into the capillaries of everyday life to the extent that no place as such (as opposed to everyplace) is the privileged repository of the spirit. But it is equally true that twentieth century theology was vitalised through its crises. For Karl Barth, the crises of the twentieth century had the effect of showing him the pure truth of the life of Christ which provided the yardstick from which we could see the gap between what is demanded of us and what we have done. Above all, twentieth century German theologians had re-embraced the eschatology that the nineteenth century had abandoned. In this respect, they had joined up with the philosophers. Perhaps Mol-tmann's use of Bloch is a perfect example of the new twist that occurred: philosopher borrows from theology and is deployed by theologian. In some cases, as in Paul Tillich and Wolfhart Pannenberg, the line between philosophy and theology is very hard to discern indeed.

Significantly, the great fusion of philosophy and theology in Germany during the first part of the twentieth century was not repeated after World War II. A possible third apocalypse was too much. So many of Germany's leading thinkers had sullied themselves through connection with Nazism or Stalinism that the messianic longing itself became suspect. This was the sober position of Hans Blumenberg, one of Germany's post World War II philosophers, who argued that one of modernity's great benefits was that it offered people an alternative to the religious longings that had created so much damage. Adorno's student Jürgen Habermas's stark moralistic mode of Marxism, shorn of any messianic traces, is another example of the new German reluctance to fuse politics with philosophy and religion.

Just as significantly, and as was suggested at the start of this introduction, the tropes of messianism have risen to prominence in French philosophy, and it is no accident that there has been an increasing philosophical interest there, as well as Italy, in religion and theology. Those like Voegelin have made a powerful case for the dangers of the transposition of religious symbols onto the plane of the mundane, and it is very understandable that theologians are divided about the value of philosophy deploying religious tropes (for some an exercise in idolatry; for others, an indication of the divine presence in the human mind). It is also true that philosophy and theology in Germany in the first half of the twentieth century remain incredibly rich streams, initiating and feeding into the increasingly urgent dialogues of today.

# Part One

# Apocalyptic and Messianism in Twentieth Century German Theology

## Robert W Jenson

In theology, the nineteenth century lapped over into the following two decades; the twentieth century, as a theological history with a certain specific identity, began just after World War 1. The dominant theology of the chronological century's first twenty years was still the liberal theology of the nineteenth century—indeed its last brilliant efflorescence with Troeltsch, von Harnack and Herrmann. The twentieth century's German theological beginning can be dated by the publication of one book: Karl Barth's commentary on Paul the Apostle, *The Epistle to the Romans*, whose two main editions nicely bracketed 1920. Even those who abominated the book had to respond to it. Whether the twentieth century has yet ended, in Germany or elsewhere, is hard to say—which suggests that it has not.

This book is not just on German thought in a certain period. It has a theme: apocalyptic, messianism and—what for theology is more or less the same thing—redemption. And in those pre-war and wartime decades of the chronological century, apocalyptic moods and, in a loose sense, messianic and redemptive movements were of course very much afoot in philosophy and the arts, to say nothing of politics.

Nietzsche, the author of the twentieth century's book of revelation, *Thus Spoke Zarathustra*, died in 1900. That year was the very hinge of artistic and other movements throughout Europe, all bent on deconstructing the bourgeois grasp of reality, and trusting the collapse itself to reveal a new—something. In 1900 Picasso made his famous trip to Paris, where the heavens opened to him and Cezanne was in the middle of his *Bathers* series, which were at least as subversive as Picasso's deconstructions. Moving to Germany, Edvard Munch exhibited his *Love and Death* paintings in the Berlin Secession of 1902, infuriating the establishment and reigniting German expressionism. Arthur Schoenberg composed 'Transfigured Night' in 1899, and the first truly atonal composition in 1909. At the end of the war, Walter Gropius, who was to be founder of the Bauhaus, spoke for a generation of artists and thinkers of all sorts when he proclaimed: 'A world has been destroyed; we must seek a radical solution.' In 1917 Lenin triumphed in Russia, and in 1919 Communists and right-wing *Freikorps* (we would now say paramilitaries) fought in the streets of Berlin. But official *theology* was, in those first two decades, not yet much given to revolutionary or apocalyptic moods.

One specific legacy of liberalism was decisive for the way the story would in fact unfold. A necessary historical condition of the way things actually went was theological liberalism's structural anti-Judaism—which infected also many who thought of themselves as conservative or confessional.

The heart of so-called 'liberal theology' was historical-critical study of Scripture: crudely put, one is saved by association with Jesus and one associates with him in the same way as with any historical figure, by seeking him behind the literary relics. It is generally understood that exegetical use of historical-critical methods was theologically driven by the intention to free Christianity from the burden of Paulinism and churchly dogma. It is perhaps not quite so often appreciated that liberal historical-critical study was equally driven by intention to free Christianity from the burden of sharing Scriptures with Judaism. As it was in fact done, historical-critical study turned the Old Testament into a collection of artifacts from a vanished culture, perhaps useful as background for the New Testament but hardly authoritative. It crystallised Jesus himself from the also lamentably Jewish Gospels as a guru who could have appeared anywhere. When Albert Schweitzer observed that the various pictures of 'the historical Jesus' remarkably resembled each their delineator, he might also have observed that none looked very Jewish. Von Harnack spoke for all his liberal colleagues when he castigated the church for its 'backwardness that is unable to free itself from the Old Testament'. Two consequences of liberation from the Old Testament, and so of the church's connection to Judaism, must be noted.

Firstly, a theological establishment bent on severing the church's connection to Judaism, by effectively excising the shared Scripture, is not in the best position to resist pagan anti-Semitism when it appears. Secondly, and more important for our immediate purposes, the apocalyptic vocabulary and logic of the New Testament are severed from their determinate content, which is told in the Old Testament. They become, as it were, free-floating and liable either to make a

rhetoric of crisis as such, or to be filled out from whatever epoch or
ideology effectively takes the place of the Old Testament. What, for a
central example, is the New Testament's 'Kingdom of Heaven', if we
are not to turn to the Old Testament and find that it is the coming of all
nations to Zion, and the universal peace thereby established? It can
then be 'the kingdom of moral ends', or it can be the triumph of
socialism, or it can be the moment with no content at all—or it can be a
thousand-year empire of the Nordic races.

*[margin handwritten note: OT grounds apocalypse— tells what is coming exactly]*

## I

With Barth's *The Epistle to the Romans*, in the 1922 edition that made the
great sensation, together with essays grouped around it, the
theological twentieth century began with a bang. A theological *persona*
invaded the scene that was apocalyptic enough in itself, and brought
with it Feuerbach and Nietzsche (in the form of his disciple Overbeck),
a little bit of Marx and sundry rebellious Christian movements from
decidedly below the liberal salt. To this day, there is no reading like
Barth's *The Epistle to the Romans* for exciting a seminar of intelligent and
rebellious late adolescents who are interested in religion. Here indeed
was a theology animated by an apocalyptic sensibility—a theology that
baffled and angered that last generation of integral liberalism who had
been Barth's admiring teachers. Moreover, Barth's commentary
established the *sort* of apocalypticism that would characterise much of
the century's theology. Everything that followed in the train of *The
Epistle to the Romans*, and much theology done in opposition to it,
shared a very specific way of appropriating the Bible's apocalyptic
rhetoric and logic.

It became a slogan: 'Christianity that is not altogether eschatology
is no Christianity', which could just as well have been: 'Christianity
that is not altogether apocalyptic is no Christianity'. For what shaped
the logic and rhetoric of *The Epistle of the Romans* and of what would be
called 'dialectical' or 'crisis' theology, was not the eschatology of, say,
Amos; it was the eschatology of parts of Daniel or some chapters of
Ezekiel, and of the intertestamental apocalyptic writings—the radical
sense of a *termination* of history, as we now experience it, and of the
coming, precisely in this termination, of something utterly different.

In Barth's commentary history, whether humanity's history or an
individual history, is unpredictably crossed by the 'line of death'. We
are on our way—and we are stopped. And *that* we are stopped is all

that can be said. Death is of course and proverbially the one certain and just so uncertain future. This radical futurity of death can draw a line of death across life in time at any moment and it is the function of the church's proclamation to point to that line in any present moment. My life is brought to a halt, whenever and however; and no more can be said. Nor does the line of death afford a glimpse of new life on the other side of the line; the apocalyptic age to come does not reveal itself except by not revealing itself.

As is always noted in essays on this book, Barth provided an interpretive image in the preface to the second printing of the second edition. Time, he proposed, is like a circle and eternity like a tangent line; probably he should, for greater clarity, have said time is a cylinder and eternity a tangent plane. Inhabitants of the cylinder's surface, moving around it, will be stopped when they encounter the line of tangency; but since a line of tangency has no extension on either the cylinder or the plane, they will perceive nothing but the sheer fact of being stopped.

The apocalyptic of *The Epistle to the Romans* is a powerful vision, or non-vision, and dwelling with it can release a torrent of both energy and cerebration. But it obviously abstracts to just one moment of the apocalyptic logic that indeed underlies the apostle Paul's letter to the Romans. For in the actual apocalyptic writings of Scripture and its milieu and in the New Testament theology created on their template, when the End comes a new heaven and earth are created on the other side. And when this death and resurrection cast their line in advance, the new world and the life in it are 'uncovered'; they are seen and heard and can be *narrated*, with whatever imagery the vision provides. In the Bible, the plane of eternity is *reflected* on the cylinder of time as a line of death with *thickness*, an interruption of our story whose new story can be *told*.

We may ask what it is in Barth's commentary that shrinks death and resurrection to an extensionless, existential point on the time line. Diagnosis is not difficult. This apocalyptic of the existential moment is but a late instance of many instances where pagan antiquity's way of relating time and eternity has misshaped Christian theology. If one defines eternity as the *absence* of time (as the ancients generally did), if indeed one defines time and eternity as logical contradictories, so that everything is either temporal or eternal and nothing can be both except in myth, then, for central example, the obviously mortal Jesus just cannot be 'of one being with the Father'. It took the church nearly three centuries to find the nerve to say that nevertheless he is. So in the present case, since time and eternity are contradictories, there can be no extension in eternity of an event in time and there can be no extended event in time that is a meeting with eternity. It is the peculiar relation of Barth's apocalypticism to actual apocalyptic that is both the genius and the disaster of the book and much else.

There is an undeniable correspondence of this theology's emergence with the crisis of political and economic liberalism in Germany —and of course elsewhere. The story of young Barth in his parish of Safenwil remains paradigmatic. He had to preach, from texts he did not select himself, and which the relentlessly straightforward young man could not simply read around. As he struggled with the Bible, a 'strange new world', as he put it in another famous saying, opened to him, just as to every apocalyptic seer. He tried to think what he had to say to his working-class parishioners, and had to conclude that the bourgeois religion he had been trained to cultivate had nothing for them; that his pastoral responsibility carried him outside the world construed by liberalism. And from over the border, he watched liberal Europe disclose its inner, and indeed constituting, violence.

*The Epistle to the Romans* made Barth a sudden celebrity, and his celebrity gathered (as was wont to happen in Germany) a *Kreis*, a circle, a movement of the like-minded. There was Barth, there was Rudolf Bultmann as a sort of approving uncle, there were Emil Brunner and Friedrich Gorgarten, there was Barth's lifelong preacher ally, Edward Thurneysen, and there were others. Since they were Germans, they naturally published a journal—*Zwischen den Zeiten* (*Between the Times*) whose very name tells you what united them. For what is there *zwischen den Zeiten*, between the times? Theologically, there is that dimensionless perch between time and eternity, between death and resurrection. Culturally, there is the breathless moment between deconstruction of the established grasp of reality and the gift of a new one—the moment of Cezanne's *Bathers*. Politically, there is revolution. And in Germany all of these were there at once. The circle around *Zwischen den Zeiten* held together only ten years. The group agreed: there is a crisis, the old centre cannot hold. Having said that, what do you say next? Faced with that question, they found they could no longer speak together.

Many of the old comrades remained more faithful to the line of *The Epistle to the Romans* than did its author. Most notably faithful was Rudolf Bultmann. The whole famous program of 'existential interpretation' and demythologizing is simply a consistent carrying-out of the sort of apocalypticism contained within Barth's commentary. When the word of the cross sounds in my ears, when I hear of death as gift, when I hear that someone died for me, then my life stops. And this moment, exactly as in *The Epistle to the Romans*, has no extension: what Bultmann means by 'myth' is any attempt to give the moment of revelation temporal extension by narrating it, even by saying *who* died for me. The Cross is salvific precisely for the reason given by Barth: the moment of death interrupts my time without itself occupying any part of that time. In the salvific word of that Cross—'One has died for you'—narrative is in fact replaced by a timeless doctrine, by the Lutheran doctrine of justification without works.

It may be thought that Bultmann's disciples corrected him here; after all, they even launched a 'new quest' for the historical Jesus. But they recouped the narrative of Jesus in a particular way: what happened with the Jesus-event was that faith 'came to word', and if we look at Ebeling's or Fuch's analyses of the word that calls for faith and of 'faith' itself, we find the same temporally contentless event, the same substitution of 'only believe' for 'He is risen'.

## II

I have just mentioned Lutheranism. One cannot speak of twentieth century German theology—whether Catholic, Reformed or Lutheran—without speaking of Martin Luther. In the present context, we must note that a major part of twentieth century German theology took place as Luther-research, *Lutherforschung*. The Luther-scholars were for the most part embarrassed by Luther's actual apocalyptic expectations, and passed over their significance for him—every great man, they said, has his peculiarities. Great effort, however, was expended in bringing Luther in line with the specific kind of apocalypticism we have just been considering. In particular, one of Bultmann's disciples, Gerhard Ebeling, created an interpretation of Luther as a sort of precursor of Bultmannian 'existential interpretation', which dominated Luther-reception in Germany and the United States for decades. Ebeling made Luther's distinction of law and gospel into a general hermeneutic, indeed a hermeneutic of being:

the law kills the project of the one who hears it—in the apocalyptic rhetoric of this exposition, it kills the hearer; the gospel gives new life; and there is no temporal space between these two events. Nor indeed does the new life occupy time, since immediately the law comes again. And precisely in this unextended moment, God and faith 'come to word'.

Friedrich Gogarten's word for that moment that interrupts history, without establishing itself in history, was 'crisis'. And because the moment is without content of its own, because the crisis is, so to speak, crisis sheerly as such, it can be analogously identified with whatever crisis we think is at the moment going on around us—thereby, after all, achieving something like temporal reality. For Gogarten, the crisis at hand was the crisis of German culture and civilization as perceived by so many at the time, and, for a time, he too found in National Socialism a *persona* apocalyptically suited to the moment. If the crisis of time is not (as in Scripture) the end of one time and the beginning of another, if it is instead an historically empty event, then it can happen again and again, and then there can also be many analogously messianic leaders, each for his moment. Why not then Hitler for *die deutsche Stunde* (for Germany's time)? Here we encounter an instance of an apocalyptic theological interpretation of the German crisis of a very different sort to that of Barth or Bultmann. When Karl Barth read my dissertaion he discovered I had cited Gogarten on a point. He rebuked me: '*Wie können Sie **den** zitieren?*' ('How can you cite **him?**').

### III

There were and would be less dialectical theological interpretations of the German crisis. The great Ernst Troeltsch, in his last post-war years in Berlin, came to believe that Germany could be saved only by an all-powerful state, and that disestablished Protestantism should survive as the personal source of moral courage within such a state. What he would initially have thought about National Socialism, is hard to say, which is itself a dispiriting observation.

Lutheran confessional theologians, like Werner Elert or Paul Althaus, had replaced the Old Testament in a way different from that of the dialectical theologians. Following their understanding of Luther's two-kingdoms doctrine, and of his hermeneutic of the Old Testament as the book of the Law, they located Israel in the Kingdom on the left hand as a particular nation with her particular law, and were then in position to take Germany and German law as the equivalent, for Germans, of Israel and Israel's law for the Israelites. Thus, they effectively made a canon of *Deutschtum* (Germanness) and Paul, instead of Old Testament and New Testament. There could even be a sort of messianism in the kingdom on the left hand, a messianism of the state and civil society, in what would prove a disastrous analogy to Israel's hope.

It would be too much to say such Lutherans supported the Nazi movement; they just could not see how to oppose it—and indeed sometimes saw in it a glimmer of messianic hope for Germany. When not too long after World War II, I studied at Heidelberg, whose theological faculty was staffed with veterans of the church struggle, a professor running out of attention could get a chorus of jeers simply by finding some way to mention Erlangen.

## IV

Barth himself took a different tack. He perceived that construing the intersection of time and eternity as the tangent to a circle, so that the intersection is a point with no extension on either, finally leaves the church with nothing to talk *about*. Called to teach future preachers at Göttingen, Münster and Bonn, he could not remain with the positions of *The Epistle of the Romans*; yet neither could he abandon the rigour of the time-eternity dialectic. The position to which he worked may be so described: having for a first time pondered classical Chalcedonian Christology, he relocated the time-eternity dialectic as the inner dialectic of Christ's own existence, as a version of the two-natures doctrine. The sheer contradiction of eternity to time, and the dialectical unity posited in the contradiction, make the structure of the God–man's reality.

In one way, this tames the apolcalyptic jolt which Barth's earlier writing had delivered. But in another way it embraces all reality in the apolcalyptic moment. The immense dogmatic which in *Church Dogmatics* emerges from this move, is nothing short of a christological ontology—an interpretation of all being as the reflection of the meeting of time and eternity in Christ. And the christological content which now is seen in the eschatological moment, the God–man *narrative* which now can be told of it, gave Barth leverage he would not otherwise have had, in the approaching and truly apocalyptic confrontation with the Nazi effort to take over the church.

Which brings me to the point where I can be a little autobiographical. I came to Heidelberg in 1957. My supervisor was a veteran of the church struggle, Peter Brunner; and the first lectures I attended were by a young war veteran, Wolfhart Pannenberg, who was to become a permanent discussion-partner. These two are the figures with whom I want to conclude. Each in his own way laboured to overcome two closely linked determining features of the apocalypticism whose story we have followed: firstly, the reduction of biblical apocalyptic's new age to a timeless moment; and secondly, the displacement of the Old Testament. Both laboured to reclaim the Bible's own apocalyptic, in which the termination of history is not a dimensionless moment but itself occupies history, and in which the new thing that appears in that termination is again a history, if of a new kind.

Peter Brunner is not well known, though in the States there is some revival of his influence. In his own time he had little following; this was, I think, mostly a consequence of his ponderousness. He had been in fact a dramatic figure of the church resistance—there is even a novel based on those years of his life. He was a theologically interesting sort of Lutheran Barthian. And he was a somewhat unexpected, given his demeanor, speculative thinker.

A decisive goal of his thinking was to restore historical extension to the event of faith. Where the dialectical theology had its sheer apocalyptic moment, Brunner has what he called *die eschatologische Schwelle*, the 'swell' before the wave of history breaks. It is on that swell that the church and believers ride. Thus the apocalypse-moment of the dialectical theology lifts up and out into an historical space: into the space of the church's liturgical life and of concrete enactment of the commandment of love for the other. Moreover, history with its apocalyptic pattern is not only our history; it the history of God with us and so of God himself—God's own life has an apocalyptic structure. There is a history that is at once God's history and ours, eternal history and temporal history, and it is apocalyptic. God not only has a Messiah; his being is messianic, and his whole creation is an apocalypse. Reading Brunner on any particular locus without knowledge of the whole structure, one could suppose his thought was merely conservative. But it was in fact perhaps the most consistently and biblically apocalyptic-messianic theology of the century.

Wolfhart Pannenberg returned from World War 11 appalled by the fragmentation of life and thought enshrined in mid-twentieth century institutions and actually celebrated by the century's loudest academics. As an intellectual, his lamentation for the human world's fragmentation became specific as lamentation for the consequent frag-mention of intellectual life—which made philosophy be one thing, science something else and left theology as an actual outsider. Taught by one of the last great representatives of traditional German education—Heidleberg's professor for Old Testament, Gerhard von Rad—Pannenberg found the coherence of all things in the apocalyptic literature's vision of universal history. The peoples and empires in all their diversity lead to one great conclusion, the *Zukunft*, in which Barth and Bultmann and others located God. And the forcibly divided truths of the various disciplines terminate willy-nilly in one truth: God is at the end.

We can know all this because we know that great End. And we know that great End because it has been enacted ahead of time among us, as the life, death and Resurrection of Jesus. From that starting point, Pannenberg wrote sociology, history, philosophy of science, formal metaphysics, both substantively and methodologically. He made apocalyptic the formal principle of any and all pursuits of knowledge.

Brunner and Pannenberg were together at Heidelberg, and respected each other but were not *simpatico*. Being young and American, I naively asked Brunner what lectures I should hear. Perhaps Pannenberg? He said, 'You can do that. He is an intelligent person. Perhaps he is a bit too intelligent.' Nevertheless, they can, I think, be paired as twentieth century German theology's most consistent apocalyticists.

## V

Christian theology is intrinsically apocalyptic and messianic; apart from particular circumstance, it is always apocalyptic and messianic. Nevertheless, it is true that modernity's great theological project was to suppress apocalyptic, and to make messianism into guru-worship. And it can indeed be said that in twentieth century German theology, the suppressed stream burst out—for both good and evil, and even if, through most of the century, with a certain shamed face.

# Theodicy Between Messiansim and Apocalypse

## Engelhard Weigl

'The discrediting of creation and the call for a Messiah are in a reciprocal relationship.'[1]

Between the religious wars and the formation of the modern state in the seventeenth century and the beginning of the twentieth century, philosophy and political theory had been united in combating and suppressing all messianic and apocalyptic trends. World War I changed that. The apocalyptic experience of 1914–1918 and the misery and despair in its aftermath sent a generation of German theologians, philosophers and literary theorists back to the apocalyptic and messianic traditions within Europe, shared by both Christians and Jews. Those traditions had been eclipsed in Germany by Leibniz's anti-apocalyptic theodicy and those philosophers in Germany, including Kant, Fichte and Schelling, who, at least in this respect, remained in Leibniz's tracks. It was not simply that the familiar opposition of religion and modernity suddenly changed and that religion was no longer perceived as the adversary obstructing the emancipation of mankind, as Marx and Heine, Feuerbach and Nietzsche would have it. Rather, the crisis of the war forced this generation to see both its plight and its solution in the interlinking of theological (especially eschatological) and philosophical terms. Outside theology, the *eschaton* was still secular, even if the symbols for making sense of past, present and future were not. Certainly, the reintegration of religious contents, once removed from their traditional transcendent context, did have some disastrous results, as was all too conspicuous in the messianic and apocalyptic dimensions of fascism and Stalinism. But the totalitarian

---

1.  Hans Blumenberg, *Matthäuspassion* (Frankfurt au Maim: Suhrkamp, 1988), 273. Thanks to Ewe Weigl for her translation of this paper. Where quotes from German sources appear these are also her translations.

misappropriation of religious symbols did not exhaust the entwining of secular and religious symbols and aspirations, which continued to play such an important role in philosophy, theology and literature in Germany in the first half of the twentieth century. It is still an open question what long term philosophical value there is in the fusion of religious tropes with secular philosophical concepts. But it remains an important one and is a major reason, why so many German thinkers from the first half of the twentieth century still exercise their fascination.

## 1. Apocalyptic and messianic traditions and currents

The first source of apocalyptic writing is the Book of Daniel, dating from the second century before Christ, followed, among others, by the books of Enoch, Ezra and, most importantly, by the Revelation of John. For the apocalyptic writers, the onset of the rule of God is immanent. The book of Daniel says that the kingdom of God falls down like a rock crushing the old kingdom: the kingdom of God and the Son of Man (a messiah of transcendental origin) will define the new aeon. These ideas dominate the history of Christianity until the seventeenth century. A scheme of four successive empires followed by the Last Judgment, which would prepare the way for the fifth divine and eternal kingdom, was the undisputed framework for all who pondered the course of history. In this view, all history is largely a history of anticipation. There is a constant expectation of the last days on the one hand and the continued delay of the world's end on the other. How immanent this expectation was adjusted according to the situation, but the basic configuration of the end of time (the *eschaton*) was fixed. The mythical overtone of the Apocalypse of St John could be adapted to fit current circumstances and the apocryphal prophecies simply varied a relatively small number of figures who were to appear in the last days of the world (such as the Angel Popes, The Emperor of Peace or predecessors of the Antichrist such as Gog and Magog). However much these ideas about the end of time varied, the presence of the Roman Empire was unquestioned: as long as it lasted the final downfall was not immanent. The Emperor was the *katechon*, the ultimate defender, against the Antichrist. During the period of the Reformation all these figures seemed to step out into historical reality. Luther saw the Antichrist on the Holy See and Rome as the Whore of Babylon while the Catholics saw Luther as the Antichrist. The Peasant Revolt and the increasingly militant fronts forming within the schismatic Church appeared as the final civil war preceding the Apocalypse. The Turks besieging Vienna in 1529 were seen as the unleashed forces of Gog. Luther said at the time: 'The Turk will go to Rome, as Daniel's prophecy announces, and then the last day will not be very distant.'[2] Luther often said that Doomsday was close and that it had to be expected if not the present year, then the next.

The expectations of the Christians were juxtaposed with the hopes of the Jews for the appearance of the Messiah. For the Jews, too, apocalyptic thought always included elements of both horror and consolation—intricately entangled. Scholem always stresses that:

> The Bible and the apocalyptic writers know of no progress in history leading towards redemption. Redemption is not a result of inner-worldly develop-ments, as in the modern Western reinterpretations of Messianism since the age of Enlightenment . . . It is rather the intrusion of transcendence into history itself; in this destruction however it changes, because it is affected by a light that shines from somewhere completely different . . . The apocalypticists have always held dear the pessimistic view of the world. Their optimism, their hope is not directed towards whatever will be born from history, but towards that, which will rise in its destruction and will finally be free of all obstructions.[3]

As different as Christian and Jewish apocalypses might have been in detail, eschatological ideas peak in both religions during the crisis of the seventeenth century. In England at the time of Oliver Cromwell apocalyptic-chiliastic expectations escalate around 1640 culminating in the belief that the time for last decisions had come, a time when everything would be completely renewed. Not only was penance the dictate of the moment, it was also not enough that every individual Christian, every religious community was compelled to live according to God's commandments—the whole nation, was compelled to do so.

---

2.  Martin Luther, *The Table Talk or Familiar Discourse*, translated by William Hazlitt (London: David Bogue, 1848), 360.

3.  Gershom Scholem, 'Towards an Understanding of the Messianic Idea in Judaism', in Gershom Scholem, *The Messianic Idea in Judaism* (London: Allen and Unwin, 1971), 10.

Many of the eschatological testimonies of the seventeenth century stem from England, especially from the Puritans, while on the Continent there were Lutherans and Calvinists in particular, as well as other Protestant communities in the Netherlands, in France, Poland and Hungary. Fear and hope are evident in the growing number of leaflets at that time which accompanied the appearance of major comets. One can adequately interpret the prophetic-eschatological messages of the seventeenth century only against the backdrop of the difficult living conditions of that time, which can justly be characterised as a profound crisis. Since the worries of the present were so immense and the fear of the future so overwhelming, hope concentrated on a direct intervention by God—be it Judgment Day, the return of Christ or the beginning of the millennium, the 'Thousand-year Reich'. This intervention would put an end to all earthly misery and reward the pious for their fidelity.

Constant suffering accompanied by hopes for the coming of the Messiah were also widespread among the Jews in the seventeenth century. In the years after the Polish pogroms, in which more than 250,000 Jews were massacred and more than 700 Jewish communities annihilated, it became evident how immense the pressure was that Jews had to endure at that time in Europe. A paradigmatic moment was when in 1665 news from Egypt reached the Jewish communities that a new Messiah had come and they were gripped by tremendous excitement. In the hour of their greatest need the Redeemer had come—at least that is what it looked like. His name was Sabbatai Zevi and Nathan of Gaza, his prophet, spread his messianic word. However, when Sabbatai Zevi had to prove that he was the true Messiah, he failed miserably. He had announced that he would go to Constantinople and there depose the sultan and in doing so would begin his messianic rule. But when he landed in Turkey he was taken prisoner and given the alternative by the sultan to convert to Islam or to be executed as an insurgent. Sabbatai Zevi chose to convert, and all hopes he had inspired were dashed. His apostasy was sobering for many Jews, but the number of those who clung to their messianic hopes was also considerable. They developed a special theory, seeking to find a justification for the action of Zevi. His apostatic conversion is seen by his followers as confirmation that he was indeed the Messiah. The old writings and traditional documents were reinterpreted and made to fit the unexpected events. According to Scholem, Sabbatainism is by far the most important and extensive movement in the history of post-Christian Judaism.[4]

In the memoirs of the Jewish woman Glückel von Hameln (1646–1724), the eager anticipation that had gripped the Jews on hearing of the new Messiah is apparent:

> At that time people started talking about Sabbatai Zevi. But 'woe betide us who have sinned', we did not experience it as we had been told and as we had almost imagined it. When I remember how young and old people atoned for their sins then—the whole world knows about it. O, Lord of the World, how we had hoped that you would show mercy towards your people Israel and redeem us; we were like a woman sitting on a birthing stool suffering great pains and contractions. She thinks that after all the pain and suffering she would be delivered of a child, but all she bore was wind. My dear Lord and King, this is what happened to us. All your dear servants and children throughout the whole world worked hard at atoning, at praying and doing good deeds and your beloved people Israel sat on the birthing stool for two or three years, but nothing came of it but air . . .Oh the joy we experienced when receiving letters telling us of Sabbatai Zevi is impossible to describe . . . Some sold house and home and everything they owned for they hoped to be redeemed any day.[5]

Jewish messianism and Christian eschatological postulations came together in a surprising way. Whether Christian and Jewish hopes influenced each other, however, is still being disputed. Scholem maintains that both movements evolved independently of each other. But for our purpose it is important to point out that we can observe a similar phenomenon in Germany after World War I. The revival of messianism by Jewish intellectuals in the 1920s was matched in

---

4. See Gershom Scholem, 'The Crisis in Tradition in Jewish Messianism', in *The Messianic Idea in Judaism*.

5. Glückel von Hameln, *Denkwürdigkeiten der Glückel von Hameln*, edited by Alfred Feildenfeld (Bodenheim bei Mainz: Philo, 1999).

Protestant theology by Karl Barth's sudden insight that 'if Christianity be not altogether thoroughgoing eschatology, there remains in it no relationship whatever with Christ'.[6]

## 2.Theodicy as anti-apocalypse

The experience gained in a century of murderous wars and confrontations made it necessary to defuse and integrate the religious energies unleashed into the world of Europe by Luther, Zwingli and Calvin. And that resulted in the possibility of an unforeseen future that was there to be opened up and developed. The genesis of the absolute state is linked to the fight against all kinds of prophecies, be they religious or political. The state demands a monopoly of any foretelling of the future by actively suppressing any apocalyptic or astrological predictions. The philosophers actively supported the state interests. In 1670 Spinoza, in his *Tractatus Theologico-Politicus*, undertook the most consistent critique of prophecy. This was followed by Bayles's *Pensées diverses sur la comète* (1682) and Fontenelle's *Histoire des oracles* (1686). The most successful instrument of the Enlightenment in dealing with apocalyptic fears proves to be the book *Theodicy*, as devised by Leibniz in 1710. The critical implications of this book were not immediately apparent. Heinrich Heine called it his 'weakest work',[7] and it induced his adversaries to accuse Leibniz of 'blissful idiocy'.[8] As its title implies, this book was written in defense of God's goodness in the face of the undeniable existence of evil in this world. The complete title of the book, published in 1710 in Amsterdam, spells out its claim more precisely: *Essais de Théodicee sur la Bonté de Dieu, la Liberté de l'Homme et l'Origine du Mal* (*Essays on Theodicy concerning God's Goodness, Man's Liberty and the Origin of Evil*). The examination of the most important qualities of God, that is, his greatness and his goodness, leads to the question theodicy has to answer. Theodicy has to describe the relationship between God and his creation and has to clarify the connection between human liberty and God's providence. The three elements of metaphysics—God, world and man—are interconnected. God is the cause of the world in which humans live in liberty. That God created

6.  Karl Barth, *The Epistle to the Romans*, translated by Edward Hoskyns (Oxford: Oxford University Press, 1968), 314.
7.  Heinrich Heine, *Sämtliche Werke*, Volume 9 (Frankfurt am Main: Kindler, 1964), 206f.
8.  Heine, *Sämtliche Werke*, 207.

the best of all possible worlds is a consequence of his omnipotence and his goodness. *Theodicy*, § 7, states: 'If it had not been the optimum of all worlds, he would have created none at all.'[9] This is the basis for the 'optimism' in Leibniz's philosophy. The consequences of his proposition are far reaching and touch on the three concepts of messianism, apocalypse and redemption. The responsibility of man for his own world is justified through the optimism argument: since God created the best of all possible worlds, it is man's task to complete this world, God having fulfilled his role.

With the argument of Leibnizian optimism—and this constitutes the central sphere of Leibniz's metaphysical subtlety in the face of theology—the world is made independent of the divine sphere. For the best of all possible worlds must be independent in order to satisfy its own metaphysical qualities. God's influence on the world, which operates according to its own, (though God-given) laws, is limited to creation. The best of all possible worlds cannot operate dependently; if it were dependent, it would not be the best; therefore, it must be autonomous. There simply is no need for God to intervene. This means the end of worldly contingency, the end of the world's dependence on God. The debate with Clarke and Newton illuminates most clearly Leibniz's opposition to the late medieval theology of voluntarism to which Newton still adhered. According to this theology the world continues to exist only because God persistently sustains it. The world is not only created out of nothingness, in every moment of its existence it needs to be prevented by God from returning to nothingness.

An event in the middle of the eighteenth century rekindled apocalyptic fervour. The great earthquake of Lisbon in 1755 provoked a sermon from Pastor Johann Melchior Goeze in Hamburg:

> Our heart trembles when we vividly imagine how many thousands of souls the abyss has devoured in Lisbon. But is the abyss solely under the palaces of Lisbon? We may set foot wherever we like, but we will always have the abyss beneath us. As soon as the Lord speaks it will open up. As soon as God gives orders it will open wide its jaws. How insignificant are humans

---

9. Gottfried Wilhelm Leibniz, *Die Theodizee* (Hamburg: Meiner, 1968), 101.

who seem to live with such certainty. O sinner! How
great is the danger you are in.[10]

The almighty God who with the earthquake reminds humanity of
the impending end of the world is a God whose will is unfathomable
for humans. Everything can change totally in an instant. Humans are
refused any confidence in the world. The future is cast in a cloud of
uncertainty; the world is seen as being radically contingent.[11]

Against this theology of a *creatio continua*, of the absolute
dependence of the world on God, Leibniz pits his argument of the best
all possible worlds, a world that sustains itself. The best world is also
the most reliable, a *perpetuum mobile*. The more the world is seen as
stable, as functioning according to its own laws, the less need there is
for redemption. Hermann Samuel Reimarus (1694–1768) writes frankly
about the consequences of Leibniz's philosophy, although it was not
published at the time.[12] In a stable world there is no room for
eschatology, just as there is no room for sin, redemption and God's
grace. This meant that the New Testament and Christ's death on the
cross had to be reinterpreted. Having learnt from the experience with
the pretender Messiah Sabbatai Zevi, Reimarus sees in Jesus not
simply a failed Messiah. He assumes that there is a difference between
what Jesus himself taught and what the apostles later wrote about
Jesus. Reimarus starts with the questioning of the content of Jesus'
teaching. This can be condensed into the following: 'Be converted, for
the Kingdom of God is near'. The Kingdom of God, however, has to be
understood according to the Jewish tradition, as neither John the
Baptist nor Jesus explains the term anywhere. Jesus must be seen as
part of the Jewish religion. He assumes the messianic expectations
without correcting them in any way. According to Reimarus Jesus
considers himself a political Messiah, a scion of David, who would
reveal himself to be the messianic liberator of his people, the one who
had been promised in the prophecies of the Old Testament. 'Under the

---

10.  Johann Melchior Goeze, *Zwo Predigten, welche durch das fürchterliche,
     und so weit ausgebreitete Gericht Gottes im Erdbeden veranlasset
     worden* (Hamburg: JC Brandt, 1756), 5.

11.  Hans Blumenberg, *Legitimität der Neuzeit* (Frankfurt am Main: 1966),
     121.

12.  Hermann Samuel Reimarus: *Apologie oder Schutzschrift für die
     vernünftigen Verehrer Gottes*, edited by Gerhard Alexander, 2 Volumes
     (Frankfurt am Main: Insel, 1972).

apostle's whitewash',[13] Reimarus detected Jesus' plan for a political rebellion. 'The apostles and other disciples may well have encouraged him in this, because they themselves still had the vain hope, or rather the desire, that he should redeem Israel and start his own kingdom, a process in which they would participate eagerly. *Summa*, the risk was taken.'[14]

The kingdom of God, however, was the political kingdom for which thousands of Jews suffering under the Roman yoke were waiting. With the arrest and crucifixion of Jesus hopes of the disciples were shattered. Reimarus interprets the new religion of Christianity as a way of dealing with this disappointment. How did they overcome this devastating event? By falling back on the second version of Jewish hopes for the Messiah, which were initiated in Daniel and still discernable in apocalyptic thinking. According to that tradition the Messiah was destined to appear twice, once in human meekness and then in the full glory of the clouds of heaven. Since the first *systema*, as Reimarus calls it, was destroyed by the death of Jesus, the disciples came up with the second one and found followers to wait with them for the second coming.

In Jewish theology, too, the importance of the Messiah vanishes under the influence of theodicy. In his book *Golgatha und Schleblimini* (1784), the Christian thinker Georg Hamann reproaches Moses Mendelsohn, the foremost Jewish philosopher of the Enlightenment, for not having anything to say about the Messiah. In 1822 the Kant scholar, Lazarus Bendavid, went one step further in the first edition of *Zeitschrift für die Wissenschaft des Judentums* (1842) (Journal for the Study of Judaism), when he wrote, 'that the expectation of a Messiah does not constitute an essential article of the Jewish faith'.[15]

## 3. Idealism's extension of theodicy

The optimism of theodicy remained viable well past Voltaire's *Candide* and was defended successfully by Kant even after the cataclysmic earthquake of Lisbon in 1755. But new difficulties arose, demanding new solutions. According to Kant the world is full of deceptions, full of

---

13. Reimarus, *Apologie*, Volume 2, 145.
14. Reimarus, *Apologie*, Volume 2, 159.
15. Lazarus Bendavid, ' Ueber den Glauben der Juden an einen künftigen Messias' in *Zeitschrift für die Wissenschaft des Judentums*, Volume 1, Number 2, 1842: 225.

antinomies, of unavoidable contradictions; it is therefore dreadful. This insight incriminates the creator at a new level and demands a radical solution. An honourable acquittal of God—that is, a theodicy—can obviously only be achieved if proof can be established that it is not God who is responsible for this terrible world (since he does not control it), but that it is someone else's responsibility. Explicitly, that it is the responsibility of humans or, as Fichte and Schelling put it, of the 'I'. And it is this evidence, as Odo Marquard[16] has demonstrated, that constitutes Idealism. While Leibniz defends God by claiming autonomy for the world, Idealism defends God by claiming autonomy for man. Seen from this perspective, Idealism is not an attack on God but rather comes to his defense. Acknowledging the evil in the world, Idealism in fact defends God against the blasphemous reproach that he had created the evil. God is in fact exonerated. And out of the idealist theodicy developed the modern philosophy of history. The only creator who could then be asked by humans to make the world better than it had already been made, would be humans themselves. And any improvement within the framework of Idealism means improvement of the legal relationships under which humans live.

But the burden of the new task set for humans soon became too heavy to bear, and so the philosophers of German Idealism looked around for support, which they found in nature and God. In the early philosophy of Schelling it was nature and, from Kant's *Critique of Pure Reason* onwards, and increasingly after 1800 in Fichte and Schelling, it was God. According to Marquard, however, this return of God into philosophy does not call into question the philosophical theodicy of Idealism; the autonomy proposition remains valid. God is called upon, but at the same time he seems increasingly unreal. Four core approaches seem to be important here:

> The first: God is—but only postulated.
> The second: God is—but only as a god of ideas.
> The third: God is—but only in the distant future.
> The fourth: God is—but he is the 'completely different'.

All these attempts at a philosophical theology of Idealism, only briefly outlined here, call on God while at the same time making him

---

16.   Odo Marquard, 'Idealismus und Theodizee' in *Schwierigkeiten mit der Geschichtsphilosophie* (Frankfurt am Main: Suhrkamp, 1973), 52–65.

unreal. This means that the only one responsible for the unfortunate state of the world remains man.

## 4. The return of the theological

Theodicy was finally crushed in the theologically inspired critique of Idealism after World War 1.[17] War and revolution are the two experiences dominating the philosophical-theological discussions of the time, as Eugen Rosenstock expresses it in the title of his book *Die Hochzeit des Krieges und der Revolution (The Golden Age or the Marriage of War and Revolution)*. Total collapse and revolution made the world go out of joint in 1919, a crucial experience for German intellectuals. In literature, philosophy, theology and art a change of generation took place, and with it came the consciousness that one stood at a crossroads in regards to world history. From Dada to Spengler, from Communism to Dialectical Theology, from the disciples of Dostoyevsky, Nietzsche and George to the more moderate Max Weber, all of them saw this time as a 'deciding moment' in world history. And it was to the vivid images of religious language, from the storehouse of history, that they turned. The Messiah and the Apocalypse became references for them all and the 1920s became a melting pot of religious and secular ideas. 'Time craves a decision', is how Rosenstock, a Jew turned Christian, expressed the prevailing atmosphere. He wrote:

> What are ideals and organizations good for? Only something extraordinary can help, only credibility of a kind that can reintroduce miracle into daily life. All Protestants and Catholics have to make a decision today, whether they want to foster the modern age with its greco-national Idealism or Christianity. The Modern age and Idealism are dead.[18]

---

17. See, for example: Karl Barth, *Der Römerbrief* (1922); Emil Brunner, *Die Mystik und das Wort* (1924); Friedrich Gogarten, *Illusionen: Eine Auseinandersetzung mit dem Kulturidealismus* (1926); Eugen Rosenstock-Huessy, *Angewandte Seelenkunde* (1924); Franz Rosenzweig, *Der Stern der Erlösung* (1921); Martin Buber, *Ich und Du* (1923).
18. Eugen Rosenstock-Huessy, *Die Hochzeit des Krieges und der Revolution* (Würzburg: Patmos, 1920), 197.

The attack on Idealism and modernity is aimed at the unreal God of Idealism and the hubristic autonomy of man. The experience of war, the daily confrontation with death, had led to the disintegration of the philosophical God. Starting with Kierkegaard, a struggle began against the abstractions Western philosophy had worked with since Descartes. Rosenstock makes this very clear:

> For Descartes' sentence—*cogito, ergo sum,* I think therefore I am, which in precise logical terms equals 'I am I', ie A=A, the following grammatical sentence has to be substituted: God called me, therefore I am. I was given my own name, therefore I am . . . *'To abstract'* is only a welcome foreign word for the process of this escape, this withdrawal. Philosophy has only recently been diagnosed by a wise man [Franz Rosenzweig] as world-angst and fear of death. All abstractions in fact aim to escape the actual situation here and now. They shirk the responsibility of the answer: that is me and that is where I am at.[19]

Language is for Rosenstock not just God's creation, not just *creatio ex nihilo,* but also *creatio continua,* God's continuing creation that has reverberated in us ever since Adam and will do so until the Day of Judgment. This I (first person singular), outside of the expansive You (comprising God, parents and one's people), is without life and leads only a shadowy or ghostly existence. The constitution of the I, as an autonomous one, as Idealism describes it, is not only presumptuous but also proves to be fictitious, acquiring eerie characteristics from the point of view of a believer. And it is exactly these eerie traits that the critics of modernity have detected in the modern human condition —especially in people living in big cities.[20]

One might see parallels with Kafka's story *'A Report for an Academy'* which was interpreted by his friend Max Brod as a scathing critique of the assimilated Western Jew. And at the same time, Scholem notes in his diary:

---

19.  Eugen Rosenstock-Huessy, 'Angewandte Seelenkunde' (1916, 1923), in *Die Sprache des Menschengeschlechts* (Heidelberg: Erster Band, 1963), 766f.

20.  See: Rosenstock-Huessy, *Die Sprache des Menschengeschlechts,* 221.

The question, what exactly makes up the Western influence on Jews, is a very difficult one. It is about the phenomenon of a ghostification of a specific form of existence. The modern Jew is set as the absolutely negative: the historical existence that has turned ghostly out of its own accord.[21]

After World War I many Jewish intellectuals experienced the alienation from their traditional milieu as threatening and this led them on a search for the religious roots of their identity. In Frankfurt, which after Berlin had the second largest Jewish community, the Rabbi Nobel laid the foundation for a Jewish renaissance. Among the young men this charismatic leader attracted were Leo Löwenthal, Siegfried Krakauer, Erich Fromm, Ernst Simon and Franz Rosenzweig. The encounter with the Jews from Eastern Europe, who had fled the pogroms to the West during and after the War, had left a deep impression on these intellectuals. Franz Rosenzweig, who became the director of the New Jewish Adult Education Academy in Frankfurt in 1920, said about this fruitful confrontation: 'In the morning I learn in the East, in the afternoon I teach in the West'. The most eminent and, for Rosenzweig, the most important collaborator at the Academy was Martin Buber, who taught comparative religion at Frankfurt University. They worked together on a new German translation of the Hebrew Bible.

The search for the religious sources of Jewish identity could not be separated from the reasons for the loss of identity that had contributed to this crisis. Walter Benjamin depicts the capitalist nature of the present as 'hellish' and contrasts it with the 'heavenly' prehistoric times:

> The idea of progress must be based on the idea of catastrophe. That things have gone this far is the catastrophe. Catastrophe is not what threatens to occur at any given moment. Strindberg's conception: Hell is

---

21. Gershom Scholem, *Tagebücher nebst Aufsätzen und Entwürfen bis 1923*, Volume 2 (Frankfurt am Main: Jüdischer Verlag, 2000), 330f.

nothing that stands ahead of us—rather, this life in the present.[22]

Benjamin's analysis of the conditions of the modernity is centred on this reflection about the decline of 'experience'. For him, the Neo-Kantian reduction of experience as something restricted to this world of objects is part of the decline. He distinguished between two words for 'experience', *Erlebnis* and *Erfahrung*. For him, the latter is grounded in cultural tradition, a concrete totality reflected largely in religion. The course of the war and its aftermath had hardened into a certainty that even the utterly unimaginable could become reality. What had actually already occurred was beyond what had been imaginable before the war, and this not only devalued all previous experience, but also called into question the meaning of experience as such. How could experience be possible if all criteria for meaningful coherence had been invalidated? Walter Benjamin expressed this quite clearly in 1936:

> Experience (*Erfahrung*) has fallen in value. And it looks as if it is continuing to fall into bottomlessness. Every glance at a newspaper demonstrates that it has reached a new low, that our picture, not only of the external world but of the moral world as well, overnight has undergone changes which were never thought possible. With the [First] World War a process began to become apparent which has not halted since then. Was it not noticeable at the end of the war that men returned from the battlefield grown silent—not richer but poorer in communicable experience? What ten years later was poured out in the flood of war books was anything but experience that goes from mouth to mouth. And there was nothing remarkable about that. For never has experience been contradicted more thoroughly than strategic experience by tactical warfare, economic experience by inflation, bodily experience by mechanical warfare, moral experience by those in power. A generation that had gone to school on a horse-drawn streetcar now stood under the open

---

22.   Walter Benjamin, 'Central Park', in *New German Critique*, 34 (1985): 33–5.

sky in a countryside in which nothing remained unchanged but the clouds, and underneath these clouds, in a field of force of destructive torrents and explosions, was the tiny fragile human body.[23]

The modern age appears to be a permanent catastrophe, a repetition of 'eternal and constantly new agony',[24] leading to utter desperation. Confronted by a damned universe, which is at the mercy of machines and industry, of fashion and commodities and turns humans into machines incapable of memory and experience, the only hope lies in the belief in the Messiah, who does 'not only come as a saviour' but who also 'overcomes the Antichrist'. 'The Messiah stops history; the Messiah does not appear at the end of a development.'[25] And in Benjamin's view, the concept of the Third Reich is the present (that is, pre-Hitler) embodiment of messianic thought.[26]

In the crisis following World War 1 these thinkers'—who would be seen by a later generation as being a part of a 'philosophical extremism'[27]—main concern was, according to Krakauer's wording, 'to lead an expelled people back into the old-new sphere of the divine reality.'[28] According to Benjamin, 'the religious and historical blindness of the Enlightenment' applies to 'the entire modern age'.[29] He wants to replace the concept of experience, which is limited to the mathematical and scientific sphere, with one that includes the religious sphere, a concept developed in critical appreciation of Kant's concept of experience. Ernst Bloch's first book *The Spirit of Utopia*, published in 1918, and Georg Lukács' *The Theory of the Novel* published in 1916, exerted an influence on young intellectuals that should not be underestimated. For Bloch the factual world, the empirical reality, is characterised by alienation and exploitation, by decay and misery; the

23. Walter Benjamin, *Illuminations*, edited and with an introduction by Hannah Arendt (London: Fontana, Collins, 1982), 83f.
24. Walter Benjamin, *Gesammelte Schriften,* Volume 5 (Frankfurt am Main: Suhrkamp, 1972), 178.
25. Benjamin, *Gesammelte Schriften*, Volume 1, Part 3, 1243.
26. Benjamin, *Gesammelte Schriften*, Volume 1, Part 2, 695.
27. Norbert Bolz, *Auszug aus der entzauberton Welt: Philophischer Extremismus zwischen den Weltkriegen* (München: Fink, 1989).
28. Quoted in Siegfried Krakauer, *Schriften*, Volume 1 (Frankfurt am Main: Suhrkamp, 1978), 11.
29. Benjamin, *Gesammelte Schriften*, Volume 2, Part 1, 159.

modern age is a 'coffin of god-forsaken being'.[30] For Lukács too, the war experience had intensified apocalyptic premonitions to such a degree that he describes the time, following Fichte's wording, as 'the era of total sinfulness'.[31] For him the modern novel is the 'expression of transcendental homelessness', a 'mirror image of a world completely out of joint'.[32] Lukács interest in Jewish messianism is directed towards the heretic tendencies personified in Sabbatai Zevi and Jakob Frank, the same two who Gershom Scholem would be fascinated by a few years later.[33] The recourse to radical religious ideas is common to all authors of philosophical extremism. With Bloch it is the revival of chiliastic models; with Benjamin it is the realization that these are in fact messianic times. The desire for unity, the longing for the absolute, arises from the experience of the first total war, the epitome of catastrophe in the beginning of the twentieth century, which affected all participating nations at a deeper level than any other major historical event since 1789, maybe since the upheavals in the wake of the Reformation in the sixteenth and seventeenth centuries.

## 5. Theodicy and messianic minimalism

After 1945, after the failed attempt of 'philosophical extremism' to break out of the 'iron cage' of a 'demystified world' (Max Weber), a time of self-reflection sets in, focusing on the political outcome of the messianism of the Weimar Republic. In his book *The Heritage of Our Times*, Ernst Bloch had, in 1935, analysed the alarming misuse of chiliastic and messianic ideas by the Hitler movement:

> In a unique way Nazism has mobilized for its own
> ends not only the economic ignorance but also the still
> valid images of hope and chiliasm of earlier
> revolutions . . .[34] Germany still listens, as has been

---

30. Ernst Bloch, *Geist der Utopie* (1923 edition) (Frankfurt am Main: Suhrkamp, 1964), 208.
31. Georg Lukács, *Theorie des Romans* (Darmstadt/Neuwied: Luchterhand, 1979), 13, 158.
32. Lukács, *Theorie des Romans,* 12.
33. Georg Lukács, *Dostojewski: Notizen und Entwürfe* (Budapest: Akadémiai Kiadó, 1985), 156, 172.
34. Ernst Bloch, 'Zur Originalgeschichte des Dritten Reiches', in Ernst Bloch, *Erbschaft dieser Zeit* (Frankfurt am Main: Suhrkamp, 1962), 206.

shown, to the old dreams of Saviour and Empire, even
if they are presented by fraudsters . . . Two main
motives have excited revolutionary consciousness from
the 12th to the 16th century. The motive of the Saviour
and the motive of the third empire, finally even the
Thousand Year Reich, to which the saviour-liberator
will lead [35]

In contrast to Bloch, the critique of Hans Blumenberg in his book
*The Legitimacy of the Modern Age*, published in 1966, aims at a deeper
level. He puts forward an alternative to the theologically motivated
critique of modernity by resorting to Leibnitz's theodicy again. In his
apology for modernity, he argues that its position in religious and
historical terms was not a wrongful position, but one that was credible,
justified and legitimate. With the argument of theodicy, the question of
evil in its Gnostic and eschatological dimensions was already included
and dispersed with at the same time. Blumenberg's argument is in fact
very Leibnitzian: If God comprises everything that is good, if he is
necessary and good, then because of his omnipotence, he could have
created only the best of all possible worlds. The consequence of God's
perfection is that his creation is also perfect and does not need his
intervention to operate. With this argument, 'evil appears to be less
clearly the physical evil inherent in nature, and more and more
undeniably because of its technological reinforcements as the result of
human action'.[36] Humans are burdened with the responsibility for
evil, while God is exonerated. According to Blumenberg, theodicy is
the result of human self-assertion against the overwhelming claims
and demands of late medieval theology. Blumenberg's way of thinking
which uses all concepts in the interest of human self-assertion, does not
allow concepts that claim the absolute truth. By disqualifying absolute
concepts as theological concepts pushed too far, he avoids the political
and totalitarian coincidences that mark the theories of Nietzsche and
Heidegger, Theodor Adorno, Arnold Gehlen and Carl Schmitt.
Following in the tradition of Ernst Cassirer, he chooses as a guiding
figure not the radical, negative theological Nietzsche, but the ironic,
concept-wary, humane Goethe.

---

35.   Bloch, *Erbschaft dieser Zeit*, 194.
36.   Hans Blumenberg, *Säkularisierung und Selbstbehauptung* (Frankfurt am
        Main: Suhrkamp, 1974), 68.

Of central importance to our context is the efficacy of Blumenberg's approach in defusing the historical fear of the apocalypse. He offers three counter arguments. Firstly, he argues the perfection of the world, seen as guaranteed by the theodicy argument, makes the new concept of the world resistant to all radical changes. This means, secondly, that the evil present in this world has to be overcome by inner-worldly means. The coming to terms with evil becomes a pragmatic problem that humans have to solve amongst themselves. Blumenberg's modern pagan age is without hope of a transcendental improvement but therefore without fear of an apocalypse. So, thirdly, history has no meaning outside of itself. Since absolute concepts have no validity, it is evident that the claim for justification of history through an apocalyptic Last Judgment is just one of the 'great questions and great hopes that overstretch our imagination only to disappoint us'.[37]

Since the expectation of a Messiah has a reciprocal relation with the bad name given to creation, and since, according to Leibniz, a critique of the creation demeans God, the creator, we can only hope for what Blumenberg calls messianic minimalism. This would be the belief in a messiah whose coming would not be perceptible. 'The unnoticeability is the condition of perfection; only that excludes a perception of imperfection at all points in time . . .'[38]

Messianic minimalism as described by Blumenberg is characteristic of the philosophy and literature produced in Germany after 1945. Only in the poetry of Paul Celan is messianism still present, albeit in a hermetic language difficult to decipher. Scholem criticises Jewish messianism with the argument that 'life [is] lived in deferment',[39] life is put on hold in anticipation of the coming Messiah, turning life itself into a preliminary, provisional stage.

As far as I am aware, the only one to adopt the messianic and apocalyptic motives of the Weimar Republic without moderation following in the footsteps of Walter Benjamin is the Jewish philosopher Jacob Taubes. According to him the experience of fascism and Stalinism does not affect the theological content of his philosophy, which in the tradition of apocalyptic thinking tries to fathom the structure of being and time as a limited time period. In his lectures, *The*

---

37. Blumenberg, *Säkularisierung und Selbstbehauptung*, 103. See also: Wilhelm Schmidt-Biggemann, *Geschichte als absoluter Begriff* (Frankfurt am Main: Suhrkamp, 1991), 124.
38. Blumenberg, *Matthäuspassion*, 277.
39. Scholem, *The Messianic Idea in Judaism*, 35.

*Political Theology of Paul,* held in Heidelberg shortly before he died in 1987, he critically examined Adorno, Bloch and Blumenberg to create space for a radical understanding of messianism. With his critique of the autonomy of man and his insight into the illusory promise of happiness made by industrial culture he picks up the threads of the critique of Idealism so prevalent in the 1920s. Taubes reads Benjamin's 'Theological-political Fragment' as a close parallel to Paul's epistle to the Romans 8:

> And for Benjamin it's important to note, first, that he maintains the Messiah and doesn't let it drift into a neutrality, which isn't a matter of religious history but an article of faith. Compared to this Bloch is just wishy-washy, and especially Adorno. Think of *Minima Moralia,* the last part. There you can tell the difference between substantial and as-if, and you can see how the whole messianic thing becomes a *comme si* affair. That is a wonderful, but finally empty, line, whereas for the young Benjamin it's substantial. It's shaken by experience. Of course I don't want to say that it's identical with Paul in a strictly exegetical sense. I want to say: This is said out of the same experience, and there are hints in the text that confirm this. These are experiences that shake Paul through and through and that shake Benjamin through and through after 1918, after the war. That's what I'm talking about.[40]

In this way Jakob Taubes, in his role as a Jewish thinker in Germany, carries on a theological-philosophical tradition that would otherwise have become extinct in the aftermath of Hitlerism and Stalinism.

---

40. Jacob Taubes, *The Political Theology of Paul* (Stanford: Stanford University Press), 74.

# Part Two

# 1

# In Light of 'The Light of Transcendence': Redemption in Adorno

## David Kaufmann

'In the end hope, wrested from reality by negating it, is the only form in which truth appears.'[1]

Adorno's mentor and close friend Walter Benjamin maintained rather famously that historical materialism can easily 'be a match for anyone if it enlists the services of theology'.[2] Given Robert Hullot-Kentor's claim that 'theology penetrates every word' of Adorno's writing,[3] it is worth asking precisely what Adorno might have meant when he invoked the notion of 'redemption', which, I will argue in this chapter, is central to his thought. Adorno maintained that in order to avoid the pitfalls of the immanence of myth and the myth of immanence (which have plagued both bourgeois and socialist theory) thinking must not shy away from transcendence, that is, from the metaphysical tendency to treat concepts as facts. Redemption is both the content of a properly chastened transcendent thinking and its proper goal. Because a redeemed world would be qualitatively different from the present dispensation, transcendent thought must take care to approach this content negatively or through the affective intimations that constitute 'metaphysical experience'. If we follow the outlines of Adorno's

1. Theodor Adorno, *Minima Moralia: Reflections From Damaged Life*, translated by EFN Jephcott (London: Verso, 1974), 98.
2. Walter Benjamin, 'On the Concept of History', in *Selected Writings*, edited by Howard Eiland and Michael W Jennings (Cambridge MA: Harvard University Press, 2003), 4 Volumes, Volume 4, 389.
3. Theodor W Adorno, *Kierkegaard: Construction of the Aesthetic*, translated by Robert Hullot-Kentor (Minneapolis: University of Minnesota Press, 1989), xi.

thinking, we can see that the concept of redemption and the realm of metaphysics are not the sworn enemies of freedom that the anti-clerical Enlightenment thought they were. Rather, metaphysics and redemption form a constellation—that is, they stand in close correlation and tension—with freedom and serve as the necessary prerequisites for any meaningful praxis. In order to see how Adorno can hold this position, it makes sense to begin with the famous final aphorism of *Minima Moralia* and see how its claims are borne out in Adorno's post-War writings, particularly in the last section of *Negative Dialectics*.

Here, lightly edited, is the final paragraph of *Minima Moralia*:

> The only philosophy which can be responsibly practiced in the face of despair is the attempt to contemplate all things as they would present themselves from the standpoint of redemption. Knowledge has no light but that shed on the world by redemption: all else is reconstruction, mere technique. Perspectives must be fashioned that displace and estrange the world, reveal it to be, with its rifts and crevices, as indigent and distorted as it will appear one day in the messianic light . . . It is the simplest of all things, because the situation calls imperatively for such knowledge . . . But it is also the utterly impossible thing, because it presupposes a standpoint removed, even though by a hair's breadth, from the scope of existence, whereas we will know that any possible knowledge must not only be first wrested from what is, if it shall hold good, but is also marked, for this very reason, by the same distortion and indigence which it seeks to escape. The more passionately thought denies its conditionality for the sake of the unconditional, the more unconsciously, and so calamitously, it is delivered up to the world. Even its own impossibility it must at last comprehend for the sake of the possible. But beside the demand thus placed on thought, the question of the reality or unreality of redemption itself hardly matters.[4]

---

4.    Adorno, *Minima Moralia*, 247.

For all his insistence on negativity and for all the sheer grimness of his philosophy (especially in that darkest of his meditations during the war years, *The Dialectic of Enlightenment*) Adorno was the sworn enemy of despair. He argued consistently that responsible thought could not succumb to despair because absolute despair is nothing less than a performative contradiction. Despair bears all the pain of disappointed hope, and this pain thus acknowledges the power of hope. It contains a protest that things should indeed be different. If despair is absolute, it cannot be despair, but will rather be experienced as something more emotionally neutral, like acceptance. While absolute despair looks like critique, it really affirms the existing state of the world because it refuses to posit an alternative. For this reason Adorno castigates it as 'the final ideology'.[5] Eschewing ideology, responsible thought must embrace hope and all hope, it seems, points towards redemption.

Adorno claims that knowledge requires this hope. Once redeemed, the things of this world will present themselves as they truly are, freed from abstractions of the exchange principle (which eliminates their particularity) and from subjective reason (which makes them depend on the subject, not themselves, for their meaning). We see a prefiguration of such a blissful state in children's play:

> The unreality of games gives notice that reality is not
> yet real. Unconsciously they rehearse the right life . . .
> In existing without any purpose recognizable to men,
> animals hold out, as if for expression, their own names,
> utterly impossible to exchange.[6]

Real knowledge of the things of this world posits a situation in which they can appear as they are in themselves. Redemption, then, what Kant calls a regulative principle—it is necessary for rational thought, but not necessarily true of the world as it stands.[7] Its validity is prospective.

---

5.  Theodor Adorno, *Negative Dialectics*, translated by EB Ashton (New York: Continuum, 1973), 373. Because this translation—the only one yet available in English—is notoriously incorrect, I will amend it without comment where necessary to accord with the German. I will cite the page references to Ashton's translation for the reader's convenience.

6.  Adorno, *Minima Moralia*, 228.

7.  See Susan Neiman's nice formulation: 'If reason ·is constitut-ive—capable of knowing the world as a whole—then the world that is

The task of responsible thinking—to assume the standpoint of redemption—is particularly difficult in a dispensation that is presently determined by exchange and subject-centred reason. How then can we begin to imagine the world *'as it will appear one day* in the messianic light'? Adorno suggests we strive for that standard strategy of High Modernist aesthetics—estrangement.

But such estrangement is not easily achieved. Thinking finds itself in a deeply paradoxical position. On the one hand, it seeks to distance itself from what is, from the present relations of existence, but there is no thought that does not rely on those relations. They serve as the ground of all possible thinking. In this way, all right thinking must acknowledge its imminence. It can only derive from the world as it is. On the other hand, it cannot rest with that world if it is to be truly critical. It must also attempt to transcend that world, to present something that is different. And so thinking finds itself in an inexorable bind. It tries to imagine things as they would appear 'unconditionally' but by denying its own conditionality, it misunderstands itself. In the end, it is tempted by the worst form of ideology. It hails the conditioned as the unconditional, the mediated as the absolute, the immanent as in fact the transcendent. It can come to salute the world as it is as the best of all possible worlds—or as the only possible world. It thus legitimates all the existing illegitimate forms of domination.

So as not to dupe itself into believing in its own unconditionality or fall into a bitter acceptance of its own irrevocably conditioned position, thinking has to take self-reflection to the length of self-negation ('Even its own impossibility it must at last comprehend for the sake of the possible.') Thus the last sentence of this final aphorism contains less pathos than might first appear. Thinking cannot fool itself into thinking that redemption is real, that is, that it has been achieved (or, extending this line of thought a bit further, that it is a certainty). But it cannot afford to assume that redemption is not possible, or else it would cease to be responsible thought.

This brief commentary on the last section of *Minima Moralia* should make it clear that Adorno belongs squarely to a long tradition of left-

---

given to us must be reasonable. If reason is regulative, it is possible that human action can make it more so.' It should be clear that my discussion of Adorno emphasises precisely this Kantian aspect of his thought. Susan Neiman, *The Unity of Reason* (New Haven: Yale University Press, 1994), 203.

wing utopianism. It should also be clear that he marks his difference from a good deal of that tradition by taking redemption, not utopia, as his goal. Though raised a Protestant (he was born of a converted Jewish father and a Catholic mother[8]) Adorno clearly does not have the Christian model of redemption in mind. He is not proposing salvation through Christ's death. Adorno quotes Nietzsche approvingly to disparage the Christian God's self-sacrifice: 'The guilt sacrifice, in its most repulsive and most barbaric form: the sacrifice of the innocent for the sake of the guilty!'[9] Truth be told though, because Adorno sees all exchange as a form of unnecessary sacrifice, the literal notion of redemption—buying a prisoner's freedom from bondage—holds little interest for him. As far as Adorno is concerned, no exchange can ever be 'fair' (or adequate) because all exchanges create false equivalences and thus ignore particularity. Exchange always falls into the trammels of mythical, not responsible, thought: 'Exchange is the rational form of mythical ever-sameness'.[10] Adorno seems to be thinking, rather, of something like redemption of the children of Israel from Egypt in which no exchange takes place. But he goes even further, because, as we shall see, the passage into freedom he imagines entails the recuperation—if only semantic—of loss. He is counting on something quite close to Paradise.

Adorno's arguments therefore go beyond the rational calculations of traditional political utopianism. To understand why Adorno would go this far, we have only to look at the task that 'historical materialism' has set itself. It rejects what it takes to be the musty spiritualism of metaphysics and the notion that it is mind, not labour, that determines the course of history and the path to freedom. To put metaphysics back on its feet, materialism feels that it must stick closely—too closely—to immanence. It mistrusts metaphysics' tendency of treating concepts as if they were facts, as if they could be freed from their material determinations.[11] Metaphysics is famously blind to these deter-

---

8.    See Evelyn Wilcock, 'Negative Identity: Mixed German Jewish Descent as a Factor in the Reception of Theodor Adorno', in *New German Critique*, 81 (Fall 2000): 169–87.

9.    Adorno, *Minima Moralia*, 98.

10.   Theodor Adorno, 'Progress', in *Critical Models*, translated by Henry Pickford (NY: Columbia University Press, 1998), 159.

11.   This definition of metaphysics comes from Theodor W Adorno, *Metaphysics: Concept and Categories*, translated by Edmund Jephcott, (Stanford: Stanford University Press, 2000), 4, 7.

minations and is in turn blindly determined by them. Even though metaphysics tries to drive a wedge between the transcendent and the existent, between the conceptual and the phenomenal, it ends up turning the transcendent into a weak apology for the existent.[12] All too often, then metaphysics becomes an affirmative mask for illegitimate domination by painting avoidable suffering as both necessary and as meaningful. But, as Adorno points out in a number of places, materialism's desire to cleave to the existent ends up in the same ideological trap. It casts a mythical spell over what exists by making it appear ordained by an inexorable fate: 'For myth is nothing other than the closed relation of immanence, of what is.'[13] Its strict loyalty to the immanent makes materialism view the contingencies of the world as if they were necessities. It therefore curtails the possibility of freedom.

For Adorno, then, it is an error to try to swap materialism for metaphysics. Responsible, emancipatory thought must hold transcendence and immanence in what he calls a constellation—a tension that cannot be resolved by conflating the two terms.[14] Metaphysics as pure conceptuality constitutes an important moment in thought, although it has to be inoculated against its worst apologetic tendencies. This inoculation is achieved through metaphysics' native capacity for reflective self-negation, its dual interest in destruction and recovery. According to Adorno, metaphysics is notable for rescuing thought by mortifying it.[15] Metaphysics can therefore be properly emancipatory, because its commitment to the concept leads it to conceive of possibilities beyond the present state of the world. It can begin to think the qualitatively different and new. For Adorno, this is the value of metaphysical constructions such as Kant's notion of the intelligible world: 'The concept of the intelligible is the self-negation of the finite mind . . . The mind thinks what would be beyond it.'[16]

Truly liberating thinking will thus have to learn to tarry with transcendence. At the same time, it will need reflective self-negation in order to figure forth a realm that will not just look like a gauzy version of our present existence. Thought will seek transcendence in a 'concept

---

12.  Adorno, *Metaphysics: Concept and Categories*, 100.
13.  Adorno, *Negative Dialectics*, 402.
14.  See my 'Correlations, Constellations and the Truth: Adorno's Ontology of Redemption', in *Philosophy and Social Criticism*, 26 (2000): 562–80.
15.  Adorno, *Metaphysics: Concept and Categories*, 20, 51.
16.  Adorno, *Negative Dialectics*, 392.

of something which is not, and yet is not a pure nonbeing'.[17] So, 'the transcendent is and it is not'.[18] To see the transcendent as merely nonbeing is to fall into immanence. To see it as actually existing is to succumb to delusion. Hence, responsible thought hovers between its positive and negative poles. In the process, it keeps open a space for true alterity and for the hope that a different world could come into being.

This hope leads Adorno to hazard a series of bold claims. Transcendence, properly pursued, leads *all* thoughts to converge 'upon the concept of something that would differ from the unspeakable world that is . . .'[19] This *something*, superior to this world, is redemption itself. Adorno is therefore claiming that all responsible thinking leads to the thought of redemption. Truly free thought will of necessity 'flow into transcendence, down to the idea of a world that would not only abolish present suffering but revoke the suffering that is irrevocably past'.[20] The abolition of present suffering is a laudable and predictable goal. Less predictable is the desire to 'revoke [*widerrufen*] the suffering that is irrevocably past'.

What does Adorno mean here? To revoke in German means literally to 'unsay' and I suspect that with this 'unsaying' Adorno is reiterating Benjamin's thesis about the 'weak messianism' of every present age, that it can secure and thus redefine the defeated hopes of the past.[21] In a very Benjaminian aphorism, Adorno claims that 'no other hope is left to the past than that, exposed defencelessly to disaster, it shall emerge from it as something different'.[22] The disaster that constantly faces the past is that the victors will win again and will succeed in obliterating all memory of the sufferings of the defeated. Their defeat cannot be undone, of course, but it does not have to be complete or absolute. In a different set of circumstances, with the original victors vanquished and with a new set of social relations in place, new meanings can be ascribed to the catastrophes of the past. Unfettered thought will not only want to defeat the sufferings of the present. It will seek to make whole the losses of the past.

---

17.  Adorno, *Negative Dialectics*, 393.
18.  Adorno, *Negative Dialectics*, 375.
19.  Adorno, *Negative Dialectics*, 403.
20.  Adorno, *Negative Dialectics*, 403.
21.  Benjamin, 'On the Concept of History', 389–90.
22.  Adorno, *Minima Moralia*, 167.

We still live in the 'unspeakable world that is'. So if thinking is going to be responsible, it will have to remember that its representations of redemption will always bear the taint of the dispensation it wants to escape. It will have to remind itself that its depictions of a redeemed existence will not show the truth of that existence, but will be a figure or a semblance of it: 'What finite beings say about transcendence is the semblance [*Schein*] of transcendence; but . . . a necessary semblance.' Transcendent thought will only produce fictions, but these are unavoidable. They will not be problematic if their fictionality is constantly borne in mind. For this reason, aesthetics and art are of a piece with metaphysics. They contribute to responsible thinking, because for Adorno, the object of aesthetics is the very 'rescue of semblance' through negation. [23]

Adorno makes the emphatic—even exuberant—claim that the semblance that is art's necessary mode is underwritten by the legitimate hope that its intimations will eventually prove to be true: 'Art is semblance . . . but its semblance, its irresistible part, is granted it by what is not semblance.' Art bears witness to redemption itself: ' . . . No light falls on men and things without reflecting transcendence . . . Semblance is the promise of nonsemblance.'[24] There are two concomitant ways of reading this last statement. One is logical and the other is temporal. To say that something is semblance is to assume that there is something that is not *Schein*; it is to posit a truth that lies behind or beyond that *Schein*. If you say that something is mere semblance, you are claiming that there is a realm of nonsemblance. Now, this nonsemblance might just be hidden because we are looking in the wrong place, or it might exist on another plane (beyond the spatio-temporal, say). Alternatively—and this is where the temporal dimension comes in—you could argue that we have to wait for this nonsemblance to come forth because we have not yet created the social relations from which it could emerge. In other words, the realm of nonsemblance is the realm of redemption. And we have not yet achieved redemption.

A good example of art's redemptive hope, of the promise inherent in aesthetic semblance, occurs in Adorno's description of the animal scherzo of Mahler's Third Symphony:

---

23.  Adorno, *Negative Dialectics*, 383.
24.  Adorno, *Negative Dialectics*, 404–05.

> Its light-beam falls on that perverted condition that,
> under the spell of the self-preservation of the species,
> erodes its esssential self and makes ready to annihilate
> the species by fatefully substituting the means for the
> end it has conjured away. Through animals humanity
> becomes aware of itself as impeded nature and of its
> activity as deluded natural history; for this reason
> Mahler meditates on them. For him, as in Kafka's
> fables, the animal realm is the human world as it
> would appear from the standpoint of redemption,
> which natural history itself precludes . . . Desolate and
> comforting at once, nature grown aware of itself casts
> off the superstition of the absolute difference between
> them.[25]

The perversion of our 'natural' drive for self-preservation into an end in itself leads us to destroy ourselves in the name of survival. Mahler's scherzo reveals this perversion and thus allows us a glimpse of the 'essential self' of our species. The music indicates what we could be once we have been freed from the error of pursuing self-preservation at any cost. In Kafka and Mahler, human history is presented as sheer fate, where freedom and humanity are confined under the supposedly immutable 'laws of nature' (survival of the fittest, supply and demand, etc). Mahler depicts, however negatively, what the world would look like once these 'laws' were repealed by redemption. (Or following Kafka, it is precisely this repeal that will bring on redemption.) Mahler, like Kafka, uses the animal kingdom as a cipher of a redeemed humanity, for whom nature represents neither a terrifying alterity nor an irremediable fate. Thus the animals show us what it would mean to be truly human, although less in an image than an after-image of the music.

Redemption thus flashes up in the artwork's play of semblance. It also flashes up in what Adorno terms 'metaphysical experience'. It is striking how important Kafka is for his notion of redemption. Adorno's first use of the optical metaphor for redemption comes in a

---

25. Theodor W Adorno, *Mahler: A Musical Physiognomy*, translated by Edmund Jephcott (Chicago: University of Chicago Press, 1992), 9.

reference to Kafka,[26] and his subsequent discussions of redemption tend to mention Kafka or to rely on turns of phrase he uses in his writings on Kafka. Similarly, when Adorno writes about metaphysical experience (*metaphysische Erfahrung*—which could also be called lived metaphysical experience or metaphysical knowledge), he tends to rely on the figure of Proust.

Following Proust, Adorno suggests that we have an intimation of the thing in itself—the thing in its 'absolute indissoluble individuation'[27]—when we feel happiness, or rather, when we anticipate or remember happiness. In happiness, we begin to experience a realm where the phenomenon and its concept coincide. We can see such a possibility of coincidence in the concept of the proper name, especially in the doctrine of the name of God.[28] Another instance in which the general and the particular come together in an uncoerced unity would be the Kantian definition of the artwork as purposefulness without a purpose, that is, as having the structure of a general law, but being a law only unto itself.

Metaphysical experience is metaphysical in a precise sense. It gives us an intimation of the thing-in-itself beyond the determinations of space and time. Hence metaphysical experience provides us with a premonition, though not a proof, of immortality. Not surprisingly, Adorno's example of such a premonition comes from Proust and, even less surprisingly, from a moment where the German translation of *The Captive* makes Proust sound uncannily like Kafka himself:

> But Proust's spirit was completely metaphysical in the midst of a world that forbids the language of metaphysics. Only once, in *The Captive*, does he open a crack, so hastily that the eye has no time to accustom itself to such light. Even the word he uses cannot be taken at its word. Here, in his depiction of Bergotte's death, there is actually a sentence whose tone, at least in the German version, echoes Kafka. It reads: 'So that

---

26. Theodor Adorno and Walter Benjamin, *The Complete Correspondence 1928–1940*, translated by Nicholas Walker (Cambridge MA: Harvard University Press, 1999), 66.

27. Adorno, *Negative Dialectics*, 373.

28. See my 'Adorno and the Name of God', in *Flashpoint*, 1:1 (1996) at www.flashpointmag.com/adorno.htm.

the idea that Bergotte was not wholly and permanently dead is by no means improbable' (510) . . . The idea that leads to this statement is the idea that the moral force of the writer whose epitaph Proust is writing belongs to an order other than the order of nature, and for this reason it holds out the promise that the order of nature is not the ultimate order.[29]

Proust's use of a double negation in his discussion of Bergotte's death (it is not improbable that he was not in fact completely dead) is a proper hedge for metaphysics, which cannot admit of empirical proof. At best, we can only be provided with a hint and nod that death is not the absolute end. It is precisely the moral force of Bergotte's writing that serves as a bridge to immortality. In a good Kantian way, the moral realm here stands for a freedom and a concomitant immortality that lie beyond the merely natural realm of necessity and law. We cannot see this realm or know it. We can only sense that it is there.

Adorno's interest in metaphysical experience leads to Proustian moments in his own prose, such as this foretaste of paradise in the child's return after vacation:

> To a child returning from holiday, home seems new, fresh, festive. Yet nothing has changed there since he left. Only because duty has now been forgotten, of which each piece of furniture, window, lamp, was otherwise a reminder, is the house given back its Sabbath peace, and for minutes one is at home in a never returning world of rooms, nooks and corridors in a way that makes the rest of life there a lie. No differently will the world one day appear, almost unchanged, in its constant feast-day light, when it stands no longer under the law of labour, and when for homecomers duty has the lightness of holiday play.[30]

---

29. Theodor Adorno, 'Short Commentaries on Proust', in *Notes to Literature*, translated by Shierry Weber Nicholsen, (Columbia: Columbia University Press, 1991), 2 Volumes, Volume 1, 183.

30. Adorno, *Minima Moralia*, 112.

Just as for the Jews, the Sabbath is supposed to provide an image of a redeemed life, so for the child returning home, the light of vacation—a time that seems, to the child at least, free from the cares of duty, from the getting and spending of everyday existence —transforms the home. Vacation provides the distorting and estranging perspective that reveals, for however short a time, the standpoint of redemption.

For Adorno, then, metaphysical experience, art and responsible thinking all begin to bathe the world in the light of redemption. They all point to transcendence but refuse to nail down its specifics. For all this, Adorno cannot be a complete agnostic about the relation between redemption, history and praxis. He has to provide some indication of how redemption might be achieved or else his philosophy will truly fall into the resigned passivity, which his critics have ascribed to it.

In a critique of the tendency to reduce the notion of progress to technology, Adorno singles out Augustine for praise because Augustine refuses to dissolve the concepts of history, progress and redemption into each other. To get rid of human history and equate progress with divine intervention is to lose the horizon of human action completely. It leads to nothing more than an eternity of quietism. If, on the other hand, you assume that redemption will be the mechanical outcome of a linear historical progress, then you strangle all emancipatory praxis in the crib. You idolise history by transforming it into a natural process. You permanently defer any demand for moral action. To put it another way, to depend on supernatural intervention or on its supposed opposite, the 'inexorable march of freedom', amounts to the same thing. It means surrendering the openness of future to the closed certainties of a mythical fate.

Augustine escaped both temptations, because he 'realized that redemption and history can exist neither without each other nor within each other but only in tension'. This tension is explosive because it 'finally desires nothing less than the sublation of the historical world itself'.31 Redemption requires intervention in history, but it is the intervention of human actors pursuing moral, not natural, ends:

> Good is what wrenches itself free, finds a language, opens its eyes. In its condition of wrestling free, it is interwoven in history that, without being organized

---

31.   Adorno, 'Progress', 147.

unequivocally toward reconciliation, in the course of
its movement allows the possibility of redemption to
flash up.[32]

History does not necessarily lead to redemption. It allows
goodness, which is constituted by a constant, vigilant resistance to evil,
to appear for however short a time. Redemption is therefore the
product of a series of struggles, of a constant waking up and of a
continuous stepping out. These struggles do not line up to form a neat
and easy narrative, but they do entail fighting against all illegitimate
domination, including the technological domination of suffering
nature. [33]

Adorno invokes redemption as a corrective to the idolatry of linear
progress. He is thus able to reassert both the need for and the risk of
moral action. Real progress, he argues, does not want to be an end in
itself, but seeks to 'cut short the triumph of radical evil'. But in the end,
there will be no final victory over such evil, because 'we live in the
perpetual danger of relapse'.[34] Redemption, which has yet to happen
for the first time, will not be limited to that first time. It will have to be
won over and over again. This final claim does seem to diminish
redemption by making it something less than conclusive, but this is the
cost that Adorno is willing to pay for maintaining freedom. He wants
to ensure that redemption remains a strictly human achievement.
Responsible thought, art and metaphysical experience are there to let
us know that redemption is possible. Moral action then puts this
possibility into play.

Redemption is an important category in Adorno's philosophy. It
stands in constant tension with immanence. It serves as the goal and
the content of all transcendence. The secularised version of redemption
is of course utopia—theology cleansed by reason and returned to the
spatio-temporal world. Adorno will not accept utopia in this way
because it does not go far enough. He preserves the theological term
precisely because its scandal is salutary. It provokes thought and it
refuses to give up anything of hope. Habermas and his followers have
been keen in their criticism of this aspect of Adorno's thought. Given
the importance of affect and intuition in his account of metaphysical

---

32.  Adorno, 'Progress', 148.
33.  Adorno, 'Progress', 150.
34.  Adorno, 'Progress', 160.

experience, it is worth asking if the truth of Adorno's work might not ultimately lie in the pathos of its desires: 'Truth is inseparable from the illusory belief that from the figures of the unreal one day, in spite of all, real deliverance will come.'[35]

---

35.   Adorno, *Minima Moralia*, 121.

# 2

# From Invisible Redemption to Invisible Hopeful Action in Karl Barth

## Geoff Thompson

Messianism, apocalypse and redemption are among those themes that both implicitly and explicitly have most forcefully separated Christian theology from modern thought. Precisely because they are inseparable from the themes of judgment and finality, and because they have not infrequently been (mis)appropriated by the fanatics, they are at the heart of those elements of Christianity which most offended the sensibilities of modernity's thinkers. Additionally, these ideas have frequently been aligned with world-denying forms of Christianity rightly attacked by the critics. Any Christian theological development of these themes cannot ignore that criticism and is under some obligation to demonstrate that by holding to such convictions (rather than abandoning them) Christianity does not at all license any flight from this world.

There is perhaps no more important test case of such a challenge than the Swiss Protestant theologian, Karl Barth (1886–1968). After a century or more of the deferential and revisionist protestant theology which preceded him, Barth emerged as a theologian committed to retrieving and developing Christianity's core convictions—in part because, in his view, such a Christianity better addressed the critics than did the revisionists, and better addressed the human condition than did modernity itself. Even if the themes of messianism and apocalypse were not developed as independent themes, and even if he never got to write his definitive text on redemption,[1] Barth's early and

---

1.  Barth intended to conclude his multi-volume *magnum opus, Church Dogmatics*, with an account of the doctrine of redemption. Declining health and energy levels in his mid-seventies led him to leave the work unfinished without the concluding volume.

epochal writings were infused with eschatological concerns, a fact which alone made him a seminal figure in the twentieth century theological discussion about hope. Those early writings emerged whilst Barth was serving as a pastor in Safenwil (1911–21) where he was forced to wrestle with the demands of Christian ministry at a time of crisis and uncertainty. This struggle resulted in him abandoning the German liberal protestant tradition in which he had been trained, and subsequently led him to a succession of three academic posts in Germany[2] before being expelled by the Nazis in 1935. He then returned to Basle where, as Professor of Dogmatics until 1962, he continued to develop a theology in which themes of eschatology and human hope, although now taking their place on a much larger doctrinal canvas, continued to claim his attention.

The context in which Barth's theology first emerged was marked by 'an intoxicating combination of nihilism and eschatological consciousness.'[3] Modernity's confidence in itself had been shattered. Barth's response to this crisis was distinctive. Whereas some secular thinkers were prepared to address the crisis by retrieving explicitly theological themes without their classical content, Barth retrieved classical theological themes but he did not merely retrieve their classical theological content. He radically 'Christianised' that content by taking with full seriousness the centrality of Jesus Christ to Christian theology. As will be demonstrated below, any interest in messianism was conditioned by the identity of Jesus the Messiah, and any interest in redemption was structured by the conviction that Jesus Christ is the redeemer.

In this paper some elements of Barth's early engagement with the climate of crisis will be sketched, and some features of the theological agenda which this engagement set for him will be noted. The paper will then move to outline how his conviction that redemption was focused in the future of Jesus Christ, far from evading the 'nihilism and eschatological consciousness' of the age, contributed a very specific Christian understanding of hope and human freedom.

During his time in Safenwil Barth was deeply engaged with Swiss religious socialism. At the height of his involvement, he would even

---

2.    Göttingen, 1921–5; Münster, 1925–30; Bonn, 1930–5.

3.    Richard H Roberts, 'Barth and the Eschatology of Weimar: A Theology on its Way', in *A Theology On Its Way: Essays on Karl Barth*, edited by Richard H Roberts (Edinburgh: T&T Clark, 1991), 171.

write, 'Real socialism is real Christianity in our time'.[4] Ulitmately, Barth would adopt a more critical posture towards socialism. Nevertheless, it exposed him to a set of theological ideas that were to prove pivotal for his developing theology. In the background to the socialist movement were the father and son, Johann and Christoph Blumhardt. Johann had died in 1880 and Christoph died in 1915, but not before he had made a deep impression on Barth. The Blumhardts' contribution was to bring a strong conviction about the immediate power of God into conversation with the social and cultural crisis. But added to this immediacy, was the scope of this power. It was not a power confined to the church. According to Christoph Blumhardt, as quoted by Barth, the world 'as a whole . . . needs and awaits a thoroughgoing redemption and renewal, not through religion, but through the real power of God'.[5] Here was a tentative theological discourse that allowed socialism to be understood as a sign that God was at work in the world, and involved in the crisis of modern society. Even as socialism lost its grip on Barth's own imagination, the lessons from the Blumhardts remained.

These lessons are seen in Barth's first two book-length scholarly works: two separate commentaries (published in 1919 and 1921 respectively) on Paul's letter to the Romans. That Barth's contribution to the cultural crisis now takes the form of biblical commentary is itself of enormous significance. Barth has discovered the 'strange new world of the bible' and has set himself apart from the liberal theological tradition.

In the first commentary Barth declares that 'in the messianic present, inaugurated by the decisive turn in heaven, a life process is opened up on earth'.[6] A *messianic present* is a present not devoid of hope: 'there is life, which is grounded through the fullness, the outpouring of the grace of God . . . and now organically unfolds itself.'[7] The Blumhardtian emphasis on the power of God is now

---

4.    Karl Barth, 'Jesus Christ and the Movement for Social Justice', in *Karl Barth: Theologian of Freedom*, edited by Clifford Green (London: Collins, 1989), 114.

5.    Karl Barth, 'Past and Future', in *The Beginnings of Dialectical Theology*, edited by James Smart (Richmond: John Knox Press, 1968), 41.

6.    Karl Barth, *Der Römerbrief. Erste Fassung, 1919* (Zurich: TVZ, 1985) (my translation), 167.

7.    Karl Barth, *Der Römerbrief. Erste Fassung, 1919* (my translation), 195.

intensified by stressing the priority of God, and the particularity of the
Incarnation. There might be a life process opened up on earth, there
might be life 'organically' unfolding itself, but it is inaugurated by a
'decisive' turn in heaven which, as it were, plays itself out on earth.
The language of 'organic growth' or 'unfolding process' was not,
therefore, intended to refer to any possibilities already existing in
history.

To the priority of God and the particularity of the Incarnation of the
first edition Barth adds to the second edition a radical eschatology. He
had come to understand the relationship of heaven to earth, of God to
creation and of eternity to time in terms of radical contrast. This is
given classical expression in what is probably the most quoted passage
of the book, that is, the passage on the Apostle Paul's: 'For in hope we
are saved. Now hope that is seen is not hope. For who hopes for what
is seen? But we hope for what we do not see, we wait for it with
patience (Paul 8: 24,25).' Barth comments:

> Could we wish anything else that this saving hope
> should always be declared at the cross, should always
> set a boundary against everything in our world, and
> should always manifest itself at that boundary. Were
> we to know more of God than the groans of creation
> and our own groaning; were we to know a Jesus Christ
> otherwise than as crucified; were we to know the Holy
> Spirit otherwise than as the Spirit of Him that raised
> Jesus from the dead;
> . . . there would be no salvation. *For hope that is seen is
> not hope* . . . If Christianity be not altogether
> thoroughgoing eschatology, there remains in it no
> relationship whatever with Christ. Spirit which does
> not at every moment point from death to the new life is
> not the holy Spirit . . . All that is not hope is wooden,
> hobbledehoy, blunt-edged, and sharp-pointed . . . there
> is no freedom, but only imprisonment; no grace, but
> only condemnation and corruption; no divine
> guidance, but only fate; no God, but only a mirror of
> unredeemed humanity. And this is so, be there never
> so much progress of social reform and never so much
> trumpeting of the grandeur of Christian redemption.

> Redemption is invisible, inaccessible, and impossible,
> for it meets us only in hope.[8]

These last two sentences crystallise two of the important themes of the book. The first theme is the attack on both the religious and political status quo—to which even the call to political revolution is subjected.[9] Barth's language is severe. The cross casts its shadow over all seemingly healthy life: the 'tenacity of [religious] men is disturbed, shattered and dissolved'.[10] Seen in the light of the resurrection 'every concrete thing that we appreciate as life and fullness, as great and high, becomes primarily a parable of death'. The second feature is the way Barth problematically reinforces this talk of the invisibility of redemption by depriving it of temporal continuity. This is evident in his famous geometrical metaphors with which he describes the revelation of God in the resurrection of Jesus the crucified:

> As Christ, Jesus is the plane which lies beyond our
> comprehension. The plane which is known to us, He
> intersects vertically from above . . . In the resurrection
> the new world of the Holy Spirit touches the old world
> of the flesh, but touches it as a tangent touches a circle,
> that is, without touching it.[11]

This same way of thinking also sees Barth move from speaking, of a *messianic present*, as he did in the first commentary, to speaking of the particular identity of the Messiah: 'Jesus as the Christ, as the Messiah, is the End of History.'[12]

What emerges through this period is that Barth's engagement with the world of crisis and the quest for redemption assumes particular theological contours: from the Blumhardts and the religious socialists he developed the conviction that God was a real power, able to be a real force and presence in an unstable and uncertain world. His reading of the bible has taught him the complete priority of God. His

---

8.  Karl Barth, *The Epistle to the Romans*, translated by Edward Hoskyns (Oxford: Oxford University Press, 1968), 314.

9.  See Barth, *The Epistle to the Romans*, 481–5.

10. Barth, *The Epistle to the Romans*, 239.

11. Barth, *The Epistle to the Romans*, 29f.

12. Barth, *The Epistle to the Romans*, 29.

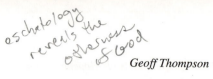

discovery of eschatology has taught him the complete otherness of God, as revealed in the cross and resurrection of Jesus.

These theological developments are important because they indicate that Barth, whilst deeply engaged with his context, is not exhaustively determined by his context. Barth does speak of crisis in the second Romans commentary, but he speaks of the crisis which, as it were, lies behind the crisis.[13] The power of God, 'being completely different, is the *krisis* of all power'.[14] Or, more concretely, 'Philosophers name this crisis of human perception—the Prime Cause: the Bible beholds at the same crossroads— the figure of Jesus Christ'.[15]

By the time Barth had completed the second commentary, he had accepted a professorial chair at Göttingen. He now begins a remarkable theological journey, in the early stages of which he discovers the genre of dogmatics, and it will be this genre in which he develops his theology and which will ultimately issue in his fourteen volumes of *Church Dogmatics*. In the course of this work, Barth recognised that to speak of the invisibility, inaccessibility and impossibility of redemption was itself inadequate. In the second volume of the *Church Dogmatics* he would write that although 'confident to treat the far-sidedness of the coming kingdom of God with absolute seriousness, I had no such confidence in relation to its coming as such'. He acknowledges the need for correction because he believed the biblical passage at issue ascribes a teleology 'to time as it moves towards a real end'.[16]

Formally, Barth's correction is twofold. It involves, on the one hand, developing an account of the relationship of time and eternity which excludes opposition between them. He does this by incorporating time into the concept of eternity. God's eternity is not timelessness but 'pure duration'[17] in which there is 'no opposition or competition or conflict . . . between present past and future'.[18] There is, therefore, a 'positive relationship of eternity to time', which consists

---

13.  See Barth, *The Epistle to the Romans*, 46.

14.  Barth, *Epistle to the Romans*, 36.

15.  Barth, *Epistle to the Romans*, 10.

16.  Karl Barth, *Church Dogmatics*, edited by GW Bromiley and TF Torrance (Edinburgh: T&T Clark, 1956–77), Volume II, part 1, 635. All subsequent references to the *Church Dogmatics* will be in the form of *Church Dogmatics*, volume number/part number, page number.

17.  *Church Dogmatics*, II/1, 608.

18.  *Church Dogmatics*, II/1, 612.

'in the fact that eternity faithfully accompanies time on high'.[19] Secondly, as well as positively relating time to eternity and thereby giving an account of God in the present, he develops the future dimension of eschatology. On the basis of the positive relationship of eternity to time he argues that 'we really do have to seek God in the perpendicular relationship . . . in each present of our time', but on the basis of the future eschatology 'we have also to seek Him in the future'.[20]

The material basis of both this positive assessment of time, and the retrieval of the future dimension of eschatology is Jesus Christ. The affirmation of the present does not rest on any principle of hope. Nor does the confidence in the future rest on any generic priority of the future.[21] Indeed, echoing earlier themes, 'Redemption does not mean that that world and we ourselves within it evolve in this or that direction. It means that Jesus Christ is coming again.'[22] Barth defines the life of hope that waits for this redemption: it is to 'move towards (the) final and yet also . . . immediate future . . . in confident, patient and cheerful expectation of His new coming'.[23]

Does Barth's increasing focus on Jesus Christ amount, however, to simply yet another endorsement of a world-denying Christianity? Answering these questions requires an investigation of Barth's mature reflections on hope and redemption.

---

19.  *Church Dogmatics*, II/1, 623.
20.  *Church Dogmatics*, II/1, 624.
21.  In this respect Barth's position will continue to fail to satisfy critics such as Moltmann and Pannenberg. In fact, in the late 1950s (still several years before Moltmann's *Theology of Hope*) Barth was already registering his disquiet at the impact of a generic eschatology on Christian theology. Eschatology, he wrote, 'has suddenly been extended to cover and explain the transcendent character of all the subjects and contents of theological discussion. In addition, it has come to be either completely or almost completely equated with the strangely empty because negative concept of the uncontrollable . . . The only trouble is that little importance can now be attached to a particularly eschatological sphere of hope as Christian expectation of the future, or to hope itself as a particular dimension of Christian existence' (*Church Dogmatics*, IV/3, 912).
22.  *Church Dogmatics*, II/1, 78.

That a future redemption still awaits does not, in Barth's particular combination of doctrinal and conceptual moves, diminish the present. The final coming of Jesus Christ does mean that the present is provisional, but as Barth would write to Jürgen Moltmann after reading the latter's *Theology of Hope*,[24] not 'merely provisional'.[25] As before, these are not merely formal considerations about the present and the future. They stem from the material considerations of who Jesus Christ is and the nature of his present life. To unpack this cluster of ideas, the following three questions will be asked: Who is this Jesus Christ? Why is his life a history? Why is the present not merely provisional?

*Who is this Jesus Christ?* He is the one who, truly God, truly human, achieves the reconciliation of God and humanity through his life and his death on the cross. He is the mediator of the covenant between God and Israel, and the one who reveals its meaning for the whole world. He is the Messiah who has fulfilled Israel's hopes. In Jesus Christ, 'the Messianic secret was not just penetrated but removed altogether'.[26] The resurrection is the declaration of this completed reconciliation. Following the resurrection Jesus is universally present in the power of the Holy Spirit. In his risen form of existence he does not cease to be the reconciler, and he continues to live the life, albeit in a different form, through which he reconciled the world to God. Thus he still lives as the suffering Jesus Christ. The resurrection does not mean that some other truth, perhaps more purely sanguine and less confronting, is to be declared. What he was in his earthly life he remains in his spiritual form. 'It is in this form of suffering, as the wholly Rejected, Judged,

---

23.   *Church Dogmatics*, IV/3, 902.
24.   Jürgen Moltmann, *Theology of Hope: On the Ground and Implication of a Christian Theology* (London: SCM Press, 1967).
25.   See Karl Barth, *Letters 1961–1968* (Edinburgh: T&T Clark, 1981), 174.
26.   *Church Dogmatics*, IV/2, 14. Barth's resistance to ascribing any general messianic quality to time or history independently of the identity of the Messiah, is extended to the way he understands Israel's history as messianic. Israel's history is messianic 'only because it is not merely impelled by an idea or conception of the Messiah, but the Messiah himself exists and takes from in it, so that its witness is His self-witness, and the announcement of its mystery his self-announcement, the announcement of His coming, his appearing' (*Church Dogmatics*, IV/3, 66).

Despised, Bound, Impotent, Slain and Crucified, and therefore as the Victor, that He marches with us and to us through the times, alive in the promise of the Spirit.'[27]

*Why is his life a 'history'?* In line with the dynamic categories of his thought, Barth writes that Jesus Christ Himself and the reconciliation which he has achieved 'is an event': 'It is a drama, which can only be followed, or rather, experienced and recounted.'[28] Yet an even more precise point needs to be made. It is a history not just because it is moving towards a goal. Barth's more precise answer is as follows:

> The necessity of a historical understanding . . . results supremely from the fact that His light, Word and revelation no less than His life, covenant and reconciliation, are challenged by an opposition which encounters them and His . . . rule thus consist[s] practically in the overcoming of this challenge.[29]

For all that Jesus is the light of life, this time is 'not only the sphere of the light of life shining in it'.[30] Indeed, neither the affirmation of the present nor the confidence in Christ's coming redemption translates into a na ve optimism about the present. Indeed, it translates into something quite different:

> The sphere of our time and history is not then, the theatre of a decrease of darkness, as we might suppose, but rather of its intensification and increase. The New Testament give us not the slightest grounds for regarding the era *post Christum* as one when the human contradiction . . . shows any signs of decrease, but rather as a period of its augmentation together with that of the Word of God.[31]

The distinctive feature of Barth's account of this conflict is that whilst the conflict is real, its result is assured. In seeking to characterise

---

27.  *Church Dogmatics*, IV/3, 390.
28.  *Church Dogmatics*, IV/3, 166.
29.  *Church Dogmatics*, IV/3, 166.
30.  *Church Dogmatics*, IV/3, 392.
31.  *Church Dogmatics*, IV/3, 392.

this relationship between Jesus and the darkness, he denies that it is dualistic ('We do not have an equilibrium of opposing forces'[32]) and that it is monistic ('The power of light is not so overwhelming in relation to that of darkness that darkness has lost its power altogether'[33]). Rather it is a dynamic teleology: 'If from the very first there can be no doubt as to the issue of the action, there can also be no doubt there is an action, and that it is taking place, and can thus be described only in the form of narration.'[34]

*Why is the present not merely provisional?* To a degree the stress on the conflict between light and darkness is its own negative answer to this question. But there is also a more positive answer, and of the various moves Barth makes in his exploration of this whole question it is perhaps the more overtly conceptual. It focuses on what he terms the threefold form of the *parousia*. He proposes that Easter, this present time of the Spirit, and Jesus' future definitive coming are 'one continuous event' in three different forms: 'Always and in all three forms it is a matter of the fresh coming of the One who came before. Always and in different ways it is a matter of the coming again of Jesus Christ.'[35] Whilst acknowledging that he is going beyond the strict use of the term *parousia* in the New Testament, he believes he can extend the term to all three because in all three 'we have to do with the one new coming of Him who came before'.[36] Then in order to guarantee the distinctions within this unity, he appeals to the Trinitarian concept of *perichoresis* and its particular strategy of speaking of unity-in-distinction. The three forms 'are mutually related as the forms of this one action by the fact that each of them also contains the other two by way of anticipation or recapitulation, so that without losing their individuality or destroying that of the others, they participate and are active and revealed in them'.[37]

The point to be emphasised here is that this conceptuality allows Barth to stress the particularity of each of the forms, but in such a way that the relationship between them is neither merely sequential nor merely cumulative. Each form is to be understood as Jesus'

---

32.   *Church Dogmatics*, IV/3, 168.
33.   *Church Dogmatics*, IV/3, 168.
34.   *Church Dogmatics*, IV/3, 168.
35.   *Church Dogmatics*, IV/3, 293.
36.   *Church Dogmatics*, IV/3, 294.
37.   *Church Dogmatics*, IV/3, 296.

'manifestation in effective presence' and 'is not more in one case or less in another'.[38] If the life of Jesus Christ has a dynamic teleology, he is not subject to—and nor is the dynamic teleology to be confused with—any cumulative process. His present—whilst being united to his past and future and conditioned by them—is not determined by them. The reason for this is that it is not a formal dynamic teleology but Jesus Christ Himself who remains the subject of this history. The different forms of the *parousia* correspond 'to the willing and fulfillment of the action of its one Subject, Jesus Christ'.[39]

This intense focus on Jesus Christ, as definitive of spiritual realities, is no less challenging to conventional Christian piety than it is incredible to secularists and offensive to the contemporary proponents of generic spirituality. The christological particularity also separates Barth's account from the Hegelian idea of history as the self-realisation of spirit. For Barth it is Jesus' history which is the 'origin, meaning and goal of all occurrence',[40] it 'impinges upon and includes within itself all history'.[41] But more than a mere framework, it is also, says Barth, a 'self-multiplying history'; 'it reproduces itself'.[42] Barth continues: 'It evokes its own reflection in the world and among men in the form of Christian knowledge of what has taken place in Jesus Christ'.[43] What is done in Jesus Christ 'should express and assert itself'; 'it should be effective and visible'.[44] Such is the ground of the existence and life of the Christian community. This is not to say that this history is only reproduced in the church, or that the church is its only form of reproduction. There is, writes Barth, in relation to the Christian community on the one hand and the world on the other, 'a distinct yet not an absolute but only a fluid and changing frontier'.[45] (The lessons about the scope of God's power, learnt from the Blumhardts and the religious socialists, were never forgotten by Barth.) Nevertheless, it is the Christian community which is commissioned to know and share in this history. And as it does so, this visible, effective, ecclesial

---

38. *Church Dogmatics*, IV/3, 293.
39. *Church Dogmatics*, IV/3, 293.
40. *Church Dogmatics*, IV/3, 211.
41. *Church Dogmatics*, IV/3, 191.
42. *Church Dogmatics*, IV/3, 212.
43. *Church Dogmatics*, IV/3, 212.
44. *Church Dogmatics*, IV/3, 211.
45. *Church Dogmatics*, IV/3, 192.

reproduction shares not just in the fact, but also the form of Jesus' history. This visible Christian history 'resembles its origin, theme and content [and] comes up against non-recognition, resistance and contradiction'.[46]

It is this which involves Christian people being summoned to 'rise up in rebellion against the regime'[47] of darkness. The significance of this aspect of Barth's theology has been highlighted in recent years by Professor John Webster, and here I am drawing on his work in particular.[48] Such rebellion is 'similar, parallel, and analogous to the act of God Himself',[49] and as analogous it is both like and unlike God's act.

> Strictly speaking, we can engage only in continual beginnings of resistance, in continually new steps in the allotted direction . . . Even in its best forms our resistance, within its limits, will on good grounds never be more than a very feeble and not a perfect work. Nevertheless, undertaken in obedience and ventured with humility and resoluteness, it will not just be unlike God's act but also like it, running parallel to it on our level, a modest but clear analogue . . . [50]

Thus does Barth ascribe dignity to visible, hopeful action; a derived dignity to be sure. Nevertheless, precisely because it is a dignity derived from God revealed in Jesus Christ, it is not a limiting

46.  *Church Dogmatics*, IV/3, 212.
47.  Karl Barth, 'The Christian Life', in *Church Dogmatics,* IV/4, translated by Geoffrey W Bromiley (Edinburgh: T&T Clark, 1981), 174.
48.  In particular see John Webster, '"Assured and Patient and Cheerful Expectation": Barth on Christian Hope as the Church's Task', in *Barth's Moral Theology: Human Action in Barth's Thought,* edited by John Webster (Grand Rapids: Eerdmans, 1998), 77–98; John Webster, *Barth's Ethics of Reconciliation* (Cambridge: CUP, 1995); and John Webster, 'The Christian in Revolt: Some Reflections on *The Christian Life*', in *Reckoning with Barth: Essays in commemoration of the Centenary of Barth's Birth,* edited by Nigel Biggar (London: Mowbray: 1988), 119–44.
49.  Barth, *The Christian Life,* 175.
50.  Barth, *The Christian Life,* 175.

derivation. Nor is it an action whose dignity is threatened by being derived, or whose reality threatens that from which it is derived. As Webster says, 'there is a community of agency between God and humanity'. It is an account of freedom that stems from 'the fact that the history of God and humanity is a history with two subjects and agents'.[51] As such, Christians are caught up in the same revolt against the disorder of life against which Christ's own mission is directed:

> The general plight against which Christians are commanded to revolt and fight is the disorder which both inwardly and outwardly controls and penetrates and poisons and disrupts all human relations and interconnections. Disorder arises and consists in deviation from order. The human race exists in such deviation. The order from which it deviates is the form of an obedient life of people in fellowship with God which includes as such the corresponding form—the guarantee of human right, freedom and peace—of a life of people in fellowship with one another. The former includes the latter because God is not an egoistic supreme being remote and alien from man and ruling over him as fate. He is the God of man, his Creator, Lord, Helper and Judge. Furthermore, man for his part does not belong to anybody or to any powers. He belongs to God and is the man of God as God is the God of man. In the revelation of this order, in the declaration of its divine righteousness as the basis and guarantee of human righteousness, God is the One he is, the God who is gracious to man as such, who affirms all men, and who in so doing works all things together for their good.[52]

This text draws together many of the themes addressed in this paper. Barth's point is this: to belong to God revealed in Jesus Christ and to hope in the redemption which Jesus Christ is, is in a very particular way to be oriented not away from the world but freely oriented towards the world in the same manner as God is.

---

51. Webster, *Barth's Ethics of Reconciliation*, 187
52. Barth, *The Christian Life*, 210f.

In the early parts of this paper, Barth's earliest theology was placed in the context of the cultural crisis. Clearly Barth was engaged with wider cultural discussions of messianism and redemption. Yet as his theology developed he became increasingly focused on Jesus Christ who, as Messiah, had already filled Israel's and the world's hopes, and who, in his future coming, is himself redemption. In the end, Barth does not respond to the cultural crises with a principle of hope, or any interest in a generic priority of the future. Initially his focus on Jesus Christ, led him to speak of the invisibility of redemption. Subsequently, through developing a more comprehensive account of the relationship of eternity to time he could speak of the proper theological significance of this present era. Yet this too, was not merely a formal issue. This era draws its significance from the life history of Jesus Christ as he moves, in conflict with a still-to-be-vanquished darkness, from his resurrection to his final coming again, which is redemption. This history, he argues, is a self-multiplying history, evoking reflections in the world of humanity. Upon these foundations, hope is no longer invisible. It is visible, taking the form of acts of covenantal obedience which resist the disorder of the human condition. Such visible hopeful action is true freedom and subjectivity. Redemption for Barth, therefore, is framed by an eschatology which, in the words of John McDowell, takes its 'cue less from a desire to provide the narcotic of a secure "way out" than an unavoidable risky pilgrimage *through* and engagement *with* the pressures and strains and futilities of our unlit and unwritten futures'.[53]

---

53.   John C McDowell, *Hope in Barth's Eschatology* (Aldershot: Ashgate, 2000), 215.

# 3

# 'Hope, Yes, But Not For Us': Messianism and Redemption in the Work of Walter Benjamin

## Bram Mertens

On 2 December 1960, Albert Salomon wrote to Gershom Scholem about his plans to write a book on Benjamin, saying:

> It is, of course, valid to state his position as an unorthodox marxist, unorthodox because his Marxist critique is overshadowed by the radicalism of his unorthodox Jewish existence.
>
> His experience of the human lot as a communion of suffering and that the totality of the Condition Humaine is only intelligible to theological categories, is a genuinely revolutionary attitude which merges with the Marxist radicalism in a Messianic perspective.
>
> His rediscovery of guilt, grace, redemption, sacrifice, freedom in dedication and salvation in spite of our knowledge that the throne of God is empty indicates the heroism and the Majestitia of the Human Situation.[1]

The author gratefully acknowledges the support of the British Academy in preparing this chapter.

1. Quoted in Gershom Scholem, *Briefe*, 3 Volumes, edited by Itta Shedletzky and Thomas Sparr (München: Beck, 1994–1999), Volume 2, 261.

It seems a shame that Salomon's project never came to fruition, as this short sketch captures the essence of Benjamin's thought better than more hefty tomes have managed to do so far. The description of Benjamin as both an unorthodox Marxist and an unorthodox Jew is wonderfully accurate. In a letter to Ludwig Strauß Benjamin himself admitted freely that he never received a proper (religious) Jewish education: 'I hardly need to tell you that I received a liberal education . . . As a religion [Judaism] was distant, as a nationality unknown.'[2] By the same token, Benjamin's brushes with Marxism came only relatively late in his life, and even then he appears to have garnered most of his knowledge from reading Karl Korsch. It is also a fundamental truth that Benjamin's work can only properly be understood in theological categories, as much as it is often not written in theological terms. Yet it is equally true that Benjamin was never a theologian *pur sang*. Although we have no direct evidence either way, the throne of God was most probably empty to him, and whereas he was convinced that history could not be understood in a-theological terms, he also insisted on the necessity of secularising this theology by constructing his philosophy of history around the very profane concept of human happiness. 'The existence of God is not a problem', writes Scholem,[3] and this is perhaps the perfect legend to Benjamin's philosophy. His main concern is not to prove the veracity of a religious belief or an ideological system—there are far more pressing problems in his time—but to show that until the Messiah comes, we have only been given hope 'for the sake of the hopeless'.[4]

The concept of redemption, or *Rettung*, is one of the most prominent concepts, theological or otherwise, throughout Benjamin's work. The first and least exposed version of redemption comes from Benjamin's notoriously complex *Ursprung des deutschen Trauerspiels*, or *Origin of the German Mourning Play*, published in 1925. The theoretical

---

2.   Walter Benjamin, *Gesammelte Briefe*, 6 Volumes, edited by Christoph Gödde and Henri Lonitz (Frankfurt am Main: Suhrkamp, 1995–2000), Volume 1, 69–70.

3.   Gershom Scholem, *Tagebücher nebst Aufsätzen und Entwürfen bis (1923)*, 2 Volumes, edited by Karlfried Gründer und Friedrich Niewöhner (Frankfurt am Main: Jüdischer Verlag, 1999–2000), Volume 1, 304.

4.   Walter Benjamin, *Gesammelte Schriften*, 7 Volumes, edited by Rolf Tiedemann and Herman Schweppenhäuser (Frankfurt am Main: Suhrkamp, 1974–99), Volume 1, 201.

framework of *Ursprung des deutschen Trauerspiels*, expounded in the now infamous foreword, is Benjamin's response to the Marburg neo-kantianism which dominated his university years. The redemption which is central to the book, therefore, is the (quasi-) metaphysical *Rettung der Phänomene*, or the salvation of the phenomena, whereby the latter term is understood in opposition to the platonic Ideas or the kantian *noumena*, the things-in-themselves. Benjamin's specific form of *Rettung der Phänomene* is twofold. Firstly it seeks to redeem everyday empirical phenomena from the instrumental rationality which he feels pervades the post-Enlightenment scientific world view. According to Benjamin, the perspective of modern science demeans everyday phenomena as it reduces them to fundamentally passive objects of knowledge, which he defines tersely as a 'having'.[5] The relationship which the scientific rationality spawned by the Enlightenment entertains with the object world is a possessive one, even a predatory one. It seeks to get hold of the objects and classify them according to 'higher' principles, thereby not only devaluing the object world in epistemological and moral terms, but also stripping the objects of their specificity and uniqueness, both in time and in space, in order to grasp or understand them (the German word for to understand, *begreifen*, also includes the word *greifen*, a word with a slightly aggressive undertone meaning to grasp or to clutch).

Benjamin counters what he considers to be a defective viewpoint by redefining the relationship between objects on the one hand and ideas and concepts on the other, and by insisting at the same time on a fundamental distinction between truth and knowledge. If he defined knowledge as a 'having', then truth is defined as a 'being': 'Truth is an intentionless being constructed out of ideas. The correct relationship towards it is therefore not [extracting a] meaning in [an attempt at] knowing, but immersing [oneself] and disappearing into it.'[6] With a methodological *prise de position* typical of Benjamin's work, he shifts the emphasis away from an active, intentional and predatory approach to the object world which seeks to extract a commodity called knowledge, and suggests in its place a more passive, receptive and contemplative mind-set which allows a truth, although not necessarily *the* truth, about the object world to reveal itself. The receptivity of this method automatically turns truth into a given, quite literally

---

5.   Benjamin, *Gesammelte Schriften*, Volume 1, 209.
6.   Benjamin, *Gesammelte Schriften*, Volume 1, 216.

something which is offered to the inquiring subject and which must thus necessarily come from outside the subject, assuming, in other words, the form of a revelation. Indeed, it is with the definition of truth as an intentionless being that the *Erkenntniskritische Vorrede* takes an emphatically mystical turn, and it comes as no surprise that the ultimate intentionless being which determines the revelation of ideas themselves is revealed as the Name. This mysticism, however, establishes the radical separation between the world of ideas and the object world in such fundamental terms that any immediate contact between the two spheres is now no longer impossible. Yet this is the point where Benjamin's second *Rettung der Phänomene* opens up the possibility of a mediated contact between the spheres of the ideal and the real, and thus of truth and world.

The kind of mediation described by Benjamin follows directly from his insistence that knowledge can be wanted but that truth has to be revealed, and thus can only be hoped for, not unlike the Messiah himself. The mediator Benjamin introduces is, predictably, a linguistic one: it is the concept or *Begriff*, which allows the idea to manifest itself as a constellation. Using an image from Goethe, Benjamin describes this process as follows:

> Ideas . . . are faustian mothers. They remain dark when the phenomena do not stand by them and gather around them. Bringing the phenomena together is the task of the concepts, and the division which takes place in them through the activity of the discriminating mind is all the more meaningful because it achieves a twin aim: the redemption of the phenomena and the representation of the ideas.[7]

It is, in other words, almost as if the idea becomes visible and truth is revealed at the moment when a spark jumps between two poles which do not touch each other: a positively charged pole which we can see (that is, the object world) and a negatively charged pole which we cannot see until the spark illuminates it (that is, the idea). Without this sudden connection, the phenomenal world would remain fragmented and meaningless, and the world of the ideas would forever run on a

---

7.    Benjamin, *Gesammelte Schriften*, Volume 1, 215.

line parallel to the object world but never touching it, remaining unrevealed.

But *Ursprung des deutschen Trauerspiels* is not only concerned with this epistemological and metaphysical version of redemption. One of its main thrusts is a re-evaluation of an almost forgotten art form, considered by critics to be a poor and uninteresting relation of the literary production immediately preceding and following it. This art form, as the book's title suggests, is the baroque *Trauerspiel* or 'mourning play', dark and melancholy plays heavy with apocalyptic allusions and allegorical representations of a world in decay, which were seen in stark contrast to what critics in Benjamin's day considered to be the more interesting and intellectually ambitious literatures of the Renaissance and the Classical era. The latter literature was dominated by the category of the symbolic, promising an immediacy and totality of experience which baroque literature did not, could not and would not deliver. As an art form, *Trauerspiel* was, therefore, largely ignored by critics in Benjamin's time, as it did not fit into the comfortable pattern of a continuous tradition. If it was discussed at all, it was in an attempt to somehow fit it into the continuity of a literary and cultural tradition by explaining it away as a symptom, taking the form it did as a necessary reaction to or a product of its turbulent historical circumstances. Benjamin calls this kind of insincere reappraisal a *Würdigung*, which reduces the artwork to a function or a reflection of a historical era, and which is at best more apology than redemption. Yet what he objects to most in any attempt at reappraising past art forms in these terms is that it glosses over every discontinuity and every note of dissonance sounded against the perceived uninterrupted course of the—in this case literary—tradition. The idea that not all tradition is good tradition, and that the wrong kind of (pseudo-) redemption would in fact be worse than no redemption at all, returns very forcefully in the *Passagen-Werk*, or the *Arcades Project*, Benjamin's unfinished magnum opus:

> From what are the phenomena redeemed? Not just, not even in the first instance, from the disdain and the disrepute into which they have fallen, but from the catastrophe that is their representation as 'patrimony', as a certain kind of tradition has it. They are redeemed by pointing out the leap [that is, discontinuity] within

them. There is a kind of tradition which is
catastrophe.[8]

Benjamin again insists that the moment when true knowledge
about an object or a work of art reveals itself is at the point where there
is a rupture, a discontinuity, where the object reveals itself to be a
fragment. It is no coincidence that Benjamin has chosen the baroque
*Trauerspiel* as the art form with which to illustrate this opposition of
tradition and discontinuity, not only because he interprets it as a
forgotten and outmoded form, but also because the dominant mode of
expression of the *Trauerspiel* itself is allegory. Benjamin opposes
allegory to symbol, whereby the latter expresses immediacy, organic
totality, transparency and presence, and the former expresses and
indeed consists of displacement, fragmentation, deferral and absence.
In what Benjamin calls the antinomy of allegoresis, allegory recycles
images and objects which it lifts out of their original context,
emphasising the fragmentation of the unredeemed object world but at
the same time redeeming the objects by using them in the allegorical
image.

At this point, *Ursprung des deutschen Trauerspiels* explicitly
introduces the third and specifically theological meaning of
redemption, namely the salvation of the finite and mortal world. In
order to do this, Benjamin uses the theological triad of paradise, fall
and redemption. In his version of the pattern, the fall constitutes a
descent from unity into duality, represented by the biblical story of the
tree of the knowledge of good and evil, which introduces this duality
into the world, but which also introduces duality into the word,
separating meaning and form. Language in prelapsarian paradise is
the divine, undivided and unmediated language of names, rather than
signs, in which all creatures have but one name which is at one with
their being. The fall into human language, which also creates human
language as an entity distinct from divine language, introduces
difference, division, multiplicity, convention and mediation. The
prelapsarian and postlapsarian states are not simply separated by
time, they are qualitatively absolutely different states: they no longer
speak the same language, so any reference a fallen humanity makes to
the state of paradise is already essentially and necessarily allegorical.
But to Benjamin, allegory also describes the state of creation after the

---

8.    Benjamin, *Gesammelte Schriften*, Volume 5, 591.

fall. It has become fragmented, lifeless and devoid of meaning, forced back into a mute and passive objectivity. Whereas in the state of paradise, still according to Benjamin, mankind and creation came together in the divine act of naming with which God charged mankind, the world remains mute after the fall, and any meaning assigned to it by mankind is conventional, transitory and arbitrary. The further this process goes, the more of the 'original' meaning is lost, the more allegory becomes the only way in which to make sense of a decaying world.[9] And thus the concept of redemption described in *Ursprung des deutschen Trauerspiels* comes full circle, as the allegorist is the only one who is able to bring the object world closer to redemption in what seems like an extremely paradoxical way: precisely by emphasising, reinforcing, thematising and using its unredeemed state.

The theology which Benjamin uses throughout his work (witness the version described above) is neither a fully-fledged and closed system, nor is it a straightforward and unproblematic theology. Theology in the work of Walter Benjamin is an ambiguous, yet constant presence, a framework which he uses to order his thoughts, but also an outdated and endangered mode of thinking which is itself in need of redemption. For these reasons, Benjamin tends to conceal the theological patterns in his texts, a strategy which he himself thematises so famously in his allegorical image of the dwarf in the chess machine, in which the dwarf of theology, 'which is small and ugly nowadays, and cannot show itself under any circumstances', animates and manipulates the outward machinery which represents historical materialism.[10] Thus, for the most part, Benjamin's work only contains fleeting allusions to the theological patterns that so frequently inhabit them, and it is only rarely that the reader catches a glimpse of this hidden mechanism. One such rare moment is the short text entitled *Theologisch-politisches Fragment*, an esoteric text in the proper sense of the word, as it was never published during Benjamin's lifetime and only rarely revealed to a very close circle of friends. In this fragment, most likely written around 1921, Benjamin seeks to define the concept of the messianic in relation to history and the world, and in doing so reveals the pattern which underlies the concept of redemption as expounded in *Ursprung des deutschen Trauerspiels*. As he writes in the apodictic opening sentences:

---

9. Benjamin, *Gesammelte Schriften*, Volume 1, 398.
10. Benjamin, *Gesammelte Schriften*, Volume 1, 693.

> Only the Messiah ends the course of history, more
> precisely in the sense that he redeems, ends and creates
> its relationship to the messianic. This is why no
> historical entity can seek to relate to the messianic on
> its own accord. This is why the Kingdom of Heaven is
> not the *telos* of the historical *dynamis*: it cannot be set as
> a goal. From a historical perspective, it is not the goal,
> but the end. That is why the order of the profane
> cannot be built around the notion of the Kingdom of
> Heaven, that is why theocracy does not have a political
> sense, but only a religious one.[11]

The *Theologisch-politisches Fragment* puts a strong emphasis on the
separation between this world and the Kingdom of Heaven, to the
extent that any desire to establish the Kingdom of Heaven on earth is
fundamentally impossible. The messianic expectation of humanity
cannot take the form of an attempt to actively bring about redemption,
for redemption is a category of the Kingdom of Heaven and thus
entirely meaningless on earth, it should rather be a contemplative
receptivity which is prepared, but does not expect. The advent of the
Messiah not only redeems the world, but also establishes the
relationship between the world and the Kingdom of Heaven, thus in
effect ending the world and putting an end to history. Like the realm
of ideas and the realm of objects in *Ursprung des deutschen Trauerspiels*,
the Kingdom of Heaven and the world are best visualised as two
parallel lines into infinity that neither touch nor cross, but will
coincide into one if the Messiah comes. And this 'if' is crucial, because
Benjamin accepts the eschatological aspect of messianism, but
resolutely refuses to define it as a teleological movement. Especially
towards the end of his life he insists ever more dramatically that the
advent of the Messiah is not a given, and he contrasts his conception of
the messianic sharply with a secular faith in human progress on the
one hand and a teleological religious faith on the other.

It is the latter which comes under heavy fire in the *Theologisch-
politische Fragment*, in which he stresses that the religious desire to
establish a theocracy, or the Kingdom of Heaven on earth, is politically
meaningless, exactly because of the radical and necessary separation of

---

11. Benjamin, *Gesammelte Schriften*, Volume 2, 203.

the spheres of the worldly and the divine. The world we live in, the 'order of the profane', cannot and should not hold up the idea(l) of the Kingdom of Heaven as its ultimate aspiration, because it cannot know what it desires. Instead, Benjamin establishes the very worldly concept of happiness as the focal point for humanity and as the driving force behind the messianic intensity: 'The order of the profane should be built around the idea of happiness.'[12] This seemingly paradoxical refusal to put religion at the very heart of his messianism is what makes Benjamin's theology a fundamentally negative theology. In fact, performing a conceptual *volte-face*, it is the explicit turning away from theology which Benjamin defines as the driving force behind the messianic intensity:

> If one arrow points into the direction into which the dynamic of the profane moves, and another arrow indicates the direction of the messianic intensity, then the quest for happiness of a free humanity may well derive from the former direction, but just as one action is capable of reinforcing a reaction in the opposite direction, the profane order of the profane is capable of bringing forward the advent of the messianic Kingdom. So the profane may not be a category of this Kingdom, but it is the most pertinent category of its closest approach.[13]

This construction is analogous to the epistemology of *Ursprung des deutschen Trauerspiels*, in which the diametrically opposed realms of the ideal and the phenomenal are radically separated, but paradoxically in need of one another in order to be revealed or to be meaningful. By the same token, the orders of the profane and the messianic will come closest to one another, close enough for a spark to connect them, when they are at their furthest remove. Whereas in the *Trauerspiel* book, meaning emerged when two extremes entered into a constellation, here the suggestion seems to be that the messianic moment—and hence redemption—can be brought about by forcing the extremes of the profane and the divine into a constellation at the very moment when the opposition between them is at its starkest.

---

12. Benjamin, *Gesammelte Schriften*, Volume 2, 203.
13. Benjamin, *Gesammelte Schriften*, Volume 2, 203–4.

From this perspective, too, Benjamin's theology can be termed negative, as the advent of the Messiah and the establishment of the Kingdom of Heaven can only be brought about by pushing the world into the opposite direction, in other words, by emphasising the profane.

However, Benjamin's critique of teleological messianism was not exclusively nor even mainly aimed at its religious or theological varieties. Following the likes of Marx, Weber and Freud, Benjamin saw a structural similarity between a religious teleology which looks towards the future with impatience and confidence, assured of the advent of the Messiah and the Kingdom of Heaven, and a secular teleology which expects the ultimate and inevitable realisation of its utopia, whether this should be a classless society or a liberal free-market democracy. Significantly, Benjamin criticised both the bourgeois ideology of progress, exemplified in the Enlightenment idea of infinite perfectibility, as well as the classical Marxist notion that the dictatorship of the proletariat and the subsequent classless society are necessary stages in an inevitable historical process. His criticism was reserved particularly for the fact that both of these ideologies put their faith in a gradual development of history, which Benjamin's brand of messianism emphatically rejects: 'The Messiah interrupts history, the Messiah does not appear at the end of a development . . . Progress bears no relation whatsoever to the interruption of history.'[14] As he made clear in the *Theologisch-politisches Fragment*, the only point of contact between a postlapsarian world and a redeemed world is when the Messiah or the messianic moment interrupts the continuity of history and brings history itself to a halt. Even speaking in entirely secular terms, this principle still holds. His philosophy of history therefore seeks to concentrate on the discontinuities within the apparently constant flow of history and tradition. He speaks of the necessity to point out the jump or leap within phenomena, works of art or tradition itself, to lift a historical period or event out of the continuum of history, or in more violent and apocalyptic terms, of the necessity to blast an era out of the historical continuum or to detonate history itself. Particularly in his later essays on Baudelaire and the Parisian arcades, Benjamin develops the notion that humanity has been lulled into an inert acceptance of the idea that history will run its unstoppable course and that events follow one another seamlessly,

---

14. Benjamin, *Gesammelte Schriften*, Volume I, 1243.

logically and inevitably. His main concern in the unfinished *Passagen-Werk*, summarised in *Über den Begriff der Geschichte* (*On the Concept of History*), was to propose not only that an interruption or a reversal of this continuum of history is possible, but also urgently necessary.

By contrast, the teleological ideologies which Benjamin criticises so heavily go hand in hand with a view of history in which the past is not only truly over, but also explained away as a necessary stage on the way to the ultimate goal, which therefore comes marginally closer with the passing of time. Benjamin diagnoses this as the modern condition, and according to him, it is nothing less than catastrophic: 'The concept of progress is to be rooted in the idea of the catastrophe. That it "goes on like this", *is* the catastrophe. It is not what is immediately ahead of us, it is what is happening right now.'[15] What Benjamin proposes to counter this ideology with is another *volte-face.* Whereas the teleological ideologies look towards the future, Benjamin's historian has his face turned resolutely towards the past. The most enduring image of this is of course the Angel of History, based on a drawing by Paul Klee called *Angelus Novus* which Benjamin had bought in 1921. This image conveys not merely Benjamin's critique of the 'bourgeois' concept of history, but also the sense of urgency and the sheer helplessness of the historian who is confronted with the paradoxical task of interrupting the course of history:

> [The Angel's] face is turned towards the past. Where *we* see a chain of events, *he* sees one single catastrophe, which incessantly heaps ruin upon ruin and slings them in front of his feet. He would like to stay, to wake the dead and to restore what has been torn asunder. But a storm blows from Paradise, a storm which has caught his wings and which is so strong that the Angel can no longer close them. This storm unremittingly drives the Angel into the future, to which he has turned his back, while the mountain of devastation before his eyes grows to high heaven. What we call progress is this very storm.[16]

---

15. Benjamin, *Gesammelte Schriften*, Volume 5, 592.
16. Benjamin, *Gesammelte Schriften*, Volume 5, 697–8.

Benjamin's turn towards the past has more than one side to it. Having exposed the theological impossibility, the philosophical impotence and the epistemological irrelevance of a teleological orientation, it is logical that he should focus on the past and present in order not only to understand history but also to be able to intervene into the historical process. This intervention should be taken quite literally, as the 'historical materialist', who Benjamin holds up as the ideal historian, is not a distant and passive observer who seeks to explain *post facta* how a given historical event fits into a logical and ever-progressing chain of events. On the contrary, the task of the historical materialist is to discover the discontinuities in the historical process, its fissures and its ruptures, and to point out those forgotten objects, people and events which did not make it into the accepted historical narrative. One note for *Über den Begriff der Geschichte* summarises this very tersely as a 'fundamental aporia': 'The history of the oppressed is a discontinuum. —It is the task of history to get hold of the tradition of the oppressed.'[17] According to Benjamin, there are two distinct sides to the historical process, the losing side and the winning side. What he disparagingly calls the 'pedestrian conception of history'[18] both represents and romanticises the winning side, in very literal terms the victors of wars, military or economic, and in figurative terms those who have seen their ideas, ideals, art and tradition become the dominant force to the exclusion or denigration of all else. As was the case with the notion of *Würdigung*, which sought to explain a work of art not in its own terms but as a function of historical events, the historiography of the victors refers to the vanquished not in their own right but in order to establish and confirm its own superiority. By contrast, it is the task of the historical materialist to write the history and establish the tradition of those who have been forgotten, vanquished or superseded: 'History has the task not only to get hold of the tradition of the oppressed, but also to found it.'[19] In doing so, the historian seeks to show that things have not changed, that we are still involved in the same historical process in which some will triumph and some will be left by the wayside. Benjamin's historical materialism aims to represent this other side of history in such a way as to produce a sudden and intense awareness of this

17. Benjamin, *Gesammelte Schriften*, Volume 1, 1236.
18. Benjamin, *Gesammelte Schriften*, Volume 1, 1242.
19. Benjamin, *Gesammelte Schriften*, Volume 1, 1246.

unredeemed state of history in a single image: 'It is not the case that the past sheds its light on the present, or that the present sheds its light on the past: the image is the point where the past suddenly enters into a constellation with the present.'[20]

To Benjamin, this is an emphatically ethical task, which stands at the very centre of the *Passagen-Werk* and which he formulates in explicitly theological terms. Significantly, however, the moral obligation is not predominantly towards the present, but in the first instance towards the past. As he writes in the second thesis of *Über den Begriff der Geschichte*: 'Like every generation that came before us, we have been given a *weak* messianic power, to which the past has a claim.'[21] The historical materialist seeks to answer the moral call of the past in what could almost be termed the ritual observance of *Eingedenken*, a uniquely evocative word which is translated as either remembrance or mindfulness, and which lies somewhere in between the two. The act of remembering seeks to perform a small but never insignificant *restitutio in integrum*, if only by doing as little as simply refusing to accept the finality of past suffering. *Eingedenken* can therefore be called messianic, not just because it seeks to ritually redeem the past, but most importantly because it asserts the necessity of a messianic redemption at some point, lest the catastrophe that is the history of human suffering continues for all eternity.

*Eingedenken* is a fundamentally theological concept, and as such carries with it its own unmistakable paradox. This paradox was highlighted by Max Horkheimer in a letter he wrote to Benjamin in 1937: 'The injustice of the past has happened and is finished. The vanquished really have been vanquished. In the final analysis, your statement is a theological one. If one takes the unfinishedness [of history] seriously, one has to believe in the Final Judgement.'[22] Benjamin responded to this letter twice. He sent one answer to Horkheimer himself, in which he explains in conspicuously secularised terms what the ramifications of refusing to accept the finality of past suffering might be. Admitting that there is a certain finality to defeat, he maintains that it is after all not the dead who should remember, but that it is the responsibility of the survivors to honour their obligation towards the past by remembering that they have a place in history only

---

20.    Benjamin, *Gesammelte Schriften*, Volume 5, 576.
21.    Benjamin, *Gesammelte Schriften*, Volume 1, 694.
22.    Quoted in Benjamin, *Gesammelte Briefe*, Volume 5, 495.

because others have not. The vanquished, Benjamin maintains, may have lost the war, but they did not lose their history:

> I always considered it an important question as to what is meant by this odd figure of speech, to *lose* a war or a trial. The war or the trial are after all not the stake but the act that decides on the stake. In the end, I explained it as follows: for him who loses the war or the trial, those events are truly finished and lost to *his* praxis; for the partner who won, this is not the case. Victory bears its fruits entirely differently from the way in which defeat has its consequences.[23]

Benjamin's second response to Horkheimer's objection came in the notes for the *Passagen-Werk*, in which he does not hide the theological inspiration of the concept, but states categorically that the very possibility of Horkheimer's objection proves the absolute necessity of understanding history in theological terms:

> The corrective of this way of thinking lies in the notion that history is not only a science but nothing less than a form of remembrance. What science has 'determined', remembrance can modify. Remembrance can turn the unfinished (happiness) into something terminated and the terminated (suffering) into something unfinished. That is theology; but in remembrance we have an experience which forbids us to understand history in a fundamentally a-theological way, however little we are allowed to attempt to write it in unambiguously theological terms.[24]

As a historian who keenly feels the moral claim which the suffering of the past lays upon the present, there simply is no other legitimate way of writing history without sinking into barbarism. The only thing that is left to the forgotten millions who were subjected to oppression, who saw their hopes dashed and their voices silenced, is the dignity of a memory which the present must uphold at all costs. Benjamin's

---

23.  Benjamin, *Gesammelte Briefe*, 486–7.
24.  Benjamin, *Gesammelte Schriften*, Volume 5, 589.

unsent reply to Horkheimer conveys with painful accuracy the paradox which he was forced to leave suspended over the unfinished *Passagen-Werk*: the fundamental inability to change history in theological terms combined with the equally fundamental inability to understand it in any other way. Countering this paradox with another one, Benjamin writes that the only task we have left to us is to restore hope to those who are already beyond it: 'What we want from posterity is not gratitude for our victories but the remembrance of our defeats. That is consolation: the consolation which there can only be for those who no longer have any hope of consolation.'[25] It is unclear at which point Benjamin seems to have given up hope, but then it is only the truly hopeless to whom hope can be given. In the end, Benjamin's philosophy remains infused with the messianic paradox that requires a leap, not so much of faith but of hope against hope that any second might just be 'the small gate through which the Messiah could enter'.[26]

---

25. Benjamin, *Gesammelte Schriften*, Volume I, 1240.
26. Benjamin, *Gesammelte Schriften*, Volume 1, 704.

# 4

# The Fate of Hope in Hollow Spaces: Ernst Bloch's Messianism

## Frances Daly

## 1. Introduction

The question of the existence of redemption and the messianic has long troubled its many thinkers. Even at the height of its conceptual resuscitation in the early decades of the twentieth century, the most willed-for sense of apocalypse was shrouded in fear and doubt. Thus Walter Benjamin spoke of a necessarily weak messianic power, endlessly indebted to an unrecompensed past;[1] Martin Buber wrote of the mysteries still accessible yet 'buried under debris';[2] Ernst Bloch referred to the possibility of a 'forestalled Apocalypse', a time lost to discontinuity and without the ability for any correlation to so disparate an age to reach us;[3] and, rather less sanguine still, Franz Kafka had declared the existence of an abundance of hope but insisted that none was for us.[4]

Today, these questioning, searching explorations of the radical kingdom have receded, although not without in any sense

---

1.   Walter Benjamin, *Illuminations*, translated by Harry Zohn (New York: Schocken Books, 1969), 254.
2.   Martin Buber, *I and Thou*, translated by Walter Kaufmann (New York: Charles Scribner's Sons, 1970), 174.
3.   Ernst Bloch, *The Spirit of Utopia*, translated by Anthony A Nassar (Stanford: Stanford University Press, 2000), 271. Bloch had originally called this work *Music and Apocalypse* but changed it, apparently under pressure from his publisher.
4.   This was Kafka's response to the following question put to him by Max Brod: 'So could there be hope beyond this particular manifestation of the world?' Franz Kafka, in discussion with Max Brod, cited by Walter Benjamin, 'Franz Kafka–*Zur zehnten Wiederkehr seines Todestages*', in *Über Literatur* (Frankfurt am Main: Fischer, 1959), 159.

disappearing, living on in various different ways and not without certain tensions, I would argue, via a range of diverse theological and philosophical ideas.[5] Many of these theorisations are attempts to imagine a state of being, existence or divinity in which the idea of a redemptive value available to us—in experience, values or faith—is some type of a reconnection with who we are or could be and, thus, is a kind of bringing to account current absences of, or barriers to, such a realization. Whilst many current conditions of an anticipatory consciousness are markedly different from those of the troubled hope of the early twentieth century, what is nonetheless clearly recognisable is the existence of many of the same processes—the same 'scrambling up a cliff', the same cage 'in search of a bird', the same worship of idols borne of fear to which Kafka had alerted us.[6] And thus whether what confronts us is a similar confirmation of estrangement or whether it is also evidence of a distorted, disappointed or inaccessible hope, what the messianic might mean is surely a fundamental issue. The central question that emerges on this basis is whether in continuing to address a sense of the 'darkness that is closing in' we are also able to recognise the existence of any 'distant, questionable, ponderable star'[7]—the sort of difficult redemptive possibility which Bloch and a number of other

---

5.   Those ideas with considerable currency in contemporary philosophy that express something of a sense of the redemptive might include those such as: responsibility and sacrificial altruism in the work of Emmanuel Levinas; of transcendental experience and the experience of freedom and presence in Jean-Luc Nancy; and the idea the ambiguous 'sea of the possible' that Jacques Rancière finds in the dreams and utopian visions of the emancipatory movements of the nineteenth-century. See, for example, Emmanuel Levinas, *Totality and Infinity: An Essay on Exteriority,* translated by Alphonso Lingis (The Hague: M Nijhoff Publishers, 1979); Jean-Luc Nancy, *The Experience of Freedom,* translated by Bridget McDonald (Stanford: Stanford University Press, 1993); Jacques Rancière, *The Nights of Labor: The Workers' Dream in Nineteenth-Century France,* translated by John Drury (Philadelphia: Temple University Press, 1989).

6.   Franz Kafka, 'Reflections on Sin, Suffering, Hope and the True Way', in *Wedding Preparations in the Country and Other Posthumous Prose Writings,* translated by Ernst Kaiser and Eithne Wilkins with notes by Max Brod (London: Secker & Warburg, 1954), 39–40, 49.

7.   Ernst Bloch, 'Recollections of Walter Benjamin', in *On Walter Benjamin: Critical Essays and Recollections,* edited by Gary Smith (Cambridge, Massachusetts: MIT, 1991), 343.

thinkers of the period found in the discontinuities of the twentieth century—and to understand in what sense this amounts to an engagement with the messianic.

If the messianic can be understood as a type of venturing beyond what exists, the present time suggests an horizon of possibility but one that can perhaps best be described, in Blochian terms, as that of a forestalled hope. It is impossible to ignore the context of a profound impoverishment of the spirit where much of the legacy of more questioning times has been dissipated. A widespread scepticism in relation to hope is a rather prosaic, but nonetheless symptomatic, response to an extended period of willful deceit and the near collapse of concepts of ethics. Various types of hope—in the ending of injustices and the overcoming of conflicts and destructiveness—have clearly been disappointed and, perhaps, more than simply disappointed, have withered and transmogrified into a detachment without any promise of change. But this tells us little about whether hope and the dynamic fuelling the dissolution of connections between potential and change have been displaced, or whether the problem is more in our ability to engage with a 'weak messianism'. Our present time is characterised neither by the complete absence of hope nor by its consistent or obvious presence. This is what makes an investigation of messianism a difficult and yet vital task for us today.

## 2. Ernst Bloch and the topos of possibility

Bloch is perhaps one of the least well-known or understood of the major figures of twentieth century German philosophy in the English speaking world[8] and yet his corpus is frequently referred to as 'one of the great works of the human spirit', as work of 'visionary breadth' and 'epic voyage', as George Steiner writes.[9] Bloch's transformative, unfinished ethics of becoming and world-in-process presents a hugely ambitious, difficult project that sees questions of self, other, world, heritage, culture and eschatology all brought together as a fundamental way of approaching the basic questions of 'Who are we?'

---

8.  There are many reasons as to why this is the case—not by any means have all of his writings been translated from the German, and some of his central texts have appeared only recently in English.

9.  George Steiner, *TLS* (3 October, 1975); George Steiner, *Extraterritorial: Papers on Literature and the Language Revolution* (Harmondsworth: Penguin, 1972), 176.

and 'Where are we going?' as the highly gnostic, apocalyptic opening words of Bloch's *magnum opus, The Principle of Hope*, pose.[10] In this work he elaborates principles and archetypes of the future—chief amongst these being the guiding images of hope—through which he is able to understand fragments of 'anticipatory illumination' in which humanity attempts to engage with, and overcome, oppression, alienation and disillusion. 'Thinking', Bloch says, 'means venturing beyond'.[11] And in this tendency to anticipate he sees something powerful and unconcluded at work, 'a true soul-spirit of utopia'.[12] It is in this connection between soul and forward-dreaming—the exodus that Bloch feels is posited in the very experience of our identification with each other—that we are able to come to challenge the insufficiency that we sense in lived reality.

For Bloch, the messianic is expectation and intention towards possibility in a human, an historical and a more indefinable, mysterious sense, and is concerned decisively with the ability to transcend, or step outside and above, to achieve transformation by way of the contradictions of experience and imagination. A sense of the future entails the duality of something hoped for and the ability to bear witness to an unrealised messianism of the present. It is in this manner that Bloch is able to explore the breadth of human yearnings and expectation, and is able to understand the connections between spiritual and philosophical consciousness. This is not without considerable difficulties, for as much as some basis of human intention might be present in types of unfulfilled, expectant consciousness suggestive of the presence of hope and this incompletion and dissatisfaction appear most animated precisely in 'the nothingness of

---

10. Theodotus, for example, writes: 'It is not the bath (washing) alone that makes us free, but also the knowledge: who were we? what have we become? where were we? into what place have we been cast? wither are we hastening? from what are we delivered? what is birth? what is rebirth?', *Excerpta ex Theodoto* 78.2, quoted in George MacRae, 'Apocalyptic Eschatology in Gnosticism', in *Apocalypticism in the Mediterranean World and the Near East*, edited by David Hellholm (Tübingen: JCB Mohr, 1983), 320.

11. Ernst Bloch, *The Principle of Hope*, 3 Volumes, translated by Neville Plaice, Stephen Plaice and Paul Knight (Cambridge, Massachusetts: MIT, 1995), Volume I, 4. This work originally had the working title of *System of Theoretical Messianism*.

12. Bloch, *The Spirit of Utopia*, 254.

this godless world',[13] this can only be judged against what might equally threaten to overwhelm any active anticipation of human dignity. We will concern ourselves here primarily with Bloch's critiques of the problems of theism and modernity, because it is with these that we can not only appreciate Bloch's unique contribution to an understanding of messianism but situate the problematic terrain the messianic occupies in the contemporary world.

## 2. Wishful images of the fulfilled moment

### 2.1 The Promethean myth

Bloch's earliest memories recreate with telling impression the landscape of modernity that was in process across cities in nineteenth century Europe. Born in Ludwigshafen in 1885, Bloch could see the fading beauty and opulence of the neighbouring Mannheim, on the other side of the Rhine, becoming eclipsed by the new, bleakly industrial town of his birth, its factories and functional production the promise of the construction of all that is 'lifeless and subhuman', an accelerating disquiet of serviceability and 'joyless comfort' that would lead, ultimately, not only to the functional result of 'craven mass junk' but to a type of misery, a 'pervasive destruction of the imagination'. Amidst this expression of the retreating, 'endangered spirit', Bloch also perceived other processes that for him hinted at a quite different impulse shaping humanity and an image of the world. His immediate landscape presented the 'nonsynchronism' of an existence torn between modern, secularised society and community, between industrialised homelessness and reactionary nostalgia, between 'forgotten essence' and tradition. It is a world that attempts to embellish the 'same mangy . . . ulcerous abominations as before' and in this presents a mirror 'where we glimpse our future'. This confusion of tendencies brings with it a sense of a void to be filled that Bloch views more generally as a tendency partly satisfied in dreams. Dreams can present to us the human ability to construct alternatives to current reality. And this contradictory state seeps into the given in unpredictable ways. Thus modernity is at one and the same time the desolation of a commodified functionality with a 'vague reluctance' underlying it, and 'that tragic battle' over authority, which Bloch takes as the basis of human experience, the battle between 'Lucifer and the

---

13.   Bloch, *The Spirit of Utopia*, 223.

demiurge'. Something 'stirs and seethes' even, and perhaps most particularly, in the 'charmless and empty'.[14]

If in his understanding of modernity Bloch were merely indicating the constant presence of warring tendencies of hope and fear—the 'murder of all light in this prison, madhouse, mortuary that is this earth' and, in return, 'the sublime'—his case for the messianic would seem to us today overly extenuated. But Bloch argues something beyond this: that we long for the 'darkness of the lived moment' because it is here that the inner dream world, given expression to by the darkness, can be conveyed to an awakening process. We 'await the dark', where 'our strange, inner dreamwork may go and strike undisturbed'.[15] The problem here, as he recognises, is not only in the way in which humanity 'dwells in thick darkness'[16] and whether it is possible to differentiate sinking gloom from darkness and waking dream from dream but whether in the darkness there is necessarily promise, the weight of what he calls the 'Messiah-dream' that is filled with the 'hope that lies before us', the religious *Humanum*.[17] It is relatively simple to accept that there are guiding images, virtues and aesthetic hope-contents to be found in what is deeply anticipated in present human experience and what is pre-figured of the future, and that this anticipation or pre-appearance is illumination, yearning and imagination, rather than mere momentary flights of fancy, whim or fantasizing. But if we can distinguish hope as the intention towards possibility from escapism by the directing act of informed hope (varying levels of pre-figuration in the quest for self-knowledge or meaning, in wonder and curiosity, in love and passion) then we need to know how we can confront this question of being in a world that so displaces its meaning. An engagement with the messianic means something beyond 'mere inwardness' or the 'empty promises of the other world'.[18]

Bloch's critique of modernity indicates powerfully the contradictions involved in reclaiming any informed response. He

---

14. Bloch, *The Spirit of Utopia*, 11, 12, 13, 32, 223, 25, 35.
15. Bloch, *The Spirit of Utopia*, 222, 144.
16. I Kings 8, 12, quoted in Ernst Bloch, *Atheism in Christianity*, translated by JT Swann (New York: Herder and Herder, 1972), 28 and *The Principle of Hope*, Volume 3, 1197.
17. Bloch, *Atheism in Christianity*, 31.
18. Bloch, *The Spirit of Utopia*, 5.

refers to the modern world as a strange 'hollow space'.[19] He clearly sees a world that has become both more sceptical and more restless, where despair, discontent and fraudulent hope emerge out of increasing contradictions between technological control and its 'decorative-individualistic' appropriation, between rationalist lies and anti-mythical suspicion.[20] He accords to the 'inhuman'—the seemingly external, uncontrollable processes of life—a power, a 'slimy, gelatinous, unpredictable, arbitrarily stalling, falsely complex, moody, maliciously fortuitous and intermittent element' that shapes our ability to act. But alongside what he often refers to as a time of 'the capitalist laceration of all life-connections', the nothingness of 'this age of a distant God',[21] he maintains that there is 'a creative, reflecting consciousness that demonstrates manifold ways of transformation', that is capable of splintering time into messianic, utopian moments.[22] And with this he contends not merely that we possess a capacity to change but that we actively 'want to explode our darkness'.[23] At one level this can read as assertion and yet Bloch's examination of such periods by way of archetypes of human expression contains a compelling insight into the contradictions of modernity. For it is here that a recognition emerges that something is not quite right, that there is 'something missing', as he expresses it, using a Brechtian term.[24]

As a consequence, Bloch's patently Fichtean view of an early twentieth century world of 'consummate sinfulness' seems, disturbingly, equally relevant to us today. What remains of a world of unfreedom, he writes, 'is the desperation of not really believing in anything, of first needing a presentiment and then already seeing the end, and closing the path'.[25] Whilst the conclusion we might draw

---

19. Ernst Bloch, *Heritage of Our Times*, translated by Neville Plaice and Steven Plaice (Cambridge: Polity Press, 1991) 347, 341; Ernst Bloch, *The Utopian Function of Art and Literature: Selected Essays*, translated by Jack Zipes and Frank Mecklenburg (Cambridge, Massachusetts: MIT Press), 222.

20. Ernst Bloch, *Literary Essays*, translated by Andrew Joron and others (Stanford: Stanford University Press, 1998), 7.

21. Bloch, *Heritage of Our Times*, 115; Bloch, *The Spirit of Utopia*, 222.

22. Bloch, *The Utopian Function of Art and Literature*, 30, 218.

23. Bloch, *The Spirit of Utopia*, 222.

24. Bloch uses this idea in a well-known discussion with Adorno. Bloch, *The Utopian Function of Art and Literature*, 15.

25. Bloch, *The Spirit of Utopia*, 172.

from this is bleak, the path, he reminds us, is not merely that given to and profaned by us. Genuineness had not already been completely discovered in us only to be concealed again as a negative transcendence. Moreover, the 'anamnesis of the modern age' is also evidence of a re-remembering and rescuing of what is sacred from the 'world's unknowing and error'. Thus the 'questions of our souls, of our religious conscience', he argues, 'still burn, undiminished', 'their absolute claims unredeemed' even though the *'kairos'*, the right moment, has not been realised.[26] With this comes a sense of exodus, of journeying and probing that brings the Promethean myth and its idea of the subversive human spirit into a relation with wishful religious images, those images, as we will shortly consider, that reveal most clearly a 'murmuring with intent'.[27] There remains an unlost heritage even at times of 'no breadth', 'no inner threshold', 'no gathering conscience of the Absolute'.[28] The figure of Thomas Münzer suggests to Bloch a past that is remembered as a way to obligate and enthuse us, as a 'warning that comes from searching, getting lost, possibly finding'.[29] There is something accumulative to this history even though it is here that, as in Benjamin's sense, the fragments of messianic time are splintered. The more terrible the abyss, the more restless and empty an encounter with the world is, the more the human drive to go through emerges as the only possible way to continue.

Modernity certainly has, in the place of ancient myth, brought with it the seeming assent to the fable of master and servant. But in this it opens itself to uncertainty. This is a world that degrades and humiliates but it is also a world in which doubt festers and this doubt is 'the space in which human life drives upwards'.[30] The figure of Prometheus is central to Bloch's understanding of this. Prometheus, the chained and yet undefeated, can be the victim or victor of his own hubris, but with the benefit of his heaven and earth-storming qualities will never succumb to a flat, given reality where desire and creativity

---

26.  Bloch, *The Spirit of Utopia*, 2.
27.  Bloch, *Atheism in Christianity*, 54.
28.  Bloch, *The Spirit of Utopia*, 3.
29.  Ernst Bloch, *Thomas Münzer: als Theologe der Revolution* (Frankfurt am Main: Suhrkamp, 1969), 13.
30.  Bloch, *Heritage of Our Times*, 371. See also: '"Talking with Ernst Bloch: Korcula, 1968": A discussion between Michael Landmann and Ernst Bloch', in *Telos*, 25 (Fall 1975): 168.

exist.[31] Through art we are capable of being 'like a cyclone through the given'.[32] Does this engagement with the given also mean that the aspect of transcendence is necessarily always available? Bloch's messianism follows from a sense of engaging with what has not yet been completely realised—something that is present in yearnings and dreams and in this way is neither a return to the past nor a philosophy of predictions of the future but an engagement with the hopes of everyday life through which one is able to trace the symbols and allegories of an unfinished world. Humanity's dream, its 'oldest daydream', he claims, is to overcome all those conditions in which the human being has been degraded, subjugated, forsaken and treated with contempt.[33] Whether or not the dream continues, we know more certainly that it has failed to be realised, or perhaps has been repeatedly disappointed but nonetheless struggled for, and in this it bears testimony to the present. If what is acknowledged is a latent sense of the encounter between self and other, an aspect of which is the possibility of radical transformation, then we are less concerned to qualify hope in terms of a univocal relation to transcendence. Let us consider the place of images of religion for Bloch in order to pursue the problem of the transcendent within his messianism.

## 2.2 'And the time of the wolf will pass away and the time of the sheep will enter': Theology and radical expectation

If we are led to suspecting that our present circumstances make the task of revealing an impelling relation through despair and hope more difficult, it is also worthwhile considering that this relation and its very tensions exemplified in a sense of a constant slippage between light and dark, knowing and unknowing, is precisely what has always constituted the subject matter of messianism, a tradition whose origins are to be found not only in the extensive Jewish apocalyptic literature that we are aware of from around 200 BC but also in many earlier variants from Ancient Egypt, Mesopotamia and Persia. The earliest concepts of messianism deal with the ideas of transformation and expectation as tendencies that emerge within the context of a state of turmoil or chaos, a world of a primordial darkness in which oppression, uncertainty and difficulty constitute the content of much

---

31. Bloch, *The Principle of Hope*, Volume 3, 1195.
32. Bloch, *The Spirit of Utopia*, 31.
33. Bloch, *Literary Essays*, 344.

experience. Thus there is the 'time of darkness' from the Nag Hammadi texts, the 'times grown old' in Ezra, the 'time of wrath', as we find in the Damascus Document or a time of 'interval', as in the Apocalypse of Daniel, or the 'time of the wolf' derived from Zoroastrian dialogues. Bloch is particularly interested in Babylonian astral myths, in Confucius and Lao Tzu, in the couplet of suffering and rebellion adopted by Moses from the Kenites, the state of night becoming light in the teachings of Mani, the redemptive idea in Buddhism, as well as in the early Greek figures of Cadmus and Orpheus as bringers of salvation from the time of plague or the land of the dead.[34] With these understandings of the transition of the world we often find some idea or imagery of time, of finality and renewal that gives structure to and interrupts human actions with a sense of the temporal. And in this we encounter also the idea of the possibility that extended periods of sorrow or insecurity present to human awareness. The ideas of purification through suffering, of witnessing and reckoning, revelation and salvation are fundamental elements of such approaches.

There is much that is useful in setting out the processes of a developing contradiction that can repeatedly indicate what it is that is as yet not possessed as a form of possibility or anticipation. The theoretical basis of much messianic thought is just such a depiction of the content of unfulfilled existence, emphasizing as it does the contradictory relation of the, as it were, negative impulse of the object of dissatisfaction in terms of a productive combination of anxiety and hope. Gershom Scholem, for example, summarises this paradox of apocalyptic thinking as the intertwining of elements of dread and consolation that are expressed in utopian, sometimes conservative, but more usually 'restorative' terms, the latter, terms that return to or recreate conditions of the past as an ideal.[35] Whilst one can easily recognise the intention of this summation—to provide a sense of the dynamic that exists within messianic thought—stated as such it fails to express one of the pivotal issues characterizing the messianic. This is the sense of an impulse that presents us with something more than a sense of the distance or negation of fear or dread from or against hope.

---

34.  Bloch, *The Principle of Hope*, Volume 3, 1203, 1204.
35.  Gershom Scholem, *The Messianic Idea in Judaism and Other Essays on Jewish Spirituality*, translated by Michael A Meyer and Hillel Halkin (New York: Schocken Books, 1978), 10, 3.

What this requires is a sense of a 'venturing beyond', or a 'being hope in totality', as Bloch calls it, that provides not only tensions within fermenting images of past and future, hope and despair, but a sense of worth that oppressedness or suffering alone cannot provoke. This 'explosive hope', as Bloch again refers to it, hope as a type of vigilance ultimately bound to a questing freedom, a hunger, is then something different from wishful thinking, unmediated hope or the expression of an objectivised teleological relation.[36] This means that hope exists not merely in relation to its opposite but is related to a purposive content—a realm of freedom—that makes of hope a watchful, open category of possibility in which the intervention of subjectively active contradiction is vital. This relation then shifts our understanding of the process of an impelling relation of hope and fear from that of a constant negation or paradox to that of open possibility. Hope, Bloch argues, holds 'the condition of defeat precariously within itself'. It stands not merely within the realms of potential salvation and damnation but 'within the topos of objectively real possibility' and within the indeterminacy of the historical process. We cannot take comfort from types of objectivist automatism, believing that times of crisis will give way to perfection, darkness to illumination, annihilation to rebirth.[37] Servitude needs to be actively rejected, freedom anticipated.

If this 'dangerous hope' points to a danger that need not necessarily be dreaded or feared because it indicates a type of self-possession pitted against some external object, rather than a vague, often debilitating inwardness, what is the significance of this? For as much as there is an openness in Bloch's understanding of hope, there is also a difficulty in grounding the conditions of what he variously refers to as murmuring, the vital trace, contention or the upright gait, in anything other than a primordial presentiment.[38] The idea of witnessing as the ability to take possession of one's waking dreams within the 'comprehended darkness of the lived moment' by way of an engagement with the profound meaning of human dignity cannot be simply assumed to emerge from an informed sense of the contradictions of the age, as we have previously considered. How an

---

36. Ernst Bloch, *The Principle of Hope*, Volume 3, 1193.
37. Ernst Bloch, 'Dialectics and Hope', in *New German Critique*, 9 (Fall 1976), 7.
38. Bloch, *Atheism in Christianity*, 27, 28.

expanse in which the 'world of the soul' can appear requires an engagement in the world that directs us towards the self-encounter that is always the question of our relation to each other. This longing for 'the fullness of the manifestation to oneself' and of what is meant of the relation between I and We, is most fully expressed in religion, for here, Bloch contends, an anticipation posits an ultimate 'pre-existence of our selves in total involvement' where not even disinterested enjoyment is present.[39] It is a 'transformed existing', a transfiguration or transformation, rather than simply pre-appearance. Religion is 'radical longing', a 'longed-for authenticity'.[40]

In the wishful image of religion, Bloch detects the development of types of commitment to mystery, particularly to the ideas of exodus and the utopia of the kingdom. Even in its most 'cobbled together' and 'ghost-ridden' occultist forms he sees the expression of tensions, fermenting images and imagined worlds but also a type of defiance, something self-willed.[41] The religious figure, he argues, 'is no longer a squashed worm'. Used surrealistically, these tensions can reveal a sense of astonishment and an appreciation of the 'dream space of the unconditional'. There are for Bloch different levels of meaning within religious ideas. Where religious feeling contains something of the divine and the miraculous it can, at its best, enable us 'to see around the corner, where different, unfamiliar life may be going on'. This is an important element because a sense of exodus, a longed-for future, acts against reconciling people to given reality and its ideologies, and instead places them in a position of protest and summoning. A sense of venturing beyond that places community at the core of its commitment is what Bloch sees in prophetic founders of religion who are contrastive rather than conformist, in protests and hopes and in movements where a sense of worth is struggled for against oppression and exploitation. These commitments are suffused with an impulse that is never a static or apologetic myth but a humane, eschatological, explosively posited messianism. There is a clear distinction, then, between a morality of bland rationalizations that attempts to make existence more superficially ethical and a theology of community in

---

39.  Bloch, *The Spirit of Utopia*, 3, 33.
40.  Bloch, *The Principle of Hope*, Volume 3, 1201, 1203. Here, Bloch draws a contrast with the anticipatory in art, which he argues posits solely pre-appearance.
41.  Here Bloch has in mind everyone from Sabbatai Zevi and Joseph Smith to Rudolph Steiner and Madame Blavatsky.

which the wishful content of religion is that of 'a feeling at home in the *mystery* of existence'. For it is here that the self experiences a reverence for depth and infinity, a sense of mystery and the divine. It is as much this sense of mystery that gives to religion its militant light as does active hope. It enables one to grasp the essence of the world 'in tremendous suspense', and allows fear to resound as reverence. And the contents in the 'unfathomed depths of existing' are, in the religious ineffable, 'given the sign that they are not forgotten' or buried.[42]

It is easy to see why Bloch describes his utopian, messianic philosophy as 'revolutionary gnosis'.[43] For him the intention of the religious kingdom involves atheism or the elimination of an hypostasised God in order to open oneself to what he calls 'the real Possible in the sense of mystery'. Religions of protest and heresy can express archetypes of freedom, the Kingdom, and a sense of life force. They set out on the basis of the centrality of the darkness but understand this moment as a manifestation of redeeming knowledge, via such images as that of the serpent or the motif of Lucifer as the light-bearer. These images place the content of salvation as that which is accessible within the self, the godly or messianic self, the self capable of transformation. It is here that the upwards drive can become a drive forwards within an awakened consciousness.[44]

## 3. Conclusion

What are we to make of this theorization of human aspirations for a radically transformed self and world within our present circumstances? It is difficult for us to imagine a time more destructive of both human dignity and a hope for change. Undoubtedly at great cost and against the continuing presence of forms of resistance, we have nonetheless been absorbed into a landscape of barbarism, of carelessness and disregard, a world in which death has been thoroughly debased and life attenuated. We accept or tolerate a banal, suffocating conformity and a culture of 'objective mendacity'. Distraction and boredom characterise a meagre existence. We have, as Bloch says, mastered the art of fear in a terrible fashion. And whilst other times have undoubtedly harboured such doubt and have felt concerned for what this means for human consciousness, our age has

---

42. Bloch, *The Principle of Hope*, Volume 3, 1184, 1188, 1193, 1196, 1198.
43. Bloch, *The Spirit of Utopia*, 279.
44. Bloch, *The Principle of Hope*, Volume 3, 1199, 1278.

witnessed the destruction of much intention towards an unalienated future within creative, potentially oppositional space as well. We are left to ask what might obligate or enthuse us today? Have we become too reconciled to the abyss? Has a commitment to community been too damaged by the failure of religious hope to challenge the given, or of little more than a listless, indulgent, self-parodying accommodation to have greeted the long, drawn-out commodification of modernist culture? And does this culture still offer any of the subversive potential it once did in ways that might give the messianic current meaning?

The opening sections of Bloch's first major work start by considering the problem of nearness—we stand too close to ourselves to see ourselves completely and are too near those objects external to us to fully appreciate our relation to them. And yet we want to occupy the space that is there between the self and other, between ourselves and our world. For this we need the perspective of hope—the long, sunlit corridor with a door at the furthest end.[45] The corridor can of course only be illuminated when the capacity to create images of a better life, images driven at their most fundamental by a searching, a hunger, a wish to overcome dissatisfaction, is activated. Without this element of hope the door remains firmly shut and the world 'that is sometimes helpful, sometimes hostile, sometimes indifferent' 'pitches senselessly back and forth'.[46] We recognise this currently in forms of cultural exhaustion and paralysis and a cynicism signalling an emptiness of spirit and lack of creative imagination, in a greedy, insecure triumphalism that flattens out any sense of alternative and insinuates its mediocrity globally.

It is in just such an existence that we are bound to ask whether the messianic is still available to us. For Bloch, such periods of *'Zeitwende'* remain an opportunity for self-reflection; they are times of anticipation and acknowledgement that something else is possible. In the wishful images of religion and the guiding elements of redemptive commitment, which Bloch saw as so inextricably linked, there remains a search for a disclosure of the meaning of human existence. We feel the need to understand what a longing is for and why our deeds need to be directed towards realizing who we are. Bloch's understanding of an educated or informed hope, one that encompasses guiding images

45. Bloch, *The Spirit of Utopia*, 9.
46. Bloch, *The Utopian Function of Art and Literature*, 59; Bloch, *The Spirit of Utopia*, 1.

of the journey of humanity and its not-yet realised content of a 'venturing beyond what is', is a theorization of a fluctuating amalgam of possibility and witnessing through which emancipation is struggled for against both a stale, self-satisfied dismissal of longing and its instrumental appropriation. It provides us with a state of bewilderment rather than despair, a 'concrete disillusionment'.[47] With a sense of what is involved in that act of taking hold of the life-force and an openness to the mystery of the depths of humanity's situatedness in the world, we are better able to see the problem of a freedom and of a messianism that is always qualified by the human. The current parlous state of a theoretical engagement with the contradictions that this entails makes the concept of messianism seem only all the more tenuous. And yet types of anticipation persist. The messianic as the existence of an object hoped for and a hope inspired by it, as Jürgen Moltmann defined it, rests uneasily within contemporary existence— but only as similarly uneasily, it seems to me, as George Steiner's more recent claim that we exist within conditions of the 'eclipse of the messianic'.[48] Steiner's view would seem to take into account the very altered place of hope in current life, where the idea of the future has lost much credibility and what remains to be hoped for often contracts to an empty escapism. But his contention that it is only literalists and fundamentalists who await the true coming of a Messiah or the actual rebirth of history strikes at overdrawn and overly predictable targets, suggesting as it does that, at its most complete, the messianic has been merely a definitional, programmatic solution to chiliastic presumptions, which clearly it is far from limited to. The messianic instead more usually addresses the problem of a fractured, contradictory existence steeped in hope and fear, belief and disbelief, promise and disappointment, and it is for this reason, as much as it is for the reality of what remains unrealised, that any basis for hope can persist.

What gives cause to an uneasiness in us today is, I feel, that a dialectical flow between human strength and shadow, between recalling the past and anticipating the future, between the question and a comprehension of our current darkness, might be decisively interrupted, perhaps even curtailed, in a way that seriously threatens

---

47. Bloch, *Atheism in Christianity*, 239.
48. Jürgen Moltmann, *Theology of Hope: On the Ground and the Implications of a Christian Eschatology*, translated by James W. Leitch (Minneapolis: Fortress Press, 1991), 16; George Steiner, *Grammars of Creation* (London: Faber & Faber, 2001), 7.

any sense of possibility. The ability to transform might well begin, as Bloch thinks, with unfulfilled need and the inadequacy of the achieved form of existence but it is difficult for us to not also ask how any viable recognition of possibility and the non-resignation of desire for a better reality might emerge, and then to contemplate what it might actually emerge as, given the pervasiveness of types of alienation and the menacing presence of a return to barbarism.

Bloch contends that beyond all our exhausted, false attempts there is the one presentiment, conscience and salvation that arises, 'unbroken in spite of everything, from the deepest part, that is, the realest part of our waking dreams: that is, from the last thing remaining to us, the only thing worthy to remain'—this is the absolute question of our relation to each other.[49] It is perhaps in the persistence of this question—as damaged and as threatened as it presently is—that we can locate a basis for hope. But more importantly still, Bloch writes persuasively of a need to *learn* hope, as much as we have learnt fear, and I think that it is perhaps here that we can most see something available to us in order to venture beyond. Barriers, he tells us, are there to be crossed, and if they are felt as such, they already have been.

---

49.   Bloch, *The Spirit of Utopia*, 3.

# 5

# Redemption after Nietzsche? The 'Acceptance of Guilt' in Bonhoeffer's Christology

## Max Champion

Dietrich Bonhoeffer (1906–45) was hanged for his part in a conspiracy to assassinate Hitler. A Lutheran pastor and son of humanist parents, he understood the force of Nietzsche's attack on religion and reason. He basically accepted Nietzsche's critique of ignoble religion but not his solution in the revival of paganism. Bonhoeffer met his objections by advocating a Christ-centred form of faith and discipleship that was sacrificial and life affirming. His own life and thought reflected his belief that Christians are called to share God's suffering in the world by speaking and acting boldly in the face of tyranny and cowardice. His doctrine of reconciliation acknowledged the overcoming of sin and guilt in Christ in such a way that people become stronger, not weaker (as Nietzsche thought).

### 1. Nietzsche's critique of Christianity: 'Dionysus versus the Crucified.—'

Our chief interest is Nietzsche's criticism of Christianity, which formed one part of his attack on Western culture as a whole. In *Twilight of the Idols* he blamed rationalists and theologians alike for trying to shield people from their noble, life-affirming instincts. The philosophers are 'honourable idolaters of concepts who kill the life in what they worship'[1] who falsify 'the testimony of the senses'.[2] And the Church,

---

1.  Friedrich Nietzsche, *Twilight of the Idols* (1888), in *The Portable Nietzsche*, edited and translated by Walter Kaufmann (New York: Viking Press, 1968), 479.
2.  Nietzsche, *Twilight of the Idols*, 480.

with its attack on pride, greed, revenge and the 'will to power' is 'hostile to life' when it should have been 'spiritualising and deifying desire'.[3]

In a chilling passage, which anticipates the rise of Nazism, Nietzsche says that Christianity, following Judaism, 'represents the counter-movement to any morality of breeding, of race, of privilege: it is anti-Aryan religion par excellence'.[4] It is a sick, slavish religion, which lacks humanity, vision and courage. Moreover, the Church is an ideological institution, which helps timid people cope with weaknesses of mind, body and spirit. It deifies fear, envy, vengeance, resignation, decency and humility and promotes self-denial as a means to assuage guilt and avoid passionate, joyful commitment to life:

> the feelings of devotion, self-sacrifice for one's neighbour, the whole morality of self-denial must be questioned mercilessly and taken to court . . . There is too much charm and sugar in these feelings of 'for others, not for myself,' for us not to need to become doubly suspicious at this point and to ask: are these not perhaps—*seductions*![5]

The consequences of Christianity's subversion of noble sacrifice are severe—for God and humankind. The 'madman' who brings a lantern into the market place at noon looking for God[6] pronounces judgment on the Church: humankind is diminished because it has killed the noble God.

In response to the collapse of rational-humanism and Judeo-Christianity, Nietzsche proposed the 'revaluation of all values' and 'sounding out idols' by the restoration of what he called 'Aryan humanity' based on the concept of 'pure blood'. Thus 'nobility' shall be restored to both God and humankind. The dehumanising effect of (enlightened) reason and (Christian) faith shall be followed by the resurrection of our true human nature. After the exposure and

---

3.    Nietzsche, *Twilight of the Idols*, 487.
4.    Nietzsche, *Twilight of the Idols*, 504.
5.    Friedrich Nietzsche, *Beyond Good and Evil*, in Kaufmann, *The Portable Nietzsche*, #33, 235. See also, Friedrich Nietzsche, *The Antichrist*, in Kaufmann, *The Portable Nietzsche*, #17, 584.
6.    Friedrich Nietzsche, *The Gay Science*, in Kaufmann, *The Portable Nietzsche*, # 125, 95–6.

abandonment of the futile search for totality and unity in God or universal values, we shall be free to 'redeem' ourselves through heroic life-affirming acts.

Nietzsche is drawn to the Jesus who exemplifies anti-rational faith and inclusive love which accepts life as it is and experiences the eternal in the midst of the world, but he is particularly critical of the primitive Christian idea of redemption (which he blames on Paul and the Church). Believing that Christ died for the remission of sins is 'most revolting' and 'most barbarous'. It is unworthy of a noble religion. 'What gruesome paganism!'[7]

When, however, we realise that the beliefs and values of (the Christian) religion and (enlightened) humanism are really attempts to avoid living in the present without props, the terror of nihilism confronts us. Only then can we find the resources within us, our own 'will to power,' to live in the midst of suffering and joy; and thus to experience redemption.

Nietzsche's antipathy to Christ crucified for our sins is strongly expressed in *Thus Spake Zarathustra.* Being redeemed, here, means accepting one's fate and acting serenely and heroically in the present without regret about the past. 'Redemption' is not to be found in healing the body or forgiving sins. Zarathustra refuses to heal the weak because they will lose their spirit. Being sick is better for individuals than being timid, apathetic or dispirited. 'To redeem the past and to transform every "It was" into an "I wanted it thus—that alone do I call redemption!"'[8] The past cannot and should not be undone by mercy, healing or justice. We must become reconciled to time so that we act heroically in time.

This life-embracing attitude is 'redemptive' because it confronts us with the necessity of accepting the past without regret. Thus Nietzsche seeks redemption from sin and guilt by denying their historical and temporal reality. We must be redeemed from wanting to be redeemed! Instead of trying to have our guilt expiated by the Christian God, we should learn to act nobly, without God, under the necessity of guilt and suffering.

---

7.  Nietzsche, *The Antichrist*, 616. In this context 'paganism' means 'primitive superstition,' not the neo-pagan 'celebration of life' which he advocates.

8.  Friedrich Nietzsche, *Thus Spoke Zarathustra* (Great Britain: Penguin, 1972), 161.

In summary, Nietzsche's account of redemption flatly contradicts the Christian account. ' . . . With no more contrasts existing, there can be no more "concept of guilt and punishment". Sin, any sort of distance in the relationship between God and man, has been abolished.'[9] Jesus died 'not to redeem mankind but to show how one must live—by non-resistant, non-judging, suffering love'. Redemption is achieved when people learn to live fully in the present joys and challenges of life. In experiencing the 'heavenly bliss which Jesus experienced and achieved by his way of life, they will know "the psychological reality of redemption"'.[10]

Thus, Nietzsche powerfully declared the incompatibility of Christian and neo-pagan forms of redemption. The decisive difference is dramatically stated at the end of *Ecce Homo*: 'Have I been understood? Dionysus versus the Crucified.—'[11] Nietzsche clearly saw that the battle between Christianity and neo-paganism would intensify, the open-ended hyphen indicating a long, possibly eternal struggle, for supremacy.

This unrelenting critique is 'neo-pagan' in that it appeals to human nature and demythologises nineteenth century Christian beliefs. Indeed, it is a nihilistic form of romanticism with its 'protest against the subordination of life to reason and rational civilisation; the search for intensity of experience; and the desire for communion with the natural forces'.[12] For Nietzsche, the death of the Christian God is the redemptive moment when ecstatic pagan religion is reborn:

> Is the pagan cult not a form of thanksgiving and affirmation of life? Must its highest representation not be an apology for and deification of life? The type of a well-constituted and ecstatically overflowing spirit! The type of a spirit that takes into itself and redeems

---

9.   Karl Jaspers, *Nietzsche and Christianity* (Henry Regnery: Gateway, 1937), 20–1.

10.  Jaspers, *Nietzsche and Christianity*, 17.

11.  Friedrich Nietzsche, *Ecce Homo* in *The Basic Writings of Nietzsche*, edited and translated by Walter Kaufmann (New York & Toronto: Random House, 1966), 791.

12.  Wilhelm A Visser t'Hooft, *None Other Gods* (London: SCM Press, 1937), 151.

the contradictory and questionable aspects of existence.[13]

## 2. Bonhoeffer's deconstruction of Nietzsche: Christ crucified for others

Nietzsche's challenge demanded a theological response which addressed the questions without being daunted by them. Bonhoeffer accepted the force of nineteenth century critiques of religion in general and of Nietzsche's in particular. Individuals and communities make God in their own image to justify their causes, overcome their weaknesses, satisfy their needs and bolster their private faith. As Bonhoeffer was painfully aware in the crisis engulfing the world in the 1930s and 1940s, many Christians were loath to take decisive action on public issues which did not affect them directly. The German Christians, the Evangelical Lutheran Church and the Confessing Church were more concerned about self-preservation (of their religious influence) than self-sacrifice (in the fight against tyranny).

The central point in Bonhoeffer's critique of religion is the absolute distinction between Christ-centred reconciliation and 'redemption myths'. He could say that 'redemption is at the heart of the Gospel'[14] but, also, more typically, that the idea of 'redemption' had become more difficult and remote in a 'world come of age', which is no longer interested in 'religious questions'.[15] The fundamental problem with 'religions of redemption' is that they draw people out of the world instead of placing them more fully in the world. They treat God as a stopgap for our incomplete knowledge of nature, death, suffering and guilt. They prey on psychological weakness and intellectual ignorance and encourage the idea that faith is an escape from personal, scientific and political challenges.[16]

---

13. Friedrich Nietzsche, *The Will to Power: An Attempted Transvaluation of All Values,* translated by Walter Kaufmann and RJ Hollingdale (London: Weidenfeld & Nicolson, 1968), 542. He also refers to the clash between Dionysian religion, which accepts harsh suffering as part of life, and 'the god on the cross' religion, which signifies redemption from life.

14. Dietrich Bonhoeffer, *Letters and Papers from Prison,* edited by Eberhard Bethge (London: SCM Press, 1971), 14.

15. Bonhoeffer, *Letters and Papers from Prison,* 324–9.

16. See Bonhoeffer, *Letters and Papers from Prison,* 281–2; also 311 and 341f.

In contrast, the Old and New Testaments insist that 'this world must not be prematurely written off'. The crucial difference is that, where redemption myths try to overcome the barrier between death and eternity, Israel is freed from Egypt to live before God as God's people on earth. The resurrection of Jesus reinforces the 'this-worldly' character of faith. Thus, the Church must reject the idea that:

> Redemption now means redemption from cares, distress, fears, and longings, from sin and death, in a better world beyond the grave. The difference between the Christian hope of resurrection and the mythological hope is that the former sends a man back to his life on earth in a wholly new way which is even more sharply defined than it is in the Old Testament. This world must not be prematurely written off; in this the Old and New Testaments are as one. Redemption myths arise from human boundary experiences, but Christ takes hold of a man at the centre of his life.[17]

The way in which Christ encounters human beings is developed positively in Bonhoeffer's Christology by focusing on what it means to be truly human. It is not enough to criticise religiosity in the cause of self-affirmation. Nietzsche's disdain for self-sacrifice and the Christian idea of remission of sins must be met by its life-affirming alternative in the self-giving love of Christ for the world. Two closely inter-related themes are apposite: what it means to be persons-in-community and what it means to act on behalf of others.

### 2.1 Being persons-in-community

Bonhoeffer first articulates a general concept of social relations in which (a) 'person' is understood in relation to 'community' and (b) 'humankind' is understood as 'being in Adam' (unredeemed) or 'in Christ' (redeemed).

---

17.  Bonhoeffer, *Letters and Papers from Prison*, 336–7. The seriousness with which Bonhoeffer took Nietzsche is evident in his positive 'non-religious interpretation of biblical concepts' for a 'world come of age'. See also: 311–2, 325–9, 341, 344–6, 358–62. See, too, his appreciation of the Song of Songs: 'It's a good thing that the book is in the Bible, in face of all those who believe that the restraint of passion is Christian (where is there such restraint in the Old Testament?)', 303.

The essential nature of our 'human being' is not to be found either in the 'isolated individual' who places him/herself in the truth or in communities claiming to embody the truth in themselves. We live in a web of reciprocal relationships; we are persons-in-community, called to act responsibly in the disordered world which God, nevertheless, loves. Thus, says Bonhoeffer, we are essentially social, both in our spiritual nature (as creatures) and in our existentiality (as sinful creatures).

We must not let a false anthropology distort our understanding of the human reality. Our specific 'human being' is not constituted either by 'individuals' for whom 'society' is a problem or by 'the masses' for whom 'individuality' is a problem. Thus, while the concept of the pure individual (upon which individualism and collectivism both depend) is an abstraction, the concept of the person entails the concepts of community and humankind.[18] Therefore, in fidelity to biblical anthropology, Bonhoeffer rejected the choice between 'individualism' and 'collectivism'.[19]

### 2.2 Acting on behalf of others

Bonhoeffer does not merely describe the general conditions for 'being human.' Nor is he primarily interested in describing an alternate biblical theology of 'human being.' Instead, he is concerned with what it means that the person of Christ has acted on behalf of humankind and, consequently, what it means for the Body of Christ to act on behalf of others.

In developing his Christology and ethics, Bonhoeffer distinguishes between two basic forms of sacrificial action: the 'ethical' and the 'Christological.' The 'ethical' or 'penultimate' form is also different-tiated in two ways. There are 'structures of the responsible life' in which citizens exercise representative functions for others.[20] And there

---

18. See Dietrich Bonhoeffer, *Act and Being*, translated by B Noble (London: Collins, 1962), 11–72, where he criticises both idealist and essentialist philosophies for separating the (acting) individual from its universal condition (of being) and for failing to distinguish between (unredeemed) life 'in Adam' and (redeemed) life 'in Christ,' thus falsely investing the thinking-and-acting self with power to know reality directly.
19. See Clifford Green, *Bonhoeffer: A Theology of Sociality* (Revised edition) (Grand Rapids: Eerdmanns, 1999), 41–2, footnote 53.
20. Dietrich Bonhoeffer, *Ethics*, edited by Eberhard Bethge and translated by Neville Horton Smith (London: Collins Fontana Library, 1964), 224f.

are actions which entail the 'voluntary acceptance of an evil by one person in another person's place' in a particular situation (country, debt etc).'[21] In Bonhoeffer, the primary focus is on the importance of costly action in general and its relation to the costly love of God in Christ. Thus, while 'humanly heroic love' belongs to the highest form of ethical responsibility, it 'does not involve the other man's self-responsibility . . . In acknowledging it a man does not set his whole ethical person at stake . . .'[22]

The 'Christological' form of vicarious action, therefore, is qualitatively different from both forms of ethical action. What Christ has done on behalf of others is *sui generis*. A person is not in his debt only in a particular situation but 'he acknowledges Christ as acting vicariously for his entire person, and thus owes his entire person to him.'[23] The vicarious action of Christ for humankind is unique, both in substance and scope. It cannot be understood from general concepts of sociology or ethics but only in relation to Hebrew faith, with which Christian faith is integrally connected. Thus,

> The people is to repent, but it is not a question of the number who repent, and in practice it will never be the whole people, the whole church, but God can so regard it 'as if' the whole people has repented. 'For the sake of ten I will not destroy it' (Gen 18:32). God can see the whole people in a few individuals, just as he saw and reconciled the whole of mankind in one man.[24]

It is notable that Bonhoeffer develops the concept of vicarious action, not in relation to the Jewish cult, but to the prophetic role within and outside Israel. In describing Christ as mediator (*Mittler*)[25] and representative (*Stellvertreter*), he presupposes the Jewish concept of

---

21.  Dietrich Bonhoeffer, *Sanctorum Communio: A Dogmatic Inquiry into the Sociology of the Church*, translated by R Gregor Smith (London: Collins, 1963), 114 and footnote 36 (on page 223).
22.  Bonhoeffer, *Sanctorum Communio*, 114 and footnote 36.
23.  Bonhoeffer, *Sanctorum Communio*, 114 and footnote 36.
24.  Bonhoeffer, *Sanctorum Communio*, 83–4.
25.  Dietrich Bonhoeffer, *Creation and Fall. Temptation*, translated by John C Fletcher (New York: Macmillan, 1978), 48–57; and Dietrich Bonhoeffer, *Christology* translated by John Bowden (London: Collins, 1966), 61–7.

'the few acting on behalf of the many'. This strong sense of a person or group acting on behalf of the entire covenant community, and of the covenant community acting on behalf of the nations, is at the heart of his Christology. The distinctive mark of Christ's vicarious love is that he alone acts 'on behalf of the world'. He is the 'one righteous man' in whom humanity is redeemed, whose intercessory role is exercised specifically in relation to idolatry and inhumanity.

> In a manner which passes all comprehension . . . God Himself sets out on the path of humiliation and atonement, and thereby absolves the world. God is willing to be guilty of our guilt. He takes upon Himself the punishment and the suffering which this guilt has brought upon us. God Himself answers for godlessness, love for hatred, the saint for the sinner. Now there is no more godlessness, no more hatred, no more sin which God has not taken upon Himself, suffered for and expiated. Now there is no more reality, no more world, but it is reconciled with God and at peace. God did this in His dear Son Jesus Christ. Ecce homo![26]

The reference to '*ecce homo*' is crucial for understanding Bonhoeffer's method. First, he locates the vicarious action of Christ in the sinlessness of a crucified man. It is in the innocent, suffering humanity of Jesus that God is to be seen.[27] Second, he challenges Nietzsche at the critical point where he tries to deconstruct Christianity, the cross. Third, Christ's guilt-bearing action on behalf of others is portrayed as the free expression of God's love for the ungodly (Romans 5: 6ff). Jesus is not a helpless victim.[28]

Christ's 'acceptance of guilt' (*Schuldübernahme*) on behalf of the sinful world is at the centre of Bonhoeffer's Christology to express the divine purpose of Christ's incarnation, crucifixion and resurrection. In love for humankind God takes guilt seriously as the reality which afflicts every aspect of human existence. Only the righteous one who

---

26. Bonhoeffer, *Ethics*, 70–1. See also: Bonhoeffer, *Sanctorum Communio*, 113–14.
27. See John 19:4, 5.
28. 'Freedom from sin and the question of guilt are inseparable in him,' in Bonhoeffer, *Ethics*, 241. See also: Bonhoeffer, *Christology*, 113.

created time and came into the midst of the world at a particular time
can cancel guilt. Thus, what he had done, as the Lord of time, is 'in
time' and is efficacious 'for all time'.[29]

In this expression of guilt and innocence we come to the heart of
the matter and the most difficult idea of all: sin is forgiven and guilt
cancelled through the death of an innocent person. Bonhoeffer tacitly
admits the problem that appalled Nietzsche (and others) when he says
that it may seem to deny moral responsibility.[30] He argues that it does
not do so because it is a theological, not a moral, concept.

This is not a clever argument to avoid valid criticism, but a way of
expressing the reality of divine love for sinful humanity, for which
there is no adequate analogy. Guilt, in Bonhoeffer, is not simply to be
equated with individual feelings so despised by Nietzsche. It is a
reality which effects our universal 'human being-and-actions' in
rebellion against God and our personal-and-collective refusal to live in
truth. We incur guilt because of the theological fact that, at the heart of
every person and community, is the desire to become like God and
place ourselves 'in the middle'. Thus, guilt is the common heritage of
humankind and the fault of every person.[31]

In Bonhoeffer, the locus of the redemption which Christ has
affected is personal, corporate and universal in scope. Christ stands 'as
man' in the centre of the earth as the one who, by virtue of his guilt-
bearing love, is *pro me* (me), *pro nobis* (us) and *pro aliis* (others). While
the vicarious love of Christ 'for all' is always central, there is a subtle
shift of emphasis in the Christology from the personal and ecclesial to
the worldly. This reflects Bonhoeffer's deepening awareness, under the
pressure of events, of the scope of Christ's guilt bearing love.[32]

---

29. Bonhoeffer, *Sanctorum Communio*, 114.
30. Bonhoeffer, *Sanctorum Communio*, 114. For a criticism of Bonhoeffer,
    which fails to recognise his focus on Christ's loving identification with
    human guilt, see: Dorothy Soelle, *Christ the Representative: An Essay in
    Theology after the 'Death of God'* (London: SCM Press, 1967), 92–7.
31. 'Guilt is inconceivable, inexplicable and inexcusable . . . [and] as a
    creature of God I have committed a completely anti-godly and evil act,
    and that for that very reason I am guilty—and moreover, inexcusably
    guilty . . . The guilt rests upon me alone . . .', in Bonhoeffer, *Creation
    and Fall*, 65.
32. See Ernst Feil, *The Theology of Dietrich Bonhoeffer* (Philadelphia:
    Fortress, 1985), 75–6, 92–6. In his earlier work, Bonhoeffer spoke of
    Christ being *'pro me'* (me) and *'pro nobis'* (us), the latter referring

We can now see how Bonhoeffer challenges Nietzsche's critique of the Church's Christology. He focuses on the vicarious humanity of Christ who acts on our behalf to set us free from placing personal and collective ideals at the 'centre' of life, and freedom from guilt means living fully in the world before God. Thus, Christ's being-and-acting *pro aliis* is not a 'gruesome primitive idea' but the sign of self-giving, guilt-bearing love for others, a reality for which there is no satisfactory analogy.[33]

Bonhoeffer's Christology is both 'reformed,' in focusing on Christ's liberation of humanity from guilt, and 'modern,' in responding to Nietzschean criticisms of life-denying guilt. It is worked out through the interplay between helpful concepts of social relations in general, Nietzsche's critique of Christianity, and theological-biblical concepts of what it means to be persons-in-community. Each part does not, however, have equal weight. The vicarious guilt-bearing humanity of Jesus is the 'ultimate' towards which all social and ethical life moves and from whom they receive their 'relative' freedom. Because what God has done in Christ is *sui generis*, the 'ultimate' cannot be derived from the 'penultimate.'[34] General concepts cannot express the unique person and work of Christ. Only he has represented each person, group and humankind in their guilt and freedom. Only he can rightly be called the incarnate 'man for others'[35] who has 'redeemed' humankind from 'redemption myths' so that people can engage in positive 'non-religious interpretation' of biblical texts for a 'world come of age.'[36]

---

primarily to the Church. Later, in the *Letters and Papers from* Prison, 381ff, the primary focus is firmly on Christ '*pro aliis*' (others) and the incarnate, crucified and risen Jesus is described as the 'man for others'.

33. Christ's vicarious action contains elements of 'ethical sacrifice.' His ministry is one of healing and mercy to sufferers who could not help themselves in a particular situation. However, there is another dimension which cannot be described as 'ethical.' Christ's self-giving love for others, which embodies the love of God for sinful humanity, is guilt-bearing love which cancels guilt and restores fellowship with God and one another.

34. For the importance of this relation in Bonhoeffer's theology, see: Bonhoeffer, *Ethics*, 120–87.

35. Bonhoeffer, *Letters and Papers from Prison*, 381ff.

36. Bonhoeffer, *Letters and Papers from Prison*, 311–12, 325–9, 341, 344–6, 358–62. The use of these terms shows how seriously Bonhoeffer

## 2.3 *The church and guilt*

Bonhoeffer's Christology is the foundation of his ethics and ecclesiology. In 'Ethics as Formation',[37] he contrasts ethics which begin with God's guilt-bearing love for real human beings and 'theoretical' ethics which does not seek reconciliation with real (sinful) persons. Although not explicitly stated, his frequent use here of *'ecce homo'* in relation to Christ rejects Nietzsche's criticism of 'the crucified' at the end of his last work, *Ecce Homo*. He deconstructs Nietzsche's 'gruesome primitive idea' by placing the 'acceptance of guilt' at the centre of a truly 'Christian' ethic. Christian community must be conformed to Christ's love for real people who are both enmeshed in guilt and responsible for resisting particular manifestations of self-deification and communal arrogance. The church is called to share in the sufferings of the world by accepting guilt 'in Christ'. Christian ethical commitment, therefore, will not be concerned to act with a 'pure conscience' but to do what is necessary to oppose evil.[38]

This entails the church confessing guilt *(Schuldbekenntnis)* in particular situations in which the state and the church refuse to carry out their God-given mandates. As a result of his disillusionment with the cowardice of the Confessing Church in not protecting Jews and other vulnerable people in the face of Nazi atrocities, Bonhoeffer wrote a 'Confession of Guilt'[39] which identifies its origin in self-justification and looks for renewal of personal, ecclesial and national life 'in Christ'. Typically, he says that:

> The church confesses . . . her timidity, her evasiveness,
> her dangerous concession . . . She was silent when she
> should have cried out because the blood of the
> innocent was crying aloud to heaven. She has failed to
> speak the right word in the right way at the right time.
> She has not resisted to the uttermost the apostasy of

---

regarded Nietzsche's critique. He had seen too much of this kind of Christianity!

37. Bonhoeffer, *Ethics*, 64ff.
38. Such guilt-bearing action was necessary to counter the cowardice of reasonable, pious folk who were concerned for self-preservation. Bonhoeffer's decision to take part in the conspiracy incognito exemplifies his Christ-centred ethics.
39. Bonhoeffer, *Ethics*, 110–16.

faith, and she has brought upon herself the guilt of the
godlessness of the masses . . .[40]

Bonhoeffer's guilt-bearing Christology led him to a profound
understanding of the personal-and-collective nature of guilt in German
culture, which was steeped in Christian theology and enlightened
philosophy. It also shaped an ethic which challenged particular evils
without denying the shared responsibility of all.

His Christ-centred theology was not a theoretical exercise but the
expression of reality which shaped a practical, life-affirming ethic
within a community which participates in the sufferings of God in the
world. Therefore, we may say that, for Bonhoeffer, the Church is the
body whose members confess their own guilt in the light of the
liberating guilt-bearing love of Christ. A Christian is 'in a state of
solidarity with the other man's guilt, but my dealings with him take
place on the basis of the life-principle of vicarious action (which) can
become fundamental for the church of God in and through Christ'.[41]

This is completely different from the pre-occupation with guilt
against which Nietzsche railed. Instead of focusing on fear and
weakness, Bonhoeffer enables a person to see the reality of the human
situation in the light of the vicarious sin-bearing love of God in Christ.
It frees us to confess (personal) sin as part of the (collective) sin of a

---

40. Bonhoeffer, *Ethics*, 112–13. See also on 114:'She is guilty of the deaths
of the weakest and most defenceless brothers of Jesus Christ.' In his
poem, 'Night Voices in Tegel', (Bonhoeffer, *Letters and Papers from
Prison*, 349–56), Bonhoeffer uses darkness as a metaphor for the
collective power of guilt which forces prisoners to 'share the guilt' with
the perpetrators. Bonhoeffer does not excuse the crimes of the Nazis but
insists that all Germans, as heirs to civilised culture and reformed faith,
have ignored political lies and human suffering out of concern for self-
preservation. Therefore, all of us, he says, in a typically inclusive way,
must come before God 'as confessors of our sins' and 'await the wiping
out of our guilt'. See the commentary in Johann Hampe, *Dietrich
Bonhoeffer, Prayers from Prison* (Philadelphia: Fortress 1978), 62. For
a modern confession inspired by Bonhoeffer, see Hiroshi Murakami,
'What has the Japanese Church Learned from Dietrich Bonhoeffer?' and
'Confession of Guilt by Today's Japanese Church: Prepared by the
Japan Bonhoeffer Society [1985]' in *Bonhoeffer's Ethics: Old Europe
and New Frontiers*, edited by Guy Carter and others (Kampen, The
Netherlands: Kok Pharus, 1991), 217–25.
41. Bonhoeffer, *Sanctorum Communio*, 107.

particular nation (Germany), culture (the West) and Church (German Evangelical Lutheran and Confessing Churches). And it enables us to face our universal propensity to deify personal and collective goals without retreating from costly action which may be necessary in the face of specific evils.

### 3. The legacy and promise of Bonhoeffer's challenge to Nietzsche

We are now in a position to assess whether Bonhoeffer's guilt-bearing Christology offers hope of redemption after Nietzsche. The following summations are pertinent:

First, post-modern Western culture has largely accepted Nietzsche's analysis of the timidity of the (Christian) religion and the futility of establishing universal religious and moral principles on rational grounds. The 'celebration of life', the mass appeal to passion, the rejection of personal guilt, scorn for the church's teaching on redemption and pre-occupation with immediate concerns are signs of the neo-paganism which Nietzsche foresaw and welcomed. Although Bonhoeffer agrees with Nietzsche's analysis of 'religions of redemption', he also saw the dreadful impact of revitalised and nihilistic romanticism.

Second, the 'will to power', which has filled the vacuum left by a loss of confidence in the 'will of God', is more often expressed in behaviour that is akin to the herd mentality (despised by Nietzsche) than in heroic individuality which faces the tragic necessity of life without rational or religious props. While Bonhoeffer accepts Nietzsche's criticism of weak-willed religion, he rejects the idea that, by a heroic act of will, human beings can redeem themselves. In his Christology, therefore, he portrays Jesus as the strong man who, in fidelity to the will of God and in love for others, willingly bears the consequences of idolatrous and inhuman expressions of the 'will to power'.

Third, the clash between Dionysus and the Crucified is usually interpreted as the choice between the secular-pagan strength and vitality of life and religious-Christian weakness and repudiation of life. Where Nietzsche considered them to be incompatible, Bonhoeffer brings them together in a way which acknowledges much of Nietzsche's critique while categorically rejecting his pagan presuppositions. Crucified love and costly discipleship are signs of deepest love of others, the earth and God. The 'penultimate' must neither be confused with the 'ultimate' nor abandoned by it.

Fourth, is the dispute over the meaning of 'sacrifice'. Where Nietzsche rails against sugary acts of self-sacrifice and self-denial, Bonhoeffer puts them at the centre of what it means to live in the midst of the world. He counters Nietzsche's charge that such actions are ignoble by showing that the incarnate, crucified and risen Christ is the 'man for others' whose powerful goodness and mercy enables human beings to be strong in faith, hope and love. He thereby demythologises Nietzsche's 'noble sacrifice'.

Fifth, in response to Nietzsche's charge that the Christian account of redemption from guilt is fundamentally 'gruesome paganism', Bonhoeffer's Christology centres on the vicarious action of Christ in taking upon himself human sin and guilt. He achieves this by implicitly rejecting Nietzsche's 'redemption of redemption' and his assertion that the Christian doctrine of redemption is dependent on human weakness and sin. Thus, Bonhoeffer sets Christ's 'acceptance of guilt' at the centre of his account of the reality of God and our vocation in the world. Bonhoeffer repudiates Nietzsche's thesis that the past does not need to be redeemed. Past actions and inactions led to Nazism! We cannot exonerate ourselves simply by plunging into the present in a spirit of tragic heroism. We are called to live in the midst of life, no matter how dreadful, with a confidence born of faith in God's providential, suffering love which is revealed and embodied in the Person of Christ. Therefore, while he agrees with Nietzsche that the human problem is caused by religion, Bonhoeffer denies Nietzsche's assertion that there is no need to seek redemption from guilt and that we should heroically bear the present and ignore the past. 'Man cannot absolve himself of guilt. Otherwise, Christ would have died in vain.'[42]

Sixth, Bonhoeffer entirely rejects Nietzsche's strong criticisms of Jews and the Old Testament. Christianity is indissolubly wedded to Israel. As such, Bonhoeffer criticises all idealistic attempts to establish Christianity 'within the limits of reason alone' (Kant) as if the historical and theological link to the Jewish covenant could be transcended. He clearly distinguishes between disagreements about Judaism and hateful anti-Semitism. The church's silence over crimes against Jews, while defending her right to preach the Gospel, was, to Bonhoeffer, the outcome of a flawed theology which had its counterpart in the philosophy of people like Nietzsche.

---

42. Bonhoeffer, *Creation and Fall*, 76.

## 4. Conclusion

Although Bonhoeffer basically agrees with Nietzsche's critique of Christianity (and the Enlightenment) for being lifeless, passionless and inward, he does not accept his solution to the dismantling of life-denying redemptive myths. Instead of turning to a vitalistic philosophy of life and heroic participation in the present, Bonhoeffer centres on the triumphant, suffering love of God 'in Christ' which takes place in the midst of the world and enables us to love the earth and real (sinful) people while challenging evil. Thus, his Christology is shaped by the crucifixion which is understood, not as the craven rejection of life, but as the place where the strength, vitality and nobility of Christ's sacrificial and redemptive action is revealed as costly love for all.

The consequence of this for what it means for human beings to live fully in the world before God is an ecclesiological ethics which is centred on our participation in the vicarious guilt-bearing love of Christ. The confession of guilt and self-sacrificing love come together in his Christology.

Bonhoeffer's response to Nietzsche is not only a matter of past historical interest. His Christ-centred critique of Nietzsche, and its implications for ethical action and Church practice, provides a profound insight into the place of guilt and redemption in our personal and collective relations today. He also speaks to a world where the deification of personal and collective ends still causes so much misery. Having seen the strengths and weaknesses of Nietzsche's critique of guilt, and being prepared to die as one who bore the guilt of a nation in which he shared, Bonhoeffer can help us to recognise the 'proper uses of guilt'[43] and the dangers of 'collective guilt'.[44] His Christ-centred ethics can speak to post-modern culture where it is fashionable to ridicule the idea of 'personal guilt' (as being repressive for individual dignity) while welcoming the idea of 'collective guilt' (as being necessary to restore dignity to oppressed groups).

---

43.   Thomas Oden, *Guilt Free* (Nashville: Abingdon, 1980), 80ff, 101.
44.   Matthew Scully, 'Viktor Frankel at Ninety: An Interview', in *First Things*, 52, (April, 1995): 39–43.

# 6

# Apocalypse, Messianism and Redemption in Martin Buber's Dialogical Thought

## Cecil Schmalkuche

Martin Buber was a prominent Jewish writer and speaker, whose long life (1878–1965) spanned tumultuous and divisive times for humanity and in particular for Jews. Throughout his life Buber affirmed the necessity of dialogue as essential for human survival. This dialogical theme resonates in Buber's treatment of messianism, apocalypse and redemption. Buber placed 'dialogue' or 'meeting' (*Begegnung*) above all other concepts, even space and time. The *real* life needs an 'I-Thou' (*Ich-Du*) dialogue to survive. Writers in English have tended to use the word 'Thou' to capture the single number and intimacy of *Du*. This is not a meeting of a subject with an object but a subject with another subject, a *Beziehung* or 'relationship'. It can occur between humans, with nature and with God, the eternal or absolute Thou. This meeting is fully mutual, direct or *present* but incomprehensible. Without it a human does not really exist as an 'I'.[1]

Over against this Buber describes the subject-object relation as an I-It meeting, a *Verhaeltnis* or 'relation'. It is not mutual but indirect and comprehensible. The relation is really totally subjective too, because one does not need to go outside one's self when relating to an It. One must go out to meet a Thou but not an It.[2] All relations, even those with God, can become I-It meetings, indeed at times they must. 'The *It* is the eternal chrysalis, the *Thou* the eternal butterfly', says Buber.[3] He successfully applied this thesis to all areas of life and knowledge,

---

1. Martin Buber, *Ich und Du*, *Das dialogische Prinzip* (Heidelberg: Lambert Schneider, 1973).
2. Buber, *Ich und Du*, 7–21.
3. Martin Buber quoted in Maurice Friedman, *Martin Buber: The Life of Dialogue*, (London: Routledge, 2002), 66.

whether in religion, philosophy, education, politics, ethics, psycho-
therapy, art or literature. This chapter is primarily concerned with the
religious and political dimensions of his work.

It is impossible to understand Buber's basic thesis without coming
to terms with his faith in the God of the Hebrew Scriptures. For him
the bible is not a book but a voice.[4] It relates the greatest dialogue
between heaven and earth. (Buber's ears were tuned to dialogue by the
host of Hasidic tales, which filled his childhood). On Mount Sinai God
initiates and sustains an I-Thou meeting and dialogue. When God
speaks and reveals his name from the burning bush, Buber translates
the Hebrew divine name as 'I-will-be-there' (*Ich-werde-da-sein* or *Ich bin
da*), rather than the conventional translation 'I-am-who-I-am' (Hebrew
*Ehyeh asher ehyeh* Exodus 3:14). Instead of three tenses, past, present
and future, biblical Hebrew has two: finished and unfinished. The
form *ehyeh* and the name YHWH for God are unfinished or continuous
forms. So for example, according to Buber, the Decalogue cannot be
understood unless it is a direct address to people today and not just
information. Consequently the people of Israel, even though they had
settled in Canaan, could be addressed as if they themselves were
present in the desert (Joshua 24). When translating the Bible with Franz
Rosenzweig, Buber endeavoured to capture its living voice by using
units, which matched the human breath (*Atemzuege*) and reflected the
Hebrew syntax.[5] The bible exhibits what Buber calls 'my foremost,
essential conviction that my relationship with God is tightly bound to
the relationship with my fellow human.'[6]

The word 'apocalypse' means 'revelation' or literally 'uncovering'.
From his dialogical understanding, 'apocalypse' means for Buber the
Torah or the Bible: that is, humans' meeting with God's presence or
voice. Apocalypse is a powerful Presence, which contains the eternal
Thou of he-who-reveals-himself, *your* Creator.

In an essay of 1954 called, 'Prophecy, Apocalyptic and the
Historical Hour', Buber calls this revelation 'prophetic' in order to
differentiate it from 'apocalyptic'.[7] Just as there are two forms of
dialogue (I-Thou and I-It) so too faith can go in two ways—prophetic

4.    Martin Buber, *Biblical Humanism* (London: Macdonald, 1968), 235.
5.    Friedman, *Life of Dialogue*, 284.
6.    Buber, *Ich und Du*, 122.
7.    Martin Buber, 'Prophecy, Apocalyptic and the Historical Hour', in
      Martin Buber, *Pointing the Way* (London: Routledge and Kegan Paul,
      1957), 192–207.

or apocalyptic, encounter or escape. It goes without saying that Buber
rejects the apocalyptic way. The following comparison shows why:

> *Whereas the prophet, as God's mouthpiece, speaks to a people,*
> The apocalyptic author writes a book.
> The prophet is called to a task that involves his body and life,
> But the apocalyptic author writes a literary fiction.
> *The prophet breathes in history, in the fullness of decision,*
> But the apocalyptic author points to a coming age, beyond time,
> where all is predetermined.
> The prophet remains free to 'turn',
> But the apocalyptic author is caught in original sin and destiny.
> The prophet speaks from 'the hour of the highest strength and
> fruitfulness of the Eastern spirit'
> But the apocalyptic author from 'the decadence of its cultures and
> religions'.
> *The prophet undergoes inner transformation, a 'turning',*
> While the apocalyptic author 'obliterates . . . individual resolutions
> and actions'.

Today the word 'prophet', means a foreteller of the hidden future.
However, the root meaning of the Greek word *prophetes* (*nabi* in
Hebrew) is a 'forthteller', a spokesperson or interpreter of current and
past events. The true prophet faithfully speaks the present, divine
Word, which may declare a disaster or judgment. Buber recognises
that God's revealing himself presupposes his 'hiding himself' (Isaiah
45:15), an essential element of genuine dialogue and indeed of
revelation itself.[8]

The prophet as an 'anointed one'(the literal meaning of 'messiah')
introduces Buber's attitude to Messianism.

In his biblical writings, such as 'Moses', 'The Prophetic Faith' (*Der
Glaube der Propheten*), 'The Kingship of God'(*Koenigtum Gottes*) and
'The Anointed One'(*Der Gesalbte*), Buber investigates thoroughly the
development of the reality that God is the King who shares his role
with humans.[9] He shows that the Sinai covenant contains a sac-
ramental mutuality between Above and Below, between God and the

8.  Martin Buber, *Two Types of Faith* (New York: Macmillan 1951), 130.
9.  Martin Buber, *'Schriften zur Bibel'*, in Martin Buber, *Werke*, Volume 2
    (Muenchen: Koesel-Verlag, 1964).

people of Israel. Even though the people surrender to God's grace and power, *both* parties enter freely into dialogue.

Later the Judges remained directly dependent on the Spirit and its charisma or 'anointing' in order to judge. They possessed neither office nor succession. In faith they had to wait for grace, for God's spontaneity. Of course this freedom allowed the people to refuse God's dialogue. Nevertheless, from Sinai until the Judges, the Lord is clearly King. His people, however, longed for a visible human king, who would bring security by power. Even though the judge Gideon refused to be king (Judges 8:22,23), the people eventually received what they desired. Saul was chosen and anointed.

Now an ongoing struggle between heaven and earth, between God and king or prophet and king began, in which successive kings desired monologue not dialogue. They preferred autonomy not anointing; a restricted cultic god, not the free, dynamic YHWH, whose prophetic Word demanded a turning back to dialogue, to justice and righteousness throughout the kingdom.

The recurring failure of judge and king to preserve dialogue and divine kingship between God and people culminates in Isaiah's prophet and messianic figure.[10]

Buber's work, *Der Gott der Leidenden*, (The God of Sufferers), not only provides the climax and goal of his messianic journey but also lays the foundation for Israel's future identity in the world and for Buber's personal vocation.[11] Many of God's servants (for example, Abraham, Jacob, Moses, David, Isaiah, Jeremiah and Job) had to go through the dark night of suffering in order to experience the nearness of YHWH. The suffering servant of Isaiah, however, also carries the burdens of the people's sins in order to 'return' the people to YHWH. As servant, the prophet becomes the living tie (*die lebendige Verbindung*) between God and people.[12] Unlike the king, the prophet is powerless. It is precisely this vulnerable state of powerlessness that, breaking through the illusion of the powerful king, facilitates the Word of dialogue. So while the prophet's suffering fulfils his anointing, the king's 'power' prevented fulfilment.

The suffering of YHWH and of his people meet in the servant. The God who seems to hide his face, to withdraw from dialogue, chooses to

---

10.   Buber, *Biblical Humanism*, 237–8.
11.   Martin Buber, 'Der Gott der Leidenden', in *Werke*.
12.   Buber, *Werke*, 481.

be nearest the suffering servant. In 'Two Types of Faith', Buber describes this experience:

> ... the new questioning of the justice of God arises, of the meaning of suffering, of the value of human effort on behalf of the right way, which surged up ... in the miseries of the Babylonian exile. Its effect has been preserved in the outcries of Jeremiah, the dialectical *theologoumena* of Ezekiel, the accusing speeches of 'Job', the Psalms of tormented souls and the songs of the suffering servant of God ... So man penetrates step by step into the dark which hangs over the meaning of events, until the mystery is disclosed in the flash of light: the *zaddik*, the man justified by God, suffers for the sake of God and of His work of salvation, and God is with him in his suffering. [13]

So, paradoxically, God suffers from his own actions, as he regards the suffering servant as his intimate dialogue partner, in the same way as he had loved Israel. [14] Just as formerly Israel was chosen, now the servant is chosen (Isaiah 42:1). Suffering unites both the personal 'servant' (*ebed* in Hebrew) and servant Israel.

Buber develops this 'unity by means of suffering' theme further. When Israel suffers, especially for other nations, it becomes the suffering servant of Isaiah . Furthermore, whoever undergoes Israel's suffering is the *ebed*, and he or she is Israel, who glorifies YHWH. [15]

Commenting on 'Deutero-Isaiah', chapters 51–3, Buber states:

> Here for the first time a prophet had to proclaim an atonement fulfilled through the suffering of the people ... through a series of 'servants of the Lord', a series at the beginning of which the speaker sees himself. An epoch such as ours, entangled in guilt and far from atonement, can learn something great from this prophet, but it cannot take anything directly from him.

---

13. Buber, *Two Types*, 144.
14. Buber, *Werke*, 481.
15. Buber, *Werke*, 483.

> Here something not dependent upon our wills shines
> on us comfortingly.[16]

It is obvious that Buber includes himself and his audience. Here the dialogue that YHWH desires may begin with them as potential servants. Buber himself participated in the messianic suffering servant role as he found himself in a life of dialogue. Being at dialogue's disposal brings one to the threshold of redemption. As he wrote in 1928: 'We cannot prepare the messianic world, we can only prepare for it'.[17]

The question arises, 'redemption (*Erloesung*) from what?' When Buber wrote the foreword for his collected essays in 'Pointing the Way' in 1957 he revealed an important learning curve in his life that helps answer this question. Even though he disagreed with an essay that he wrote many years ago he included it in the collection in order to make a salient point. The essay, which is titled 'The Teaching of the Tao', presents the redemption of an individual as unification with the universal Tao, of the self with the 'all-self'. Buber perceives that this teaching cuts one off from self -knowledge, from the existence as a human,

> the existence into which he [sic] has been set, through
> conception and birth, for life and death in this unique
> personal form. Now he no longer stands in the dual
> basic attitude that is destined to him as a man: carrying
> being in his person, wishing to complete it, and ever
> again going forth to meet worldly and above-worldly
> being over against him, wishing to be a helper to it.
> Rather in the 'lower' periods he regards everything as
> preparation for the 'higher'. But in these 'higher hours'
> he no longer knows anything over against him: the
> great dialogue between I and Thou is silent; nothing
> else exists than his self, which he experiences as *the self*.
> That is certainly an exalted form of being untrue, but it
> is still being untrue. Being true to the being in which

---

16. Martin Buber, *Pointing the Way* (London: Routledge and Kegan Paul, 1957), 199.
17. Buber, *Pointing the Way*, 137.

and before which I am placed is the one thing that is needful.[18]

Consequently Buber seeks redemption from any irresponsibility, from being untrue to where he has been placed or from any escape from the concrete self. In reality this reflects an escape from dialogue into an aimless wandering, which Buber fearlessly designates as 'evil'. Evil must be recognised before dialogue or redemption can begin.

In his book *Images of Good and Evil*, Buber describes the good as a movement in the direction of home, while evil has no direction; it asserts itself as the goal, a self-made being.[19] Whereas humans need affirmation, evil asserts absolute self-affirmation. During World War 11, Buber wrote an essay in Hebrew entitled 'People and Leader'.[20]He traces the dangerous phenomenon of a leader without a teacher, through Mussolini, Hitler and Jacob Frank, an eighteenth century Jewish pseudo-messiah. Here are men who must be worshipped in order to believe in themselves. They know no goals, no morals, no power or truth apart from themselves. Buber quotes Goering as saying, 'I have no conscience, my conscience is called Adolf Hitler,' and Frank as saying, 'I have come in order to abolish all laws and all doctrines, and my desire is to bring life into the world . . . You shall rid yourself of all laws and doctrines and follow after me, step by step'.[21]

Despite the dreadful persecution of the Jews and the self-absolutising of these leaders, Buber refused to absolutise evil. He affirmed only one absolute, without whom one cannot believe in oneself. Since God remains the ultimate source of good and evil ('I make weal and create woe,' Isaiah 45:7), evil itself cannot be conquered but loved and redeemed through transformation.[22] Not only politicians but theologians, philosophers and sociologists should beware of 'eclipsing God' through separating him from life, by containing him in the sacred. Buber fears the separation of the sacred from the secular, mystery from reality, the God-encounter from the

---

18. Martin Buber, 'The Teaching of Tao', in Buber, *Pointing the Way*, 31–58. (I have retained the English translation of *Mensch* as 'man' and *man* as 'he'.)

19. Martin Buber, *Images of Good and Evil* (London: Routledge and Kegan Paul, 1952), 13–52.

20. Martin Buber, 'People and Leader', in *Pointing the Way*, 148–60.

21. Buber, *Pointing the Way*, 152–4.

22. Friedman, *Life of Dialogue*, 16.

human-encounter, the ideal from the actual, the end from the means and responsibility from the individual, as an escape from God. Nietzsche's cry, 'God is dead', Sartre's free invention of values and Heidegger's claim that the appearance of the divine depends on human thought, all indicate a turning away from the reality of God.[23]

The turning of God and humans towards one another constitutes a pivotal theme for dialogue, and therefore redemption, in Buber's thought. He strives to preserve the holistic dynamic of the Hebrew original (*teshuva* from *lashuv*, 'to turn'), which includes the turning of the whole person, whether in the message of the prophets, of John the Baptist or of Jesus. The bible uses the same Hebrew verb for God and people. God has turned away from his anger towards Israel, so the prophets call the people to turn back to God (Hosea 11:1-11). Similarly, John the Baptist and Jesus proclaim the presence of the Kingdom of God, the call to repentance (or turning) and to faith (or trust).[24]

As with Job, the turning arises out of a dark, purifying suffering, which perceives God's hand reaching down to him and in taking it realises that 'my redeemer lives' (Job 19:18). Although human action is enclosed in God's gracious action, it is still real and responsible.[25] Despite the human's infinitely subordinate position, this mutual turning of two partners toward one another initiates a precious dialogue.[26] On the human level and perhaps also on the divine, both partners turn to each other and thereby confirm each other mutually. In fact, 'the historical continuation of existence depends on the turning'. [27]

Again and again Buber returns to 'trust' as an essential ingredient of dialogue and its goal, redemption. In his essay 'Trust and Mistrust', Buber differentiates between putting one's faith in a leader and trusting him. The former relationship is founded on the leader alone, whereas the latter stands on a common standard or truth, which the

---

23.   Martin Buber, *Eclipse of God: Studies in the Relation between Religion and Philosophy* (New York: Harper & Brothers, 1952).

24.   Buber, *Two Types of Faith*, 24–7. With Friedman I have translated *teshuva* as 'turning', rather than 'reversal' (as used by RG Smith) or 'return' (*Umkehr*), *The Life of Dialogue*, xxi, xxii.

25.   Friedman, *Life of Dialogue*, 15–6.

26.   Buber, *Two Types*, 27.

27.   Martin Buber, 'Hope for this Hour', in *Pointing the Way*, 203, 225. See also Buber's *Werke*, 34: '*In . . . Augenblick der Umkehr ein Gespraech mit den Menschen wird*'.

trusted leader serves. Even the latter's errors point toward the truth. So Buber writes, 'To trust a man, that means to believe in the truth which one can serve, in the truth which does not exist by our grace, but by whose grace we exist . . .We need leaders whom we follow not for their sakes, but for the sake of the one they serve . . . They lead in that they teach'.[28]Clearly, the relationship of trust involves I-Thou dialogue, whereas 'faith in a leader' may remain at the I-It level. Many years later Buber characterised the faith of Israel as a persevering trust in YHWH and that of Christianity after Jesus' life as a creedal 'leap of faith', which says, 'this is true'.[29]

Buber translates YHWH's word to King Ahaz via Isaiah as, 'If you will not trust, you will not be confirmed (Isaiah 7:9, Hebrew, *Im lo ta'aminu ki lo ta'amenu*),[30] whereas the New Revised Standard Version renders the text 'If you do not stand firm in faith, you shall not stand at all.' Buber's translation presupposes a dynamic dialogue and relationship, whereas the NRSV tends to objectify a solitary stance.

When considering the 'redemptive' work of a psychotherapist in 'Healing through Meeting', Buber boldly rejects the clinical 'objectifying of a patient' who has been entrusted to, and trusts in, the psychotherapist. He advises that the therapist must acknowledge his/her guilt, must pass through the 'crisis of the paradox of his vocation', and must step outside of himself into a relationship where 'self is exposed to self.'[31]While still today psychotherapists meet lonely patients in private rooms, Buber's words strike home: 'A soul is never sick alone, but always a between-ness also, a situation between it and another existing being. The psychotherapist who has passed through the crisis may now dare to touch on this'.[32] Buber implies that the therapist should share the patient's sickness, for healing to take place. By establishing a dialogue of trust, the psychotherapist confronts *existential mistrust*, which itself is a sickness, denying the *existence* of the other; hence the choice of the adjective *existential*. Buber showed that in human relations, ideologies can lead to 'boundless simpli-fication', which have 'contributed decisively to the development of existential

28. Buber, *Mamre: Essays in Religion* (Melbourne: Melbourne University Press, 1946) 62, 63.
29. Buber, *Two Types*, 9.
30. Buber, 'The Demand of the Spirit and Historical Reality', in *Pointing the Way*, 189.
31. Buber, 'Healing through Meeting', in *Pointing the Way*, 93–7.
32. Buber, 'Healing through Meeting', 97.

mistrust', leading to the 'destruction of trust in human existence'.[33] And he concludes that 'existential mistrust of all against all prevents any meaningful negotiation over the *real* differences of interest'.[34]

In a world of specialists with their esoteric, alienating jargons, Martin Buber's holistic thought appears attractive. His 'panorama' comes from the bible. In an article titled 'Redemption', Buber highlights a theme, 'unique in literature', which is found in the psalms and prophets: Zion as the centre of the future, redeemed world.[35] Since Zion is the heart of the world, the renewal of the world and of Zion coincide. Once the foreign 'anointed one', Cyrus, had liberated Israel and the nations, God gave the task to the servant of YHWH and through him the peoples are bound together (Isaiah 45:1; 49:7). The servant is chosen, not self-appointed (Isaiah 42:1). Similarly the people of Israel are chosen, YHWH says to Zion, 'You are my people . . . I have put my words in your mouth' (Isaiah 51:16). She shall be the herald and pioneer of divine dialogue in a redeemed, peaceful world. God's dialogue with Zion should be heard as an overture to his dialogue with the whole world.

It is against this backdrop that we can understand Buber's corporate consciousness, his high level of responsibility to all people, his unity of thought and his indestructible passion for dialogue. When he was awarded the Peace Prize in Paulskirche, Frankfurt in 1953, Buber identified the two fronts of an imminent 'battle', *homo humanus* against *homo contrahumanus*, as being far more dangerous than the so-called cold war. He said,

> In Germany, and especially in German youth, despite their being rent asunder, I have found more awareness of it (the *battle*) than elsewhere. The memory of the twelve-year reign of *homo contrahumanus* has made the spirit stronger, and the task set by the spirit clearer, than they formerly were.
>
> Tokens such as the bestowal of the Hanseatic Goethe Prize and the Peace Prize of the German Book Trade on a surviving arch-Jew must be understood in

---

33.  Buber, 'Hope for this Hour', 224, 227.
34.  Buber, 'Prophecy, Apocalyptic and the Historical Hour', in *Pointing the Way*, 205.
35.  Buber, 'Redemption', in *Biblical Humanism*, 160–5.

this connection . . . The survivor who is the object of such honours is taken up into the high duty of solidarity that extends across the fronts . . . This duty is, in the present hour, the highest duty on earth. The Jew chosen as symbol must obey this call of duty even there, indeed, precisely there where the never-to-be-effaced memory of what has happened stands in opposition to it . . . The busy noise of the hour must no longer drown out the *vox humana,* the essence of the human which has become a voice. This voice must not only be listened to, it must be answered and led out of the lonely monologue into the awakening dialogue of the peoples. Peoples must engage in talk with one another through their truly human men if the great peace is to appear and the devastated life of the earth renew itself.

The great peace is something essentially different from the absence of war.[36]

Buber goes on to argue that fighting begins where speech has ceased and that no human conflict can really be resolved through killing. It is only in a crisis that a 'turning' and the healing powers of salvation are encountered. Our difficulty in praying (addressing God, regardless of belief) and our inability to talk with each other reveal the same lack of trust in Being. For Buber, dialogue—even with an enemy—affirms and confirms one's opponent as an existing other as both sides face a common enemy, Satan, whose Hebrew name means 'the hinderer'.[37]

During the 1930s Buber carried out a dialogue with Mahatma Gandhi which threw into relief the roles of religion and politics in the redemption of a people. In his essay, 'Gandhi, Politics and Us', Buber differentiates the two thus:

---

36.  Buber, 'Genuine Dialogue and the Possibilities of Peace', in *Pointing the Way,* 234.
37.  It is interesting to note that in this address Buber refers to himself in the first person, then in the third person singular and finally in the first person plural; thus following the popular pattern of the psalter.

Religion means a goal and a way, that is, a journey
*Whereas politics implies an end and a means to success.*
Religion preserves the unconditional which contradicts
*The political conditionality of the situation.*
Religion is sacred but not binding, ('God's love cannot
be measured by success'),
*Whereas politics is unenlightened but powerful.*
'Only in the great *polis* of God will religion
*And politics be blended into a life of world community*
wherein neither religion nor politics will any longer
exist.'[38]

Despite their differences, Buber claims that religion and politics need each other just as religion and society need each other, like spirit and body, address and response.[39] For the 'redemption' of public life he prefers religious means to political:

> The real evil in politics is the 'political means'. . . to win
> over other men through imposing views on them. But
> in public life (as elsewhere) it is possible and necessary
> to employ religious instead of political means; to win
> others through helping them to open out. He who
> attempts this may appear weak in the midst of the
> political tumult . . . There is no legitimately messianic,
> no legitimately messianically-intended, politics. But
> that does not imply that the political sphere may be
> excluded from the hallowing of all things. The political
> 'serpent' is not essentially evil, it is itself only misled; it,
> too, ultimately wants to be redeemed.[40]

By the end of the 1930s Buber had lost some of his optimism. Growing anti-Semitism pushed him into apologetics for his people. Gandhi not only suggested that the Jews in Germany use *satyagraha*, or soul-force, in response to the Nazis but that Zionism and Jewish settlements in Palestine were unjust to the Arabs who possessed the

---

38. Buber, 'Gandhi, Politics and Us', in *Pointing the Way*, 131.
39. Martin Buber, 'Three Theses of a Religious Socialism' (1928), in *Pointing the Way*, 112–4.
40. Buber, *Pointing the* Way, 137.

land. Buber rejects Gandhi's redemption by passivism, highlighting the massive difference between the Indian majority who opposed British rule, and the Jewish minority who were in danger of being exterminated. Furthermore, Buber regards the possession of land as necessary, as part of a mission from above. An idea cannot become holy, 'but a piece of land can become holy'.[41] Buber belonged to the *Ichud* (Union), which strove for peace between Arab and Jew. His hope came from their common faith and love for the land and from their common father Abraham, who had heard the word of blessing (Genesis 12:1-3) fulfilled in children (Isaac and Ishmael) and received the gift of land. The land became the necessary *reality* behind the symbol.[42] No matter what the form of the political structure it should never be absolutised as it has a mediate, dependent role. Redemption depends on the maintenance of wholeness and immediacy; a direct, divine dialogue, which renders to God what is his. Where there is Word and prayer, address and response, there is hope for the individual and the country.

Buber concisely outlines the possibilities and limits of redemption in a key statement on the relationship between Jewish Messianism and Redemption:

> I firmly believe that the Jewish community, in the course of its renaissance, will recognize Jesus; and not merely as a great figure in its religious history, but also in the organic context of a Messianic development

---

41. Buber, *Pointing the Way*, 142.
42. The common desire for the land of Israel has led to death, despair and walls of division. The land has become an It, coveted and divided, not a Thou, sanctified by being a means of access to each other, bringing blessing and dialogue. Surely consequent developments go beyond Buber's cautious concession: 'I do not want force. But if there is no other way of preventing the evil destroying the good, I trust I shall use force and give myself up into God's hand . . . (to) fight for justice . . . to fight lovingly'. See Buber, 'Three Theses of a Religious Socialism', in *Pointing the Way*, 146). The blood of both sides cries out from the ground. In this land, religion and politics have met tragically, with unclean lips and dirty hands. However, Buber says, 'We cannot leave the soil of tragedy, but in real meeting we can reach the soil of salvation after the tragedy has been completed'. See: Friedman, *The Life of Dialogue*, 335.

extending over millennia, whose final goal is the
Redemption of Israel and of the world. But I believe
equally firmly that we will never recognize Jesus as the
Messiah Come, for this would contradict the deepest
meaning of our Messianic passion . . . There are no
knots in the mighty cable of our Messianic belief,
which, fastened to a rock on Sinai, stretches to a still
invisible peg anchored in the foundations of the world.
In our view, redemption occurs forever, and none has
yet occurred. Standing, bound and shackled, in the
pillory of mankind, we demonstrate with the bloody
body of our people the unredeemedness of the world.
For us there is no cause of Jesus; only the cause of God
exists for us.[43]

In 'Hope for the Hour', he focuses on what is at the base, the
'anchor,' of the Messianic and expresses his longing for a 'civilisation
of dialogue':

The hope for this hour depends upon the renewal of
dialogical immediacy between men. But let us look
beyond the pressing need, the anxiety and care of this
hour. Let us see this need in connection with the great
human way. Then we shall recognize that immediacy
is injured not only between man and man, but also
between the being called man and the source of his
existence. At its core the conflict between mistrust and
trust of man conceals the conflict between the mistrust
and trust of eternity. If our mouths succeed in
genuinely saying 'thou', then, after long silence and
stammering, we shall have addressed our eternal
'Thou' anew. Reconciliation leads towards reconciliation.[44]

Buber's legacy is an on-going challenge to humanity. He insists that
human existence is ultimately dependent on its response to the
creative, divine address and that the tracing of this primary
relationship can be found in the face of the other in our human

---

43.   Friedman, *The Life of Dialogue*, 332.
44.   Buber, 'Hope for the Hour', 228–9.

relationships. He reminds us that powerlessness is the prerequisite for any dialogue and that real dialogue preserves a tension between distance and nearness, solitude and intimacy, concealing and revealing. As with a tree, here growth occurs 'in between', not within. It is the interface that carries life and growth. Buber challenges us to break through to a new authenticity. He did not write a *systematic* theology or philosophy, as that would reduce the direct I-Thou 'happening' (*Erlebnis*) to an I-It experience (*Erfahrung*). Even if justice were *organised* for all, the real problem would remain: are we able to say 'I' and to hear 'thou', to say 'Thou' and to hear 'I'.

# 7

# Redemption and Aesthetic Imagination: The Messianism of German Expressionism

## Lisa Marie Anderson

While most of the chapters in this volume are concerned primarily with the themes of messianism, apocalypse, and/or redemption in the work of a major thinker or thinkers, this essay takes up the Expressionist movement dominant in German literature throughout the 1910s and into the early 1920s as a relatively unified body of thought, and examines the central roles of messianism and redemption in the development—and decline—of that thought.[1] The Expressionist movement pervaded all facets of German intellectual and cultural life in the early twentieth century, from the visual arts (one thinks of artists like Max Beckmann, Ernst Ludwig Kirchner, Ludwig Meidner, or Emil Nolde), to music (Paul Hindemith, Arnold Schönberg, Anton Webern), to philosophy (the early works of Ernst Bloch are decidedly 'Expressionist'), to the literature which is in focus here.

The foregoing notwithstanding, 'Expressionism' is among the most controversial appellations in German cultural history, as much disagreement remains as to how the identifier may even be defined. A fundamental source of this difficulty is the evolution which the term 'Expressionism' underwent even within its heyday. As early as 1919, Walter Rheiner pointed out that the label had outgrown its original role of 'opposition to Impressionism', and no longer addressed 'a technical or formal problem, so much as a worldview . . . an

---

1. The scope of this essay does not permit a thorough analysis of the apocalyptic strain within German Expressionism, equally pivotal though it is in the ideology of the movement. I have examined the relationship of Expressionism's apocalypticism to its overarching messianic tone in *The Encoding of Desire: Reflections of Contemporary Messianism in German Expressionist Drama* (2004).

epistemological, metaphysical, ethical mentality'.[2] What, then, are the phenomena that unify this 'worldview' as essentially 'Expressionist'? What 'thread' connects this body of literature in terms of language, style, themes and motifs? This essay takes as that thread Expressionism's concern with the messianic, with the possibility or indeed imminence of redemption via a messiah-figure. To a significant degree, it is the fervent desire for this redemption which defines the contours of German Expressionism, yielding a highly elucidating phenomenon which may be called Expressionist Messianism.

The present analysis of Expressionist Messianism concentrates primarily on the plays and playwrights of the period, as well as the reception thereof. While an equally messianic spirit pervades the widely read poetry of Gottfried Benn, Georg Heym, Jakob van Hoddis, Ernst Stadler, Georg Trakl and Paul Zech, as well as Expressionist prose (despite its status as the movement's least common genre) like Alfred Döblin's *Berlin Alexanderplatz*, the Expressionist stage represented the optimal pulpit from which visionaries could diffuse their gospels of redemption. In 1919, Hugo Zehder called the theater 'the tribune, from which the poets will proclaim' their messianic purpose, namely 'a new confraternity of humanity'.[3] And Ernst Toller's short essay 'Zur Revolution der Bühne' ('On the Revolution of the Stage'), likewise written in a quasi-religious style, demonstrates the extent to which Expressionism's messianic mission to provide redemption operated in a specifically dramatic setting:

> Our dream is a great community between stage and audience, a community of attitudes towards life and the world, a community of ideas, a cooperation, pregnant with connections, between listeners and actors, a glowing unity of all involved.[4]

---

2.  Walter Rheiner, 'Expressionismus und Schauspiel', in *Die neue Schaubühne*, 1/1 (1919): 14–17. Unless otherwise noted, translations from the German are my own.

3.  Hugo Zehder, 'Zeit, Theater und Dichter', in *Die neue Schaubühne*, 1/1 (1919): 1–3.

4.  Ernst Toller, *Gesammelte Werke*, edited by John M Spalek and Wolfgang Frühwald (Munich: Carl Hanser Verlag, 1978), Volume 1, 113–14.

Accordingly, the plays themselves contain clear indicators of their centrality for Expressionist Messianism. The preponderance of these dramas falls under one of the subgenres *Verkündigungsdrama* (proclamation plays), *Wandlungsdrama* (conversion plays), *Märtyrerdrama* (martyr plays), or *Stationendrama* (station plays), all of which are, as the names suggest, consistently imbued with the language and motifs of redemption. While playwrights like Johannes R Becher, Ludwig Rubiner, Carl Sternheim and Fritz von Unruh played instrumental roles in shaping Expressionist drama and its understanding of redemption, the analysis undertaken here focuses upon the work and reception of four well-known and representative Expressionist dramatists: Ernst Barlach; Georg Kaiser; Ernst Toller; and Franz Werfel.

Before examining the plays and playwrights in any detail, however, it is crucial to establish a conceptual framework of what is meant by 'messianism' in this case. This is no easy task, even for the relatively limited purpose at hand, as evidenced by Gert Mattenklott's reminder that 'there is not *one* messianism, the invention, rise and fall of which we can report'.[5] He suggests that one think instead of a 'characteristic constellation', central to which are the respective relationships between three elements: aesthetic imagination; religious imagination; and politics.[6] Taking separately each of these three strands provides comprehensive insights into the Expressionists' messianic project—simply stated—to redeem their society.

Working backwards, it might seem most apparent to characterise this project as a *political* one. Indeed, the messianic spirit of the early twentieth century, like the messianic currents which have historically arisen in the Jewish and Christian traditions, was incited primarily by political developments. The Expressionists' overarching desire for redemption was the result of the anxiety effected by the corrupted state of their bourgeois society, numerous failed revolutions, and above all, the devastation and dehumanisation of World War I. This desperate scene was the impetus for the Expressionists' propagation of a messianic vision of human and societal renewal.

---

5.  Gert Mattenklott, 'Mythologie Messianismus Macht', in *Messianismus zwischen Mythos und Macht. Jüdisches Denken in der europäischen Geistesgeschichte*, edited by Eveline Goodman-Thau and Wolfdietrich Schmied-Kowarzik (Berlin: Akademie, 1994), 179–96.

6.  Mattenklott, 'Mythologie Messianismus Macht', 179.

Rather than aligning itself with any concrete political program, however, this vision was articulated primarily in terms of a rather vague social criticism and, eventually, overwhelming historical pessimism. So politically quiescent, in fact, did the Expressionist movement remain, that those within it who sought true political effectiveness broke away from the literary identification altogether, and began referring to themselves collectively as the Activists. Among the remaining Expressionist literati, only Toller, a devout socialist, produced a body of work consistently political in nature. His political mission remained a thoroughly messianic one, as demonstrated by the ecstasy of the hero in his quintessential proclamation play *Masse Mensch (Masses and Man)* (1920): 'Our work, our Cause! O holy words!'[7] Indeed, Carsten Schapkow has aptly characterised Toller's 'attempted combination of savior-symbolism with Socialist ideas' as being 'clothed in a prophecy in which Toller understands himself to be the savior'.[8] But Toller found little support among his contemporaries, who, according to Wolfgang Paulsen, one of the foremost scholars of German Expressionism, utterly lacked 'genuine political motivation'.[9]

Turning, then, to the second factor proposed by Mattenklott, one cannot fail to be struck by the prevalence with which Expressionism borrowed from traditionally *religious* forms of messianism its expectant desire for the redemption of mankind via a messiah-figure, as well as its quest for the (re)establishment of a kind of paradise on earth. Accordingly, the frequency with which Expressionist Messianism is articulated in rhetoric and imagery coopted from Jewish and Christian scripture is too great to be anything other than blatantly intentional, with the majority of these references relating directly to the messiah. To begin with biblical rhetoric, it is astounding how commonly the Expressionists appropriated, for example, Jesus' proclamation that he and his kingdom are 'not of this world'.[10] The Expressionist writer

---

7.  Ernst Toller, *Seven Plays*, edited by Ernst Toller, Mary Baker Eddy and Hermann Kesten, translated by Ashley Dukes, Edward Crankshaw, Hermon Ould and Vera Mendel (New York: Liveright Publishing, 1936), 137.

8.  Carsten Schapkow, 'Judentum als zentrales Deutungsmuster im Leben und Werk Ernst Tollers', in *Exil*, 16/2 (1996): 25–39.

9.  Wolfgang Paulsen, 'Introduction', in *Expressionism Reconsidered. Relationships and Affinities*, edited by Gertrud Bauer Pickar and Karl Eugene Webb (Munich: Fink, 1979), ii.

10. John 8:23.

and theatre director Kurt Heynicke announced in 1918: 'Our kingdom is not of this world. But it shall rule on this earth . . . '[11] And Paul Nikolaus' essay 'Das Theater als Erlösung' ('The Theatre as Redemption') insisted: 'Now our kingdom is not of this world; our brains do not acknowledge the borders of the horizon, our hearts no thermometer'.[12]

Many authors chose to embody this same otherworldliness in their protagonists, who then served as vehicles for their authors' appropriation of a messianic persona. By foregrounding in their work exemplary characters speaking in proclamatory rhetoric, Expressionist writers proselytised for their own visions of redemption. One of the most telling examples is found in Werfel's early dramatic endeavor *Die Versuchung. Ein Gespräch des Dichters mit dem Erzengel und Luzifer* (*The Temptation. The Poet's Discussion with the Archangel and Lucifer*) (1913). Here the poet-hero is heralded as 'the medium which connects [God] with the world'.[13] As a result, the poet may claim that 'the laws of man, even his moral laws, are not mine, since I stand in relation to wholly other, higher powers'.[14] An angel tells him:

> Now you know fully that your kingdom . . . is not of this world . . . And to be the messenger, the intercessor, the despised in this world, this is your fate. No laws, no morals apply to you, for you are one of us eternal spirits.[15]

The specific choice of the poet as otherworldly hero is significant, as it renders the author's self-representation via his messianic mouthpiece completely transparent.

Even more common than biblical rhetoric in Expressionist literature, however, is biblical imagery. In 1920, Rudolf Friedmann-Brook wrote of the visual arts of the period:

11. Kurt Heynicke, 'Die Herrschaft des Geistes', in *Der Freihafen*, 1/3 (1918): 33.
12. Paul Nikolaus, 'Das Theater als Erlösung', in *Der Freihafen*, 2/9 (1919/20): 129–32.
13. Franz Werfel, *Gesammelte Werke. Die Dramen*, edited by Adolf Klarmann (Frankfurt: S. Fischer, 1959), 28.
14. Werfel, *Gesammelte Werke'*, 37.
15. Werfel, *Gesammelte Werke'*, 39.

> The art of our time is fraught with religious desire almost to the point of overflowing; packed into the exhibitions are images, effectively schematic by nature of their repetitive content, of always the same crucifixion, the mother of God, and self-portraits with a cross on one's forehead . . .[16]

The same may be said of Expressionist literature, which teems with biblical iconography. When the protagonist of Kaiser's *Von morgens bis mitternachts* (*From Morning To Midnight*) (1912) considers a Cranach painting of the Garden of Eden, he identifies strongly with its representation of Adam. The remainder of this station play recounts his quest for the 'Promised Land'. The biblical diluvian narrative is the basis for Barlach's Expressionist retelling *Die Sündflut* (*The Flood*) (1924). In Werfel's *Bocksgesang* (*Goat-Song*) (1921), a character is sacrificed as a burnt offering, and his role as such is proclaimed by a character described as a 'prophet'. Iconography from the Gospels' Nativity accounts, complete with infant characters who provide redemption for the cast of characters, dominates plays like Barlach's *Der Findling* (*The Foundling*) (1922) and Werfel's *Die Mittagsgöttin* (*The Midday Goddess*) (1918). The imagery of the Eucharist shapes the action of *The Foundling*, as well as of Kaiser's famous conversion play *Die Bürger von Calais* (*The Burghers of Calais*) (1914). The title character is betrayed by a Judas-figure in Toller's *Hinkemann* (1923). A stunning number of Expressionist protagonists are martyred in a manner consciously and directly related to Jesus' crucifixion, including the heroes of Kaiser's *From Morning To Midnight* and *The Burghers of Calais*, Werfel's *Juarez und Maximilian* (*Juarez and Maximilian*) (1924), and Toller's *Die Wandlung* (*Transfiguration*) (1918). And Barlach's *Der arme Vetter* (*The Poor Cousin*) (1918) takes place entirely on Easter Sunday, with a persistent preoccupation with resurrection. Finally, imagery of the Apocalypse lends a highly messianic tone to Werfel's *Paulus unter den Juden* (*Paul Among the Jews*) (1926) and Toller's *Die Maschinenstürmer* (*The Machine Wreckers*) (1922).

Even the most cursory examination of the Expressionists' contemporary reception demonstrates a remarkably similar employment of biblical motifs, as many commentators praised the new

---

16.   Rudolf Friedmann-Brook, 'Kunst und Religion', in *Freie deutsche Bühne*, 2/5 (1920): 115–17.

generation of writers and their 'literary works of redemption'[17] in messianic language: 'Recent literature is action, Golgotha its image. Painfully it tastes the bitterness of each Station of the Cross for the sake of fruition'.[18] The dramatists whose work is in focus here were, it seems, especially successful in portraying themselves as veritable saviors. A contemporary of Werfel's called him a 'poet, preacher, prophet' who 'takes the cross upon himself . . .', to whom 'God has revealed his spirit'.[19] Likewise, Toller was dubbed 'a gentle Apostle, filled with his mission'.[20] And Barlach was once hailed 'a justified prophet and miracle worker in the ecclesia'.[21] Taken together, Expressionist attempts to appropriate a messianic persona via cooption of biblical rhetoric and imagery, and contemporary reception of that persona as such, demonstrate the centrality of the messiah-complex within the Expressionist identity. This model of messianic desire assigns responsibility for the redemption of society to the writer, and allows for the assumption of a soteriological mission that elevates the Expressionists above the rest of humanity.

However, despite the frequency with which its desire for redemption is encoded in highly religious and even directly biblical language and metaphor, Expressionist Messianism remains an essentially secular phenomenon. Michael Beintker has described the process of secularisation whereby the 'messianic idea leaves the Life-World of faith and is transformed into a historical-philosophically deducible target'.[22] This is precisely the case for the Expressionist generation, comprised of individuals dwelling in the relative secularism of the early twentieth century, and enamored especially of the decidedly nonreligious philosophy of Friedrich Nietzsche. The secularism of Expressionist Messianism is witnessed, for example, in

---

17.  Willi Handl, 'Dichtungen der Erlösung', in *Freie deutsche Bühne*, 23 (1920): 538–43.
18.  Anonymous, 'Die kommende Dichtung', in *Romantik*, 3/1 (1920): 8–10.
19.  Ernst Jockers, 'Franz Werfel als religiöser Dichter', in *The Germanic Review*, 2 (1927): 40–63.
20.  Quoted in Robert Bruce Elsasser, *Ernst Toller and German Society* (Ann Arbor: University of Michigan, 1973), 218.
21.  Hans Ehrenberg, 'Barlach: Bildner und Dichter', in *Eckart*, 5/6 (1929): 241–50.
22.  Michael Beintker, 'Der Zerfall des säkularisierten Messianismus als Herausforderung für jüdisches und christliches Denken—Eine Problemanzeige', in *Messianismus Mythos Macht*, 167.

its quest for the 'promise of Judeo-Christian religion . . . in this world and without God, by the deeds of man alone'.[23] Thus, the texts of literary Expressionism were mapped onto the theological and Christological discourses of messianism in the Jewish and Christian traditions not out of religious conviction, but primarily because the biblical idiom remained a more effective medium for communication with an audience (whose redemption was believed to be at stake, after all) than the Nietzschean one. In this respect, the Jewish writer Toller spoke for his contemporaries when he declared his awareness that 'all Europeans have absorbed elements of Christianity in school and in literature, in their surroundings and their landscape'.[24]

What remains, then, is the recognition that the Expressionists' essentially literary articulation of messianic desire was rooted far more in *aesthetic* principles than in any truly religious or political brand of messianism. Indeed, Paulsen has called the movement a 'transitional artistic phase' 'dominated primarily by aesthetic and artistic concerns',[25] and perhaps no facet of Expressionism bears out this claim better than its preoccupation with redemption via a messiah-figure. The ardent cry for redemption issuing forth from the Expressionist stage failed to define the contours of the redemption it sought, and thus remained a purely aesthetic gesture. So enrapt in their messianic project were the Expressionists, that the literary and theatrical articulation of their desires seemed to them a sufficient catalyst for the onset of redemption. This was a generation of ecstatic youth who forgot that 'very little in literature has ever affected the course of events' or ushered in, in the absence of a concrete social framework, 'a new way of thinking'.[26]

The strongest indicator that Expressionist Messianism arose from a predominantly aesthetic longing, and had its zenith in a conviction of a purely aesthetic nature, is the loss of faith endemic to the movement in its later phases. One of the most significant aspects of this particular messianic desire is the very ambivalence towards it, which became pervasive. Most Expressionists eventually relented from their impassioned message of societal redemption, choosing instead to critique the

23.   Heinz Abosch, 'Hoffnung und Wahrheit. Ernst Blochs Philosophie in der Praxis', in *Neue Zürcher Zeitung* 100 (1986): 53.
24.   Toller, *Gesammelte Werke*, Volume 1, 116
25.   Paulsen, 'Introduction', ii.
26.   Wolfgang Paulsen, 'The Tradition of Revolt', in *Expressionism Reconsidered*, 4.

very messianic desire, which had come to dominate the contemporary intellectual scene. The disaffected rejection of the messianic promise is acerbically articulated, for example, in remarkably similar scenes penned by Barlach and Werfel. A character in Barlach's *The Foundling* castigates the messianic mentality in general, but is certainly referring to the mode of Barlach's age:

> if the practice of birthing saviors were to become fashionable, we would soon have a world full of such creatures. Where does it end?—here a savior, there a savior, each one making himself more important than the others.[27]

And in Werfel's *Spiegelmensch* (*The Man in the Mirror*) (1920), a high priest proclaims: 'I tell you, your Redeemer is near!'[28] and three characters respond with utter disbelief and criticism. 'I'm getting old waiting for this savior', one complains, while another challenges: 'Do you know the address, name or residence of the messiah?'[29] The third respondent offers a rather callous explanation for the lag in redemption: 'The savior is delayed at the tavern'.[30] Such satirical comments not only trivialise and even vulgarise the originally sacred motif of the messiah's imminence, they further betray a growing awareness of the failure of messianic ideology. Such an awareness is also articulated by the messianic protagonist at the end of *The Man in the Mirror*, who laments: 'Belief in election, action and mission/. . . Asthmatically it shrinks away . . . The deed does not come! Even adventures come rarely, / And at best, one has amused oneself'.[31]

Toller's later work likewise articulates this resignation of the redemptory mission. Just three years after its publication, Toller recanted the entire premise of his quintessential conversion play *Transfiguration*: 'I don't believe anymore in a transfiguration to "new" humanity'.[32] A decade after that, Toller reflected specifically upon the inefficacy of the movement's messianic desire in his post-Expressionist

---

27. Ernst Barlach, *Das dichterische Werk*, edited by Klaus Lazarowicz (Munich: R Piper, 1956), Volume 1, 308.
28. Werfel, *Gesammelte Werke*, 193.
29. Werfel, *Gesammelte Werke*, 193.
30. Werfel, *Gesammelte Werke*, 193.
31. Werfel, *Gesammelte Werke*, 184.
32. Toller, *Gesammelte Werke*, Volume 5, 66.

autobiography (1933), chastising 'the youth of a whole generation' (his own) which 'worshiped false gods, and believed in false prophets', 'look[ing] for their salvation not to reason, work and responsibility, but to a spurious savior'.[33] Toller's mature writings, like those of so many other 'reformed' Expressionists (most notably Werfel), are characterised by a mood of relative sobriety which enables (among other things) a condemnation of the Expressionist Messianism in which he had once partaken:

> Everywhere the same lunatic belief that a man, a leader, a Caesar, a Messiah, will suddenly appear and work a miracle; will suddenly arise and take upon his shoulders all responsibility for the future; will master life, banish fear, abolish misery, create a new people, a new kingdom of splendor; will suddenly appear endowed with supernatural powers to transform the old Adam into a new man![34]

Of course, the Expressionists' withdrawal from and critique of their own weighty proclamations about their mission to redeem society coexisted with the venom of numerous critics external to the movement. No less influential a thinker than Gershom Scholem, himself an advocate of a far less feverish brand of messianism (rooted in religious and political traditions), had attempted to serve as a voice of reason as early as 1917, warning that 'one does not build houses out of desire, and a movement cannot base itself upon speaking again and yet again of desire . . . '[35] And only two years later, the author and theater critic Max Herrmann-Neiße had declared: 'The desire of our contemporaries is too great for fulfillment'.[36] Most illustrative, however, is the exasperation articulated by Camill Hoffmann in 1920:

> Enough already with the dramas in which people throw themselves down humbly, indict and mangle

---

33. Ernst Toller, *I Was a German*, edited and translated by Edward Crankshaw (New York: William Morrow, 1934), Introduction.
34. Toller, *I Was a German* 5.
35. Gerhard Scholem, 'Jüdische Jugendbewegung', in *Der Jude*, 1 (1916/17): 822–5.
36. Max Herrmann-Neiße, 'Entzweiung und Magie', in *Die neue Schaubühne*, 1/2 (1919): 33–6.

themselves, take the guilt of all upon themselves, each a Lord Jesus Christ . . . Enough already with this entire literature . . . all of this Judeo-Christian didacticism, which is evaporating into ever more shadowy abstractions.[37]

It was precisely its sheer aesthetic nature which led to the eventual abandonment of Expressionist Messianism. Most political and certainly most religious manifestations of messianic desire are founded upon tenets not easily shaken, upon deep-seated beliefs. This is why one speaks of a messianic *tradition* within Judaism and within Christianity, or of the messianic *tradition* within certain enduring forms of political ideology such as Marxism. Expressionist Messianism, in contrast, could not align itself with any broader redemptory project, nor was it ever able to establish itself as literary tradition in its own right, precisely because the principles in which it was rooted were rather vacuous beyond any self-servingly aesthetic merit. Once true political aims had been proved lacking, all that remained was to encode a fervent desire for redemption in ecstatic biblical rhetoric and recognizable biblical imagery. But this process of encoding was, at heart, an aesthetic one, promptly resigned when it failed to achieve its objective, such that the end of Expressionism in a decidedly unredeemed world signaled the end of its messianic mission, and thus of the movement itself.

---

37.   Camill Hoffmann, 'Max Brods sentimentale Groteske', in *Die neue Schaubühne*, 2/10 (1920): 275–6.

# 8

# Messiah as Dandy: Aesthetic Fundamentalism in the Writings of Stefan George and his Circle

## Martin Travers

The discourse of transcendence in modern German thought crosses the boundaries between the theological and the secular. If we return it to its historical context (and specifically to the period between 1890 and 1933), we can see it best as informing a certain practice or set of practices, whose goal lay very much in the *Diesseits* (this world) rather than the *Jenseits* (the beyond). Many artists, writers and theorists of this period sought to transcend the processes of modernity in a re-fashioning of selfhood through style. Theirs was an aesthetic funda-mentalism, which expressed itself as pose, gesture, in short as the articulation of the body as lived ornament. They adopted in many cases the forms and rhetoric of traditional religion, but they did so in a way that allowed them to embrace the comportment of a religious calling without embracing its theological content.

The first major study of this discourse of secularised transcendence was Ernst Bloch's *Erbschaft dieser Zeit* (*Heritage of Our Times*), written between 1924 and 1935 (and later expanded). The book is, amongst other things, an analysis of the populist status of the ideology and culture of National Socialism, and the way that its ideology usurped and integrated a variety of pseudo-religious discourses into its own. It mobilises, in however a travestied fashion, key themes and symbols from paganism, the medieval period (its Chiliastic redemptionism), German Romanticism (the forests, 'the Volk', the 'enchantment of the soil'), as well as more contemporary phenomena (anthroposophy, the occult, and even Catholic liturgy) which it incorporated into its own political iconography of religious revivalism. These were all, for Bloch, incongruous examples of the persistence of atavistic wish-fulfilment in an advanced industrial society, a phenomenon that Bloch summed up in his famous notion of '*Ungleichzeitigkeit*' or 'Non-Contemporeity'.[1]

The strength of Bloch's approach was that he took seriously the surface of Nazified culture, its style. We need, however, to take Bloch's concern with the surface one step further. He himself pointed the way in the chapter 'Amusement Co, Horror, Third Reich', where, discussing the appeal of the Nazi message, Bloch notes: it is 'not the theory of the National Socialists but rather their energy which is serious, the fanatical-religious strain which does not merely stem from despair and stupidity'.[2] Bloch, it is true, did not go beyond this, believing that this secularised religiosity would soon fall apart in the light of 'concrete-materialist reason'.[3] But the broad conceptual span of his work and its impressive detail permitted him to reconstruct the synthetic nature of National Socialist ideology in a remarkable way, to link authors, texts and cultural formations that would not, because of the lack of any apparent political affinity, otherwise be brought into alignment, but were, nevertheless, part of the movement of the *irratio* that helped bring the Nazis to power.

For Bloch, one of those authors who most represented this eclectic movement of the *irratio* was the poet-seer Stefan George (1868–1933). Bloch saw in George an emissary from one of those 'diverse crypto-religions of which an alienated and lacking age was full'. He further castigated George (and his followers) for their 'remoteness' ('*Entlegenheit*') from the exigencies of the real world, for taking flight into a costume world of Greco-Roman fantasy.[4] But this was not really what Stefan George and his followers did. Or, to be more exact, they did do this, but not so they could escape from reality, but in order to enter it more deeply, and on their own terms.[5] Theirs was a flight not

---

1.  Ernst Bloch, *Erbschaft dieser Zeit* (Frankfurt am Main: Suhrkamp, 1985), 69.
2.  Bloch, *Erbschaft dieser Zeit*, 67. And Michael Landmann (one of George's later disciples) put it in exactly the same terms: 'what attracts me about the movement is not its content but its energy (*Impuls*). Quoted from Stefan Breuer, *Ästhetischer Fundementalismus: Stefan George und de Deutsche Antimodernismus* (Wissentschaftliche Buchgesellschaft: Darmstadt, 1995), 236.
3.  Bloch, *Erbschaft dieser Zeit*, 149.
4.  Bloch, *Erbschaft dieser Zeit*, 101 and 201.
5.  Indeed, they would have rejected all attempts to typify them as exponents of irrational excess. George took great pains to distance

of 'distance' but of symbolic proximity. Indeed, their writings, both poetic and theoretical, and the terms in which they organised themselves as a cultural formation, force us to rethink notions such as the political and the apolitical, the secular and the religious, the profane and the pious, the worldly and the transcendent.

But certainly 'distance' is a trope that appears throughout their writing, whenever they seek to define their policy towards the public and the social sphere, in general. In his earliest writings, George had assertively distanced himself from those trends within contemporary German literature, such as Naturalism, that had engaged with social issues. As he noted in the very first edition of his journal, *Blätter für die Kunst (Journal for the Arts)* (1892–1904), the publishing organ for what would later be called the *'George-Kreis'* ('George Circle'), and founded by George, together with Carl August Klein, in 1892. The journal saw itself as servicing the needs of a 'select community of artists and art lovers,' who were construed, in a way typical of the aristocratic demeanour adopted by George, not as a public (indeed, its first editions, as with George's poetry, had a purely private circulation), but as an intimate circle of *'Gleichgesinnten'*, those 'few companions who are intimately known to us'.[6] They were to become the guiding spirits of a new poetic renascence in Germany, whose task it would be to return verse to its classical function in liturgy and ritual.[7] Even the

---

himself from groups such as the *'Kosmiker'*. As he exhorted in 1904: 'Do not mistake the idol for the god, the ghost for the spirit, the seer for the sorcerer'. Quoted in Breuer, *Ästhetischer Fundementalismus*, 40. Indeed, Bloch's synthesizing perspective is perhaps too inclusive at times.

6. Thus Klein to Hugo von Hofmannstahl in 1892, as quoted in Michael Winkler, *George-Kreis* (Stuttgart: Metzler, 1972), 11.

7. The journal ceased publication in 1919. For an account of its history, written from within, see Friedrich Wolters, *Stefan George und die 'Blätter für die Kunst'* (Berlin: Bondi, 1930). The élitism of George and his acolytes was also reflected in the manner with which they published their work: in small, hand crafted editions, with ornate iconography and script. Even the idiosyncratic choice of lower-case formatting throughout his poems (breaking with conventional German syntax) represented a conscious stance against the ethos of mass production, and further served to highlight the aristocratic uniqueness of George's writing. For a detailed account of George's publishing strategy, see Dieter Mettler, *Stefan Georges Publikationspolitik: Buchkonzeption und verlegerisches Engagement* (Munich: Saur, 1979).

typography of the journal—with its parchment-like paper, its carefully worked binding, ornamentation, vignettes and other forms of decoration—seemed to embody the spirit of anti-commercialism. To retain its aesthetic integrity, the journal self-consciously avoided topical themes and even book reviews.[8] As George notes in the first edition:

> the name of this publication already indicates what it is trying to achieve: it seeks to serve art and, in particular, poetry, avoiding everything that has to do with society or the state. It wishes to see the development of a spiritual art on the basis of the new sensibility: in short, it seeks to encourage an art for art's sake.[9]

We are here in familiar *fin de siècle* territory—or so it would seem: the poem as the verbal icon, internally wrought without external reference, its ontology one of mood and suggestion, of esoteric arabesque, of music even (everything aspires to be it), a *via ductus* between the aesthetic will of the poet and the refined sensibility of the reader. But George adds something new to this model: a constructivist rhetoric that moves beyond the ethereal into something much more pragmatic. So much is clear from his manifesto, *Über Dichtung* (*Concerning Poetry*). Here we learn that art has nothing to do with the 'petty rationalism and the discords of life' or with a desire to 'have an effect' or to 'say something,' but is a product of aesthetic organisation *within the text*. George explains: 'The relationship of the individual parts to one another, the logical progression of the one out of the other are the defining features of great poetry.' In short, the poem is a means of structuring subjectivity, and George's poetic is characterised by a concern that the formal elements of the poem do not remain 'unrestrained,' but should be integrated into a closed totality. For 'the strictest measure is at the same time the greatest freedom.'[10]

If we read this paradigmatically, and extend it into the political realm, it is clear where it leads. But even if we stay within the personal, the implications are apparent: art is the means to a refashioning of self.

---

8.　　See Winkler, *Georg-Kreis*, 10.
9.　　*Der George-Kreis: Eine Auswahl aus seinen Schriften*, edited by Georg Peter Landmann (Stuttgart: Klett-Cotta, 1980), 15.
10.　　Stefan George, *Werke*, 2 Volumes (Stuttgart: Klett-Cotta, 1984), Volume 1, 530.

This George made clear elsewhere, in the fifth edition of the *Blätter für die Kunst*, where he wrote in an essay that the goal of his poetry was to instil '*Haltung*' ('attitude', 'bearing'). As he further explained: 'What is essential is the artistic '*Umformung*' ('remodelling', 'remaking') of a life—what sort of life that will be is, for the present, entirely irrelevant'.[11] And the transformation is to be a total one; that is the all-important proviso. Poetry is not something you practise as an extension of your life; it is your life, or, rather, the means to its transcendence. George's essay is an espousal of a personal credo that reproduces at the level of a cultural programme the redemptionist ethos of a religious faith. It is Dandyism with a messianic purpose.

This notion of the remaking of self runs, as does the liturgy that will make that process possible, throughout George's poetry, from *Hymnen* (*Hymns*) (1890) and the *Pilgerfahrten* cycle (*Pilgrimage*) (1891), through to *Algabal* (*Elagabalus*) (1892), and *Das Jahr der Seele* (*The Year of the Soul*) (1897). The very titles of many of the poems included in these volumes are revealing: 'Prayer', 'Consecration', 'Procession', 'Blessing' and 'Response'.[12] In a later poem, *'Templer'*, ('Knights Templars'), from the volume *Der siebente Ring* (*The Seventh Circle*) (1907), the poet extols the redeeming power of a new elite of youth who represent 'the body which is spiritualised, and the spirit which is embodied'.[13] The two varieties of selfhood are bonded together through ritual and participation in cultic ceremony. Without this participation, there is no redemption, even when such participation leads to the death of the individual involved. This is the message of the poem *'Das Geheimopfer'* ('The Cultic Offering') from *Die Bücher der Hirten- und Preisgedichte* (*Poems of Pastoral Lore and Celebrations*) (1895). *'Das Geheimopfer'* depicts the process of an Attic-pagan ceremony that culminates in a blood sacrifice. The poem begins by describing how the two anonymous officiants start their journey 'reconciled and redeemed', as they travel through field and meadow to the place of the ceremony. The narrating voice explains in the final stanza how, when the time comes, the two prepare themselves to assume the ultimate role:

---

11.   Quoted in Winkler, *George-Kreis*, 19.
12.   See Hansjürgen Linke, *Das Kultische in der Dichtung Stefan Georges und seiner Schule* (Munich: Helmut Küpper, 1960), 21–22.
13.   George, *Werke*, Volume 1, 256.

When we are adorned with
The choicest decoration of youth
Then bound fast
To the pillars of bronze
By the seer who raises
The veil before God.
Then we tremble and look
In shuddering power
In consuming pain
In glowing intoxication
And die in eternal longing.[14]

'*Das Geheimopfer*' turns upon a paradox quite central to George's *Weltanschauung*: the notion that, through ritual, personal sacrifice becomes an empowerment of self. Even those who do not choose this form of redemption are, nevertheless, capable of transfiguration through it. The *Algabal* cycle, published in 1892, evinces many of the major qualities of George's early poetic idiom: an introspective *Weltschmerz* (world-weariness), combined with a sensuous feel for the aesthetic surface—of experience, of body, gesture and ornament —which is allied to a notion of power whose exertion is purely the affirmation of a superior will. The central figure is the young Roman emperor known as Heliogabalus (204–222), because he worshipped the sun god, Baal. His corruption, cruelty and penchant for ritualistic self-deification were infamous, even when compared with the behaviour of the other Roman emperors of the period.[15]

In George's volume, Heliogabalus traverses the entire range of the poet's poetic *personae*: he is, '*Im Unterreich,*' the quintessential aesthete, the creator of a *paradis artificial,* an elaborate subterranean palace in which nature has been banished by stone and rare metal, artefacts that represent a sublime confirmation of that artistic will to form that was enshrined in the Symbolist credo.[16] But at other times, he exercises his power with a totally amoral regard for life that has its source in his conviction in the aestheticised moment. This is the case in '*Wenn um der zinnen kupferglühe hauben*' ('When copper glows around those pinnacles

---

14.  George, *Werke*, Volume 1, 701.

15.  Michael M Metzger and Erika A Metzger, *Stefan George* (New York: Twayne, 1972), 60.

16.  George, *Werke,* Volume 1, 45–7.

of pewter'). The poem tells of how Heliogabalus' enjoyment of a moment of sensual calm is destroyed by a Lydian slave who, whilst kneeling to the Emperor, frightens the imperial doves. In the poem (not cited here) there is no preparation for what follows; no justification of the act, not even a grammatical preparation.

> The doves flutter anxiously towards the roof
> "I gladly die because my master was startled"
> A broad blade already in his breast,
> A red pool staining the green floor.[17]

One state leads transitively to another state. The reader doesn't have to question why. The sentiments possess an unquestionable logic: the birds are disturbed; the slave is dead. What could be simpler? Ethical interrogations of the actions are redundant: even as he is being murdered, the slave is bereft of identity. We are in a world where ritual has replaced morality. This becomes even clearer in the final lines of the poem, where the slave 'returns,' not in body but as a name inscribed on the royal drinking urn, his presence restored through a final aesthetic gesture, a regal compensation for a lowly and short life.

In the two poems discussed so far, the self is transfigured through absorption into ritual, becoming a grim abstraction through its place in a ceremony of death. But at other times, the self that is styled to transcendence does not lose its human contours but has them rewritten into something larger, as the basis for the formation of personality that, on an iconic level, will transcend the purely personal. This was the case with the fourteen-year youth Maximilian Kronberger, whom George had met in Munich in 1902. A chance meeting on a street deepened into a relationship and a closer social intimacy. George, impressed by the youth's ethereal presence, soon welcomed Kronberger into his Circle, seeing in him the living embodiment of the 'spirit of the sacred youth of our people'.[18]

Kronberger (now renamed simply as 'Maximin') soon became a willing participant in the pagan pageants that George and his followers held in private homes throughout this period, where George was able

---

17. George, *Werke*, Volume 1, 48.
18. Landmann, quoted in Breuer, *Ästhetischer Fundementalismus*, 505. The reality behind the mythic reconstruction of Kronberger is appraised by Werner Kraft in his *Stefan George* (Munich: Edition Text + Kritk, 1980), 175–89.

to dramatise the ritualistic values that had earlier appeared only in his poetry. Here, in brief moments of theatrical excess, the crass impingements of the modern period could be undone. Those who took part in such pageants, dressed in costumes of Greco-Roman antiquity, sought to take themselves beyond the travails of modernity, dissolving their individual identities in figures such as Nero, Caesar, and Homer, who all embodied for George and his associates archetypal values that could not be found in the modern period. [19] George formed the spatial and spiritual centre of these ceremonies, but it was Maximin who most clearly embodied the Georgian ideal: male beauty. Writing somewhat later, George attempted to reconstruct the aura of transfigured physicality that surrounded the youth:

> His voice was particularly soothing, but even when he did not speak, his mere presence in the room was enough to awaken in all present a feeling of the warmth and resonance of youth. We willingly surrendered ourselves to the magical force of his personality, which one had merely to touch or breathe in order to be transplanted from the everyday world into a paradise of untainted majesty.[20]

What Maximin brought George was not a message but a moral exemplum written as a body. Through his beauty and the unity of his self, he transcended, in George's eyes, those existential antinomies that the poet had explored in his early poetry: the tensions between the spirit and the flesh, contemplation and action, and art and the world. 'Who is your god?' the poet asks himself in the concluding *'Eingang'* section of the *Der Stern des Bundes* (*The Star of the Circle*), published in 1914. The answer is framed in terms of the 'archetypal image,' Maximin, 'beautiful and noble,' who has it within him to mediate between the poles of spirit and matter, the ideal and the real, around which the modern era is aimlessly turning. The poem concludes with faith that Maximin has injected 'fresh sap' into the 'decayed word of the world':

19. See Robert E Norton, *Secret Germany: Stefan George and His Circle* (Ithaca: Cornell University Press, 2002), 329–30.
20. George, *Werke*, Volume 2, 524–25.

God is the highest consecration of mystery
In glowing circles he reveals his procession:
The son born from the stars he delivers
Out of spirit born the new golden mean.[21]

'Maximin lived but a short time amongst us,' George noted with laconic pathos in his *'Vorrede zu Maximin'* ('Preface to Maximin'), describing the early death of Maximilian Kronberger in 1904 from meningitis. In his short life, the loved one had offered the poet a living symbol of the 'Hellenic miracle' that George had spent his entire life seeking: a physical model of aesthetic perfection that transcended time and history. But in his death, Maximilian gave George something of even greater significance: the basis for a myth with which to challenge the disfigured and lifeless anti-culture of modernity. Friedrich Wolters, a key member of the Circle, summed up the sacerdotal import of Maximin's visitation in the following words: 'That he, after twenty centuries, as the first corporeal son of the earth a ring had consummated with the corporeality of the master, in which the love of the divine, in which the loving God had perfected himself, is the miracle that bears his name and sanctifies once more every level of earthly being'.[22]

Maximin dies, in fact, so that George may be re-born, the poet's faith in his vision of an aristocracy of the body and spirit revitalised. As Edith Landmann (the wife of Julius) expressed it: 'Life may have been destroyed in the former (Maximin), but it experiences its resurrection in the higher life of the other (George)'.[23] Indeed, throughout his short life, the boy-god is adorned with the typical sign of oblation, the *'Kranz,'* ('wreath') (I, 280, 281), as if in readiness for the ultimate sacrifice that he will be called upon to make. When the time comes, George's poetic Maximin chooses his fate in full knowledge that this final gesture is the precondition for an existence that will elevate him beyond the mundane world that he despises. His language merges a proud assertion of self with the Nietzschean disposition of *amor fati*, which seeks the embrace of fate, however tragic the consequences:

---

21. George, *Werke*, Volume1, 354.
22. Wolters quoted in Breuer, *Ästhetischer Fundementalismus*, 42–43.
23. Edith Landmann, as quoted in Breuer, *Ästhetischer Fundementalismus*, 54.

You know not who I am, but understand this:
I have not yet finished the deeds and the speech
That would make me mortal, but the time has come
For me to choose my new self.
I change but retain my original essence
I will never be like you: that decision was long
taken.
So prepare the sacred branches and the crowns
Of violets and the flowers of death made
And bring forth the purifying flame: farewell![24]

Maximin became elevated into a symbol around which George and his acolytes became filled with a new sense of their mission. The 'Kreis' became a *Bund*, an important moment of transition reflected in the title of George's next volume of poetry, *Die Stern des Bundes* (*The Star of the Covenant*), published on the eve of World War 1, in 1914. With its missionary commitment to the cult of the aestheticised self and in its unswerving loyalty to its poetic leader, the *Bund* became the organisational site of secular transcendence. Those who wished to enter this privileged realm (*Reich*) were compelled, as George made clear in one famous poem from this cycle, 'Herrn der Welt' ('Lord of the World'), to abandon all ties with their former lives. For:

This is the realm of the spirit: reflection
Of my realm, its courts and its groves.
Newly formed and reborn
Is each one here: their place of birth
Their homeland is but a distant echo.
Through the calling and through the blessing
You have exchanged your family, class and name
Fathers, mothers no longer exist.
From their sons, the chosen ones
I elect my rulers of the world.[25]

The bond between George and his followers was a highly personal one, forged during the many readings that the magister gave in the intimacy of chosen households, speaking to the initiated. Here, in an

---

24.   George, *Werke*, Volume 1, 352.
25.   George, *Werke*, Volume 1, 382.

atmosphere compounded from aesthetic reflection and sacerdotal solemnity, the spoken word combined with gesture and silence to produce a form of secularised ritual. On such occasions, George exuded a particular charisma that bordered upon religious presentation, as if he were 'a commander of a holy order from days gone by, or a fantastic messenger sent by the Knights of the Grail.[26] Retrospective accounts left by his many acolytes almost unanimously present him as an ethereal figure, an icon of ideal purity, untouchable, almost an abstraction rather than a real person.[27] This is how George appears in a hagiography by Friedrich Wolters, entitled simply *Gestalt*. The figure here being described is clearly Stefan George, but the latter is never mentioned in name, so that the aura surrounding his messianic presence might stay intact. George is elevated into an abstract principle of moral guidance. As Wolters explains: '*Gestalt* does not set out to inform us, but moulds our ideas more than any teacher; it has no moral imperative but guides us more than any law. *Gestalt* is the highest judge and the final judgment upon our actions, work and ideas.'[28]

Those who wished to belong to the *Bund* had to accept the trials of an initiation ceremony, for which George had earlier drafted a script, called 'Induction into the Order', and first published in the *Blätter für die Kunst* in 1901. Subtitled 'an ordination play' (*Weihespiel*), the 'play' featured a Grand Master who, standing at an altar surrounded by those already initiated into the Order, waits to receive the entreaties of those seeking to become members. What was important, above all, about such ceremonies (and indicative of the particular type of secular redeemerism promoted by the George circle) was the deliberate confusion of fantasy and reality, role-playing and the personal. As the chorus announces in the opening scene, theirs is: 'the most worthy guild/ the most magnificent council/figures of dreams/here become deeds'.[29] As one commentator has noted, reading the parts in this

---

26. Ludwig Thormaehlen, *Erinnerungen an Stefan George* (Hamburg: Hauswedell & Co, 1962), 9.

27. See, for example, Kurt Hildebrandt, *Erinnerungen an Stefan George und seinen Kreis* (Bonn: Bouveir, 1965), Robert Boehringer, *Mein Bild von Stefan George*, 2 volumes (Düsseldorf: Küpper, 1968), and Edgar Salin, *Um Stefan George: Erinnerungen und Zeugnis* (Düsseldorf: Küpper, 1948).

28. Friedrich Wolters, 'Gestalt', *Jahrbuch für die geistige Bewegung*, Volume 2, 150.

29. George, *Werke*, Volume 2, 555.

ceremonial pageant assumed the form of a responsory such is typical in the Catholic Mass, 'uniting the congregation through the spoken word and linking the celebrants by a shared invisible spiritual bond'.[30]

Those accepted into the *Bund* carried out their roles with devotion, being prepared to change their identities, even their very names in the process. This is how the young Friedrich Gundolf (whose original name *'Gundelfinger'* was thought to be too ungainly by George) summed up the articles of his faith in an essay entitled 'Obedience and Youth', written in 1910. Here, Gundolf exhorts all who seek to be a part of the *Bund* to nurture a 'longing for the eternal will that is fulfilled in this mortal man and the Word that he brings with him'. 'It is not the ideal of a free "personality" that these would-be acolytes should embody (Gundolf makes clear), but the willing subservience to "the compulsion of this world", a process that demands a graduation of service, from reverence to sacrifice, from self-surrender to union.' All are pathways on the road to transcendence.[31]

The *Bund* was held together not only by the ethics of ritual, but also by a sense of collective purpose. Its members felt that they were part of a 'secret Germany' whose goal it was to undo, no less, the culture of modernity. Writing years later in his history of the journal, Wolters emphasised the militant nature of the *Jahrbuch*'s project: 'The moving spirits in this intellectual movement knew that this renascence had its origins in distant forces. Theirs was no mere speculative groping in the dark, but an action directed towards a complete reversal of the intellectual temper of the age and its hollow notion of freedom. They sought a radical break with the dominant philosophical, educational and social ideologies of the period.'[32]

It is here that the redemptionist ethos of the George circle, its will to transcendence, even its sense of aesthetic self identity, meets the broader current of German thought in the modern period: in the form of a salvationist symbolism that opened up entirely new definitions of the political. This was recognised by one of George's foremost adherents, Karl Wolfskehl, who made the following remark in an essay in 1910: 'that the German finally receives a gesture, a German gesture,

---

30.  Norton, *Secret Germany*, 398.
31.  Friedrich Gundolf, 'Das Bild Georges', *Blätter für die Kunst*, 1 (1893): 47.
32.  Wolters, *Stefan George und die 'Blätter für die Kunst'*, 384.

this is far more important than ten conquered territories.[33] These were George's sentiments exactly. In one of his rare theoretical pronouncements on the political relevance of his work he said: 'New levels of culture arise when one or several original spirits manifest their vital energies, and have these energies accepted first by their immediate community and then by a greater part of the people. The original spirit makes its effect not through doctrine but through its energy: the doctrine is something that is made by its disciples.'[34]

That we are dealing here with a form of politics may not be immediately clear. One of the problems lies in the way we define notions such as 'politics' and 'the political', frequently defining the latter exclusively as a conscious or, at least, explicit stance towards a party-political platform, a coherently formulated set of polices or recognisable ideology. Following this familiar view, politics is about the winning and exercise of civic power (hence its root in *polis*), and, as such, posits the material primacy of the external world upon the agency of self and subjectivity, whose everyday terrain constitutes a force-field of competing interests in which individuals must situate themselves through democratic debate, diplomatic negotiation, power-broking or simply *force majeure*. In the work of George and his followers an alternative notion of the political came to the fore: one that was founded upon a ritualistic and cultic worldview, in which the individual finds identity not by following considerations of a material or utilitarian nature but through initiation, through the acceptance of a mission and through self-sacrifice to a higher mystical reality whose embodiment and primary force is the charismatic leader, in this case, Stefan George. Power becomes empowerment; it is not experienced at first hand, but lived vicariously through the Other. Applied to the public sphere, such an ethos can at best be described as the 'politics of the apolitical'.[35] It is a transcendence of reality that at the same time, in

---

33. See Karl Wolfskehl, '*Die Blätter für die Kunst und die neueste Literatur*,' in *Jahrbuch für die geistige Bewegung*, Volume I, 16.

34. Quoted in Franz Schonauer, *Stefan George:Selbstzeugnissen und Bilddokumenten* (Hamburg: Rowohlt, 1960), 98.

35. See Klaus Landfried, *Stefan George: Politik eines Unpolitischen* (Heidelberg: Lothar Stiehm, 1975). As Max Weber remarked within another context: 'As soon as art takes upon itself the function of inner-worldly redemption' its crosses the barrier of social differentiation and assumes holistic features that are highly relevant to the social'. See Max

certain historical situations, allows for its greatest penetration. It was George's achievement precisely to encourage a generation of readers, particularly middle class academic youth, to look upon this latter ethos as the only authentic terrain of the political.[36]

But that these two definitions of the political would ultimately converge was clear to anyone who looked deeply into the George Circle and the mystique that surrounded it. The George disciples themselves were quite frank about the political relevance of their redemptive ethos. As Max Kommerell, yet another George acolyte, noted in his book *Der Dichter als Führer in der deutschen Klassik* (*The Poet as Leader in German Classicism*) (1928): 'the poet should not replace the Führer, but he should prepare for him.'[37] But in 1928, the time was not right, as Kommerell, a student of *kairos* would have known. 'Real redemption', under these terms, had to wait until 1933, when one messianic figure left the stage (Stefan George, the year of his death), and another arrived.[38]

Weber, *Gesammelte Aufsätze zur Religionssoziologie* (Tübingen: Mohr, 1972), 555.

36. Even from its earliest days, the George Circle was concerned to find a readership amongst academic youth. See Hugo von Hofmannstahl's letter to George, 1 May 1896, as quoted in Winkler, *George-Kreis*, 67.

37. See Breuer, *Ästhetischer Fundementalismus*, 225.

38. Breuer lists the members of the George Circle (including the von Stauffenberg brothers) who joined the Nazi Party in 1933. See Breuer, *Ästhetischer Fundementalismus*, 234.

# 9

# 'In the Blink of an Eye': Apocalypse and Redemption in Martin Heiddeger

## Koral Ward

The concept of apocalypse can carry secular and historical as well as theological significance and can provide us with powerful conceptual tools for interpreting contemporary situations. Stated briefly, the apocalyptic themes which surround the philosophy of Martin Heidegger are grounded in the idea that the social and political situation of a certain time is one of crisis which appears to move inevitably toward total destruction. The crisis is in the present and, therefore, of direct and immediate concern to those whom it affects. The change which inevitably emerges from such a situation is imminent, the present cannot be held onto, it must be transcended and give way to the awaited future. The presence of a 'visionary', Messianic figure is necessary to the recognition that 'now' is the time, a fitting person who is properly situated, who recognises and is prepared to seize the possibilities that the present harbours. The culmination point of the state of crisis, the eschatological moment, cannot but give way to change and the instigation of a new order, as such it is, one might argue, the central concept of apocalypse. The sudden and decisive yet enigmatic Moment (*Augenblick*) also plays a pivotal role in Heidegger's philosophy, as a concept which allows a transcendence of the everyday temporal world and a 'revelation' concerning the very Being of human being. Heidegger advocates a return to consideration of the neglected concept of Being which, if carried out authentically, constitutes a redemption of the concept.

Ancient apocalyptic texts were motivated by socio-political situations, especially situations of political oppression.[1] Albert

---

1.  I am grateful for this observation to Dr Paul S MacDonald of Murdoch University WA.

Schweitzer in *The Quest for the Historical Jesus,* of 1909, tells us that the
holy books of the Jews were 'concerned not with the mysteries of
internal prayer or personal salvation but with the promises made by
God that he would deliver the nation from this captivity of that'.[2] The
contemporary world of Jesus, as Schweitzer tells us, was one
suppressed by a foreign power and their hope was toward a free and
peaceful Jewish state. This state would be instigated and ruled over by
God but in the here and now rather than a future, otherworldly
spiritual life, that which becomes the 'eternity' of Christian doctrine. In
the case of Heidegger, his concern is always with 'world' as that which
surrounds human being as 'Being-in-the-world', where 'world' is not
opposed to the heavenly realm, nor is it 'the 'worldly' as opposed to
the spiritual'.[3] Yet this is not to say that there is no 'spiritual' element
to his thinking as we shall see and his ontology can be seen as
redemptive even though grounded in the world. In this discussion it is
necessary to refer to the actual historical events of Heidegger's time,
his own contemporary situation being caught up within an apocalyptic
zeitgeist. Unfortunately, commentary on Heidegger's political stance
often overwhelms discussion of his ontology, his allegiance to National
Socialism in the 1930s is well documented. Heidegger considers this
movement to herald a new epoch, offering, he says, the possibility of
'an internal as well as external regeneration of the Germans.'[4]

If the literal meaning of apocalypse from the Greek *apokalupsis* is
that of unveiling in the sense of revelation, we might ask what it is that
is revealed in Heidegger's thinking. His concern is always for the
question of Being and his project is its constant uncovering, this very
'questioning' he says, 'is the piety of thought.'[5] On one level, in his
phenomenological analytic of Being in *Being and Time* of 1927,
Heidegger uses the term 'disclosure' to speak of the way in which
things come to our attention or are 'revealed' as that which can be
grasped and used. But, for *Dasein* as an entity for whom Being is

2.   Albert Schweitzer, *The Quest of the Historical Jesus* (USA: The
     Macmillan Company, 1969), 123.
3.   Martin Heidegger, ' Letter on Humanism', in *The Existentialist Reader:
     An Anthology of Key Texts*, edited by Paul S. MacDonald (Edinburgh:
     Edinburgh University Press, 2000), 242.
4.   Petzet, *Encounters and Dialogues with Martin Heidegger 1929–1976*
     (Chicago and London: The University of Chicago Press, 1993), 31.
5.   Martin Heidegger, *The Question Concerning Technology and other
     Essays* (New York: Harper and Row Publishers 1977), 35.

always in question, or as Heidegger puts it 'is an issue',[6] there might be, in *Dasein's* looking further as it were, the chance to catch sight of the very 'there' (*Da*) of our 'there-being' (*Dasein*). What is revealed is a 'vision' of Being itself, and an insight into the truth of Being. For Heidegger, the very way that human being is in the world is a 'revealing'. *Dasein's* course through life is not revealed as a fated 'inevitable course' but as 'destining' (*Geschick*), which describes how all things come to presence or are brought forth from out of Being itself and are caught sight of by *Dasein*. He posits the possibility of a 'more original revealing' and that human being can be called by 'a more primal truth'.[7] Heidegger's project is to retrieve thinking from philosophy which he considers has become 'science', fixed and frozen by theoretical considering which denies the 'direct experience' in which the world and Being is held open and in question. He wants to get back to 'the essential ground'[8] of the thinking of Being which he attributes to ancient Greek philosophy, back to a 'rigour of questioning' which can reveal 'accessible' entities 'unconcealedly in themselves', by a direct 'pre-theoretical' disclosure it gives 'access to entities *and to Being*'.[9]

Heidegger perceives his contemporary world to be moving progressively toward 'total destruction' both politically and spiritually.[10] As a young seminarian in a Catholic institution in 1910 Heidegger observes the modern world outside in its fascination with speed and novelty and laments the superficiality of concerns of what he calls the 'they', by which he means the general 'mass' of people. He considers contemporary human being to have 'become bored with themselves', and characterises their way of looking at the world as mere inauthentic 'curiosity'. This state of affairs worsens, by 1935 Heidegger says 'The spiritual decline of the earth is so far advanced that the nations are in danger of losing the last bit of spiritual energy that makes it possible to see the decline', he describes 'the darkening of the world, the flight of the gods, the destruction of the earth, the transformation of men in to a mass, the hatred and suspicion of

6.   Martin Heidegger, *Being and Time* (UK: Blackwell, 2000), 17.
7.   Heidegger, *The Question Concerning Technology*, 28.
8.   Petzet, *Encounters and Dialogues with Martin Heidegger 1929–1976*, 30.
9.   Heidegger, *Being and Time*, 187.
10.   Heidegger is not referring to 'spirit' in a theological sense but rather to the stance of man inexorably *in* the world.

everything free and creative'.[11] By the 1950s the danger reaches its apotheosis in the epoch of modern technology whose exploitative essence, as that which imposes the ordering and stockpiling of resources has its detrimental effect on human being itself. Technology, Heidegger asserts, renders human being as merely another resource, or 'standing reserve' (*Bestand*).[12] This is, for Heidegger, the reason for the endangered state of human being and its root lies in their having forgotten the meaning of Being. The meaning is, in fact, so deeply lost and completely forgotten that it is consigned to 'oblivion'; human being no longer even remembers that there is anything there to remember. I will return to the discussion of Heidegger's actual historical situation but first it is necessary to consider the importance of the present time in Heidegger's ontology.

The concept of apocalypse carries a sense of urgency, the critical present holds an anxious anticipation of change, an expectation of transcendence of the time or epoch, when one situation gives way to another, entirely new one. The counter to this anxiety is the hope that the event of the change's coming to pass will afford a redemption through whatever the change reveals. It is the very situation of impending destruction which itself gives rise to the possibility of its transcendence. For Heidegger, the present can assume a special character which not every present moment has, that of being 'authentic'. An authentic 'Present' cannot be derived from a ordinarily present 'now' of time, he tells us, without the unity of its corresponding 'ecstases' of future and 'having-been'. In using the word 'ecstases' Heidegger points to the way in which the three elements of past, present and future stand out rather than being part of the ordinary 'levelled off'[13] sequence of 'now' moments.[14] Of these three 'temporal ecstases', Heidegger asserts, the future has priority for *Dasein* whose 'facticity'[15] includes its existence as 'projection'. This means that *Dasein* has the possibility of 'projecting' its own future

---

11.  Heidegger, *An Introduction to Metaphysics*, 38.
12.  Heidegger, *The Question Concerning Technology*, 17.
13.  Heidegger, *Being and Time*, 377.
14.  Heidegger is not here using this word to speak of a state of ecstasy or a visionary trance although the language may hint at it.
15.  'Facticity' does not refer to the brute facts of existence, but a characteristic of *Dasein's* Being, the 'that-it-is'. See *Being and Time*, 174.

possibilities. It is this 'futural'[16] being of *Dasein* which compels us throughout life and onto ever new projects and gives us an expectation of change and a propensity for hope. In expressing this special sense of the present, Heidegger exploits the German for present (*Gegenwart*) which, by hyphenating *'gegen'* and *'wart'* becomes 'waiting-towards'. The 'now' of everyday temporality already seems to take on a transcendent quality as a unity of past, present and future which stand out in anticipation. From here, Heidegger elevates his concept of the Moment or *Augenblick*, which, he says, must also 'be understood, in the active sense as an ecstasis'[17] and from which can come an experience of a 'more primordial temporality',[18] that which is fundamental to *Dasein*.

In Christianity the eschatological moment as the event of 'Last things' offers transcendence, it heralds the day of judgement following which the spiritual kingdom of God in eternity replaces the earthly one of man in time. This kingdom takes its place before us in the future, the phrase 'the future life' can be taken to refer to the eternal life after death. Heidegger derives aspects of his *Augenblick* from Søren Kierkegaard whose Moment represents a transition between time and the eternal. Kierkegaard asserts that the distinction of present moments from the temporal stream can happen only when time is related to the eternal in such a way that they become one another, when the present moment is filled with the infinite. Having given significance to the present as the Moment, a renewed significance is given to the future which, Kierkegaard says, contains the past and present in a whole. For Kierkegaard the incarnation of Christ is a concrete historical event and the decisive point of departure for the eternal being or 'eternal consciousness'[19] of man. In this advent, God as 'wholly other', comes into time and history as a direct communication of the eternal. Heidegger also comes to speak of the eternal in relation to the Moment, not as a realm separate from this world, but relating to the way in which *Dasein* can bridge the 'cleavage' between temporality as ordinary everyday being 'in time' and the transcendent *'Temporality of*

---

16. Heidegger, *Being and Time*, 437.
17. Heidegger, *Being and Time*, 387.
18. Heidegger, *Being and Time*, 497, note iii.
19. Søren Kierkegaard, *Philosophical Fragments*, edited and translated by Howard V Hong and Edna H Hong (Princeton University Press, 1985), 58.

*Being'.*[20] For Heidegger, the concept of the *Augenblick*, is central to his ontology, in such a moment human being can transcend its ordinary, everyday temporal situation, such a transcendence for Heidegger is not to another spiritual realm but to an experience of Being itself as a 'pre-ontological'[21] state of *Dasein's* constitution.

The event of the moment itself, according to Corinthians 15:52, arrives 'in the blink of an eye'. This phrase is the English equivalent of the German *Augenblick* and as a visual and temporal metaphor it both names and describes the concept. Such a figurative expression points to its harbouring meaning in excess of an ordinary moment in time, it describes the moment of something happening suddenly and swiftly, bringing about a change which is momentous and decisive. Such a moment comes, according to the St Paul's First Letter to the Thessalonians, 'like a thief in the night', it cannot be brought about by human actions but only by the direct intervention of God. Otto Pöggeler, in his essay 'Destruction and Moment',[22] tells us that Heidegger's concern is with 'the philosophical indication that life-experience in general is factical, historical, and thereby oriented to the unavailable moment beyond our control'.[23] Heidegger asserts that in the 'moment of vision' 'nothing can occur', it is rather the site of 'an authentic Present or waiting-towards',[24] as Kierkegaard points out, there is no discernible moment of change we can identify as being when one state of being becomes another, or when something comes into or goes out of existence. There is only a kind of 'pause' he describes, where wonder itself 'stands in pausa and waits for the coming into existence'.[25]

In the event of a personal moment of revelation, the reason is confounded by the paradox of the infinite meeting the finite. In this state of perplexity or wonder, reason takes 'offence'[26] and cannot remain indifferent, one is pushed toward risking the leap of faith. This is the state of perplexity which Kierkegaard asserts is the proper point

---

20.   Heidegger, *Being and Time*, 39.
21.   Heidegger, *Being and Time*, 39.
22.   Otto Pöggeler, 'Destruction and Moment', in *Reading Heidegger from the Start: Essays in His Earliest Thought*, edited by Theodore Kisiel and John van Buen (New York: New York State University Press, 1994).
23.   Pöggeler, 'Destruction and Moment', 140.
24.   Heidegger, *Being and Time*, 388.
25.   Kierkegaard, *Philosophical Fragments*, 80.
26.   Kierkegaard, *Philosophical Fragments*, 49.

of departure for philosophising, it is 'with explaining the wonderful'[27] he tells us, that philosophy began. Heidegger echoes this in his insistence that a questioning stance is required for thinking, and for the direct 'pre-theoretical' disclosure in which *Dasein* catches 'sight' of its 'there'. The translators of *Being and Time* render the word *Augenblick* as 'moment of vision' and as such the term is necessarily related to 'sight' or some kind of 'insight' (*Einblick*). For Heidegger, what is attained in the *Augenblick* is the 'vision' into Being which reveals *Dasein* in its ownmost possibilities of Being, and through which *Dasein* can experience an extraordinary and 'totalizing' sense of Being.

Yet some kind of action on the part of a particular individual is necessary to this moment. What is needed is a person fitted to the task, who can risk meeting its challenge and seize its possibilities. Schweitzer sees Jesus, as 'a man of his time' who shares the beliefs of other Jews living in the constant expectation that the world is about to be remade, and who has the 'vision' to realise that 'now' is the time. For Heidegger, in relation to the *Augenblick*, there must be a person who is of a sufficiently courageous disposition to take up the possibilities which the *Augenblick* presents. Such a one must be receptive to the possibilities and in a state of readiness which he describes in his concepts of 'attunement' (*Gestimmtheit*) and 'resoluteness' (*Entschlos-senheit*). Jesus, Schweitzer says, understood *himself* to be the Messiah,[28] and there is a sense in which Heidegger sees himself as one who can redeem the present disastrous situation in philosophy and thinking which, he asserts, underlies the political and social empasse of his contemporary world.

For Heidegger, the metaphysical question of why there are beings at all, is hand in hand with the question of 'how' human beings *are* in the world, 'how things stand'[29] with them in their situation. Being 'inauthentically' engrossed in or 'lost' in the world is the usual, unquestioning mode of *Dasein's* existence, part of its 'facticity'. Heidegger uses the term 'irresoluteness' to describe 'the way things are in the "they"'.[30] An aspect of this 'facticity', then, is that human being exists as 'throwness'(*Geworfenheit*), it is 'thrown' Heidegger says, into

---

27. Kierkegaard, *Philosophical Fragments*, 240.
28. Schweitzer, *The Quest of the Historical Jesus*, 123.
29. Martin Heidegger, *The Fundamental Concepts of Metaphysics* (USA: Indiana University Press, 1995), 135.
30. Heidegger, *Being and Time*, 331.

the everyday world and also from the past toward the future. Heidegger describes this 'thrownness' as being in a condition of 'falling' into the everyday ways of 'idle talk, curiosity and ambiguity',[31] it can be understood to mean a 'falling away' in which *Dasein* avoids its authenticity (*Eigentlichkeit*).[32] Lost in its everyday concerns, Heidegger says, '*Dasein* can undergo a dull suffering' and seeks to lose itself further. But, 'In the moment of vision and often just 'for that moment', he says, existence can even gain the mastery over the 'everyday' though it 'can never extinguish it',[33] this may in a sense point to a redemption of *Dasein* from the superficial world of everyday concern and a momentary experience of the overcoming of its temporality.

In a continuation of the understanding of the authentic Present as 'waiting-towards', there are underlying 'moods' of *Dasein* which Heidegger describes as a 'heightened waiting-towards'. These existential moods Heidegger calls 'attunements' and they can afford the possibility of a transcendence of the temporal domain. *Dasein's* being 'attuned' is necessary to the experiencing of the *Augenblick,* when one is properly 'attuned' a moment can be anticipated. The main attunements are *Angst*, derived from Kierkegaard's 'dread', which occurs when *Dasein* confronts its own finitude, and *Langeweile*. *Langeweile*, along with a sensation which might be described as the drawing away of, or loss of meaning of the world, also carries the connotation of an altered temporal experience of the present, a 'lengthening of the while'.[34] These 'attunements'[35] allow the sudden and unexpected moments of experience to yield an insight, to 'sound' in one's Being, then 'all at once' one might see the world as one has never *seen* it before. An attunement can take hold of us, Heidegger says, 'in an instant like a flash of lightning' and is of an 'overpowering nature' so that it would be impossible to struggle against it, because 'it has already *transformed* Dasein'.[36] In a translators note in *Being and Time*, it is pointed out that this powerlessness (*Ohnmacht*), can also

31. Heidegger, *Being and Time*, 219.
32. Despite this word resonating with the Christian sense of a 'fall' into sin, this is not the sense in which Heidegger intends it.
33. Heidegger, *Being and Time*, 422.
34. Martin Heidegger, *The Fundamental Concepts of Metaphysics* (USA: Indiana University Press, 1995), 152.
35. Further attunements appear in Heidegger's later writing.
36. Heidegger, *The Fundamental Concepts of Metaphysics*, 136.

suggest a visionary's 'mystical trance'.[37] Heidegger describes this further as a state of 'resolute rapture' in which *Dasein* regards its ownmost possibilities revealed in a 'Situation', and holds onto them in anticipation of what they may disclose. Heidegger's use of the word 'rapture' strongly suggests a state of being carried out of oneself, but again it is important to understand that Heidegger is not referring to being transported to a heavenly realm. What is disclosed to *Dasein* most forcibly in terms of its future potentialities of Being, is its 'ownmost' possibility of death.

As Being-toward-death *Dasein* carries, in *Angst*, an underlying anticipation of this most certain of events. In the face of the threat of loss of being the meaning and significance of the world and the situation which surrounds being as a whole drains away. In authentic attunement, it is as if one is released, or freed to gaze at death and comprehend it as the ultimate possibility for one's being. *Dasein*'s own death hovers in its horizon, as a *'possibility that it has inherited'*, as a state of Being. In grasping and 'accommodating' the finitude of existence, Heidegger says, *Dasein* is rescued from the possibilities that are closest, the inauthentic 'comfortableness, shirking, and taking things lightly'.[38] *Dasein* cannot usually know, however, when to expect this moment, and neither can it, when the moment comes actually experience its own 'demise', *Dasein* can never 'have' this moment, it is 'unavailable'. In using the word 'demise' rather than 'end' Heidegger keeps the concept of death from being a final closing down of *Dasein*, it must, Heidegger asserts, be recognised as a state of *Being*.[39]

The counter to inauthentic irresoluteness is 'resoluteness', not as practical 'behaviour' but a decisive mode of being-there, in which one lets oneself be summoned out of the lostness in the 'they', into a kind of existing which, Heidegger says, is 'primordial and authentic'. It is only through resoluteness that the attunements of which we have spoken can, as Heidegger puts it, 'mount authentically' in *Dasein*. In being resolute, *Dasein* can retrieve itself from being engrossed in the everyday and hold a moment in authentic presence as the *Augenblick*.

---

37. Heidegger, *Being and Time*, 436.
38. Heidegger, *Being and Time*, 435.
39. We might extend this notion of *Dasein's* Angst regarding its own demise, perhaps the deepest Angst is in relation to the possibility of the end of 'world' and Being itself in some cataclysmic event.

Heidegger's extension of this concept as 'anticipatory resoluteness' describes the 'futural' impetus of *Dasein* but also refers to *Dasein's* way of existing authentically in understanding itself concerning its 'potentiality-for-Being', that it can take over its factical 'there' and the 'individualization'[40] into which is has been 'thrown'. 'Anticipatory resoluteness is at the same time a coming-back to one's ownmost Self.'[41] By being properly attuned and resolute, Heidegger tells us, there is a possibility, that *Dasein* can be *augenblicklich*. As an adjective in German, this word describes a state of Being of *Dasein*, it is translated in *Being and Time* as being 'in the Moment'. Heidegger says that *Dasein* can be *'in* the moment of vision for 'its time',[42] this refers to *Dasein's* 'being-historical' which comprises both the ownmost and intrinsic temporal existence within which one might experience a personal and decisive Moment, and also one's actual time in history, or one's epoch.

To return to Heidegger's own actual historical situation, a decisive Moment appears for him in 1933 when he sees Hitler as the august man of the moment. At this time Heidegger takes over the rectorship of the university of Freiburg and delivers his famous rectoral address in which he speaks of the 'greatness and glory of this dawn,' of the Reich (kingdom) and states that: 'The *Führer* himself and he alone *is* the present and future of German reality and its rule'.[43] Hitler, for Heidegger, is one of the few 'authentic and superior' men who have 'an insight into the caesura, the moment of destiny' and 'the will and power to carry it through',[44] those who can meet this opportunity in its fullness of possibilities and make the 'radical decisions' required. The apocalyptic politic of fascism appeals to Heidegger's notion of heritage and tradition but also demands a look away from an idyllic past and toward the future with a new energy and will.

At the same time as Heidegger sees Hitler as the Messianic figure for Germany he sees himself as the one who can rescue the university and return philosophy to the kind of questioning thinking in which, he says, there can be a 'privileged, unique relation' between the question

40.   Heidegger, *Being and Time*, 338.
41.   Heidegger, *Being and Time*, 338.
42.   Heidegger, *Being and Time*, 437.
43.   Martin Heidegger, 'Only a God Can Save Us:' *Der Spiegel's* Interview with Martin Heidegger, translated by Maria P Alter and John D Caputo in *Philosophy Today*, 4 (1976): 271.
44.   Heidegger, *An Introduction to Metaphysics*, 26.

and the questioner who is, he says, thereby opened up 'as a whole'.[45]
One can catch a view of oneself as this questioning being in the very
act of questioning and can 'unlock' what forgetfulness of Being has
hidden. Thus, Heidegger asserts, '*one* kind of essent persists in coming
to the fore, namely the men who ask the question',[46] those who have a
certain intelligence required to point their efforts toward the 'psycho-
spiritual process'[47] of fundamental inquiry. Hannah Arendt, writing
on the occasion of Heidegger's eightieth birthday describes how the
rumour spread concerning Heidegger's lecturing on thinking at this
time and the way in which Heidegger is regarded: 'The secret king
reigned in the realm of thinking, a realm that is entirely of this world,
but is so concealed in it that one is never quite sure whether it exists at
all'.[48]

In *An Introduction to Metaphysics*, based on his lecture courses of
1935, Heidegger comes to see the inquiry into Being as concerning not
only *Dasein* and the actual events of historical existence but the very
'spiritual destiny of the Western world'.[49] Man's forgetfulness of
Being is due to something inherent in Western metaphysics from the
beginning. Now is the time, Heidegger asserts that it is precisely
'today'[50] that the situation has arisen or come to a culmination point,
that we have both 'fallen away from' the meaning of Being and that it
is necessary to find 'our way back' to it in order to grasp and
understand the truth regarding the historical being of Germany.
Heidegger sees Europe at this time as a nation, 'in a great pincers'
between Russia and America which he considers to be metaphysically
equivalent 'in regard to their world character and their relation to the
spirit'. They display 'the same dreary technological frenzy, the same
unrestricted organisation of the average man'.[51] Europe however,
although a danger to itself because it is without 'vision' is, Heidegger
asserts, metaphysically superior and has therefore an 'historical

---

45. Heidegger, *An Introduction to Metaphysics*, 4.
46. Heidegger, *An Introduction to Metaphysics*, 3.
47. Heidegger, *An Introduction to Metaphysics*, 29.
48. Hannah Arendt, 'For Martin Heidegger's Eightieth Birthday', in *Martin Heidegger and National Socialism. Questions and Answers*, edited by Günther Neske and Emil Kettering, translated by Lisa Harries (New York: Paragon House, 1990), 207–17.
49. Heidegger, *An Introduction to Metaphysics*, 37.
50. Heidegger, *An Introduction to Metaphysics*, 40.
51. Heiddeger, *An Introduction to Metaphysics*, 37–8.

mission'[52] to grasp the opportunity for change.

Could it be, Heidegger asks, that oblivion regarding Being 'was the most powerful and most central cause'[53] of the decline of these nations. They have fallen prey to the 'sway' of technology and its reduction of 'the human spirit on earth'.[54] Heidegger's later questioning in *The Question Concerning Technology*, of the essence of modern technology aims at opening 'our human existence'[55] to this essence[56] out of which comes the type of revealing which Heidegger calls 'Enframing' [*Ge-stelt*]. The 'monstrousness that reigns'[57] as a result of 'Enframing', he tells us, represents the most extreme danger, 'the danger as such'. Due to the insidious nature of this essence of technology human being itself is 'endangered' and comes to a 'fall' where he must take himself as 'standing-reserve'. Arendt tells us 'technology's very nature is the will to will, namely, to subject the whole world to its domination and rulership, whose natural end can only be total destruction'.[58] The counter to this danger, Heidegger tells us, comes ambiguously from out of this very 'Enframing'. Due to 'the mystery of all revealing',[59] the essence of technology contains also a 'saving power' and the closer human being is to the danger, Heidegger asserts, the 'more brightly . . . the ways into the saving power begin to shine and the more questioning we become'.[60] The danger is not counterable by human activity, the action which Heidegger refers to here is that of thinking. Arendt explains, that Heidegger's concept of will comes to refer to 'thinking that obeys the call of Being' and to think in this way is to 'say the unspoken word of Being' and it is this which constitutes authentic 'doing', a doing which transcends 'all human acts'.[61]

---

52. Heiddeger, *An Introduction to Metaphysics*, 29.
53. Heiddeger, *An Introduction to Metaphysics*, 36–7.
54. Heiddeger, *An Introduction to Metaphysics*, 42.
55. Martin Heidegger, *The Question Concerning Technology*, translator's footnote, 3.
56. Here 'essence' refers not to what technology consists of in the way of its objects and their purpose but what it means, how it 'comes to presence' as itself.
57. Heiddeger, *The Question Concerning Technology*, 16.
58. Hannah Arendt, *The Life of the Mind* (New York: Harcourt, 1978), 178.
59. Heiddeger, *The Question Concerning Technology*, 33.
60. Heiddeger, *The Question Concerning Technology*, 35.
61. Arendt, *The Life of the Mind*, 175.

Heidegger, it transpires, is mistaken in the redemption he expects of National Socialism, which harbours the very opposite of a saving power. There is, however, a redemption to be found within Heidegger's ontology both in the sense of his hopes for a return to a proper engagement with the concept and in the allowing of a redemptive experience of Being itself for human being. From out of the 'danger as such' comes the 'saving power', and from out of oblivion, Being itself calls. The revelation, paradoxically, 'comes out of Being itself[62] and by 1936–8, in *Contributions to Philosophy (On Enowning)*, the *Augenblick* comes to be understood as the happening of Being, 'the event (*Ereignis*) of presencing itself'[63] and *Dasein* belongs to the *Augenblick* 'as the originary site of the disclosure of a world and of the historical destiny of the event of being'.[64] In the *Augenblick* comes the revelation of human being as an entity which understands itself in its momentariness (*augenblicklichkeit*), coming into and passing out of existence, *Dasein* partakes for 'a time' in the '*transcendens*'[65] that is Being.

---

62. In German the 'there is' in the phrase 'there is Being' is '*es gibt*', literally 'it gives', enabling Heidegger to indicate that Being gives itself.
63. William McNeill, *The Glance of the Eye: Heidegger, Aristotle, and the Ends of Theory* (New York: State University of New York Press, 1999), 116.
64. Mc Neill, *The Glance of the Eye*, 137.
65. Heidegger, *Being and Time*, 63.

# 10

# 'Writing as a Form of Prayer': Apocalypse, Redemption and Messianism in Kafka

## Luke Vieceli

The nature of Franz Kafka's relationship to the tropes of messianism, apocalypse and redemption is a troublesome one. It would appear upon first glance that these three figurations are inextricably bound up with hope, while Kafka's writing and thought is conversely hopeless. Rather than an accurate appraisal of Kafka and his work, this conception is more a consequence of the notion of the Kafkaesque that has been inferred by commentators. It would appear that this idea is one of a bureaucratic, technological nightmare, suffused with paranoia, which cannot be escaped.[1] This conception does not provide space for any understanding of the role of the theological, which is of obvious importance to Kafka. The most noticeable manifestation of this concern is the series of aphorisms Kafka writes in 1917, which he numbered and distilled into fair copy, though they were not published in his lifetime. Max Brod, upon publication, entitled them *Reflections on Sin, Suffering, Hope and the True Way*.[2] This collection essentially reveals the concerns that inform and motivate Kafka's work and life. That the tone and the figures employed in this work are markedly different to the rest of his work must be acknowledged. Thus, Kafka's writings can be

1. For a useful exposition on the notion of the Kafkaesque see Eleanor Courtemanche, 'Kafka and the Mirror of Instrumental Reason' in *Journal of the Kafka Society of America*, 1,2 (1995): 16–22.
2. For all aphorisms not otherwise sourced, see: Franz Kafka, 'The Collected Aphorisms', in *The Great Wall of China and Other Short Works*, translated by Malcolm Pasley (London: Penguin, 1973), 7–98.

*Luke Vieceli*

separated into two spheres, those that are aphoristic and those that are parabolic. These two fields, the aphoristic and the parabolic, can be seen as broadly analogous to the relationship between the Law (*halakhah*) and its explication (*midrash* or *aggadah*) within the Jewish tradition. That these two realms operate in accordance with vastly differing rules means that the identities of apocalypse, messianism and redemption must be treated likewise. This means that an analysis of the differing manifestations and functions of the two branches of Kafka's thought is necessary. In inspecting these two realms, the reasons why, along with an elucidation of how the tropes of apocalypse, redemption, and messianism are utilised, will result in their characters being brought into stark relief.

In light of the splitting of the aphoristic writings and the parabolic writings, or stories, into separate spheres, the differing concerns must be outlined. The aphorisms are a reflection of Kafka's theological position. They mirror his interests in terms of all mankind, rather than his own personal situation. It is thus that Kafka's position—in terms of modernism and the crises inherent, along with the problems facing Judaism and the loss of tradition—comes to the fore. This position is bound to an understanding of the Kabbalah as Kafka uses explicit Kabbalistic imagery in several of the aphorisms. Along with this are the similarities between the Gnostic conceptions of creation and the resulting notions of time and judgment.[3] The stories, in opposition to the aphorisms, reflect Kafka's own sensibilities; they are highly personal figurations, simultaneously reactions to, and interventions in, his own life. Indeed, the stories are the receptacles of Kafka's redemption and are subsequently related to his messianic orientation. An understanding of his position in the world is likewise necessary for an understanding of the exilic motivations of the texts produced. It should therefore be demonstrated that Kafka's concerns are not at all incongruous with those of the hope associated with apocalypse, redemption, and messianism.

## 1. Aphorisms

In the aphorisms, Kafka posits the figure of the apocalypse as that of the Last Judgment. In *Aphorism 40* he claims, 'It is only our conception

---

3.    This is not to go as far as Karl Erich Grözinger does in his book *Kafka and Kabbalah*, translated by Susan Hecker Ray (New York: Continuum, 1994).

of time that makes us call the Last Judgment by that name; in fact it is a permanent court martial'. It is this conception of time that eludes the apocalyptic formulations of traditional Judaism, which are evinced by Scholem in his essay 'Towards an Understanding of the Messianic Idea in Judaism'.[4] Indeed, it would seem that by fusing the continuity of time and the apocalypse Kafka has freed the entire process of its eschatological flavour. In so doing, he has opposed the restorative and utopian impulses inherent in the apocalypse, as there is no end point onto which these can be projected. The objection may well be made that over and above our conception of time there is an eternal Judge who will, in a manner not involving time or history, call the court martial to order and finally pass judgement. This is immaterial in terms of the apocalypse, for the apocalypse provides the basis for redemption, which in Judaism is 'an event which takes place publicly, on the stage of history and within the community.'[5]

That the apocalypse has been denuded of its finality is problematic only insofar as rabbinical Judaism is concerned. The Kabbalistic conception of the apocalypse appears to be able to deal with the issue with far greater coherency. It would therefore seem that Kafka, in terms of the orientation of his thought, was much more closely aligned to the Kabbalah than to traditional Judaism. His exact relationship to it is of some contention and is not the task at hand. Suffice to say, that while it would appear that he had only cursory contact with it, the problems he dealt with and the manner in which he dealt with them reflect the concerns and methods of the Kabbalah.[6]

The Kabbalistic conception of the apocalypse is markedly opposed to that of the apocalypticists. Whereas they claim that the apocalypse will take place at the End of Days, the Kabbalah of Isaac Luria conceives of the apocalypse as inherent in creation, thus at the very inception of days. The Kabbalists assert that God limits himself from boundless infinity to concentrated infinity in order to allow for creation, or the revealing of the world. In so doing, he has exiled

---

4.  Gershom Scholem, 'Towards an Understanding of the Messianic Idea in Judaism', in *The Messianic Idea in Judaism*, translated by Michael A Meyer (London: Schocken, 1971), 1–36.

5.  Scholem, 'Toward an Understanding of the Messianic Idea in Judaism', 1.

6.  See Walter A Strauss, 'Trying to Mend the Broken Vessels', in *Kafka's Contextuality*, edited by Alan Udoff (Baltimore: Gordian Press, 1986), 28–341.

himself from boundlessness.[7] It is this concept of exile that is the driving force and central concern of the Lurianic Kabbalah. In the act of creation, God formed vessels for his various potencies so that differing aspects of his being could have their own manifestations. Upon filling the vessels with his divine light, it proved that the vessels were not strong enough and they shattered, thus consigning creation to exile: 'nothing remains in its proper place . . . since that primordial act, all being has been a being in exile, in need of being led back and redeemed.'[8] The fragments of the shattered vessels, still infused with divine light, entered into creation. At this juncture, the act of redemption was entrusted to man, in the first instance Adam. In light of his failure to restore the shards to their proper place, Adam ensured that 'everything was thrown into worse confusion than before'.[9] Thus, for the Kabbalist, the entire history of mankind has been that of dealing with the catastrophe of creation, of striving for the reassembly of the vessels. In this sense the permanency of the apocalypse can be entertained, as man is condemned to endure the cataclysm that resonates throughout existence until the shards have been reassembled and redemption is achieved. Insofar as the apocalypse is concerned, it appears that Kafka echoes the themes of the Kabbalah. This is not to say that Kafka's writings are unequivocally Kabbalistic, but that the concerns of the two modes of thought are not dissimilar. Both emphasise exile as inherent in the world and both certainly are reactions to the conditions of exile on a social level.

Despite the preoccupation with the trees of life and death, paradise and *kenosis* that Kafka displays in his aphorisms, it appears that he renders the idea of redemption inaccessible. In *Aphorism 3*, he claims that:

> There are two cardinal sins from which all others derive: impatience and indolence. Because of impatience they were expelled from Paradise, because of indolence they do not return. But perhaps there is only one cardinal sin: impatience. Because of

---

7. Gershom Scholem, 'The Messianic Idea in Kabbalism', in *The Messianic Idea in Judaism*, 37–48.
8. Gershom Scholem, *On the Kabbalah and Its Symbolism* (New York: Schocken, 1968), 112.
9. Scholem, *On the Kabbalah and Its Symbolism*, 115.

impatience they were expelled, because of impatience
they do not return.

In this aphorism, Kafka is damning any effective action that may be
entertained in order to bring about the restoration of the sparks and
thus redemption. Traditionally in the Kabbalah, ritual practice in
accordance with the Law was engaged with, in order to restrict evil
and help hasten the messianic age. [10] Any such action is seen by Kafka
as impatience, an attempt to defraud the world of its victory.

While Kafka plays extensively with the symbolism of the Kabbalah,
the problem appears to be that this symbolism is no longer significant.
This is due to the role of tradition being undermined in a manner that
precludes it from utopian considerations. As Kafka entertains religious
considerations and themes, he is doing so from a standpoint that
denies an end or absolute. This amounts to a dislocation of the
authority of the Law and of tradition. If, as Benjamin maintains, 'his
assistants are sextons who have lost their house of prayer, his students
are pupils who have lost the Holy Writ', then ritual action would be
spurious. [11] Yet Kafka explores ideas such as *kenosis*, or the stripping
away of obstacles, to reach the divine spark:

> Before setting foot in the Holy of Holies you must take
> off your shoes, yet not only your shoes, but everything;
> you must take off your travelling-garment and lay
> down your luggage; and under that you must shed
> your nakedness and everything that is under the
> nakedness and everything that hides beneath that, and
> then the core and the core of the core, then the
> remainder and then the residue and then even the
> glimmer of the undying fire. Only the fire itself is
> absorbed by the Holy of Holies and lets itself be
> absorbed by it; neither can resist the other. [12]

The accompaniment of patience with kenosis is perhaps the only
imperative for man in regards to what Kafka terms the indestructible.

---

10. Scholem, *The Messianic Idea in Judaism*, 22.
11. Walter Benjamin, *Illuminations* (New York: Schocken, 1968), 139.
12. Franz Kafka, *Wedding Preparations in the Country and Other Posthumous Prose Writings*, translated by Ernst Kaiser and Eithne Wilkins (New York: Schocken, 1953), 99.

After the realisation of *kenosis*, whereby the spark is encountered, it appears that Kafka would counsel more patience, so that there could be no resolution of the spark with the divine and certainly no further action.

The indestructible is one of the more important figures for Kafka's spiritual excursus. He reveals his position in several places, most noticeably *Aphorisms 50, 69, 70/71*, and an unnumbered aphorism from the *Third Octavo Notebook*: 'Believing means liberating the indestructible element in oneself, or, more accurately, liberating oneself, or, more accurately, being indestructible, or, more accurately, being.'[13] This characterisation of the indestructible proves to contain the redemptive space for Kafka's vision of humanity.

Richie Robertson claims that the situation that Kafka is essentially writing about is that of self-estrangement, so that he necessarily separates being and consciousness.[14] Robertson goes further to argue that the indestructible bridges the deep chasm between the two, and leads to the freeing of the believer from isolation. In so doing he points to *Aphorism 70/71*: 'The indestructible is one; it is each individual human being and at the same time it is common to all, hence the unparalleled strength of the bonds that unite mankind.' Harold Bloom disagrees. While he subscribes to the separation of being and consciousness, he points to the circularity of Kafka's logic regarding the indestructible while claiming that 'Hope belongs to consciousness, which is destructible, not to indestructible being'.[15] Bloom believes that the indestructible manifests itself in Kafka's vision of humanity as essentially an unrelenting assault, the symbiotic relationship between the hope of the destructible consciousness and the patience of the indestructible. This often culminates in self-destruction, as Kafka states in *Aphorism 35*: 'There is no having, only a being, only a state of being that craves the last breath, craves suffocation.'

The figure of the messiah is mentioned twice in Kafka's aphoristic writing, both in the *Third Octavo Notebook*. On 4 December 1917, he writes: 'The Messiah will come only when he is no longer necessary, he

13.   Kafka, *Wedding Preparations*, 87.
14.   Richie Robertson, 'Kafka as Anti-Christian: "*Das Urteil*", "*Die Verwandlung*", and the Aphorisms', in *A Companion to the Works of Franz Kafka*, edited by James Rolleston (New York: Camden House, 2002), 101–22.
15.   Harold Bloom, *The Western Canon: The Books and Schools of the Ages* (New York: Harcourt Brace, 1994), 456.

will come only one day after his arrival, he will not come on the last day, but on the last day of all.'[16] Again Kafka is eluding the traditional apocalyptic conception of the messiah, as that of the leader of Israel who appears at the most catastrophic moment in history in order to set things right. Instead, the figure he presents to the reader is more akin to the Kabbalistic conception. Scholem states that 'when duty has been fulfilled the son of David, the Messiah, will come of himself, for his appearance at the End of Days is only a symbol for the completion of a process, a testimony that the world has in fact been amended',[17] although this is not to overstate the messianic strain in Kafka. While Scholem is talking about a conception whereby 'completion of the process' arises through the observance of the Halakah, for Kafka there can be no observance, because the role of tradition has been rendered inaccessible. Instead, that which stands in its place is patience, and as a consequence, the indestructible. This figuration moves away from the community-oriented piety of Judaism, and towards a more personal, almost mystical communion with the indestructible.[18]

It could be argued that Kafka's thought therefore leans towards a Christian conception of the messiah:

> The messiah will come once the most unbridled individualism of faith is possible, nobody destroys this possibility, nobody tolerates its destruction, and thus the graves are opened. This is perhaps also the Christian doctrine, both in the actual displaying of the example and in the symbolic displaying of the resurrection of the mediator in the individual.[19]

However, it should be pointed out that Kafka's notion of the indestructible and his theory of patience preclude the need for a mediator between man's consciousness and his being; he is merely invoking Christianity as an example. Indeed, the messiah would not seem to be a figure of significance for Kafka, the difficulties associated with his coming proving insurmountable.

---

16. Kafka, *Wedding Preparations*, 87.
17. Scholem, *The Messianic Idea in Judaism*, 47.
18. While in the Kabbalah this personal redemption is present, it must be performed with the community in mind, not for solely personal ends.
19. Kafka, *Wedding Preparations*, 86.

Kafka briefly touches upon the notion of the messiah, with inherent loose links to redemption. Likewise, he meditates on what the messianic would look like, through his enigmatic musings on paradise. In *Aphorism 84* he claims: 'We were created to live in Paradise, and Paradise was designed to serve us. Our purpose has been changed, that this has also happened with the purpose of Paradise is nowhere stated.' The purpose and topography of Kafka's Paradise is engaged as a puzzle. However, some light is shed if two other aphorisms from his collection are reflected upon, *Aphorism 64/5* states that:

> The expulsion from Paradise is in its main aspect eternal: Thus it is true that expulsion from Paradise is final and life in the world unavoidable, yet despite that the eternal nature of the event not only gives us the possibility of remaining in Paradise permanently, but it means that we may in fact be permanently there, no matter whether we know it here or not.

While *Aphorism 74* asserts: 'If what was supposed to be destroyed in Paradise was destructible, then it was not decisive; but if it was indestructible, then we are living in a false belief.' This brings us once again to the indestructible and patience. For it seems that if man is permanently in Paradise, without realising it, and if man is living in the false belief that the indestructible element has been destroyed, then consciousness is the most pertinent obstacle to the messianic. Thus, Kafka's work is orientated towards the messianic, but only insofar as the messianic is a function of being. It is at this point that the distinction between messianism and the messianic must be stressed. Messianism is a formulation that is closely bound to eschatology, where action is undertaken in the name of a concrete end point. Thus, deeds are performed with the figure of the messiah in mind, so that this figure may be hastened to revelation and the messianic age with it. This conception is to be distinguished from a messianic orientation, which is a moment in consciousness, a direction of hope projected into the future. There is not necessarily an end point bound to the idea of messianic orientation, indeed in Kafka's case an end is absent. Rather the messianic orientation is connected with time, so that it is ongoing. For Kafka this is closely linked to his ideas of the permanency of the Last Judgment, as mentioned in *Aphorism 40*, and the eternal patience required, for the indestructible to be recognised, along with the arrival of the messiah. Kafka's messianic orientation is most strongly typified in the stories, where both he and his characters are constantly striving after the hopeful moment of consciousness.

## 2. Stories

Stanley Corngold states that 'Kafka's Gnosticism . . . is a metaphysical dualism which, in the absence of an indubitable gnosis, might still be overcome by one type of practice—that is, of course, artistic practice.'[20] While Kafka's stories can be considered the parabolic expositions of his aphorisms, they can also be viewed as a reaction to the world, which he inhabited as an attempt to create for himself a redemptive space. In the aphorisms, the position that Kafka elucidates is sparse in its outlook. The function of these fragments is not unlike that of the law, their pronouncements applicable to mankind. Indeed, their impersonality is one of their striking features. The stories on the other hand, function largely in the style of parables. Thematically, in terms of messianism, apocalypse and redemption, many of the stories follow a similar line to that of the aphorisms. *Before the Law* is an apt example, where the man from the country is subjected to the ongoing last judgment of the law, which has become impossible to access. Just as the end of his life descends upon him, his infinite patience is rewarded by a glimpse at the dazzling brilliance of the promise of the law.

There are parallels between the figurations of the three tropes under consideration in both the aphorisms and the stories but it would appear that the functions of the two vary vastly. Thus, it is more useful to look at the role that the stories play for Kafka, and through what forces they are formed. The crisis point that Western Civilisation had reached in the early part of the century, up to and including the war, can only be described as apocalyptic. This, coupled with the position that Kafka occupied in the world, meant that the feeling of exile was particularly keen in his thought. He was a German speaking Jew amongst an increasingly nationalistic Czech majority in the crumbling Austro-Hungarian Empire. Writing on 25 February 1918, Kafka states:

> I have vigorously absorbed the negative element of the
> age in which I live, an age that is, of course, very close

---

20. Stanley Corngold, 'Kafka's "Zarathustra"', in *Journal of the Kafka Society of America*, 1,2, (1995): 9–15.

to me, which I have no right ever to fight against, but as it were a right to represent. The slight amount of the positive, and also of the extreme negative, which capsizes into the positive, are something in which I have no hereditary share. I have not been guided into life by the hand of Christianity—admittedly now slack and failing—as Kierkegaard was, and have not caught the hem of the Jewish prayer-mantle—now flying away from us—as the Zionists have. I am an end or a beginning.[21]

Kafka outlines his position in regards to the spirit of the age, and in particular his situation within it. He sees himself either as the end of an epoch, or conversely as the beginning of a new one. In any case, the traditional avenues of salvation are rendered inaccessible to him. As Corngold maintains, Kafka's Gnosticism is distinguished by the absence of a gnosis, where the only means of transcending the world is the practice of art. This proves to be the only avenue appropriate to the position in which Kafka finds himself.

Hence, the path taken by the stories can be considered as redemptive, and indeed messianic in orientation. While not stated as such, it would appear that Kafka's writing becomes so through its reaction to the apocalyptic and exilic milieu in which he was working. It is in this sense that Kafka posits the phrase: 'Writing as a form of prayer.'[22] He is transposing what he sees as the empty religious categories of tradition into his writing, so that his existence might be oriented in a hopeful manner. That this hope eventually turns out to remain unfulfilled, this prayer unanswered, is lamented by Kafka late in his life:

Writing is an assault on the frontiers; if Zionism had not intervened, it might easily have developed into a new secret doctrine, a Kabbalah. There are intimations of this. Though of course it would require a genius of an unimaginable kind to strike root again in the old centuries, or create the old centuries anew and not

---

21. Kafka, 'Fourth Octavo Notebook', in *Wedding Preparations*, 114.
22. Kafka, 'Fragments from Note-Books', in *Wedding Preparations*, 343.

spend itself withal, but only then begin to flower forth.[23]

It would appear that Kafka viewed his writing as potentially being a new orientation of thought, a new Kabbalah. Zionism would seem to be the antithesis of the Kabbalah, in that it stresses the end of exile. Instead of residing in the promises of the Word of God, it propagates the idea of a material home for the Jewish people. What Kafka was engaging with in his writings was the idea of an immaterial home, of creating a text that displaced the exile into secular terms. The end of exile obviously became a pervasive idea amongst many of his generation. Indeed the notion seemed to captivate Kafka's imagination; he toyed with it in a haphazard fashion for much of his life. Ultimately though, Kafka could not conceive of redemption in material terms. Moreover, as in his aphorisms his stories were an attempt to come to terms with this exile. Far more than the aphorisms, the stories seem to revel in exile, driving the idea to its limit. Stories such as *Investigations of a Dog*, *Metamorphosis* and *A Report for an Academy*, poignantly demonstrate the idea of 'Kafka's images of exile in the alien landscape of the body'.[24]

Kafka's pursuit of secular redemption, through artistic creation via the stories, is not simply the creation of a space where the ungoverned free play of the imagination may occur. Rather, the stories are regulated by the concerns and structures imposed by the aphorisms. The redemption Kafka seeks can never be realised due to the patience necessary for the realisation of the indestructible. As *Aphorism 69* states: 'There is a possibility of perfect happiness: To believe in the indestructible element within one, and not to strive towards it.' Kafka's stories are thus the impatient strivings of the artist towards the indestructible, in the hope of reconciling the temporality of the world with that of the individual; of patience with impatience. On 16 January 1922' in the same entry but preceding the above quotation, Kafka claims: 'The clocks are not in unison; the inner one runs crazily at a devilish or demonic or in any case inhuman pace, the outer one limps

23. Franz Kafka, *The Diaries of Franz Kafka 1910–1923*, translated by Martin Greenberg and Hannah Arendt (Harmondsworth: Penguin, 1972), 399.
24. Anson Rabinbach, 'Between Enlightenment and Apocalypse', in *New German Critique*, 34 (1985): 78–124.

along at its usual speed. What else can happen but that the two worlds split apart, or at least clash in a fearful manner.'[25]

It may be concluded that one of the objects of Kafka's writing is to align these two temporalities, to redeem creation with the world so that they are identical. This attempt at the reconciliation of the two spheres can be seen in works such as the last chapter of *America*, entitled 'The Nature Theatre of Oklahoma'.[26] In this scenario all of the characters that apply for a position with the theatre are granted employment as actors. The roles that they are to play are themselves: 'It's the biggest theatre in the world . . . I haven't seen it yet myself, I admit, but some of the other girls here, who have been in Oklahoma already, say there are almost no limits to it.'[27] The distinctions between art and the world are removed so that the characters are given the opportunity to strive for the resolution of patience and impatience. This reaches a near farcical conclusion after the characters have been taken on and are awaiting transportation to the theatre. While the participants are enjoying the meal laid out for them by the company they begin to voice their thanks. The ensuing gratuitous speeches result in the assembled workers having to race along the road to the train station so that they do not miss their new lives.

The ceaseless exertions that are peculiar to Kafka's characters, particularly in stories such as *The Trial* and *The Castle* can be deemed analogous to the position that Kafka himself inhabits in relation to his creations. Through incessantly writing, he was trying time and again to invoke his means of redemption, to bring into alignment the two temporalities and, therefore, create a sphere that he could inhabit. Indeed, in writing he was attempting to transcend the gross matter of life and was thus evoking a messianic world. That the manifestations of Kafka's messianic sensibilities are not in themselves explicitly hopeful need not mean that Kafka's work and thought is bereft of hope. Rather, due to his positing the stories as a means of redemption, of his striving for the messianic through literature, Kafka's oeuvre becomes permeated with hope. Indeed, it becomes prayerful.

The two styles of writing that Kafka employs correspond to the two levels of engagement he partakes in with the figures of apocalypse,

---

25.   Kafka, *The Diaries of Franz Kafka*, 398.

26.   As with all of Kafka's novels, it remains unfinished.

27.   Franz Kafka, *America*, translated by Edwin and Willa Muir (London: George Routledge & Sons, 1938), 290.

redemption, and messianism. In the aphorisms, Kafka posits the apocalypse as continuous and in unison with the Last Judgment, so that there cannot be an end point to his thought. This figuration eludes the traditional conceptions of apocalypse and is therefore reflective of the spirit of the times. The direction that is indicated by this, especially in terms of time, is instrumental on the related notions of redemption and messianism. Kafka's connection with redemption is tenuous in a conventional sense, as unequivocal action has been rendered untenable. This leads to the postulation of the indestructible and its necessary counterpart, patience. The role of patience subsequently informs the messianic, as it stresses the inaccessibility of any messianic venture. This is not to say that the messianic is hopeless and should not be strived for, rather that it is temporarily unreachable.

In contrast to the aphorisms, where a theological framework is introduced to secular renderings, Kafka's stories are his attempt at redemption; each act of writing is an effort to transcend the world and realise the indestructible, with all that this implies. As Kafka claims in his diaries, he strove to realise a new Kabbalah. Moreover, in the resultant striving towards the artistic object, he inevitably adhered to the messianic orientation of patience that he stressed so incessantly. It is this hopeful striving that Kafka's thought undertakes that is one of the most striking features of his work. As he states in *Aphorism 109*:

> 'It cannot be said that we are lacking in faith. Even the mere fact of our life is of a faith-value that cannot be exhausted.'
> 'Where is the faith-value here? One simply cannot not-live.'
> 'It is precisely in this "simply cannot" that the insane strength of faith lies; in the form of this denial it takes shape.'
> It is not necessary that you leave the house. Remain at your table and listen. Do not even listen, only wait. Do not even wait, be wholly still and alone. The world will present itself to you for its unmasking, it can do no other, in ecstasy it will writhe at your feet.

# 11

# The Battle Between Spirit and Soul: Messiansim, Redemption and Apocalypse in Klages

## Paul Bishop

---

> Whoever does *not* seek, shall find; for only he is led by the procession of the gods.[1]

## 1. Apocalypse

In the writings of the German graphologist, characterologist, philosopher, poet, and 'biocentric metaphysician' Ludwig Klages (1872–1956) we do not have to look far to find apocalypse. One of the earliest fragments in his *Nachlass*, which its author edited and published in 1944, offers a vision of 'The End of the World'.[2] Nor are these tones reserved solely for fantasies of death and destruction; a similar apocalyptic note is sounded in his central philosophical work, *The Spirit as the Adversary of the Soul* (*Der Geist als Widersacher der Seele*) (1929–32),[3] when he evokes the last decades of the nineteenth

---

1.   Ludwig Klages, *Rhythmen und Runen: Nachlass herausgegeben von ihm selbst* (Leipzig: JA Barth, 1944), 253. I should like to acknowledge the support of the British Academy and of the Faculty of Arts, University of Glasgow in the writing of this paper.
2.   Klages, *Rhythmen und Runen*, 233–4.
3.   For discussion and commentary, see Hans Kasdorff, *Ludwig Klages: Werk und Wirkung: Einführung und kommentierte Bibliographie*, 2 Volumes (Bonn: H Bouvier, 1969), Volume 1, 190–283; and Roland Müller, *Das verzwistete Ich: Ludwig Klages und sein philosophisches Hauptwerk "Der Geist als Widersacher der Seele"* (Berne: Frankfurt am Main: Herbert Lang, 1971).

century.[4] And in the same work Klages conjured up the apocalyptic fate of humankind in the following formulaic terms: 'The foreseeable end is either: the decline of all; or: the automatisation of all.'[5] In fact, apocalypse lies at the heart of Klages's conception of our individual and historical being; for Klages—as opposed to, say, Günther Anders (1902–92)[6]—there is a sense in which History begins with apocalypse, and it is in this context that his conceptions of messianism and redemption must be understood.

For those reading Klages for the first time, one way to approach his philosophy is through the mysterious Heraclitus (c540–c475 BCE), known even to the ancient world as 'the Riddler' and 'the Obscure'. If Martin Heidegger (1889–1945) considered Hölderlin, Hegel, and Nietzsche to be three Heraclitean thinkers, we might well add to this list Klages as a fourth.[7] As early as 1902, Klages recognised in Heraclitus an 'ecstatic', a 'dithyrambic writer', a kindred spirit who, like himself, saw life in terms of ceaseless flux: everything is one (*panta einai*), and everything flows (*panta rhei*). In *The Spirit as the Adversary of the Soul* Klages cites the following fragment of Heraclitus: 'death is what we see when awake.'[8] Now, the text of this fragment is corrupt, and its meaning is in dispute; here I shall follow the reading provided by Marcovich: 'What we see when awake is death, and what we see when asleep is life (reality).'[9] This reading corresponds closely to Klages's use of the passage, which is reflected in his later citation of an

---

4.  Ludwig Klages, *Der Geist als Widersacher der Seele*, 6th edition (Bonn: Bouvier Verlag Herbert Grundmann, 1981), 923.

5.  Klages, *Der Geist als Widersacher der Seele*, 1204.

6.  See Günther Anders, *Endzeit und Zeitenende: Gedanken über die atomare Situation* (Munich: CH Beck Verlag, 1972).

7.  See Martin Heidegger and Eugen Fink, *Heraclitus Seminar*, translated by Charles H Seibert (Evanston, IL: Northwestern University Press, 1993), 115.

8.  Klages, *Der Geist als Widersacher der Seele*, 814; see Heraclitus, DK 22 B 21.

9.  M Marcovich, *Heraclitus: Greek text with a short commentary* (Merida: Los Andes University Press, 1967), 248. This reading is sustained by another fragment cited by Clement of Alexandria in his *Stromatae* (DK 22 B 26), and by the view attributed to Euripides in *Gorgias* (493 a) that the whole of waking life constitutes death (for references and discussion, see the commentary in *Les Présocratiques*, edited by Jean-Paul Dumont (Paris: Gallimard, 1988), 1235–6).

(anonymous) German Romantic source: 'Inasmuch as we sleep, we live; as soon as we awaken, we begin to die.'[10]

According to Klages, in our sleep, and specifically in our dreams, we have access to images (*Bilder*) which are, he claims, ontologically prior to bodily sensations. These images should not, however, be thought of as purely visual; they are, rather, *Anschauungsbilder*, or more precisely *Urbilder*, archetypes, which are not optically perceived but rather are experienced (*erlebt*). We shall return to this notion later on. For the moment, let us retain that Klages distinguishes two modes of experience: first, 'the sensuous experience of the bodiliness of . . . images'; second, and more important, 'the intuitive experience of a reality of images'.[11] As a disciple of Herclitus, Klages regards the sleeping state as more important than the waking one.

As a result, and by contrast, the perception of the waking state is the province, not of the soul, but of the mind, the intellect, the spirit—*Geist*. Here, Klages is profoundly indebted for his notion of *Geist* to Aristotle who, in his treatise *On the Generation of Animals* (*De Generatione Animalium*), advanced the view that, in conception, the female contributes the matter of the future composite, while the male contributes the soul. The intellect, however, enters the individual at another point: it is, in Aristotle's phrase, an 'intellect from without' (*nous thurathen*).[12] Thus the model with which Klages operates is not the Cartesian dualism of body and soul or, more generally, matter and mind, but rather the tripartite (and Aristotelian) division of *nous—psyche—soma*.

As a result Klages's system is inherently conflictual, which may or may not have been a product of his persona in biographical terms, but is certainly reflected in his energetic and combative prose style. Within Klages's works the fundamental dramaturgy consists of the enmity between, on the one hand, the body and the soul, and, on the other,

---

10. Klages, *Der Geist als Widersacher der Seele*, 814.
11. Klages, *Der Geist als Widersacher der Seele*, 811.
12. Aristotle, *De Generatione Animalium*, Book 2, 736 b 27 ('Reason alone enters in, as an additional factor, from outside') and 744 b 22 ('a mind, external to them'), (Aristotle, *Generation of Animals*, translated by AL Peck (London, Cambridge, MA: William Heinemann, Harvard University Press, 1943), 170–1 and 230–1); compare Aristotle, *'De Partibus Animalium'*, I *and* *'De Generatione Animalium'*, I (with passages from II, 1–3), translated by DN Balme (Oxford: Clarendon Press, 1972), 63–4 and 159–60.

Geist. In The Spirit as the Adversary of the Soul and elsewhere Klages uses
the following image: 'Body and soul are the poles of the life-cell which
belong inseparably together . . . into which from outside the spirit, like a
wedge, inserts itself, in the endeavour to split them apart, to 'de-soul'
the body, to disembody the soul, and in this way finally to kill all the
life it can reach.'[13] Moreover, this struggle takes place on the
ontogenetic, as well as the phylogenetic, level; Klages describes the
conflict between soul and spirit as internal to each individual: 'As souls
we are inescapably intertwined in what is essentially a fleeting reality,
but as spirits we are based literally outside this reality, unable, even for
the briefest moment, to merge with it.'[14]

Under the influence of Geist, the soul's experience of the world as a
continuous stream of living shapes or images (Bilder) is interrupted,
and is replaced by the perception of a series of discrete 'objects'
(Gegenstände). As Klages emphasises, however, the key to Geist lies not
just in this mode of perception but rather in the corresponding
phenomenon of the will. For the apogee of this way of seeing the world
and of behaving within it is the mechanistic approach of Western
science which, more clearly than anything else, demonstrates the
disruptive, and deathly, intervention—from outside space and time
into the sphere of life—of the alien, a-cosmic power of Geist.

In one of his Nachlass fragments, Klages speaks of the dual reality
of, on the one hand, everyday consciousness and, on the other, the
soul, in terms of the intellectual expression of the fissure of inner being
that first entered the world of life deep in the past, and became
especially problematic with Plato and Christ. While this is not exactly
chronologically specific, nor is his periodisation of the time when the
world was not, in his terms, 'logocentric'. At the beginning of his
account of History stand the Pelasgians, an ancient people of the
Neolithic and Bronze Ages, mentioned by Homer, Thucydides, and
Herodotus.[15] The pre-historic world of Minoan Crete, Mycenean
Greece, and the matriarchal culture of ancient Aegean earn high praise
from Klages; in his account, he draws extensively on Johann Jakob

---

13.  Klages, Der Geist als Widersacher der Seele, 7; compare 755. See, also,
     Ludwig Klages, Vom kosmogonischen Eros, 2nd edition (Jena: Eugen
     Diederichs, 1926), 64.
14.  Klages, Der Geist als Widersacher der Seele, 71.
15.  Homer, Iliad, Book 2, line 840; Odyssey, Book 19, lines 172–7; Thu-
     cydides, The Peloponnesian War, Book 1, §3; Herodotus, The Histories,
     Book 1, §56–8.

Bachofen (1815–87) and his notion of *Gynaikokratie*.[16] What characterises the Pelasgians is their 'pathic consciousness', which 'thinks in symbols'.[17] Next comes what Klages calls the Promethean age, which coincides with the rise of Platonism, classical Athens, then Christianity, down through to the Renaissance; Prometheus symbolises the emergence of consciousness, the faculty of knowledge, for he 'made men masters of their minds', as the bound god in Aeschylus's tragedy puts it.[18] Finally, there is the Heraclean age—our own—in which, like the Greek hero in the legend related by Prodicos (the significance of which Klages inverts), we choose the world of work and purposiveness rather than the pleasure of the moment.[19] In this stage, symbolised by Hercules's 'drive to action' (*Tatendrang*), life becomes dependent on *Geist*, thinking dependent on willing, and knowledge becomes subject to the aims of humankind which subjugates Nature and naively celebrates the 'wonders of technology'.[20]

Klages had made a similar point in 'Humankind and Earth' (*Mensch und Erde*), an address written for the Freideutscher Jugendtag held in the Hoher Meißner in October 1913.[21] In this text he attacks 'progress', lambasts 'capitalism', laments the disappearance of the chthonic gods, draws attention to the destruction of the environment, and comments gloomily on the bleakness and greyness of the workaday world. In these accounts we find Klages's version of the

---

16. See Klages, *Der Geist als Widersacher der Seele*, 488, note 38; 1252; *Vom kosmogonischen Eros*, 240–2; *Rhythmen und Runen*, 17.
17. Klages, *Der Geist als Widersacher der Seele*, 1258.
18. Aeschylus, *Prometheus Bound*, line 442; compare Klages, *Der Geist als Widersacher der Seele*, 750–1.
19. Klages, *Der Geist als Widersacher der Seele*, 752; compare 'Bewußtsein und Leben', in *Sämtliche Werke*, Volume 3, 650 (see *Les Présocratiques*, 1062–5). For further discussion, see Erwin Panofsky, *Hercules am Scheidewege und andere antike Bildstoffe in der neueren Kunst* (*Studien der Bibliothek Warburg*, Volume 18), (Leipzig and Berlin: Teubner, 1930).
20. Klages, *Der Geist als Widersacher der Seele*, 753 and 751.
21. 'Humankind and Earth' ('*Mensch und Erde*'), original version, in *Freideutsche Jugend: Zur Jahrhundertfeier auf dem Hohen Meißner* (Jena: Eugen Diederichs, 1913); republished with slight modifications in Ludwig Klages, *Mensch und Erde: Zehn Abhandlungen* (Stuttgart: Alfred Kröner, 1956), 1–25; reissued in *Mensch und Erde: Elf Abhandlungen* (Stuttgart: Alfred Kröner, 1973).

'dialectic of enlightenment' as advanced by Theodor W Adorno and Max Horkheimer. Indeed, it is possible to find—as Axel Honneth, Georg Strauth, Bryan S Turner, and, more recently, Michael Großheim have done—striking analogies between the apocalyptic discourse of *The Spirit as Adversary of the Soul*, argued from the position of the Right, and the Left-wing critiques offered by Adorno, Horkheimer, and other representatives of the Frankfurt School.[22] (For Walter Benjamin, coming to terms with Bachofen and Klages was even 'unavoidable' [*unumgänglich*]).[23] Klages once actually described himself as 'the most *plundered* author on the contemporary scene'.[24]

## 2. Redemption

So much, then, and there has been much of it, for the apocalyptic element of Klages's thought. Where do we look for redemption? And given that, for Klages, the apocalypse has in a sense already taken place with the entrance of *Geist* into human life, to what extent can there be any redemption at all? Some of the earlier commentators on Klages emphasise those passages which seem to suggest we might come to live in harmony with *Geist*. Hans Eggert Schröder, for instance, argued that the Klagesian concept of personality embodied that successful integration of *Geist* with the demands of life.[25] Similarly,

---

22. See Axel Honneth, '*L'esprit et son objet: Parentés anthroplogiques entre la dialectique de la raison et la critique de la civilisation dans la philosophie de la vie*', in *Weimar, ou, l'explosion de la modernité: Actes du colloque "Weimar et la modernité"*, edited by Gérard Raulet (Paris: Editions Anthropos, 1984), 97–112; Georg Stauth and Bryan S Turner, 'Ludwig Klages (1872–1956) and the Origins of Critical Theory', *Theory, Culture and Society*, 9/3 (1992): 45–63; Georg Stauth, 'Critical Theory and Pre-Fascist Social Thought', *History of European Ideas*, 18 (1994): 711–27; and Großheim, '"*Die namenlose Dummheit*"'.

23. Walter Benjamin, *Briefe*, edited by Gershom Scholem and Theodor W Adorno, 2 Volumes (Frankfurt am Main: Suhrkamp, 1966), Volume 1, 409.

24. Klages, *Sämtliche Werke*, Volume 2, 1535. I am grateful to Michael Großheim for helping me locate this passage.

25. Hans Eggert Schröder, '*Vom Sinn der Persönlichkeit: Ein Beitrag zum Menschenbild von Ludwig Klages*', *Psychologische Rundschau*, 8 (1957): 207–17 (208 and 215); and '*Über den Geistbegriff bei Klages*', *Schweidewege*, 4 (1974): 113–20. Compare *Die Grundlagen der Charakterkunde*, in *Sämtliche Werke*, Volume 3, 372.

Hans Kasdorff considered it might be possible to develop a fruitful relationship between soul and *Geist*.[26] More recently, however, critics have drawn attention to the reliance of Klages's theoretical methodology on an argumentative rhetoric of inversion,[27] a n d Michael Pauen has described Klages's thought as a 'pagan gnosis', claiming that art is 'the secret paradigm' of his philosophy.[28] So where can we locate in Klages's thought the redemptive and messianic moments of his thought, if any?

On one point Klages is clear: redemption will not come through the church. He maintains that 'it was Christianity's achievement to exhaust the soul by defaming sensual passion', whereas, according to Klages, 'satisfied "bodily desire" is the necessary pledge of cosmic radiance'.[29] In an aphorism contrasting paganism and Christianity, he writes that 'Christianity was the first to pour the poison of transcendence into the spring waters of the underworld'.[30] And elsewhere he tells it is:

> impossible to think of a worse blindness than the one instigated by this Jewish sectarian and his apostles and successors . . . Before this mad masquerade of a 'kingdom to come', a 'last judgement', an 'eternal punishment' the heroes and gods had to 'creep to the Cross'![31]

Instead, Klages points us, with strong Nietzschean echoes, towards another god, Dionysos, as 'the releasing god', and to the cults of Eleusis and Lysios: 'Death in him is eternal rebirth and the meaning of life . . . Dionysos is the sign of the vortex, which is chaos when it glowingly gives birth to the world.'[32]

Yet Klages also knew, as well as Nietzsche did, that there can be no going back. 'The pagan urn shattered. Around its shards war raged, its

---

26. Hans Kasdorff, *Ludwig Klages: Gesammelte Aufsätze und Vorträge zu seinem Werk* (Bonn: Bouvier, 1984), 109 and 25.
27. See Müller, *Das verzwistete Ich*, 55; and Michael Pauen, *Dithyrambiker des Untergangs: Gnostizismus in Ästhetik und Philosophie der Moderne* (Berlin: Akademie-Verlag, 1994), 136–7.
28. Pauen, *Dithyrambiker der Untergangs*, 135.
29. Klages, *Rhythmen und Runen*, 243–4.
30. Klages, *Rhythmen und Runen*, 290.
31. Klages, *Rhythmen und Runen*, 285.
32. Klages, *Rhythmen und Runen*, 267.

fragments scattering to the four corners of the earth'.[33] So what is to be done? On the one hand, nothing: it is in some sense for Klages (always) already too late. For, as he noted in 'Humankind and Earth', 'no teaching can bring back to us what has once been lost', since 'to turn back [*zur Umkehr*] alone the *transformation of life* would help, the power to effect which does not lie in the ability of humankind'.[34] On the other hand, redemptive notes are sounded, softly and subtly, yet insistently and suggestively, in Klages's thought. For example, the conclusion to 'Humankind and Earth' sketches a redemption-via-ecology within the Nietzschean appeal to 'remain true to the earth!' (*bleibt der Erde treu!*); here Klages quotes an extensive passage from the final chapter of Eichendorff's *Ahnung und Gegenwart* (1811–12, published in 1815), which concludes—after some truly apocalyptic lines of its own—as follows:

> For the world will be turned upside down once more, a tremendous struggle will break out between the old and the new, the passions that now creep hidden will throw away their masks, and blazing insanity will throw itself with flaming torches into the turmoil, as if hell itself were let loose, justice and injustice, both sides, in blind and angry confusion. —Last of all, miracles will take place for the sake of the just, until finally the new and yet eternally old sun breaks through the horror; the claps of thunder still roll but only in the mountains, the white dove comes flying through the blue sky, and the earth lifts herself up, tear-stained like a beautiful women who has been rescued in new glory.[35]

Central to the redemptive moment here is, I think, the association of the redeemed earth, tear-stained but liberated, with something, or

---

33. Klages, *Rhythmen und Runen*, 281.
34. Klages, *Mensch und Erde*, 22.
35. Klages, *Mensch und Erde*, 24–5; citing Eichendorff's *Ahnung und Gegenwart*, Book 3, chapter 24. For further discussion of Eichendorff by one of Klages's followers, see: Hans Eggert Schröder, *Schiller – Nietzsche–Klages: Abhandlungen und Essays zur Geistesgeschichte der Gegenwart* (Bonn: Bouvier Verlag Herbert Grundmann, 1974), 403–7.

rather someone, beautiful;[36] a symbol of 'the tragic beauty of life', tragic because of the *ananke* (necessity) of transience in the Klagesian-Heraclitean world of flow and flux.[37]

Linked with this positive moment is his praise in 1922 of the 'cosmogonic Eros', a figure derived from Hesiod's *Theogony* and Phaedrus's speech in the *Symposium*,[38] whose return he had adumbrated in 1900.[39] In *Of Cosmogonic Eros* Klages sounds a potentially redemptive tone when he proclaims the primacy of the 'daemonically-living reality of the images' over the mechanical notion of the world of things.[40] And the redemptive moment in Klages can be located in his conception of the daemonic *Bild*. In 1901 Klages had written that 'only when the spirit is asleep does the soul awaken'.[41] And a year earlier in 1900 he had written of the 'primal imagery' or *Urbildlichkeit* of the world: 'Every detail of the world can in every moment become the complete possession of the soul, bathe in the colour of the essence. These are the moments of insight into the world of eternity.'[42] Klages returns to this theme in the fifth and final volume

---

36. Compare with Klages's reference in *Of Cosmogonic Eros* to Eichendorff's poem '*Schöne Fremde*' (*Vom kosmogonischen Eros*, 100). As Michael Pauen has pointed out (*Dithyrambiker der Untergangs*, 156, note 109), Klages noted in 1912 'the ecstasy of wandering' (*die Ekstase des Schweifenden*) in Eichendorff, an expression that is echoed in connection with the same poem by Adorno, who spoke in his 1957 broadcast of Eichendorff's 'wandering, erotic utopia' ('*Zum Gedächtnis Eichendorffs*', in *Noten zur Literatur* (Frankfurt am Main: Suhrkamp, 1974), 69–94 (77)).
37. In his 'Letter on Ethics' ('*Brief über Ethik*') (1918), Klages lists the wonder of beauty as one of the main ways of nourishing the soul (*Sämtliche Werke*, Volume 3, 672).
38. See Hesiod, *Theogony*, 117–22; Plato, *Symposium*, 178 f; see also Plato *Phaedrus*, 252b, 265 b-c.
39. Ludwig Klages, *Stefan George* (Berlin: Georg Bondi, 1902), 31–2.
40. Klages, *Vom kosmogonischen Eros*, 127. Of this passage Ernst Cassirer writes that 'with this basic conception Klages' doctrine is able as almost no other to do justice to the true significance of myth'. See: Ernst Cassirer, *The Philosophy of Symbolic Forms*, Volume 4, *The Metaphysics of Symbolic Forms*, edited by John Michael Krois and Donald Phillip Verene, translated by John Michael Krois (New Haven and London: Yale University Press, 1996), 25.
41. Klages, *Rhythmen und Runen*, 264.
42. Klages, *Rhythmen und Runen*, 244.

of *The Spirit as the Adversary of the Soul* when he writes: 'What, in moments of grace, moves us with daemonic power from nature or from the works of the spirits of the source, is not apprehended intellectually and constituted in the imagination, but rather it is—*released.*'[43]

## 3. Messianic aesthetic

As previously discussed, Klages distinguishes between *empfindendes Erleben* and *schauendes Erleben,* or more simply between *Empfinden* and *Schauen,* the first mode of perception having as its object the sensuous, bodily world, and the second *die Wirklichkeit der Bilder,* 'the reality of images', of *Anschauungsbilder* or *Urbilder.* To the consternation of such critics as Ernst Bloch (1885–1977)[44]—to whose own messianic and utopian *Noch-Nicht* he resolutely opposes a defiantly dystopian *Nicht-Mehr*—Klages also calls these images the 'elementary souls' (*Elementarseelen*), the perception of which constitutes a third dimension of perception he calls *Schauung.*[45] Of this mode of perception Klages writes that it constitutes 'the inner equivalent of the *reality of images* which consists of constant transformation', and that it is thus 'a sequential and completely inactive process'.[46] Hence, within Klagesian epistem-ology, perception (*Wahrnehmung*) corresponds to the dimension of the object, and intuition (*Anschauung*) to the dimension of the image (*Bild*), but *Schauung* is a *visionary experience* that reveals the dimension, not of spirit, but of soul—or souls.[47]

Within this scheme, the *Elementarseelen* belong, not to the temporal-spatial world of *Geist,* but to the sphere of *Leben.* In *The Spirit as Adversary of the Soul,* Klages writes that 'phenomenology is the science of essences', but he adds that 'the science of essences becomes the knowledge of the elementary souls'.[48] He speaks of 'the *souls* of the images of light and darkness, warmth and cold, storm and calm, of cliff

---

43. Klages, *Der Geist als Widersacher der Seele,* 1132.
44. Ernst Bloch, *Erbschaft dieser Zeit* [extended edition] (Frankfurt am Main: Suhrkamp, 1985), 330–1.
45. For further discussion, see Robert Josef Kozljani, *Kunst und Mythos: Lebensphilosophische Untersuchungen zi Ernesto Grassis Begriff der Urwirklichkeit* (Oldenburg: Igel Verlag, 2001), 63–73.
46. Klages, *Der Geist als Widersacher der Seele,* 159.
47. Klages, *Der Geist als Widersacher der Seele,* 182 and 285.
48. Klages, *Der Geist als Widersacher der Seele,* 1138; compare 1119.

and tree, river and sea, wood and desert, of sunlight and moonlight, starry sky and daylit heaven, gorge and peak'; drawing again on Heraclitus,[49] but more ominously, he adds: 'Assuming that something of the elementary souls became known to us, we could follow them right into the individual beings and in the end right into the human being, thus establishing the *essences* on which in humankind the differences of the characters of individual people, the characters of nations, races, epochs depended.'[50] Further on, Klages speaks of the 'images' as *daemons*, which he identifies with the *genius locii*.[51] Earlier on, however, Klages had spoken outright of 'the gods', commenting that the (Platonic) world of 'immobile "ideas"' offered to a certain extent the shadow-image of the reality of previous living gods':

> There are gods of water and gods even of particular stretches of water, gods of the plant kingdom as well as of a particular tree, gods of the hearth as well as of the hearth of a particular house, but also gods of the night, of the day, of the dawn, of the light, of the darkness, of the thunderstorm, of the rainstorm, of lightning, furthermore of love, friendship, revenge, reconciliation, of anger, furthermore of death, of sickness, of fertility, finally of prayer, sacrifice, exchange, healing, making war, swearing, warding off evil and so on into infinity.[52]

So on one level, it is possible to see in Klages a call for a return to polytheism or pantheism, inasmuch there are significant affinities between his outlook and the cosmogony of the ancient Greeks, who saw each individual part of the world in pantheist and pagan terms. Within a pantheist view of the world, there is no god separate from the

---

49.  'The behaviour [or character] of a human is his fate', or his 'daemon' (*ethos anthropo daimon*) (DK 22 B 119). See the discussion of this passage by Heidegger in his *Letter on Humanism*, who translates as 'the human is the habitation of the divine' See: Martin Heidegger, *Platons Lehre von der Wahrheit: Mit einem Brief über den 'Humanismus'* [1947] (Berne and Munich: Francke Verlag, 1975), 109.
50.  Klages, *Der Geist als Widersacher der Seele*, 1138.
51.  Klages, *Der Geist als Widersacher der Seele*, 1264. For further discussion, see Kozljani, *Kunst und Mythos*, 63–73.
52.  Klages, *Der Geist als Widersacher der Seele*, 202.

world; instead of god(s) nowhere, we have god(s) everywhere. Corresponding to every energy or force, associated with a crossroads, or a house, or the world, there is a god; and so every place has its *genius loci* or tutelary deity. For example, Hecate is the goddess of the crossroads, and we should leave anything we come across there as a sacrifice to her.[53] From his earlier work, *Of Cosmogonic Eros* (1922), we know that Klages regarded 'the gods' as the ancestral souls (*Ahnenseelen*), and claimed that 'the souls of the past that appear' are the 'primal images' (*Urbilder*).[54] So we might well see in Klages a thinker in the same mould as others, such as the philologist Ulrich von Wilamowitz-Moellendorf (1848–1931),[55] or the philologist and philosopher Walter F Otto (1874–1958),[56] or even perhaps Heidegger,[57] who seem to have believed that the Olympian gods in some sense actually exist.

On another level, however, we should note that, most of the time, Klages chooses to talk about *Bilder*, 'images', with its panoply of echoes and resonances in the aesthetic and visionary traditions, including the Goethean *Urbild*. Could it be that art is, as Michael Pauen has suggested, the secret paradigm of Klages's thought? Is Klages offering us a phenomenology, a (poly)theology, or an aesthetics? In a fragment from 1901 Klages wrote that 'deep art is the bridge between *nus* [spirit] and *hyle* [matter], between *Helios* [the sun] and *Gaia* [the earth];[58] further on, in distinctly mage-like, even messianic tones, Klages writes of the *Dichter*: 'Although the poet remains an individual, he remains

---

53. See Plato, *The Laws*, Book 11, 914 b. For a discussion of the vexed question of the ancient Greek 'belief' in polytheism, see Paul Veyne, *Les Grecs ont-ils cru à leurs mythes? Essai sur l'imagination constituante* (Paris:Éditions du Seuil, 1983).

54. Klages, *Vom kosmogonischen Eros*, 170 and 194.

55. Ulrich von Wilamowitz-Moellendorf, 'The gods exist' ('*Die Götter sind da'*) in *Die Glaube der Hellen*, 2 volumes (Darmstadt: Wissenschaftliche Buchgesellschaft, 1973), Volume 1, 17).

56. See Walter F Otto, *Die Wirklichkeit der Götter: Von der Unzerstörbarkeit griechischer Weltsicht* (Reinbek bei Hamburg: Rowohlt, 1963), 66 and 71.

57. In his Heraclitus seminar organised with Eugen Fink in the winter semester of 1966–7 in Freiburg, Heidegger recalled a moment on a Greek island: 'I remember an afternoon during my journey in Aegina. Suddenly I saw a single bolt of lightning, after which no more followed. My thought was: Zeus' (Heidegger and Fink, *Heraclitus Seminar*, 5).

58. Klages, *Rhythmen und Runen*, 258.

still as aspect of the cosmic flux: he is animal, star, sea, plant; he is the eye of the elements; he is matriarchal and earthly to the core. The praxis by which he expresses his inner vision is *magic'*.[59] And the following question, posed by Klages, gives substance to an attempt to go beyond the equation *Bild = Seele = Urbild* and to re-think Klages in aesthetic terms, specifically Goethean: 'Is the botanist concerned **about** the beauty of the flower, whose nature he wishes to explore, and in particular does he think that its life is unrepeatable?'[60] This question strongly implies that the botanist is not concerned about the beauty of the flower, but that the poet, revealing through language the world of essences, 'the reality of images', is.

## 4. Conclusion

Klages reflects deeply on the nature of apocalypse, and situates it far back in the remote past; what we call History is, for him, no more than the endgame in the struggle between *Seele* and *Geist*; yet for Klages, the gods have not disappeared, in the tradition of the *deus absconditus*,[61] it is just that we do not notice them, or the 'images', or the 'souls', anymore; while there can be no redemption, on his account, for the species, the messianic moment in his philosophy lies in his call for us to pay attention to 'the reality of the images'. If art is indeed the 'secret paradigm' of his philosophy, this would mean Klages is more concerned with aesthetic-visionary, rather than with magical-mystical, modes of perception; his messiah would thus be, not so much a magus, as an artist or a poet. So, when reading Klages, we might do well to

---

59.   Klages, *Rhythmen und Runen*, 261. Compare with the following fragment from 1900: 'Poetry [*Dichten*] is a kind of ecstatic vivacity. The life of the poet is inner poeticising [*inneres Dichten*]. Poetic experience [*Dichterisches Erlebnis*] is magical experience of language [*magisches Spracherlebnis*]' (243).
60.   Klages, *Rhythmen und Runen*, 276.
61.   Here lies a potential point of contact with Heidegger who, in his *Introduction to Metaphysics* (1953), criticised the misunderstanding of *Geist* as instrumental intelligence.See: *Einführung in die Metaphysik* (Tübingen: Max Niemeyer, 1966), 35–7). Yet Heidegger sought to distance himself from Klages—dismissing him in 1929, along with Oswald Spengler (1880–1936), Max Scheler (1874–1928), and Leopold Ziegler (1881–1958)—in his lectures on metaphysics, *Gesamtausgabe* (Frankfurt am Main: Vittorio Klostermann, 1975, (Volume 29/30), 112.

recall the following anecdote about Heraclitus, related by Aristotle and retold by Heidegger in his *Letter on Humanism* (1947):

> Some strangers wanted to meet Heraclitus but,
> entering his house, they saw him warming himself in
> the kitchen, and stood still where they were; but he
> asked them not to be afraid to and to come in, because
> 'even in this place, gods are present'.[62]

Given what we have said here about Ludwig Klages, we could perhaps paraphrase Heraclitus along the following lines: come in, for 'elementary souls' are also here; come in, for the 'reality of images' is everywhere.

---

62.  Aristotle, *Parts of Animals*, Book 1, chapter 5, 645 a 17; see Aristotle, *Basic Works*, 657; compare *Die Vorsokratiker*, Volume 1, 283; *Les Présocratiques*, 137.

# 12

# Moltmann's Political Theology: Messianic Hope Grounded in the Resurrection of a Crucified Jew

## Wes Campbell

*In the end is the beginning*: Eschatology is generally held
to be the doctrine of 'the Last Things', or of 'the end of
all things. To think this is to think in good apocalyptic
terms, but it is not understanding eschatology in the
Christian sense . . . To think apocalyptically means
thinking things through to their end: the ambiguities of
history must sometime become unambiguous, the time
of transience must sometime pass away; the
unanswerable questions of existence must sometime
cease. The question about the end bursts out of the
torment of history and the intolerableness of historical
existence. To echo a German proverb: better a
terrifying end than this endless terror. Eschatology
seems to search for the 'final solution' of all the
intolerable problems . . . But *Christian* eschatology has
nothing to do with apocalyptic 'final solutions' of this
kind, for its subject is not 'the end' at all. On the
contrary, what it is about is the new creation of all
things. Christian eschatology is the remembered hope
of the raising of the crucified Christ, so it talks about
beginning afresh in the deadly end.[1]

---

1. Jürgen Moltmann, *The Coming of God* (Minneapolis: Fortress, 1996),
   x–xi.

Jürgen Moltmann began in the mid-twentieth century to argue for the political character of Christian theology, the primary category being *hope* grounded in the reality of the resurrection of Jesus the crucified Jew. Such Christian theology is clearly a contemporary theology that knows the challenges posed for Christian faith by modernity. Names such as Hegel, Marx and Nietzsche feature here, as do Dilthey, Troeltsch, Adorno and Ernst Bloch. This contemporary political theology does not, however, take the path of accommodation as in Liberal Protestantism. Rather the thinkers and theorists named here, by their very criticism of God, church and Christian faith, remind the church of its own intrinsic character. The *politics* of Christian theology, as articulated by Moltmann, therefore arises from its own subject matter, namely hope of the Kingdom of God announced by Jesus of Nazareth. Such hope is possible only because of the resurrection of the crucified Jew, Jesus of Nazareth. Moltmann acknowledges that he shares this eschatological emphasis with Wolfhart Pannenberg, and both insist on the reality of Jesus' resurrection, while differing on its implications for the future.

## 1. Political theology

Jürgen Moltmann's theology is political theology. Its political character derives from the primary identity of Christian theology as such. This is theology defined polemically as a *critical* and *a mediating* task.[2]

Moltmann explicitly rejects an understanding of the theological task which isolates theology and the church from its surrounding society and critical voices. He is clearly aware, and critical, of forms of theology that sought an accommodation with modern society and thereby gave up its own distinctive character. Yet, he judges that there is no alternative but to engage in the theological task of mediation. As he outlines in *The Crucified God*,[3] church and theology are always involved in the dialectical relationship of identity and relevance, knowing the risks of loss of identity implied in that relationship.[4]

The widest reason for this task of mediation is the eschatological horizon of Christian faith. Neither theology nor the church exhausts or

---

2.    Jürgen Moltmann, *Theology Today: Two Contributions Towards Making Theology Present* (London: SCM, 1988), 59–94.
3.    Jürgen Moltmann, *The Crucified God: The Cross of Christ as the Foundation and Criticism of Christian Theology* (London: SCM, 1973).
4.    Moltmann, *The Crucified God*, 7–28.

circumscribes the realities with which theology is engaged. Rather, the reality which informs Christian theology is the eschatological horizon of the future kingdom of God and, therefore, of the coming of God. At the same time, the church lives in the misery of the present suffering world and has a proclamation of hope for the world.[5]

Moltmann outlines his case for 'theology as a mediating task':

> In historical terms, any Christian theology is a 'mediating theology' whether or not it is aware of the fact, since it mediates the Christian message that has been handed down in such a way that it falls within the horizons of the understanding of the people of a particular time. Mediation between the Christian tradition and the culture of the present is the most important task of theology. Without a living relationship to the possibilities and problems of the man and woman of the present, Christian theology becomes sterile and irrelevant. But without reference to the Christian tradition Christian theology becomes opportunist and uncritical. Historical mediation must both work to achieve the true preservation of the identity of the Christian message and see that it is relevant to the present.[6]

In contrast to previous epochs, there is no single, convincing contemporary theological response to modernity. Nevertheless, Moltmann outlines a two-fold task:

> On the one hand [mediating theology] must defend the right and significance of the Christian faith against the doubt and criticism of the modern spirit *apologetically*. On the other hand it must show that the Christian faith has therapeutic relevance to the sicknesses of the modern spirit and the perplexities of the modern world. The present day mediation of Christian faith to the modern world is always determined by apologetic

---

5.  Jürgen Moltmann, 'Mediating Theology Today', in Jürgen Moltmann, *Theology Today*, 53.
6.  Moltmann, *Theology Today*, 53–59.

interests on the one hand and by interests which are critical of culture and therapeutic on the other. That distinguishes modern 'mediating theology' from its predecessors in pre-modern eras.[7]

Understanding the modern world as a 'scientific, technological project' Moltmann says the mediating theology he describes 'calls for both adaptation and contradiction'. That approach is necessary for the sake of the world. 'Theology must accept the changes circumstances of the world in order to change these in its turn towards peace, justice and the life of creation.'[8] In the modern world the theological task is also a hermeneutical task. In 'Toward a Political Hermeneutic of the Gospel' in *Religion, Revolution and the Future*,[9] Moltmann shows that the modern world is one of crisis produced by 'criticism'. Beginning with Scripture and extending to all received dogma, criticism promised freedom from the past. Historical criticism, simultaneously understood as revolutionary criticism, opened up a gulf between past and present and made all insecure.[10]

A hermeneutical task is thus required to make sense of the relationship of past and present. A *theological hermeneutic* engages intentionally and critically both received Christian tradition and contemporary society. That is, theology is aware of its participation in and seeks a form of engagement with the contemporary society. Aware of previous attempts to deal with history and faith, Moltmann argues for a *political hermeneutic* for Christian theology, rejecting 'existentialist' and other forms of hermeneutic that seek to derive theology solely out of the preaching or life of the church.

Christian hermeneutic cannot concern itself exclusively with proclamation and language because they themselves stand in the larger political and social forum of public life. Therefore the political configuration of the church and the ethical form of the Christian life are the proper subject matter of Christian hermeneutical considerations. If the totality of Christian expressions of life or charisms must be considered in the hermeneutical significance of the Christ

---

7.   Moltmann, *Theology Today*, 54. See also: Jürgen Moltmann, *Religion, Revolution and the Future* (New York: Charles Scribner's Sons, 1969), 102ff.

8.   Moltmann, *Theology Today*, 94.

9.   Moltmann, *Religion, Revolution and the Future*, 83–107.

10.  Moltmann, *Religion, Revolution and the Future*, 83–6

event, then it becomes clear why one can no longer derive hermeneutic from a principle. Hermeneutics is then not simply the 'act of understanding written expressions of life', but of understanding all historical expressions of life within their political context. In *kerygma, koinonia,* and *diakonia,* the spirit of freedom and of the new future of God is brought into the total misery of the present. Thus we arrive at a method which is not a principle, that is, at the method of historical effectiveness in the form of a project, the experience and then the criticism of this project. Preaching needs the text as its basis and the dialogue of the congregation as a check. The church needs the Bible as its foundation and the public discussion as a check. Obedience and love need the discipleship committed to Jesus as their ground and the working out of present experience as a control. This is a hermeneutical process which encompasses the whole history of Christianity. From it arises the method of the realisation of faith, community, and free life under the changing conditions of misery in the present.[11]

Therefore serious attention must be given to preaching, the Bible and the life of discipleship, yet all within the context of a method of testing each in a lived form, and in open and public discussion. The church and its proclamation is not hermetically sealed but is in fact always involved and engaged in wider life. So, drawing upon so-called *dialectical theology,* as in the work of Dietrich Bonhoeffer, the theological task as a hermeneutical task is also a critical, political task.

Since the work of George Lindbeck,[12] among others (with the background of Karl Barth), it has become customary to regard the church as its own distinctive form of politics. This is thoroughly discussed by Arne Rasmussen, in *The Church as Polis.*[13] Moltmann argues that *political theology* is a specific theological task that emerged within Europe around the mid-point of last century, *after Auschwitz.*[14] While bearing some family resemblance, it is to be distinguished from Latin American Liberation Theology. Its roots belong in the response of Christian theology to the modern world, challenging Liberal Protestant attempts at accommodation with modern society, and taking up the

11.   Moltmann, *Religion, Revolution and the Future,* 101–2.
12.   George A Lindbeck, *The Nature of Doctrine: Religion and Theology in a Postliberal Age* (Philadelphia: Westminster Press, 1984).
13.   Arne Rasmussen, *The Church as Polis: From Political Theology to Theological Politics as Exemplified by Jürgen Moltmann and Stanley Hauerwas* (Notre Dame, Ind: University of Notre Dame, 1994).
14.   See the account in Moltmann, *Theology Today,* 87ff.

impulses of *dialectical theology* and the struggle of the Confessing Church against Nazism. This style of theology has also arisen through the recovery of the eschatological character of Christian proclamation, as expressed in Moltmann's *Theology of Hope* and, although differently, in the work of Wolfhart Pannenberg. Where for Pannenberg the resurrection is an anticipation of an open future, open for God; for Moltmann it is the promise of transformation for the whole creation. Thus the *eschatological* character of Christian faith and theology brings with it an expectation of transformation.

Moltmann enters this theological task in a double way. He notices that *hope* is constitutive of the modern world. *What may I hope for?* is one of Kant's questions. Ernst Bloch, as a Marxist philosopher who was both Jewish and atheist, rediscovered the 'principle of hope' that springs from Biblical faith. But Moltmann regards these thinkers as reminding the church that it has forgotten its own eschatological character.

The foundations of political theology belong in the resurrection of Jesus, the crucified Jew, and the hope generated there for the transformation of the whole of creation. Political theology is *mediating* theology in that it mediates between the received Christian proclamation of hope and the contemporary voices and movements for liberation. The church is that community who lives by the promise of the kingdom of God, and gives expression to its hope, in company with others, in movements for social and political transformation.

Rasmussen recognises that Moltmann has been formed within the Reformed tradition in the line of Karl Barth and detects in some of Moltmann's political theology an unacceptable acceptance of modernity if one regards the church as having its own characteristic politics. He summarises his critique in his final chapter: 'From a Mediating Political Theology Towards an Ecclesial Theological Politics':[15]

> Political theology is a mediating project. It emerged as an attempt to mediate Christianity and modernity. Central in this mediating project is a positive reception of secularisation . . . This interpretation was possible because Moltmann describes the whole history as a progressive and dialectic history of freedom

15.   Rasmussen, *The Church as Polis*, 375–82.

movements, in which the church has played a decisive role. The Enlightenment and modernity represent merely a further stage in this history. In this way he can give both Christian legitimacy to modernity and modern legitimacy to Christianity.[16]

Favouring Hauerwas' theological methodology, Rasmussen detects and approves, in Moltmann, a view of the church as a *contrast society* whose 'life of common discipleship witnesses to an alternative social and political practice'.[17]

This is a telling challenge to 'political theology' as mediating theology. However, I judge that Moltmann's mediating, political theology has not had that positive and uncritical regard for modernity, and that he regards the church as having its own politics. His eschatological horizon, however, with his Christology, regards the theological task as placed within a wider arena, opened up by the horizon of the kingdom of God.

## 2. Autobiography

Moltmann provides various autobiographical accounts to explain his work. He recalls the beginnings of his Christian faith or, better, hope. He describes his despair and the end of the war, captured and in POW camps. In contrast to some of his fellow prisoners who began to give up hope and die, Moltmann tells of coming into contact with the hope of the gospel. His life's work has been an attempt to understand and articulate that hope.[18] In another account Moltmann tells of walking through Auschwitz after the war and being overwhelmed, such that he wished the earth would open up and swallow him. Here is the encounter with the suffering and crucified God, as told in Elie Wiesel's account of the death camps, *Night*.[19]

---

16. Rasmussen, *The Church as Polis*, 375.
17. Rasmussen, *The Church as Polis*, 376, where Rasmussen refers to *The Way of Jesus Christ*.
18. Jürgen Moltmann, *Jesus Christ for Today's World* (London: SCM Press, 1994), 2. See also: Jürgen Moltmann, *The Source of Life: The Holy Spirit and the Theology of Life* (London: SCM Press, 1997), x, 1–9.
19. Moltmann, *The Crucified God*, 1, 273.

Written in 1991 in 'My Theological Career',[20] Moltmann gives an account of his theological work up to that point. He makes clear his approach to theology through one focal point, namely through the theme of hope, seeking a recovery of the eschatological in Christian theology, prompted by exegetical work and a reading of Ernst Bloch:[21]

> I began from the God who raised the executed Christ from the dead and made him Lord of the future of the world. Whereas Bloch restored to their place the social utopias in which 'the weary and heavy laden' were to be made happy, and then brought in the constitutional utopias according to which those who had been humiliated and had suffered hurt had to be given their human dignity, for me the hope 'for the resurrection of the dead and eternal life', and thus the expectation grounded in the biblical testimony to God, became important and was the foundation for accepting the social and constitutional utopias.[22]

Moltmann observes that the perspective of 'creative discipleship' proved to be the crucial element in the linking of 'historical liberation' and 'eschatological redemption'. That is, eschatology took on the realisation of eschatological hopes within history. Creative discipleship therefore acted in hope of God's future.[23] That is, eschatology now takes up the theme of transcendence as *future*. These directions involved, then, working out a *political theology*. He describes the links made with Johann Baptist Metz, and the Christian-Marxist Dialogue, Black theology with James Cone, the Latin American theology of Liberation with Gustavo Gutierrez and, beyond that, Korean Minyung theology.

Seeking a foundation for this political theology of hope took Moltmann to the cross as the 'foundation and criticism of Christian

---

20. Jürgen Moltmann, 'My Theological Career', in Jürgen Moltmann, *History and the Triune God: Contributions to Trinitarian theology* (London: SCM Press, 1991), 165–82.
21. Moltmann, 'My Theological Career', 168–9.
22. Moltmann, 'My Theological Career', 169.
23. Moltmann, 'My Theological Career', 170–1.

theology'.[24] This focus also involved a criticism of society. In *Umkehr zur Zukunft* (1970), he wrote:

> As well as working out a political theology I have resolved more strongly than ever to reflect on the significance of the cross of Christ for theology, church and society. In a culture which glorifies success and happiness and becomes blind to the suffering of others, the recollection that at the centre of Christian faith is an unsuccessful, suffering Christ, dying in shame, can open peoples' eyes to the truth. The recollection that God raised up a crucified man and made him the hope for the world can help the churches to dissolve their alliances with the powerful and enter into solidarity of the humiliated . . . [25]

## 3. The reality of the resurrection

> Christianity stands and falls with the reality of the raising of Jesus from the dead by God.[26]

The whole of Moltmann's work can be seen as an exposition of Christian hope grounded in the reality of the resurrection of the crucified Jesus. This is the presupposition of the New Testament. The reality of the resurrection is assumed by the earliest Christian proclamation.

> The confession to the person of Jesus as the Lord and the confession to the work of God who raised him from the dead belong inseparably together, although the two formulae do not coincide but mutually expound each other. A Christian faith that is not resurrection faith can therefore be called neither Christian nor faith.[27]

---

24. Moltmann, *The Crucified God.*
25. Quoted in: Moltmann, *History and the Triune God*, 171.
26. Moltmann, *Theology of Hope*, 165.
27. Moltmann, *Theology of Hope*, 166.

This is the clear statement of Moltmann's basic starting point. It is opposed to approaches which regard the resurrection as problematical, as for example Van E Harvey in *The Historian and the Believer*.[28] The reality of the resurrection of Jesus is the key to a recalling of his own history: 'It is the knowledge of the risen Lord that on which the memory of the life, work sufferings and death of Jesus is kept alive and presented in the gospels.'[29]Moreover, the reality of the risen Jesus also shapes the identity of the church and mission, and points to the future of the creation:

> It is the recognition of the risen Christ that gives rise to the Church's recognition of its own commission in the mission to the nations. It is the remembrance of his resurrection that is the ground of the inclusive hope in the universal future of Christ.[30]

Moltmann holds the reality of the resurrection to be the ground of the earliest Christian proclamation. He regards it is necessary to speak of this same reality in today's context. He takes the slogan 'God is dead' to be characteristic of modern society, not merely as a philosophical or theological statement but as that which 'seems to lie at the foundations of modern experience of self and the world' and beyond that, to 'provide the ground for the atheism that characterises the methods of science'.[31]

The affirmation of the resurrection's reality leads to a concentrated engagement with both Hegel and Nietzsche as those who have articulated the base conditions of the modern experience of the self without God. Moltmann carries out this analysis with a double intent of listening seriously to these voices and to seeking to inform and counter them with the expression of Christian hope.[32]

### 4. Confronting modernity

Moltmann understands that such a hope leads to a confrontation with modernity as the following will briefly show.

---

28. Van E Harvey, *The Historian and the Believer* (London: SCM, 1967).
29. Moltmann, *Theology of Hope*, 166.
30. Moltmann, *Theology of Hope*, 166.
31. Moltmann, *Theology of Hope*, 167.
32. Moltmann, *Theology of Hope*, 168–71.

## 4.1 'God is dead'

While Hegel and Nietzsche are taken as key figures of modernity's claim that God is dead, the 'death of God' leads Moltmann to the foundation of Christian theology itself: namely the crucifixion of Jesus of Nazareth.[33] The death of Jesus requires a fundamental rethinking of all theology—either it is the end of all theology or the beginning of a radically new Christian theology. Hope generated by his resurrection is the means that allows the church to look at the reality of this death. The death of Jesus on the cross places him in the company of suffering humanity. While this cross cannot be loved, neither can it be avoided.

In contrast to a theology that regards the resurrection as revealing or uncovering the reality of the cross, Moltmann argues that the resurrection introduces a new moment in the life of God and the creation. The shift from death to life is also the basis for hope for the future of history.

## 4.2 Historiography

Critical historiography is the product of modernity. As described by Ernst Troeltsch, the theory of continuity and analogy precludes the discontinuity implied by the resurrection. Moltmann's description of this takes up the benefits of historical work while understanding the ideological challenge. His primary concern is to make clear that basis upon which Christian faith lives in history, namely the reality of the resurrection of Jesus crucified. His approach holds to the dialectical relationship of the historical and the eschatological. Or, in other terms, Christian faith lives diachronically, as it remembers in hope the crucifixion and resurrection of Jesus, and as it looks forward in hope to the new creation on the basis of the remembrance of the resurrection of the crucified.

A clear result of the historical study that has taken place surrounding the death of Jesus points to the political character of his death. Crucifixion as a Roman punishment makes clear that the death of Jesus was a political event, carried out by the Romans. Historical research on the accounts of resurrection appearances challenge those

---

33. Moltmann, *The Crucified God*. The following sections draw from this key treatment, further developed in Jürgen Moltmann, *The Way of Jesus Christ: Christology in Messianic Dimensions* (London: SCM Press, 1990).

interpretations which treat resurrection faith as the 'rise of faith' in Jesus' followers. The collapse of the Jesus movement and his own god-abandonment was too profound to accept the 'rise of faith' explanation as an adequate explanation of the Easter faith. Rather, the rise of Easter faith has a substantial basis in a new encounter with Jesus who was crucified, and yet appears anew.

### 4.3 Modern theological eschatologies

The insistence on the reality of Jesus' resurrection leads equally to a challenging of previous eschatologies of transcendental subjectivity —whether human (Bultmann) or of God (Barth),[34] and to a direct critique of Pannenberg's notion of 'history' as indirect self-revelation of God.[35] Agreeing with the starting point taken by Pannenberg (with Rendtorff, *et al*) that 'history is that which happens between promise and fulfilment' Moltmann is critical of their departure into an eschatology which is expressed in cosmological terms of universal history.[36] The disagreement here is in the way the resurrection of Jesus is said to be historically verifiable, and is related to a general resurrection. Moreover, Moltmann engages critically with Pannenberg over the category of *apocalyptic*.[37]

To repeat, Moltmann is concerned to recover the category of both eschatology and history on the foundation of *the resurrection* of the crucified Jesus Christ. He applies this particularly as the criterion for an appreciation of the future.

### 4.4 Eschatology and apocalyptic

Moltmann, with Pannenberg—and against other forms of modern theology that had resolved the relationship of God, Jesus Christ and the world in transcendent terms—took up a renewed theological interest in the future.

Against Bultmann's present existentialist and subjectivist eschatology, and the end of history practiced in faith, Moltmann accepted positively Käsemann's observation that *apocalyptic is the mother of Christian theology*.[38]

---

34.  Moltmann, *Theology of Hope*, 45–69.
35.  Moltmann, *Theology of Hope*, 76–84.
36.  Moltmann, *Theology of Hope*, 78–9, 82.
37.  Moltmann, *Theology of Hope*, 84.
38.  See: Moltmann, *History and the Triune God*, 168.

However, by 'apocalyptic' he [Käsemann] did not mean the speculations about the events of the end of the world but the underlying question when God would really be God in his kingdom and when his righteousness would triumph in the world. But this question presupposes that this 'end of history' is still to come and is no way already present.[39]

Against realised eschatologies that had given up the future, Pannenberg and Moltmann insisted on the reality of the resurrection of Jesus for the sake of the future. However, Moltmann distinguishes his understanding of the future from Pannenberg's. He interprets Pannenberg as treating the resurrection of Jesus as the first of the general resurrection:

The important question for theology, however, is whether such an apocalyptic view of history—and moreover, one related to the general expectation of the dead—is adequate to embrace the Easter appearance of the risen Lord in the context of tradition and expectation in which it was perceived by the disciples . . . Certain as it is that that the Easter appearances of Jesus were experienced and proclaimed in the apocalyptic categories of the expectation of the general resurrection of the dead and as a beginning of the end of all history, it is nevertheless equally certain that the raising of Jesus was not merely conceived solely as the first instance of the final resurrection of the dead, but as the source of the risen life of all believers . . . The horizon of apocalyptic expectation is not by any means wide enough to embrace the post-Easter apocalyptic of the Church.[40]

While Hegelian categories lie behind the work of both Moltmann and Pannenberg, Moltmann criticises Pannenberg's adoption of the category of universal history which is resolved in terms of the 'whole of reality': 'The apocalyptic outlook which interprets the whole of

---

39. Moltmann, *Theology of Hope*, 168–9.
40. Moltmann, *Theology of Hope*, 83.

reality in terms of universal history is secondary compared with this world transforming outlook in terms of promise and missionary history.'[41]

Finally, and most critically, Moltmann judges that the cross has receded in Pannenberg's treatment of his resurrection:

> Finally from the theological standpoint it may be due to the one track character of the apocalyptic of universal history that the theological significance of the cross of Jesus recedes in favour of his resurrection. Between the expectations of late Jewish apocalyptic and of Christian eschatology stand the cross of Jesus. Hence all Christian resurrection eschatology bears the mark of an *escatologia crucis.* That is more than merely a break in the coherent historical tradition of apocalyptic expectations. The contradiction of the cross permeates also the whole existence, life and theological thinking of the Church in the world.[42]

### 4.5 Eschatology and the messianic mission

Moltmann's approach has increasingly emphasised the Jewishness of Christian hope. The recovery of an eschatological emphasis in his early work, *Theology of Hope,* owed much to *Old Testament* scholarship, particularly the 'promise-fulfilment' motif. *The Crucified God* took up the fruits of recent 'Jesus of history' scholarship while its categories were largely shaped by the formal Chalcedonian categories. Clearly the Jesus of this work is Jewish. The latter work, *The Way of Jesus Christ,* explores more intentionally the Jewishness of Jesus and the claims surrounding him:

> There is no such thing as a Christology without presuppositions; and its historical presupposition is the messianic promise of the Old Testament, and the Jewish hope which is founded on the Hebrew Bible. We can only truly and authentically understand Jesus if we perceive him and his history in the light of the Old Testament promises and the history of hope of

---

41.   Moltmann, *Theology of Hope,* 83.
42.   Moltmann, *Theology of Hope,* 83.

Israel today. What does Christology mean except messianology? . . . Finally, no Christian Christology must surrender the hope for the messiah. Christian Christology is a particular form of Israel's hope for the messiah, and it is still related to, and dependent on, the Jewish forms of the messianic hope that anteceded Christianity and runs parallel to it . . . The mission of Christianity is to be seen as the way in which Israel pervades the world of the Gentile nations with messianic hope for the coming God.[43]

The Jewishness of Jesus is therefore a constitutive element in Christian hope. The church's hope is firmly wedded to the hope of Israel for the nations. The resurrection of Jesus is tied to the God of Israel. That same God is the God of hope for a transformed creation. The church's confession of Jesus as messiah is therefore directly related to Jewish expectation of a messiah. At the same time the church must take seriously the Jewish 'no' to Jesus. This leads him to see a double-sided relationship to Jesus:

As *Israel's messiah* he becomes the *saviour to the Gentiles*. In Jesus, *Israel herself encounters the Gentiles* . . . On the other hand, *Jesus encounters Israel as the saviour of the nations*, believed and worshipped by the many from all peoples. In this form—not directly but indirectly—he reveals himself to Israel as her messiah.[44]

The implication of this approach is a 'fundamental revision of [the church's] theological tradition, for Jesus' sake'.[45]

## 5. Theological Politics

Theology that arises from the reality of the resurrection is political in character. That is, the political character of Christian theology arises from the character of the particular history of the resurrection of the crucified Jesus; not only is the crucifixion political in the sense that it was a Roman political execution, it is political in the *theological* sense

---

43. Moltmann, *The Way of Jesus Christ*, 1–3.
44. Moltmann, *The Way of Jesus Christ*, 36.
45. Moltmann, *The Way of Jesus Christ*, 37.

that the attribution of the term *Lord* to the crucified Jew challenges the claims to lordship made by the Roman Caesars; and more, the eschatological character of these events deal with the future of history and make claims for God. The God who raised the crucified Jew Jesus identifies him as Lord over other powers and authorities. Moreover, this same God, in this identification with the godless crucified one by raising him from the dead and giving him a future, challenges the ultimate power of death. Furthermore, the political character here is present historically in the form of an apostolate, who are formed as a community and live in expectation of the future coming of God's kingdom, promised in the resurrection of Jesus. That is to say, the church is a political form of life which gives expression now in hope to the coming reign of the risen Jesus Christ. Theology that takes its bearings from the risen Jesus who was crucified is therefore eschatological in character and is intentionally political.

The politics that are implied here requires of theology and church constant challenge and reformation. Christian theology engages critically with the received tradition and also with contemporary thought and society. That is necessary because the subject matter of theology is never contained within it, nor is it bounded by the church. Rather theology's horizon is the final transformed creation in the future of God as promised in the resurrection of Jesus crucified.

The criticism has been voiced that Moltmann's is merely 'armchair theology'. It is true that Moltmann has written his theology as a German Professor within German universities. He has certainly benefited from the particular relationship of state and church of post-war West Germany. Is it fair to characterise this as an armchair theology?

His autobiography demonstrates that the beginning of his work arose from the experience of prisoner of war camps. His account of the development of 'political theology' in western and eastern Europe has involved him in dialogues and activities that move him out of an armchair. Equally, his relationship to 'liberation theology' in Latin America and South Korea demonstrate that it has been a very mobile armchair! Finally, the primary concern in this theology has been for the church's faithfulness. This included a significant role in the ecumenical movement. It drew from him theological writings on justice and peace and ecology.

Moltmann's work does fit within the German academic framework. However, his work demonstrates a wider interest. His theological work is undertaken in order to prompt the church to greater faithfulness. He also engaged with issues of moment including the student rebellion, feminist analysis and the ecological crisis.

Moltmann is a church theologian who writes with hope for the whole creation. His clear understanding of the role of the church as an *apostolate of hope* clarifies the church's own distinctive *politics*. At the same time, hope in the resurrection and the transforming of the whole creation challenges the church to live for *the coming of God* in the creation. Programmatically this does not reduce the task to mere 'politics'. It does, however, imply that the church seeks conversation and partnership with those who are politically engaged and, prompted by hope, seek a transforming of the creation. The church will not seek an accommodation with the culture, and will therefore engage critically. Equally, the confession of hope will prevent the church from withdrawing into itself and will prompt it to speak and act 'therapeutically' for transformation, in the hope of the coming kingdom of God, grounded on the resurrection of the one crucified Jewish man, Jesus.

# 13

# The Horizon of the Future in the Theology of Wolfhart Pannenberg

## Christiaan Mostert

No theologian in the twentieth century has been more preoccupied with the idea of the future than Wolfhart Pannenberg. He is often mentioned in the same breath as Jürgen Moltmann, the theologian of hope,[1] but for Pannenberg hope presses the question of the nature of the future and the future reality of the one in whom hope is placed. Pannenberg was struck by the 'priority of the eschatological future' in Jesus' understanding of the reign of God, so much so that the future, rather than the past, should be seen as 'determining' the present. This demands a reversal in our ontological conceptions.[2] Working out the extent of such a reversal, in particular its implications for understanding time, was one of Pannenberg's major intellectual preoccupations.

Gerhard Sauter, a third prominent German 'eschatological theologian',[3] distinguishes three types of eschatology that made an

---

1. Jürgen Moltmann, *Theology of Hope: On the Ground and Implications of a Christian Eschatology* (London: SCM Press, 1967). The two are almost exact contemporaries. See Christiaan Mostert, *God and the Future: Wolfhart Pan-nenberg's Eschatological Doctrine of God* (London: T&T Clark, 2002), 4f. For Pannenberg's thought on hope see: Wolfhart Pannenberg, 'The God of Hope', in *Basic Questions in Theology*, Volume 2, (Philadelphia: Westminster Press, 1971 & 1983), 234–49, and Wolfhart Pannenberg, *Systematic Theology*, Volume 3 (Grand Rapids: Eerdmans; Edinburgh: T & T Clark, 1998), 173–81.
2. Wolfhart Pannenberg, *Theology and the Kingdom of God*, edited by RJ Neuhaus (Philadelphia: Westminster Press, 1969), 54.
3. See especially Gerhard Sauter, *Eschatological Rationality: Theological Issues in Focus* (Grand Rapids: Baker Books, 1996) and Gerhard Sauter,

impact on Protestant theology in the twentieth century: firstly, the *consistent* eschatology which challenged an optimistic theology of progress and a bourgeois view of Jesus in the early years of the century; secondly, the *radical* eschatology of the period after World War I, when Barth and Bultmann in their different ways turned eschatology into a radical openness to God in the *present* time, God being the 'totally other' who speaks a liberating, redemptive word into the world of human reality; and thirdly, the eschatological *theology of history*, which appeared in Germany and later in North America in the 1960s; the leading figures here were Moltmann and Pannenberg.[4]

These theologians have written about the *eschata*, the 'last things' that Christians hope for, but their concern was fundamentally with the idea of history, understood as a unified, though infinitely differentiated reality. Pannenberg suggests that God is made known in history indirectly through historical events; God is finally and unambiguously revealed only at the end of history, when the whole creation is consummated in the kingdom of God.[5] Indeed,

> History is the most comprehensive horizon of Christian theology. All theological questions and answers are meaningful only within the framework of the history which God has with humanity and through humanity with his whole creation—the history moving toward a future still hidden from the world but already revealed in Jesus Christ.[6]

It is presupposed that 'history'—we cannot speak only of particular 'histories'—has its reality only in relation to God. God has a *telos* in view for it; we can know the direction of this intentionality and are called to align ourselves with it. Pannenberg's basic *ontological* intuition is that there is a positive (though also a negative) relation between present and future reality; the present is an 'anticipation' of the future.

*What Dare We Hope? Reconsidering Eschatology* (Harrisburg: Trinity Press International, 1999).

4.   Sauter, *What Dare We Hope?* 25.
5.   Wolfhart Pannenberg, *Revelation as History* (London: Macmillan, 1968), 123–58, especially 125–35.
6.   Wolfhart Pannenberg, 'Redemptive Event and History', in *Basic Questions in Theology*, Volume 1 (Philadelphia: Westminster Press, 1970 & 1983), 15.

The basic *theological* conviction is that God's being includes God's rule over all things; God cannot be God unless God's reign over the cosmos comes in its fulness.[7] For Moltmann, the critical problem is the reality of human suffering, and the basic ontological intuition is that the present is negatively related to the future that is promised by God. This turns the theology of hope into a political theology, with an iconoclastic attitude to political power and a strong solidarity with the poor and the marginalised. The fundamental theological conviction is that, against all present reality, God promises a new creation, which God will also bring about.

Pannenberg does not accept the adequacy of the treatment of eschatology by Barth and Bultmann; neither is sufficiently historical. Bultmann, for example, relocated the eschatological moment to the present and transposed eschatological categories into existential ones. However, in Pannenberg's view, the disclosure of possibilities of existence in the present is no substitute for a properly futural eschatology. Such an eschatology loses 'its specific temporal structure, its tension relative to the future consummation'.[8] As Moltmann expresses it, 'entering into God's coming future makes possible a new human becoming'.[9] Pannenberg argues that Christianity requires a robust and far-reaching eschatology,[10] and does so for two kinds of reason: historical/exegetical and soteriological.

First, it is not possible to understand the New Testament without a thoroughly temporal eschatology. The events in which the Christian faith is grounded, together with the background ideas from which they cannot be severed, cannot be understood in a non-eschatological way. The idea of the kingdom of God, which was at the centre of Jesus' ministry, was understood in an eschatological way. The reign of God

---

7. See: '. . . God's being and existence cannot be conceived apart from his rule. Or, to put it in the language of the philosophy of religion, the being of the gods is their power. To believe in one God means to believe that one power dominates all,' in Pannenberg, *Theology and the Kingdom of God*, 55. The concepts of power and rule should also be transposed into the terms of love.

8. Pannenberg, *Systematic Theology*, Volume 3, 537.

9. Moltmann, *The Coming of God*, 24. See also Mostert, *God and the Future*, 19–25.

10. Wolfhart Pannenberg, 'Can Christianity Do without an Eschatology?', in *The Christian Hope*, edited by CB Caird and others (London: SPCK, 1970), 25–34.

was essentially a future reality, which, because of its nearness, had an impact on people in the present. Even more strikingly, without an eschatological frame of reference, little sense can be made of the resurrection of Jesus, the *sine qua non* of Christian faith. Its proper understanding hinges on Jewish apocalyptic thought. Second, Christianity makes claims about salvation in a world that offers very ambiguous evidence of being saved. Jewish critics of Christian faith have long argued that if Jesus were the Messiah, the world would look more redeemed. Seen in an eschatological perspective, however, the matter looks different:

> . . . The decisive reason why Christianity cannot do without an eschatology is that the reconciliation of the world, the presence of God, and his kingdom through Christ, have taken place only in the form of an anticipation of a future which in its fullness has not yet materialised. Therefore, the belief in the reconciliation of the world in Christ is itself based upon eschatology while at the same time it corroborates the Christian trust and hope in the future of God.[11]

Only the full manifestation of God's reconciling and salvific action in the future can settle the question of the reality or unreality of God.

These two reasons for a strongly eschatological theology are supported by several others. First, the being of God itself requires an eschatological unfolding. The idea of God and the coming reign of God are inseparable. The God of Christian understanding is not a non-temporal being, inhabiting a timeless eternity, but has 'futurity as a quality of being'. The future of God's reign is not incidental to God's being.[12] Only by demonstrating the reality of God's reign over all things can the biblical God be God. Second, eschatology has a critical function in relation to the hopes of a secular age to create the kind of world to which it aspires. Whilst the 'other-worldly' aspect of Christian faith has been the subject of serious criticism, in many respects *this* world does not 'deliver the goods'. In Pannenberg's view, eschatology:

---

11.  Pannenberg, 'Can Christianity Do without an Eschatology?', 30.
12.  Pannenberg, 'The God of Hope', 242.

uncovers the limitations of any purely secular view of personal life as well as of the social and cultural system. Eschatology exposes secular man's illusions about the possibilities of self-realisation in this world, and therefore eschatology is at the heart of a Christian realism in appraising the conditions of human existence in the present world.[13]

Pannenberg's commitment to a thoroughgoing eschatology includes a serious engagement with the strange world of apocalyptic thought, which is otherwise easily dismissed, demythologised or used simply as a metaphor for the cataclysm of a nuclear inferno. The term 'apocalyptic' means several different things. It is, first, a particular genre of literature, to which several books in the Christian Bible belong, but most of which comes from the inter-testamental period.[14] It also refers to religious ideas about God's 'plan' for world events. It also denotes a symbolic world characterised by 'the esoteric, the bizarre and the arcane'.[15] However, Pannenberg believes that in the apocalyptic character of the ministry and destiny of Jesus, notably its anticipatory structure, there is a key to solving some problems in contemporary thought.

In the 1960s Ernst Käsemann, made the now famous remark that apocalyptic was 'the mother of all Christian theology'.[16] If Jesus himself were not influenced by the world of apocalyptic, the discontinuity between Jesus and both John the Baptist and the early church, each shaped by apocalyptic, would require explanation. Pannenberg argues that Jesus' message can be understood only 'within

---

13.  Pannenberg, 'Constructive and Critical Functions of Christian Eschatology', in *Harvard Theological Review* 77/2 (1984): 124.
14.  The books of Daniel (Old Testament) and Revelation, sometimes called the Apocalypse, (New Testament) are examples from the Bible. The core of the genre includes writings such as: 1 Enoch, 4 Ezra, 2 Baruch, the Apocalypse of Abraham, 3 Baruch, 2 Enoch and the Apocalypse of Zephaniah.
15.  Paul D Hanson, 'Apocalypticism', in *The Interpreter's Dictionary of the Bible*, Supplementary Volume (Nashville: Abingdon Press, 1976), 28–34.
16.  Ernst Käsemann, 'The Beginnings of Christian Theology', *Apocalypticism, Journal for Theology and the Church*, 6 (1969): 40.

the horizon of apocalyptic expectations',[17] which is not to say that Jesus was simply an apocalyptic preacher. A more differentiated judgment is required:

> The apocalyptic broadening and transformation of the prophetic expectation for the future into the hope for God's lordship at the coming judgment of the living and the dead is everywhere presupposed by Jesus. Thus Jesus would have been closer to being an apocalyptic than a prophet in the old sense. But he also was not an apocalyptic . . . Jesus certainly thought in apocalyptic categories. But he wrote no apocalypse; rather, he proclaimed the immediate nearness of that which the apocalyptics described as the end of the course of history and called his people to repentance in view of the imminent end.[18]

Jesus' preaching of the coming of God's kingdom was apocalyptic in tone, rather than rabbinic. But he gave no detailed description of the heavenly realm. Most significantly, he announced the kingdom of God as imminent, and he complemented the theme of judgment by an emphasis on the kingdom's coming as good news. Radically and controversially, he not only called people to repent, but 'with full authority he granted to [those] he met the salvation expected in the future',[19] certain that in his activity the salvation expected in the future had broken into the present.' Pannenberg finds here a basis for his idea of the priority of the future:

> In the ministry of Jesus the futurity of the Reign of God became a power determining the present . . . Obedience to God . . . became turning to the future of the Reign of God. But wherever that occurs, there God already reigns unconditionally in the present, and such presence of the Reign of God does not conflict with its

---

17.  Wolfhart Pannenberg, *Jesus—God and Man* (London: SCM Press, 1968), 32.
18.  Pannenberg, *Jesus—God and Man*, 217.
19.  Pannenberg, *Jesus—God and Man*, 217.

futurity but is derived from it and is itself only the anticipatory glimmer of its coming.[20]

Something similar must be said in respect of the resurrection of Jesus, the other foundational element in Pannenberg's theology. The resurrection of the dead was part of apocalyptic eschatology, and no satisfactory sense can be made of the resurrection of Jesus apart from this frame of reference. It is only through the resurrection that Jesus is confirmed as the one in whom God is definitively and finally revealed. This is basic for Christian doctrine:

> Only at the end of all events can God be revealed in his divinity, that is, as the one who works all things, who has power over everything. Only because in Jesus' resurrection the end of all things, which for us has not yet happened, has already occurred can it be said of Jesus that the ultimate already is present in him, and so also that God himself, his glory, has made its appearance in Jesus in a way that cannot be surpassed. Only because the end of the world is already present in Jesus' resurrection is God himself revealed in him.[21]

The material identity between the resurrection of Jesus and what apocalyptic thought expected from the ultimate future, the general resurrection of the dead, is fundamental. To establish this identity, Pannenberg appeals to the concept of prolepsis; the resurrection of Jesus has a proleptic character. Jesus' resurrection is an event in history and an anticipation, a proleptic occurrence of the future resurrection of the dead, which will establish the reign of God over all things. If the latter were never to occur, the claim that Jesus was raised from the dead would collapse. However, if and when this eschatological promise is actualised at the end of history, the resurrection of Jesus as its proleptic occurrence within history will be confirmed. Of course, the plausibility of the (apocalyptic) idea of resurrection is decisive. Not every detail of the apocalyptic conceptual world can be binding today,

---

20. Pannenberg, 'Appearance as the Arrival of the Future', in *Theology and the Kingdom of God,* 133.
21. Pannenberg, *Jesus—God and Man,* 69. See also Pannenberg, 'Postscript', in *Revelation as History,* 2nd edition, 193ff.

but its fundamental convictions, including the resurrection of the dead in connection with the end of the world, can be plausibly argued, in Pannenberg's view. If it is rejected, Christian faith cannot be an option, and 'Christology becomes mythology'.

It is clear that Pannenberg regards close attention to the conceptual world of apocalyptic as essential for Christian theology; it provides an irreplaceable foundation for Christian theology. What is disclosed in the person of Christ is materially connected with the resurrection of the dead, the final self-disclosure of God and the establishment of God's reign over all things. Pannenberg also finds support in apocalyptic thought for his concept of universal history. It corresponds to the fact that there is one God, creator, redeemer and perfecter of all things, and that the divine 'economy' of salvation embraces the entire history of the world. If a universal history cannot be written, for the theologian the idea of a 'whole' of history is a hermeneutic necessity; God acts in relation to all things. History, says Pannenberg, 'has a unity only in the form of a divine history'.[22] Current preoccupation is mostly with the particular and the local, but the communities among whom apocalyptic ideas flourished—communities that knew suffering and feared being lost in a world under the control of hostile powers—found comfort in the idea of a single history over which God was Lord.

We now consider how Pannenberg applies some key ideas learnt from the New Testament to the area of philosophy. By philosophy he has in mind primarily ontology, concerned not with particular things but with things in general, and with what might be hypothesised about 'reality as a whole'.[23] There is a long history of cross-fertilisation between theology and philosophy. If theology understands its concern to be 'God and everything that exists' (from the point of view of its relation to God), there can in principle be no limit to the range of its concerns, including the areas of interest to philosophers. Speaking of 'the eschatological logic of the history of Jesus of Nazareth', Pannenberg speculates that this might require 'a revision of current philosophical presuppositions', particularly along the lines of an

---

22. Wolfhart Pannenberg, 'Toward a Theology of Law', in *Anglican Theological Review* 55 (October 1973): 404.
23. See Wolfhart Pannenberg, *Theology and the Philosophy of Science* (Philadelphia: Westminster Press, 1976), 68ff.

'eschatological ontology'.[24] If persuasive, this would be a contribution of Christian theology to the understanding of reality as a whole.

It is not easy to know what to do with the idea of 'reality as a whole'. Pannenberg thinks it is feasible to attempt the quest for anticipatory hypotheses of the nature and meaning of the total context of our experience.[25] If religions are integrating systems of meaning, theology, as systematic reflection on the content of a particular system of meaning, will seek to articulate this content in the most comprehensive terms possible. Any 'semantic whole', whether a sentence or a system of meaning, has a context which transcends it. 'Every specialised meaning depends on a final, all-embracing totality of meaning in which all individual meanings are linked to form a semantic whole'.[26] To bring to expression such an 'all-embracing totality of meaning' may not be attractive to philosophers, but Christian theology, with its affirmation of a God with whom everything begins and ends, must at some point attempt it, acutely aware of the provisionality of any such attempt. Pannenberg states:

> Any metaphysics, if it is to be taken seriously, can no longer claim the character of a definitive foundation, constructed of concepts, for being and knowledge. Metaphysical reflection must instead take on the form of a *conjectural reconstruction* in relation to its object, one which distinguishes itself from its intended truth while at the same time construing itself as a preliminary form of this truth. Its characteristic reflective form will thus have to be more that of anticipation than that of concept in the sense of classical metaphysics.[27]

To speak about 'reality as a whole' is not to imply that it can be other than conjectural or that it is available to us. But neither is it reducible to what exists here and now. As Heidegger reminds us, being cannot be considered apart from time; reality as a whole must be

---

24. Pannenberg, 'Afterword', in *Jesus—God and Man,* 2nd edition, 410.
25. Pannenberg, *Theology and the Philosophy of Science,* 69.
26. Pannenberg, *Theology and the Philosophy of Science,* 216.
27. Wolfhart Pannenberg, *Metaphysics and the Idea of God* (Grand Rapids: Eerdmans, 1990), 93.

understood temporally. It includes what is hidden in the future, as well as what is no longer remembered (by us) in the past. In biblical thought, broadly speaking, the future is open and God brings about new things. In the New Testament, hope is directed toward the coming of God's kingdom in its fulness, and the new life, which the reign of God will bring, is already present. What humankind yearns for will come from the future as the gift of God. What we experience in the present has its meaning from this future.

If the future is the source of the completion of things and the determinant of what they essentially are, how is their present reality—and their past—to be understood? Developing the concept of anticipation from its original theological context, Pannenberg sees everything that exists as the anticipation of its future. 'In the course of time, as long as something is, its end remains before it; still, it is what it is in anticipation of its end and from its end'.[28] Something essentially future has broken into history and is present, but the truth of the anticipation depends on the future that is not yet present. Thus the anticipation of something is always ambiguous and always requires future confirmation. Pannenberg makes both a noetic and an ontological point. Obviously, we cannot know the essence of something until it is fully disclosed in the future. But the main point is that the essence of something or someone is not determined until its end. Yet by anticipation it already possesses its essence. Things are constituted retroactively from their end;[29] and it involves a process of becoming and anticipation. 'Things [are] what they are, substances, retroactively from the outcome of their becoming on the one hand, and on the other in the sense of anticipating the completion of their process of becoming, their history.'[30]

We customarily think very differently about causality: what things are is the outcome of their antecedents. Pannenberg's ideas are, to say the least, counter-intuitive. (Some critics have seen here more than a hint of determinism, which he strongly denies.[31]) The example of human persons may help. On Pannenberg's view, what a person essentially is remains open; it is not something unchanging through time. Only when people's lives are over is their real being, their true

---

28.  Pannenberg, *Metaphysics and the Idea of God*, 88.
29.  Pannenberg, *Metaphysics and the Idea of God*, 107.
30.  Pannenberg, *Metaphysics and the Idea of God*, 107.
31.  Mostert, *God and the Future*, 175–82.

identity, established ('determined', in non-determinist sense). The point is ontological, not merely cognitive. In fact, few people consistently hold the alternative view, that the essence of a person is determined by genetic factors and antecedent experience alone. On Pannenberg's ontology of personal identity, what people are is established retroactively from the outcome of their becoming; on the other hand, it is already theirs by anticipation.

The concept of anticipation has a long history.[32] Its use outside theology is not confined to ontology, but extends into the discussion of truth, concepts, cognition and language. There is no concept or statement that cannot be regarded as having an anticipatory structure.[33] The relation between concepts and statements and what they name or express is anticipatory. Pannenberg asks, 'could it be that the anticipatory form of knowledge corresponds to an element of the "not yet" within the very reality toward which knowing is directed?'[34] Pannenberg has shown that a concept which is a correlate of 'future' and 'eschatology' has potentially radical implications for ontology.

The immediately preceding discussion has necessarily been abstract. We turn now to the subject of redemption. That Christianity is a redemptive religion was expressed classically by Schleiermacher in 1830.[35] *Redemption* is generally used to denote a situation of liberation or profound transformation; it is implied that such redemption will be observable. Since the world is neither liberated nor transformed from much that is wrong, it is difficult to claim that the world has been redeemed. It follows that there is no 'redeemer' to whom any purported redemption is attributable. This is the standard criticism of Christianity.

However, Christian faith does know a Redeemer and it speaks of a redemptive event, the cross, and of its redemptive effect. *Redemption*

---

32. See L Kugelmann, *Antizipation: Eine begriffsgeschichtliche Untersuchung* (Göt-tingen: Vandenhoeck & Ruprecht, 1986).

33. See Pannenberg, 'Concept and Anticipation', in *Metaphysics and the Idea of God*, chapter 5.

34. Pannenberg, *Metaphysics and the Idea of God*, 104.

35. 'Christianity is a monotheistic faith, belonging to the teleological type of religion, and is essentially distinguished from other such faiths by the fact that in it everything is related to the redemption accomplished by Jesus of Nazareth.' See: Schleiermacher, *The Christian Faith*, 2nd edition, edited by HR Mackintosh and JS Stewart (Edinburgh: T&T Clark, 1928), §11, 52.

comes from the world of commerce and exchange. Having lost or sold something, one might buy it back. In a Christian context the term is used metaphorically. 'It is because of the manifold ways in which humans have felt themselves to be confined, oppressed, threatened, doomed that the prospect of *redemption* has captured the human imagination.'[36] It is not surprising that such a metaphor is used to express the effect on humankind of Jesus' death.

In the company of Jesus people experienced a liberation or transformation; they might well have described it as a redemption. After Jesus' death and resurrection, this term was certainly used, among others, to describe a radically new kind of existence (Romans 3:24; Ephesians 1:7; Hebrews 9:12, 15), effected by Christ. Like the reign of God in the life of Jesus, the reality of redemption through Christ is present in a paradoxical, anticipatory way: there is an *already* and a *not yet*. The power of the (future) reign of God is already operative. Pannenberg describes its presence as 'the overpowering by God's future of all merely present occupations and concerns'.[37] The reality of redemption is, in part, evident in people's daily lives and relationships; sometimes it is obvious, sometimes not.

Even in the church, which confesses Christ as redeemer, redemption is evident obliquely rather than directly. Its experience of redemption has the same anticipatory structure that marks the nature of human being in general. The church lives by the story of its redemption in Christ, but experiences it partly in fact and partly in hope.[38] The church may never equate itself with the reign of God; it is at best an anticipatory sign of it. At best it is an anticipatory sign of the redemption that is promised eschatologically. Its life exhibits ambiguous signs of its redemption, a redemption experienced proleptically. The New Testament sees salvation as both present reality and future hope.[39] The church dare not claim to be the 'redeemed community'. It must overcome the barriers of its own ambiguous existence, as it claims that its life is an anticipation of the eschatological

---

36. FW Dillistone, 'Redemption', in *A New Dictionary of Christian Theology*, edited by A Richardson and J Bowden (London: SCM Press, 1983), 487.

37. Pannenberg, *Jesus—God and Man*, 366.

38. St Paul speaks of being saved 'in hope' (Romans 8:24).

39. Only in the Gospel of John and the letter to the Colossians is the hope of redemption understood as essentially realised.

reign of God. These barriers, as events in every time and place amply demonstrate, are very high.

In Pannenberg's three volumes of *Systematic Theology*, the breadth of Christian doctrine is articulated in explicitly trinitarian forms. This includes the discussion of the 'last things' (the *eschata*) for which Christians hope, as well as the experience of redemption in the world. As creation is the act of the triune God, so is the world's 'reconciliation', a term used especially in Protestant theology for the reality of salvation. Though etymologically distinct, 'salvation', 'redemption' and 'reconciliation' denote the same reality. Pannenberg emphasises three things in his discussion of reconciliation (redemption). First, the subject of reconciliation is God, not human-kind. It is God who reconciles the world to Godself; it is not human-kind which must effect its reconciliation to God. The death of the Son is God's reconciling act, though through the agency of human decisions and actions, and it opens the possibility for humankind to enter into this new reconciled status. Second, to speak in these terms is already to begin a trinitarian transposition. In the classical termin-ology, it is the Father who sends the Son into the world to save (redeem) it. The Father 'gives him up' for the sake of this act (Romans 8:32), though it has a correlate in the Son's giving himself to this task (John 10:18). The Spirit completes the work of redemption (reconciliation) by effecting it among and within us.

> How can others share in the reconciliation that was achieved in exemplary fashion by the incarnation and death of the Son in Jesus Christ? They can do so only as they are taken up into fellowship with the Father of the Son who became man in Jesus Christ . . . This taking up is not merely in the sense of something that happens to them from outside but as a liberation to their own identity, though not in their own power. This takes place through the Spirit. Through the Spirit reconciliation with God no longer comes upon us solely from outside. We ourselves enter into it.[40]

---

40. Pannenberg, *Systematic Theology*, Volume 2 (Grand Rapids: Eerdmans & Edinburgh: T&T Clark, 1994), 450.

Third, redemption is *already* a reality in the event in which it has its ground, the death of Jesus, but it has *yet* to reach its goal through the proclamation of the Gospel and in those who have yet to hear it. In this proclamation—in verbal and silent witness—the redemptive reign of God still breaks into the present and the Spirit still takes people into the fellowship of the triune God.

Is the world then redeemed? The answer is both *yes* and *no*. The reign of God has not come in its fullness. The world is still in bondage to the 'powers', however identified. The justice and peace of the messianic age have not come, though in acts of justice and peacemaking they are proleptically present in the world. The reign of God *has* come, for which the church gives thanks; and it is *yet* to come, for which the church continually prays. The redemption of the world, though begun in Christ and taking people into itself through the Spirit, is not unmistakeably visible. The church is called to conform its own life to the gift of redemption it has received and to work for the feeding of the hungry and the care of the needy, by which the reign of God makes itself present in the world.

The Christian claim of redemption (reconciliation) remains unconvincing in a world that looks unredeemed, unless it is understood in an eschatological sense. This is not to say that nothing redemptive has happened. For Pannenberg, the terms 'eschatology' and 'anticipation' belong together. They relate the hoped-for future to the present and see the present as a proleptic appearance of that future. The announced redemption is *already* a reality, in anticipatory form; it is *not yet* a completed reality. This eschatological tension is at the heart of Christian faith. As part of his eschatological theology, Pannenberg is drawn to some features of apocalyptic, notably its sense that the future is already real, though hidden. While the modern world sees in apocalyptic's dramatic visions only a metaphor for its own fears about the future, Pannenberg explores its sense of the power of the future, believing it to fund new ways of thinking about many things. The concept of anticipation, of ancient provenance, is especially fruitful in this endeavour. By means of it, the idea of *redemption* in a conspicuously *unredeemed* world is delivered from relegation to the realm of wishful thinking and remains a matter of hope-generating promise.

# 14

# God as Absolute Future: Karl Rahner in Relation to Messianism, Apocalyptic and Redemption

## Denis Edwards

Karl Rahner (1904–84) was trained in the classical theology of Thomas Aquinas, but he appropriates Aquinas with fresh eyes. His perspective is informed by Kant and Hegel and influenced by Heidegger, whose seminars he attended. Rahner builds on the work of Joseph Maréchal, a Belgian theologian similarly concerned with philosophy, to develop a way of doing theology that begins with the openness of the human subject. He understands this transcendental openness in the light of the Christian tradition, which he encapsulates in the idea of God's self-communication.

The words 'messianism', 'apocalyptic' and 'redemption' are not key terms in Rahner's work. In this chapter it will be argued, that while messianism is not a developed or an explicit theme, it is implicit in Rahner's concept of God as absolute future. Rahner tends to use the word 'salvation' far more frequently than the word 'redemption'. He understands salvation as God's saving, forgiving self-bestowal. This self-bestowal is given in grace, finds its radical and irreversible expression in history through the Christ-event, and attains fulfilment in the transformation of all things in Christ, in the coming of God as absolute future. Rahner uses the word 'apocalyptic' in a critical and negative way and supports a non-apocalyptic approach to eschatology.

In his *Theological Investigations* Volume 4, Rahner published an influential essay on the hermeneutics of eschatological statements,[1] the

---

1.    Karl Rahner, 'The Hermeneutics of Eschatological Assertions', in Karl Rahner, *Theological Investigations*, Volume 4 (New York: Seabury Press, 1966), 323–46.

key ideas of which are restated in his *Foundations of Christian Faith*.[2] He notes that Christians have always interpreted biblical claims about the future and, to some extent, these interpretations have always been guided by hermeneutical principles. But today there is a new context that demands a more systematic hermeneutics, a context formed by scientific cosmology on the one hand and the Bultmannian controversy about 'demythologisation' of biblical statements on the other. This means there is a need to articulate clear theological principles for interpreting the eschatological statements of the Bible and the Christian tradition.

Rahner's proposal can be summarised in the form of six principles.[3] The first is a general one: *A Christian understanding of existence includes an eschatology that really does bear on the future.* It points to what is still to come. It cannot be interpreted simply in an existential sense, as something that bears only on the present. Rahner thus stands opposed to Bultmann's radical existential interpretation and to any exclusive emphasis on realised eschatology. He sees any programme that de-eschatologises the biblical approach as contrary to the self-understanding of the Bible and the professed faith of the church.

Rahner's second thesis is also of a general nature. It asserts that *while in principle God is unrestricted in what God can reveal, we need to take into account restrictions that emerge in the history of salvation*. Rahner has no intention of placing metaphysical limits on God or of claiming knowledge of what it is possible for God to reveal in the abstract. His argument is that limitations actually emerge from the concrete history of revelation. Revelation itself determines how eschatological statements are to be read. Some readings are clearly unfaithful to biblical revelation. A person, for example, who simply puts biblical statements about the future together into a mosaic, and then understands this in a literal way as if the future of God can be imagined in a way that echoes our present, misses the biblical message. This de-eschatologises the human person and the future no longer

---

2.   Karl Rahner, *Foundations of Christian Faith* (New York: Seabury Press, 1978), 431–47.

3.   This summary attempts to clarify the expression of these principles while remaining faithful to Rahner's thought. Rahner introduces material related to thesis 4 in his thesis 3b. This has been avoided for the sake of clarity and for similar reasons one of his more general theses (number 6 in his list) has been omitted.

impacts on the present. Rahner notes that many misread biblical assertions in this way.

In a third thesis, Rahner proposes the first of two inter-related limiting statements that can guide interpretation of eschatological statements: *The future of our world in God remains radically hidden to us.* Scripture makes it clear that God has not revealed when the end will come (Mark 13: 32). Rahner insists that it is not simply the timing of the end that is hidden. Hiddenness is essential and proper to the end. The future has been announced and promised, but it is announced and promised precisely as hidden mystery. It is nothing else than the closeness of the incomprehensible God. Revelation is not the bringing of what was unknown into the region of what is known, clear and manageable, but 'the dawn and the approach of mystery as such'.[4] It is of the essence of the eschatological for it to be hidden in its revelation. This provides a criterion for Rahner for distinguishing between genuine eschatological utterances and what he calls apocalyptic ones:

> It may therefore be said that whenever we have a prediction which presents its contents as the anticipated report of the spectator of a future event—a report of an event in human history which of itself excludes the character of *absolute* mystery and hence deprives the eschatological event of its hidden-ness—then a false apocalyptic is at work, or a genuine eschatological assertion has been misunderstood as a piece of apocalyptic because of its apocalyptic style and content.[5]

Rahner uses the word apocalyptic in a particular way to describe the attitude that we already know in an eyewitness way what will happen in the future. In his view, a genuine eschatological stance will recognise that God's future is shrouded in the absolute mystery of God. This thesis, focused on divine incomprehensibility, is dia-lectically interrelated with the next thesis, focused on the nature of the human.

The fourth thesis is concerned with the historicity of the human: *The historicity of the human person means that the future is an inner moment*

---

4.    Rahner, 'The Hermeneutics of Eschatological Assertions', 330.
5.    Rahner, 'The Hermeneutics of Eschatological Assertions', 330.

*of the present*. Rahner argues that both 'anamnesis' and 'prognosis' are fundamental to the human. It is part of the human condition to exist from the past and to be referred to a future. The future is an inner moment of the human being. Knowledge of the future is part of our self-understanding in the present, and grows out of it. This suggests to Rahner that all genuine knowledge of the future is knowledge of the eschatological present. It is not a supplement to what is known in the present, but intrinsic to it. For the Christian, who views the future as God's self-bestowal, the future is truly unknown and uncontrollable. The future, then, is not only an inner moment of the present, but also the presence of a future that is uncontrollable and incomprehensible. This means that 'the eschatological future remains uncontrollable and hidden yet also present, something we really look forward to, something in the present of which we hope, dare, trust, and surrender ourselves.'[6] The future will be the fulfilment of the salvation in Christ that is already given.

The fifth thesis is that *genuine eschatology is to be understood as the fulfilment of God's self-communication in Christ and in grace*. Our knowledge of this future is limited to what can be derived from what we experience in Christ and from what we can see as its fulfilment. We do not have supplementary knowledge of the eschatological future over and above what we have in the theology of Christ and of grace, but simply the transposition of these to their fulfilment. This excludes both the apocalyptic interpretation of some Christian sects and a totally existential demythologising. In Rahner's proposal, 'biblical eschatology must always be read as an assertion based on the revealed present and pointing towards the genuine future, but not an assertion pointing back from an anticipated future into the present'.[7] To extrapolate from the present into the future is eschatology. To extrapolate from the future into the present is false apocalyptic. This kind of false apocalyptic is either fantasy or Gnosticism. True eschatology is the fulfilment promised in God's self-communication in Word and in Spirit.

The fundamental claim that genuine eschatological statements are a transposition into the future of something experienced in the present

---

6.  William M Thompson, 'The Hope for Humanity: Rahner's Eschatology', in *A World of Grace: An Introduction to the Themes and Foundations of Karl Rahner's Theology*, edited by Leo J O'Donovan (New York: Seabury Press, 1980), 158.

7.  Rahner 'The Hermeneutics of Eschatological Assertions', 337.

as grace, provides the foundation for a sixth principle: *It provides a criterion that enables us to distinguish between the form and the content of eschatological assertions*. Rahner acknowledges that we are inescapably tied to our imaginations and that images are always important in expressing religious ideas. What is fundamental is not to mistake the images for the reality. The image might be Paul's angelic trumpet or Matthew's sheep and goats. But the reality to which the images point is based upon the experience of the grace of Christ already at work in us and drawing us into a future in God.

These six principles determine Rahner's approach to eschatological claims. They clarify his view of a false apocalyptic that would seek to give a detailed picture of the future in God. For Rahner this future remains uncontrollable and incomprehensible precisely because it is the approach of God. These hermeneutical principles provide a basis for exploring Rahner's concept of God as the *absolute future*. He articulates this concept in articles that compare the Christian concept of the future to a Marxist utopian vision and to the predictions of futurologists.[8] Rahner makes a clear distinction between the *absolute* future and what he calls *this-worldly* futures. He sees the absolute future as God's self-bestowal. This is the consummation of creation and redemption promised and initiated in the life, death and resurrection of Jesus. All 'this-worldly' futures come in the ordinary dimensions of time and space as particular events or states of this world. There are many 'this-worldly' futures in our evolving world. Each of them, by definition remains open to a further future.

Christianity, according to Rahner, is a future-directed faith. It interprets the present in hope-filled openness to the approach of a God-given future. It understands the past and future history of the world within a framework of salvation history. Above all, Christianity proclaims that the dynamic becoming of the universe will end, not in emptiness, but in the divine self-bestowal. Moreover, it sees this absolute future is already at work within history. Even though the infinite and divine reality of the absolute future transcends the

---

8. Karl Rahner, 'Marxist Utopia and the Christian Future of Man', in Karl Rahner, *Theological Investigations*, Volume 6 (New York: Seabury Press, 1974), 59–68; Karl Rahner, 'The Question of the Future', in *Theological Investigations*, Volume 12 (London: Darton, Longmann and Todd, 1974), 181–201. See also Karl Rahner, 'A Fragmentary Aspect of a Theological Evaluation of the Concept of the Future', in *Theological Investigations* Volume 10 (New York: Seabury Press, 1977), 235–41.

universe, it is a constitutive element of the unfolding of the universe in history. The absolute future, this divine self-bestowal, has found its irrevocable expression and been made visible in Jesus Christ. His resurrection is the promise and the beginning of the absolute future, the transformation of human beings and the whole of the universe in Christ.

Within this context, Rahner argues that the real nature of the human can be defined as the possibility of attaining this absolute future. We are not defined by this or that goal that then opens out towards something else. We are defined by nothing less than God coming towards us as our absolute future. Absolute future is another name for God. It points to the fullness of reality, which not only comes towards us but is also 'the sustaining ground of the dynamism towards the future'.[9] God, then, is known not as one object among others that we might plan for the future, but as the ground of this whole projection towards the future.

In grace, this God comes towards each human being here and now in self-communicating love. In the incarnation, God, the absolute future, is made present within history, in a way that it credible, irreversible and explicit. The self-communication of God, in grace and in Jesus Christ, embraces the whole reality of Christian salvation. These words really say one thing: that the world attains its goal only by being saved in the absolute future that is God. Christianity, then, is the religion of the absolute future.

Rahner poses what he sees as the one real question for the human being: Is the future to which we project ourselves simply more of the same, made up of specific and limited realities, no matter how well planned or manipulated? Or does the infinite, unsurpassable future as such come towards us? He responds that, in contrast to Marxism and many other views of the future, Christianity opts for the second possibility. In making this option, Christianity also claims the presence of this future. The absolute future is the future coming to each person: it is a real possibility for each; it is offered to each; and its acceptance is the ultimate task for each. Our acts of commitment and love, our attempts to build a better future, always contain, at least implicitly, the possibility of encounter with the absolute future as such. Rahner claims that the content of Christian preaching consists of the question of the absolute future and, properly speaking, *of nothing else*. That

---

9.    Rahner, 'Marxist Utopia and the Christian Future of Man', 62.

which is specific and proper to Christianity is something utterly simple—the question of God who is absolute future. This is intelligible only from a perspective in which God has made the history of humanity and the world God's own history. The God who is bestowed on the world as its consummation and is already at work in the Word and the Spirit is not one aspect of our world, but is the absolutely incomprehensible mystery from which it comes and to which it is directed.

This God is never known as one object in the world, but is present to us in the mode of radical question. Rahner insists: 'Only when the question is posed in radical openness do we know all that is meant by God'. We are not truly open to the mystery of God as absolute future 'until every idol is shattered, the idol of an answer which fails to meet the question in all its radical breadth, and yet at the same time seeks to bring the question to an end'.[10]

Even in the divine self-bestowal, God will remain the eternal mystery to which human beings commit themselves in the ecstasy of love. Christianity in its essence is openness to the question of the absolute future which is God:

> All individual statements in Christianity, in its knowledge and life, therefore, can be understood only as a modality of this radical commitment to refuse to call a halt at any point and to seek the fulfilment of its life, its 'salvation' in something to which no further name can be assigned, something which still lies in the future and remains an eternal mystery, something which love alone can receive.[11]

Rahner insists that this understanding of the essence of Christianity does not ignore Jesus Christ. On the contrary, it is precisely what is promised to us in Jesus of Nazareth. In him alone, as the crucified and risen one, God has entered into our world as absolute future.

In Rahner's view, the role of theology is to act as the guardian of what he calls the *'docta ignorantia futuri'*. The language of *docta ignorantia* ('learned unknowing') comes from the tradition of negative theology. It is usually associated with Nicholas of Cusa (1401–64).

---

10. Rahner, 'The Question of the Future', 188–9.
11. Rahner, 'The Question of the Future', 189.

Rahner uses this expression to point to the critical role of resisting closure with regard to the future. It is theology's task to keep open the question of the future. Rahner claims that this is the theme that is always and everywhere proper to the theologian. Precisely as one who stands before the promise of God as absolute future, the Christian is called to exercise his or her creative powers to construct and work towards 'this-worldly' future goals. Rahner calls this interaction between the absolute future and planning of a 'this-worldly' future the 'utopian' factor. He argues that this Christian form of the utopian involves both a genuine commitment to this world and an assent to the absolute future, in such a way that each conditions the other.

Openness to the absolute future introduces the element of disquiet and criticism into history and impels it forward. The *docta ignorantia futuri* provides the basis for a sustained critique of the present. It challenges all assumptions that the present is the only right state of affairs. Christians may well disagree about specific plans for the future, but they are committed to the element of the unknown in the future they plan for. Rahner notes that this makes it all the more surprising that Christianity today 'has fallen under the suspicion (and not without reason) of being a conservative force which favours the present rather than the future'.[12] Hope in the absolute future also liberates us from the mindless quest for novelty. This hope is, consciously or unconsciously, both the motive and the critique of our strivings towards a 'this-worldly' future. And it is in this striving for an authentic 'this-worldly' future that hope for the absolute future is maintained.

The concept of Christianity as the religion of the absolute future has consequences for a Christian attitude to ideology. Aware that the word ideology is used in a number of different senses, Rahner specified that he is using it in the negative sense of 'a fundamental closure in face of the "wholeness" of reality, one which turns a partial aspect into an absolute'.[13] It turns what is finite into an absolute in order to achieve a practical and political effect, often attempting to determine the norm for society.

Rahner describes three forms of ideology. First, there are ideologies of *immanence*. These convert finite areas of everyday experience into

---

12. Rahner, 'The Question of the Future', 201.
13. Karl Rahner, 'Ideology and Christianity', in Karl Rahner, *Theological Investigations*, Volume 6, 43–58.

absolutes. This covers most of what is normally referred to as an ideology, including nationalism, the 'ideology of blood and soil', racism and materialism. In a second kind of ideology, the ultimate and the infinite are totalised so that the relative and the finite are cheated out of their relative rights. Rahner calls this the ideology of *transmanence*. This is the typical danger for the philosopher or the religious person. An example would be 'quietism' where involvement with the religious world removes motivation for engagement with the realities of everyday life. Finally, there is the ideology of *transcendence*, the trap of seeing ideology everywhere and thus of being unable to commit to anything. Everyday experience and religious insights are both devalued in relativism. The result is the typical Western attitude of unrestrained 'openness' that avoids all serious engagement.

Rahner considers whether Christianity itself is an ideology. There is no doubt that it can function as an ideology. Nevertheless, he argues, Christianity in itself is not an ideology because essentially it is nothing but the absolute and forgiving nearness of God in grace. Because of this, Christianity is not an ideology of immanence. The absolute mystery of the nearness of God unmasks as worthless idols all ideologies of immanence, whether they concern the nation, one's race, pleasure or any other this-worldly ideology.

Is Christianity an ideology that seeks to rise above history, either as transmanence or transcendence? Rahner's answer is that the centre of Christianity is Jesus of Nazareth in his concrete history and the experience of the Holy Spirit that is always mediated by history. Genuine Christianity does not represent any kind of flight from the world, but a full engagement with the world. The Christian can and must take history absolutely seriously[14] and cannot remain neutral regarding planning for the future. At the centre of Christianity is the one commandment of love of God and neighbour. Love of God is not something extra added on to our everyday commitments. It means that whenever someone serves humans and their dignity in absolute selflessness and commitment, they are already, at least implicitly, affirming and loving God. The relationship with others and all that this means in terms of planning and commitment is an essential element and an irreplaceable means of loving God, the absolute future.[15]

---

14. Rahner, 'Ideology and Christianity', 54.
15. Rahner, 'Marxist Utopia and the Christian Future of Man', 66.

According to Rahner, Christianity of itself has no utopian ideals for a future of this world.[16] Of course Christianity does contain some general norms, but these do not amount to any specific programme for the future. This means that Christians are called to tolerance with regard to differing views of the future within the church, and in cooperating with others in planning and pursuing political agendas. What Christianity rejects is any political programme in which nation, race, class, money, pleasure or any vision or plan is absolutised. It must oppose sacrificing and butchering human beings here and now for the sake of a dream of the future. Christianity must also defend the dignity and value of those who can make no tangible contributions to such causes.

Rahner sees hope as the acceptance of our orientation towards the incalculability and uncontrollability of God. Hope is the act by which we base ourselves in the specific circumstances of our lives, on that which is beyond our powers to control. It is that act 'in which the uncontrollable is made present as that which sanctifies, blesses and constitutes salvation without losing it character as radically beyond our powers to control, precisely because this salvific future is hoped for but not manipulated or controlled'.[17] Those who commit themselves, even implicitly, to the incalculable and the uncontrollable are committing themselves to God and to salvation. Rahner works from within the theological tradition that sees hope as one of the three theological virtues, alongside faith and love. In this tradition, a theological virtue is an attitude freely taken up by a human subject, but it comes as a gift of God, in God's self-bestowal in grace. Hope, like faith and love, is directed to God in God's self.[18] Hope bears on God who has promised God's self to us in Christ. If God's act of self-bestowal is the absolute future for the human, then hope is the grace-filled human response.

16.   Rahner, 'Marxist Utopia and the Christian Future of Man', 65.
17.   Rahner, 'On the Theology of Hope', in Karl Rahner, *Theological Investigations*, Volume 10, 245.
18.   Rahner, 'On the Theology of Hope', 254.

In Rahner's view, hope is profoundly connected to the promise of God made in Christ. The radical quality in the movement out from self, by which we move into the uncontrollable God, is based on the grace of God. And this grace of God 'finds its unique historical manifestation in Christ precisely as crucified, and thereby as surrendering himself in the most radical sense to the disposing hand of God'.[19] It is precisely in the death of Christ, understood as the most radical act of hope, that the grace of God is definitively established in our world. Our acts of hope spring from this grace of God made manifest in Christ and they find their fulfilment in the God who is revealed in Christ as our absolute future.

In our individual lives, hope finds its radical expression in death, which Rahner understands as the culmination of a life lived in faith, love and hope. But Christian hope involves not just the individual being taken up into God but the transformation of communal life and of creation itself. While acknowledging the ambiguity of the word revolution, Rahner understands Christian hope as a 'continually revolutionary attitude'. The position of Christianity on this issue is the exact opposite of what is often thought both outside and inside the church:

> The hope that is directed towards the absolute future of God, towards that eschatological salvation which is God himself as absolute, is not entertained in order to justify an attitude of conservatism, which from motives of anxiety, prefers a certain present to an unknown future and so petrifies everything. It is not the 'opium of the people' which soothes them in their present circumstances even though these are painful. Rather it is that which commands them, and at the same time empowers them, to have trust enough constantly to undertake anew an exodus out of the present into the future.[20]

Those who hope are called to set out ever anew from social structures that have become 'petrified, old and empty'.[21] Again,

---

19.   Rahner, 'On the Theology of Hope', 255.
20.   Rahner, 'On the Theology of Hope', 257.
21.   Rahner, 'On the Theology of Hope', 259.

Rahner insists, Christianity itself offers no special programme for a this-worldly future. What it offers is an imperative to Christians to venture into the future with other people, using every bit of intelligence and common sense. It lives in hope before a God, who as the absolute future, relativises and reveals the finite limits of all human plans and programmes. This line of thought leads to the conviction that living in hope involves two attitudes. First we need to take 'with absolute seriousness' the future that we can construct, because this is the 'medium of the absolute future'. And second, we need to acknowledge the absolute future as the factor in this future that we can construct, which makes its contents relative and conditional.[22]

In an article that explores the notion of the 'new earth', Rahner faces the question put by Marxism: How seriously do Christians take the world of justice, peace and integrity that they are trying to achieve?[23] What is the relationship between the coming of God as absolute future and the world that we attempt to construct? Rahner's response is that the coming Reign of God will not simply be the outcome of the history planned and accomplished by humans. Nor will it simply come upon us from outside. It will be the deed of God, but this deed of God is to be understood as the *self*-transcendence of history. In response to Marxism, then, Rahner argues that there is a dialectical tension between two statements: the first, that human history will endure, and the second, that human history will be radically transformed. This tension 'maintains in us an openness to the future while still according a radical importance to the present.' While these two provisos are kept in mind, it can be said that history constructs its own final and definitive state. It is not left behind but 'passes into the definitive consummation of God'.[24]

What confirms this, for Rahner, is that from the perspective of God, the Word of God has entered into history for our salvation, and history is embraced by God in the Christ-event. It has eternal meaning to God. From the perspective of the human, Rahner argues that if human freedom and the moral character of our actions are to have final and

---

22. Rahner, 'A Fragmentary Aspect of a Theological Evaluation of the Concept of the Future', 240.
23. Karl Rahner, 'The Theological Problems Entailed in the Idea of the "New Earth"', in Rahner, *Theological Investigations*, Volume 10, 260–72.
24. Rahner, 'The Theological Problems Entailed in the Idea of the "New Earth"', 270.

definitive existence, history itself will need to have enduring significance. Rahner sees the achievements of human beings as having final significance, as taken up into God and transformed in Christ. This means that 'the task of completing the creation and the fulfilling of it appears as an intrinsic element in the one total redemptive and divinising will of God for a world in which his self-bestowal is achieved'.[25]

In two articles at the end of his life Rahner reflects on the gap between utopia and reality.[26] We know we should build a world of justice and love, yet what we find is a selfishness that seems pervasive and virulent. We strive for structural change designed to overcome inequality and corruption and find inequality and corruption reappearing in our new construction. Rahner identifies what he sees as two false responses to this situation. One is that of the *idealist*, who finds reality hopelessly wanting and seeks to escape it. This is the response of the snob, the aesthete, the 'ideas person', the romantic and the religious escapist. The second false response is that of the *realist*. This is the response of those who take their stance in the shabbiness of life and of humanity and proceed to make the most they can out of it for themselves. They are ethical Darwinists, who take it for granted that life is a struggle and that the strongest come out on top. They defend the present social order as the best protector of their own interests. Rahner observes: 'We might add, of course, that there are such closet realists in the Church.'[27]

Both the 'pseudo-idealist' and the 'pseudo-realist' run from the tension and the perplexity of existence. Rahner argues that genuine hope will not collapse the tension between what we hope for and what we experience. Hope lives in this tension. It lives with the perplexity. The Christian stands before that utopia that is the absolute, eternal and incomprehensible God. And this absolute future reveals all other realities as inescapably relative and finite. And it is precisely this incomprehensible God who challenges us to love the earth. Christian

---

25. Rahner, 'The Theological Problems Entailed in the Idea of the "New Earth"', 271.
26. Karl Rahner, 'Utopia and Reality: The Shape of Christian Existence Caught between the Ideal and the Real', in *Theological Investigations*, Volume 22, (New York: Crossroads, 1991), 26–42. See also, Karl Rahner, 'Christian Pessimism', in *Theological Investigations*, Volume 22, 155–62.
27. Rahner, 'Utopia and Reality', 29.

hope exists in the tension between this utopia and our everyday commitments and loving actions.

Rahner sees perplexity as built into the human condition. Christianity understands it in relation to finitude and to sin. But, writing in the early eighties, Rahner argues that the experience of perplexity is growing in intensity. Our technology is making us more and more powerful, but with ever more ambiguous results. We are flooded with information from the sciences and from other sources, but decisions seem more difficult to make than ever. There are so many possible points of view that we find ourselves lost in the complexity. Rahner comments: 'Today only the simpleminded and the foolish know what should be done by individuals and groups.'[28] At the same time 'dissonant voices urge us to do a thousand things at once'.[29] Rahner argues for a 'Christian pessimism' that accepts perplexity and refuses to allow it to be repressed. He points to the words of Paul, who declares that we are 'perplexed but not driven to despair' (2 Cor 4: 8).[30] Christians hope in the midst of perplexity because they hold that God comes towards us as the all-embracing mystery of love. They know that perplexity is built into human existence because we can arrive at God's definitive realm only by passing through death, the 'ultimate and all-embracing enigma of human existence'.[31]

This kind of Christian pessimism can liberate us from the feeling that it all depends on ourselves, that with a bit more effort everything would be all right. But it must not be the pretext for a cheap resignation. It liberates us to act wisely and lovingly: 'Its function is to explain situations in which we can act realistically, fight and win partial victories, and soberly and courageously accept partial defeats.'[32] We are perplexed but do not despair because we already experience the Spirit of God, the anticipation of the fullness of the divine self-bestowal. Because of this gift of the Spirit, Christianity is a message of 'joy, courage and unshakeable confidence'. Because of this gift, we have the responsibility to 'bring about a foretaste of God's eternal reign through our solidarity, unselfishness, willingness to share and love of peace'.[33] The grace of God does not completely remove the

---

28.   Rahner, 'Utopia and Reality', 34.
29.   Rahner, 'Utopia and Reality', 35.
30.   Rahner, 'Christian Pessimism', 155.
31.   Rahner, 'Christian Pessimism', 157.
32.   Rahner, 'Christian Pessimism', 158.
33.   Rahner, 'Christian Pessimism', 160.

complexity, but it liberates us, so that complexities become the occasion and the mediation of the mystery of God. And then we can know that all our complexities are but 'forerunners and first instalments of the perplexity that consists of losing ourselves entirely through love in the mystery that is God'.[34]

---

34.   Rahner, 'Christian Pessimism', 161.

# 15

# Revolution and the Redeeming of the World: Eugen Rosenstock-Huessy's Messianic Reading of History

## Wayne Cristuado

## 1. Introduction

The name of Eugen Rosenstock-Huessy (1888–1972) will be familiar to readers of the Jewish philosopher Franz Rosenzweig. For he was Rosenzweig's teacher, friend, correspondent, and the man credited by Rosenzweig with being the single most important influence upon his own 'new thinking.'[1] He was also admired by and collaborated on occasion with Paul Tillich. But unlike Rosenzweig and Tillich, Rosenstock has been ignored within philosophical and theological circles; at least, in part, due to his belief that philosophy and theology were spent forces. Despite such (and other) admirers (WH Auden, for example, wrote a preface to his *I am an Impure Thinker*) his status in the academy is, at best, even if unfairly, marginal.

Rosenstock began his academic career as a legal historian but his work spanned many disciplines, including linguistics, church history, Egyptology, sociology and studies on the European revolutions of the last millennia. In addition, he was active in the formation of the Academy of Work at Frankfurt, a pioneer in the student-work service movement (which would be perverted by the Nazis) and chairman of the World Association for Adult Education.

---

1.    See *Judaism Despite Christianity: The 'Letters on Christianity and Judaism' between Eugen Rosenstock-Huessy and Franz Rosenzweig*, edited by Eugen Rosenstock-Huessy (New York: Schocken, 1971) and the correspondence included in the so-called *Gritli Briefe*, letters between Rosenzweig and Rosenstock's wife Margrit; a full web version of which is at http://home.debitel.net/user/gormann-thelen/eledition.htm.

While Rosenstock's corpus is vast in both its spread and sheer volume, it is held together by three methodological moves. The first, which was to be so influential upon Rosenzweig, is speech or dialogical thinking. It was a style of thinking that had been first suggested by Ludwig Feuerbach, and had particular resonance immediately after World War 1 in the intellectual climate of Germany, where it was also developed by Ferdinand Ebner and Martin Buber, quite independently of Rosenstock and Rosenzweig. The cornerstone of this idea is that we create our world through mutual responses and callings. Reality, then, is not something naturally there, but generated out of speech. In this respect it inaugurates a break with materialism/naturalism and idealism, as it neither privileges the material or the mental. It also mounts a critique of both of these positions by its questioning of the illegitimate and unquestioned grammatical privileging given by philosophy to the indicative and subjunctive moods (the domain of necessity being governed by the indicative, the domain of freedom by the subjunctive). Concomitantly, for Rosenstock, philosophy has been caught in its non-existent metaphysical view of freedom of the philosopher, a view that either dissolves it into the necessary (Hegel) or insists upon the lack of contiguity with it (Kant). For Rosenstock the survival and development of the species has, in the first instance been generated out of the imperative, and all subsequent modalities of human interaction have been built upon the vistas of our grammar. Being free means to name and call anew and to deploy and respond to all the grammatical capacities of the soul. In this all-important respect, then, Rosenstock takes the formulation 'in the beginning was the word' completely literally.

The second methodological feature of Rosenstock's thinking, developed in the years of his intense exchange of ideas with Rosenzweig, is what he called the calendar method. For Rosenstock the calendar (both secular and ecclesiastical) provides the key to the great events that underpin the collective bodies of association within which we communicate and collectively create our future and redeem our past. In keeping with the grammatical method, Rosenstock eschews a merely causal view of history. Our world is composed of various time-bodies, events whose full significance unfolds according to their own rhythms and which continue to generate associations and activities until the event has been spent. The calendar gives us a clue to those events that have been significant enough to be marked in our collective memory as creating the rhythms of our common era. The event, for Rosenstock, that overhangs all other events of our era is the event upon which all the European/ western calendars are based☐ the beginning of the Christian (common) era, the birth of Jesus.

The third methodological feature is what Rosenstock calls the 'cross of reality'. The symbol of the cross to express the fundamental four-foldness of reality is indicative of the analogical reasoning which is such an important part of Rosenstock's reading of history. But it is equally an acknowledgment of what he sees as the essentially Christian basis of speech and calendar-thinking: Christianity, for Rosenstock, by promising and setting in train a universal future pushes speech and history further than any other previous socio-political or religious formation had achieved. It commences universal history by making us all God's children. For Rosenstock, the cross of reality signifies the dynamism of everything, including ourselves: we are always caught up in the matrix of subjectivity, objectivity, 'trajectivity' (the push of the past) and 'prejectivity' (the pull of the future). There is no escape from this and any thinking, which does not act in accordance with this four-foldness, is, for Rosenstock, simply not engaging with us or our reality. Note that for Rosenstock the future is not only guided by the past, but it also guides the past. This, for Rosenstock, is the fundamental significance of the meaning of an end time, which is at the basis of the eschatological view of universal history governing Christian speech and world making. To this extent it is no exaggeration to say that every line of Rosenstock's thought revolves around the redemption of the world. For the end of humanity is to tap into the entire range of potencies that not only derive from nature, but also from each other and which are developed over time. In this sense Rosenstock sees us, as he believes Michelangelo has represented in the great painting on the roof of the Sistine chapel, as learning to receive the great spirits of the divine which God transfers from Himself to us so that we become as gods. Heaven in this sense is not in any other world, and Rosenstock strips Christianity of any Platonic residues, including the idea of immortality.

From the above it would not be misleading to infer that Rosenstock is sympathetic to the great nineteenth century aspirations of Marx and Nietzsche to the extent that he sees them as both continuing in the eschatological theological traditions, which he saw as having been abandoned by liberal Christian theology.

## 2. Jewish and Christian messianic roots of the West

According to Rosenstock, the West has been formed out of its messianic mission, a mission first understood by the Jewish people, then mutated into Christian and finally secular forms. This thesis is developed at length in *Out of Revolution.* A passage from a section on his chapter on the French revolution encapsulates the messianic perspective at the heart of his work.

> When Louis XVIII accepted the emancipation of the Jews as a fact in 1815, he accepted the great idea of humanity as conceived by the French Revolution. This humanism, or, better still, humanitarianism, in which Rousseau and Briand, Diderot and Barthou, Jefferson and Wilson, Mary Wollstonecraft and Ramsay MacDonald, were baptized, had discovered man behind men, nature behind nations, Adam behind Shem, Ham and Japhet, and the great identity of all men behind creed, faith, colour and race. It baptized Gentiledom by giving a mission to every nation. *Nationalism makes every nation* a chosen people in competition with every other chosen people in competition with all the others. *Messianism*, originally limited to the Jews, later communicated to the heathen by the Church, *is transferred by the European nationalism* born in 1789 *to the nations in general*, which now enter upon a common race of *messianic nationalism . . .*
>
> [T]he scrupulous accuracy with which one messianism (that of the Jews) was supplanted by another, more general one (that of the nations), the exactness of the correspondence between national government by inspiration and the disclaiming of any reliance on priests or prophets shows how deeply the history of Christianity delves its channels even where neither church nor dogma, neither pope nor parsons, still play any part in the drama. Pagans, Christians, and Jews carry out the commands of revelation long after

these commands have ceased to be represented by a clergy.[2]

Of course, Rosenstock's messianic view of history differs from Judaic-based messianism in that (a) there is no waiting for the identity of the messiah to be revealed (He has come) and (b) He who has already come will come again. There is an unbridgeable gulf between Jews and Christians over the meaning of the messianic and history itself, a central point in the heated correspondence between Rosenzweig and Rosenstock of 1916. Nevertheless Christians see the Jews as having a special historical role that cannot be equated with the pagans. Unlike other tribal and imperial peoples the Israelites broke with the narrative that life and death, peace and war are inevitable cycles. Instead of merely longing for a lost golden age or responding to the directions or pleas for vengeance of ancestral voices, they staked their entire existence on a future reign of righteousness and peace. While empires kept records of dynastic reigns and while the Greek historians chronicled events and myths and tall tales, the Jews' recording of history was unique in that it was the story of the stages of a people driven by its divine purpose. They began (and in their eyes completed) the Book, which is seen as the manifestation of the power of the word to reach from heaven to earth and to make God's chosen people live up to the divine image that they are.

The narrative of redemption was expanded beyond the Israelites by those Jews who saw in Jesus Christ the long awaited messiah who was not only the King of the Jews, but also the Christ, and the Son of God and the Son of Man; that is, redemption was now possible for all. These 'ands', for Rosenstock, were essential to the human chain that Jesus set in motion, a chain in which humanity learns it is always 'and this as well'. By accepting the title of the messiah, Jesus had, according to Rosenstock, freed men and women from all other messiahs, and hence from all myths which required their subjugation to one exclusive form of life or type of existence.[3] Jesus undertook to free souls from the life forms that the Spirit had created but which now entombed them. Only

---

2.  Eugen Rosenstock-Huessy, *Out of Revolution: Autobiography of Western Man* (Oxford: Berg, 1993 [1938 and 1966]), 235–7.

3.  See especially Rosenstock's unpublished essay: 'The New Nature of Christianity: A Task for Drafted Thinkers and Free Soldiers,' reel 8, item 398, in Eugen Rosenstock-Huessy, *The Collected Works on Microfilm* (Norwich, Vermont: Argo).

by a preparedness to leave behind old forms of life and die into new forms could humanity truly live in conformity to their divinity. This appropriation of our divine nature (see John 10:34) was, according to Rosenstock, rightly grasped by the early fathers of the Church. The belief in divinisation of some men was, of course, rife in the ancient world–the political divinisation of the Pharaoh, Caesar *et al*, but this was always at the expense of those who would be sacrificed to the (human) god—or the divinisation of the philosopher, magician. This was also a divinisation of and for the few and of a specific faculty and way of life.

That everyone lives off other life makes of every lived formation a sacrificial one. Jesus sided with the sacrificial victim in acknowledgment of the law of life as feeding off death. He saw in the victim the seed of the future and to that end sought to realise a new future, a new eon in which human beings could live as brothers and sisters from the sacrifice that is God himself—a move that required not only Jesus' sacrifice, but martyrs whose blood offerings were the seed of the body of the church.

The facts of death and suffering were, then, for Jesus, the starting point. The end point, though, required that each live by the divinity of each. As Rosenstock puts it, citing Gregory of Nyssa: 'Man [*Der Mensch*] should become God. But that cannot happen without all other human beings becoming God.'[4] This could begin to happen (and not just remain a hope) because it had been grasped that God had Himself provided the sacrifice. Now it could be seen that the gods do not simply sacrifice us for their pleasure (the pagans). On the contrary, we do not need to be devoured by gods who pull us here and there—the one true God loves us (the Jews)—but, adds Christ, God *also* now fulfils the promise in us. Jesus, by accepting the name of messiah but *also* being the Son of Man, creates a new body of history unifying the different bodies of time (that is, the duration of a shared form of existence) that under paganism and Judaism remained fractured and in perpetual enmity. That is why, for Rosenstock, Jesus Christ is the centre of history: humankind's direction is turned for the first time

---

4. Eugen Rosenstock-Huessy, *Die Gesetze der Christlichen Zeitrechnung*, edited by Rudolf Hermeier and Jochen Lübbers (Münster: Agenda, 2004), 280.

toward unity.[5] The pagans created empires, but any vision of brother and sisterhood was barely an idea splintered among a few philosophical communities, let alone something to be realised across the spaces and throughout the ages to come. By basing their entire lives on the divine commands of love of God and of neighbour, as Christ had done, the earliest Christians undertook to unite as one body across the times and space, thus together becoming the body of the risen Christ. No longer must the elect wait indefinitely—for the Jews the messiah's arrival 'must never happen, but it is desired.'[6] With the Christians the time had come to act because the messiah has been.

### 3. Revolution and the messianic means of the second millennium

What, then, had originally been 'revealed' to the Jews, through the faith and acts of early Christians, became, in its reconstituted form, the cornerstone of the Church. For Rosenstock the first thousand years after Christ's death led to the recreation of the body of Europe through the presence of the Church and its types (martyrs, hermits, saints, clerics, Christian monarchs and Christian subjects) and, in Western Europe, a new, a Holy Roman Empire. The unity of Christendom that had spanned the arc of the Nicene Creed to the Crusades had in the second millennium been replaced by disintegrations: the Eastern Schism, the great protracted and often bloody tensions between Holy Roman Emperor and the Papacy, the creation of national churches of the Reformation, and finally the secularised consolidation of nation states and supra-nationalist ideologies such as liberalism and Marxism.

If the Church is the signature of the first millennium, then, for Rosenstock, revolution is the signature of the second. The World War 1 was the culmination of the process of the great revolutions of the last millennium in Europe–a marriage of war and revolution (as his early book of that name put it). Each revolution, in its own unique way, had been a confrontation for humanity with the collision between the truth of the common cause of human kind in realizing the kingdom, its failure to live up to that truth and the need to fulfil it. Each revolution had passed on something enduring to subsequent generations, thus

---

5.    Eugen Rosenstock-Huessy, *The Christian Future: or the Modern Mind Outrun*, introduction by Harold Stahmer (New York: Harper and Row, 1966), 67.

6.    Rosenstock-Huessy, 'The New Nature of Christianity', 183.

contributing to a common social, political and economic vocabulary and set of institutions.

In *Out of Revolution*, Rosenstock undertakes an examination of the role that the total revolutions of the second millennium have played in the formation of 'Western Man' which itself is but the precondition of a planetary unity. There he works backwards from the Russian Revolution, through the French Revolution, to the English Revolution, to the German Reformation and then he passes from these 'secular revolutions' to the 'clerical revolutions': the Papal Revolution (of Gregory VII spreading out into the Guelphic revolution), the Italian Renaissance, the formation of the Austro-Hungarian Empire, the National Revolutions and the American Revolution. The respective contents of what he calls the secular and clerical revolutions are indicative of Rosenstock's refusal to accept Whig and Enlightenment historical nomenclature. The typology of secular and clerical is made all the more provocative by what becomes included under it—the Reformation is a secular revolution; the American revolution a clerical one! The perplexed reader is not overly helped by Rosenstock's cryptic remark that the secular revolutions were made by 'temporal powers,' while the 'Great War' is said to have dealt with 'religious aspects not represented by these four revolutions. Empires, Crusades, Churches, Citizenship and Authority were values in the World War and are values today, though of older origin than 1789 or 1688.'[7] Far more important for our purposes than what would require a lengthy examination of the development, or assessment of the adequacy of this classification (which he omits from *Die europäischen Revolutionen*, not least because America does not belong there) is the classification of revolution itself. For ultimately all the revolutions dissolve the secular/ clerical divide and the revolutions continue, for Rosenstock, the messianic mission. The messianic feature of the revolutions stems from the feature that distinguishes them from rebellions and mere civil wars: they are all attempts to change the world itself. That is, they were all conceived as world revolutions, as attempts to inaugurate an age free from the evils that had heretofore plagued humanity:

> The world Revolutions all start without reference to
> space with an absolute programme for whole of
> mankind, and a vision of a new earth. They all believe

---

7.    Rosenstock-Huessy, *Out of Revolution*, 10.

themselves to be the vessel of eternal, revealed, definite truth. Only reluctantly do they come back to the old earth. Every revolution makes the painful discovery that it is geographically conditioned.[8]

What has been unique about the West is the interplay and sequence of these cries to heaven to overturn earthly existence and thereby creating heaven on earth. Rosenstock observes the common goods that have been generated in the hells of revolution such as: the university (the scholastic contribution to the crusade started by the Papal revolution); the freedom to choose professions (a necessity forced by the Reformation with the hundreds and thousands of nuns and monks leaving their orders); freedom of property rights even beyond death (the result of the English revolution); the patents and copyright to capitalise on individual talent (the offshoot of the intellectual freedom procured by the American and French revolutions); the protection of the worker (something that the Russian revolution staked its demand for world revolution upon). Each of these achievements which Western men and women now take for granted were once 'completely irreconcilable with existing ways of life'.[9]

It is the understanding of the cross-national everyday bounties of revolution which separate Rosenstock's 'immoralist' analysis of revolution—'the category of necessity is beyond abstract good and evil'[10] and 'each great revolution accomplishes something necessary'[11]—from political philosophers like Leo Strauss and Eric Voegelin who provide Platonically based moral critiques of revolution, yet are silent on all the benefits they owe past revolutions.[12] Yet he is equally as removed from Marx and Marxist contemporaries who overemphasise the economic dimensions of revolution. 'The Russian Revolution,' says Rosenstock, 'took the guise of an economic revolution because the previous revolutions had stressed other sides of the social order'.[13] The Marxists wanted the Russian Revolution to be

---

8.    Rosenstock-Huessy, *Out of Revolution*, 457.
9.    Rosenstock-Huessy, *Out of Revolution*, 31.
10.   Rosenstock-Huessy, *Out of Revolution*, 719.
11.   Rosenstock-Huessy, *Out of Revolution*, 719.
12.   Wayne Cristaudo, 'Philosophy, Christianity and Revolution in Eric Voegelin and Eugen Rosenstock-Huessy', in *European Legacy*, 4/6 (1999): 58–74.
13.   Rosenstock-Huessy, *Out of Revolution*, 732.

the spark of the World Revolution, when, for Rosenstock, it was itself a side effect of the far greater detonation of the Great War. Yet again, Rosenstock is not an advocate of revolution, anymore than one could be an advocate of storms. For Rosenstock: 'Revolutions come as a positive effort when the fear of a complete breakdown of order preys so terribly on the bowels of men that only a great courage and a great love can open the way to a new equilibrium of powers.'[14] They are the result of countless forces accumulating over long time scales, an insight that is central to the calendar method deployed in *Out of Revolution*, and one that is so often absent in other histories of revolution, which generally work with smaller time waves.

The revolutions of the West, then, are a sequence and at the root of that sequence is something rarely realised, that the revolutions are fundamentally Christian in their character—a claim that is as likely to horrify Christians as to startle most contemporary sympathisers of revolution. In this respect, even the French and Russian revolutions are interpreted by Rosenstock under a biblical framework in so far as they are driven by the same universalistic aspirations that find first expression in the commandment to love one's neighbour and find peace on earth. While the adequacy of the proof of this claim can only be gauged by an examination of the evidence supplied throughout the whole of *Out of Revolution* (and *Die europäischen Revolutionen*) the following passage provides a neat summary of the conclusions of the argument:

> So definitely is the revolutionary process of the last thousand years bound up with the unification of thought by the common possession of the Bible that every revolution passionately claimed a special section of Biblical history as the classical text for its own drama.
>
> The popes of the Gregorian Revolution, from Victor II to Eugene III, clearly recalled the last chapter of Biblical history: the early centuries of the Church, during which the very canon of the sacred book had been fixed and developed. The Guelphic leaders, Saint Francis and his followers, as well as Innocent III, lived the passion and cross of Christ and His disciples.

---

14.    Rosenstock-Huessy, *Out of Revolution*, 473.

Luther, by enthroning the *'Predigtamt'* of the German *'Geist'* (Spirit) as the controlling power of secular government, restored the prophetic office of the time of Elias, John and Jesus. Cromwell's and William's England reinstated the Judge's function and the divine voice of public spirit which had ruled Israel before the Kingdom of David. France went in for the period before the age of revelations- natural man, the God of nature and the rights of Adam before the Fall. And Russia and we contemporaries of Bolshevism delve deep into the pre-adamitic and pre-historical forces of labour, sex, youth, primitive tribes and clans, hormones and vitamins.

This exact sequence, an inverted Biblical chronicle from 300 A D back to the first days of life on earth, was traced by revolutionaries who thought themselves completely free, individual and independent and original, and who violently opposed the terms and slogans of every other revolution, preceding or following. Yet they were all under the invincible spell of 'One Universal Language of Mankind'. The vigour of this epic unity, binding the national revolutions together was tested to the utmost by our investigation of the American vocabulary. Halfway between the English and the French, America might not have shared in this strange biblical retrogression. But this was not so at all. We found in the pamphlets and sermons of the War of Independence the figures of Noah and his sons symbolizing the new cradle of nations in these United States! Noah, Shem, Ham and Japhet, taking their places exactly between the Puritan Judges of Israel and the Rousseauist 'Adam', bear witness to the unity of 'language' throughout the Christian era, in spite of all national languages.[15]

Rosenstock's Christian vision is one stretching from Adam to today and into heaven (the future transfigured world.) There is no beyond here, no after-world, nothing like the Platonic eternity that is out of

---

15.   Rosenstock-Huessy, *Out of Revolution*, 738–9.

time. Unlike Platonism, which he sees as a sub-set of gnosticism, Christianity, according to Rosenstock, teaches the eternity of the ages, of the times upon times. It is thus not a doctrine in which the act of purification continues out of time or is undergone for a life outside of time. On the contrary, such ways of thinking, Greek in origin and common in Christendom, are, from Rosenstock's perspective, childish formulations based upon the failure to understand creation and its relationship to the process of redemption. Creation is always in time, and redemption is always of the times, which are bodies of creation.[16] This, for Rosenstock, is the actualisation of heaven and the meaning of the second coming: the realization of the meaning of creation by the integration of all of its facets and potencies across the generations.

Rosenstock's Christ, then, is very much the Christ who has brought a sword into the world and turned brother against brother, children against parents etc. For Rosenstock, the driving force behind the revolutionary is despair at suffering and the hatred at the failure of the actualisation of the perfect man whose body they are forming historically. The cross of reality is above all the suffering reality of those who have been sacrificed in the inter-penetrations that push future generations. One of the corollaries of Rosenstock's anti-dualism is that formulations such as the wrath of God and the last judgment are not projected into a beyond but take place in the world's re-making. While Jesus taught love of one's neighbour, the revolutionaries are the expression of love's failure today and the love of heaven, which the soul hungers for. Hence, Rosenstock says: 'Revolutions do nothing but readjust the equation between heart-power and social order. They come from the open and happen under the open sky. They bring about the Kingdom of God by force, and reach into the infinite in order to reform the finite.'[17]

While mechanistic philosophers, such as Thomas Hobbes, had seen the collision of appetites as simply a naturalistic process, for Rosenstock the revolutionaries were not merely following nature. Following nature means remaining in the eternal cycles, in the tragic repetitions of war and love and hate and peace. But there is nothing 'natural' about wanting to bring heaven to earth. Indeed the very names invoked mean transcending nature; revolution means redeeming our nature so that we are no longer merely natural.

16.	Rosenstock-Huessy, *Out of Revolution*, 14.
17.	Rosenstock-Huessy, *Out of Revolution*, 473.

Rosenstock says: 'The power of going up-stream is the revolutionary force in man. It is never comparable to the seasons of nature. Because man goes against the inertia of his own habits.'[18]

## 4. Conclusion

Rosenstock's anti-otherworldliness made him something of an enigma to mainstream theologians. By and large his hostility to theology made it easy to ignore him, as if he belonged completely to the secular world, a point made by Karl Löwith in his review of *The Christian Future*. According to Löwith, and much to Rosenstock's chagrin, Rosenstock had too much in common with Goethe and too little with the writers of the Gospels and epistles.[19] Certainly Rosenstock held that we belonged to the Johannine Age and that the spirit that gave birth to the church must now be housed in secular forms. Having defined himself as a 'post-Nietzschean' Christian, he also stipulated that the creed of the future 'will depend for new lease on life upon un-denominational, nameless and incognito contributions to faith'.[20] But for Rosenstock one of the great problems confronting modern men and women is that they had lost touch with the potencies of the Christian tradition and that the more recent humanist tradition lacked historical depth and the range of its truth were too diminished to help us become who we are. For him theologians, such as Karl Barth, also only exacerbated the problem by hiving off Christianity from life. Barth's making of God and His Son the absolute Other, and of the Bible 'not merely [a] sacred but [a] closed book',[21] was, for Rosenstock, reducing church history 'to insubstantial rubbish'.[22] Such theology fails to see that the world through time, not just the Book, is where the living truth of God's presence must be rendered visible. For Rosenstock, if Christianity was

---

18. Rosenstock-Huessy, *Out of Revolution*, 719.
19. Karl Löwith, 'Review' (of Rosenstock's *The Christian Future: Or the Modern Mind Outrun*), *Journal of Church History*, 15 (1946): 249.
20. Eugen Rosenstock-Huessy, 'The End of the World', unpublished essay in *The Collected Works on Microfilm*.
21. Karl Barth, *Church Dogmatics: A Selection*, edited and introduced by Helmut Gollwitzer (Louisville: John Knox Press, 1994), 72.
22. Eugen Rosenstock-Huessy and Joseph Wittig, *Das Alter der Kirche*, Volume 1, (Münster: Agenda, 1998 [1927]), 140.

to be true its truth was to be realised in its fulfilment and its becoming.[23]

Just as Rosenstock stood outside Christian theological trends, he also did not fit easily into twentieth century social philosophical trends. Unlike Benjamin or Bloch, for example, his biblical references were not tempered by an appeal to Marxism or historical materialism. It is also pertinent that just as much twentieth century social theory was taking its cue from Jewish messianism in a manner commensurate with Rosenzweig and, in no small part, due to the assertion of identity in the face of an asphyxiating totalism, Rosenstock believed there was no way around the process of unification for salvation of the world. As he put it in a letter to Rosenzweig, in a manner that typified the blunt tone adopted by both in their disputation about Judaism and Christianity:

> Do you believe that Zionism is an accident? Israel's time as the people of the Bible has gone by. The Church—not of course the church triumphant, you heretic, but pretty well the church militant—is today the Synagogue. The epoch of the eternal Jew comes to an end, just as Basque, Celts, etc. come to an end. People have their eras. In place of the eternal Jew comes again a Zion.[24]

Rosenstock did not dispute the *desire and need* for peoples to maintain their separate identities (whether Celts, Basques, Jews) within the context of the encroaching and messianic process of unification. Nor did he dispute that unification can be suffocation, and that totalising can be totalitarian. He knew this and long before post-modernism, he had insisted that there would be a proliferation of tribal reactions, regional mythologies, and anti-universalisms to counter the

---

23. Eugen Rosenstock-Huessy, *Heilkraft und Wahrheit: Konkordanz der politischen und der kosmischen Zeit*, (Amandus: Brendow, 1990), 116. Rosenstock speaks here of the 'pure beyondness of the religious of the Bathians'.

24. Rosenstock-Huessy, *Judaism Despite Christianity* (November 19, 1916), 140. Rosenzweig, in *The Star of Redemption*, had originally held that the Jews were outside of war and nationhood (only to modify this later in an attempt to establish a compromise between his own universalistic, anti-nationalist vision and the Zionists).

globalisation of the economy. Significantly, he grasped that this was a major impetus behind National Socialism—but the Nazis tried it too early and their anti-Semitism was directed at the people who 'most represent universal history'.[25] Likewise, while he also insisted that the concept of 'man' smothered too many differences to be a legitimate sociological and historical classifier—'There doesn't exist "man" in itself,' he states bluntly in *Soziologie*[26]—he also saw that it was now impossible to ignore the necessity of the process of unification. For him that necessity was the necessity of the future redemption shaping the past, the necessity of heaven.

---

25. Rosenstock-Huessy, *Out of Revolution*, 717–18. He adds: 'Possibly the Jews will contribute more than others to that universal organization of production which makes wars impossible and leads in a world wide economy'.

26. Eugen Rosenstock-Huessy, *Soziologie, Bd 1: Die Übermacht der Räume* (Stuttgart: Kohlhammer, 1956), 273.

# 16

# Redemption and Messianism in Franz Rosenzweig's *The Star of Redemption*

## Wayne Cristaudo

Franz Rosenzweig's *The Star of Redemption*[1] is increasingly recognised as one of the most important works of Jewish philosophy in the twentieth century. It is a work of philosophical and theological erudition that espouses Jewish spiritual supremacy at a time when anti-Semites were preparing for the great annihilation. Philosophy had become, for Rosenzweig (1886–1929), a sick understanding and could only be resuscitated with the addition of theology.[2] Indeed, *The Star of Redemption*, at a fundamental level, is a deeply personal contribution to existential philosophy erected on the power of redemption. After World War 1, Rosenzweig withdrew from academia and founded a *Lehrhaus*, a centre for Jewish theology and tradition. As his health deteriorated, he dedicated himself to translations of the thirteenth century poet and mystic Judah ha-Levi and, most importantly, with Martin Buber, the Bible. He saw himself as helping his people redeem the world through understanding the great powers that were active within their tradition.

There are two overriding claims which the *Star* defends and develops: one is that life is only lived in full if redemption completes it; the other is that only the Jews have fully ingested the meaning and fulfilment of redemption. In order to defend the second claim, he had to refute the alternative traditions of redemption. But if one thinks that any talk of redemption is itself nonsense, then there is little point in

---

1.  Franz Rosenzweig, *The Star of Redemption*, translated by William W Hallo (Boston: Beacon, 1972). Original publication date was 1921.
2.  Franz Rosenzweig, *Understanding the Sick and the Healthy*, translated and with an introduction by Nahum Glatzer (Cambridge: Harvard University Press, 1999).

defending and advancing that argument. This position is the atheistic/ naturalistic one that by Rosenzweig's time had become the philosophical orthodoxy. But it was an orthodoxy being challenged in the circles within which he moved, in particular by his cousins, the Ehrenbergs, and Eugen Rosenstock, all of whom had converted from Judaism to Christianity. Also influential was the leading neo-Kantian, Hermann Cohen, whose late work had been nourished by the richness of Jewish orthodoxy. What Rosenzweig saw in these friends were people thoroughly steeped in the history of philosophy who found that a life lived under the significations and rituals of religion was energised and directed in a way that the naturalists could not adequately explain, and hence could not refute.

In effect this generation had simply taken to heart the nineteenth century romantics' critique of the enlightenment—that the *philosophes* and their offspring were wildly oversimplifying the benefits of science and the cruelty, silliness and emptiness of religions. On the contrary, they argued, religion has produced rich and varied stories, communities and artistic productions, while science, irrespective of its immediate material benefits, has also led to political cruelty ('the terror' of the Jacobins), and existential and social emptiness. Science, as Nietzsche had argued, could not generate meaning; it was reliant on an existential commitment from outside of itself. But while Nietzsche (like Feuerbach before him) was appealing to a new class of myth-makers (the philosophers of the future) Rosenzweig, like his friends, saw that such a task was doomed to the failure of pulling oneself up by one's own bootstraps. The religions of Christianity and Judaism, by contrast, had thousands of years of experiences and insights woven into them. Rather than simply denying the reality of potencies and starting from year zero, what needed to be done was tap them and apply them in a manner consistent with contemporary needs and concerns.

This position was fairly widely held at the time, but the expression of it which most impacted upon Rosenzweig had its fully blown methodological treatment in a letter written to him in 1916 by Rosenstock. Rosenstock called his method 'speech thinking,' and it was a name that Rosenzweig was to retain. It was a position that had first been advanced by Feuerbach and, in slightly different variants, it was also being developed by Martin Buber and Ferdinand Ebner. Truth was not to be found in things, as the materialists would have it, nor in reason or ideas, as the idealists claimed, but in speech. Speech activates and generates truths in a manner that simply cannot be reduced to material or thought. We call and respond just as we are called and respond, and we thus continually remake the world and its truths. In this respect the truth is to be found in all the places where God, man and world intersect. That God, contrary to the naturalists of the last two centuries, could not be simply dissolved into the world or man or nothingness is due to, and remains manifest in the potencies that remain active in the life-ways of those governed by the sign of God's presence.

Religion, then, when grasped under Rosenstock's and Rosenzweig's new methodological orientation, is essentially a container of speech, a container that has emerged from the calls and responses of the speakers. That is, the way life is alive in the *names* of its reality, and the names that are invoked in prayers and festivals and the vision they generate which, finally, for Rosenzweig, culminates in 'the silent enlightenment of the completely fulfilling end'.[3] This idea of the positive truth of the beings generated culturally, socially and historically is taken over from the late Schelling and it is also behind Rosenzweig's description of his method as 'absolute empiricism'.[4]

*cf. radical empiricism*

The Introduction and much of Part One of the *Star* explicate the origin and development of philosophy while showing philosophy the new road to be taken. The post-idealist philosophers of Schopenhauer, Kierkegaard and Nietzsche had all pressed for a philosophy no longer submerged in its own abstractions, but in life itself. But even they have failed to redeem philosophy for they had nothing, apart from their own hope and their own private experience, to redeem it with. The fundamental problem of philosophy from its inception is that philosophy is only the product of one group of a community of speakers and the exaggerated and misplaced faith that previous philosophers had had in the original totalising abstractions that motivated their speculations whether their All is 'material' or 'idea' ultimately has, for Rosenzweig, no bearing on the truth / reality that can only be disclosed by speech in action. What life gives us prior to philosophy is language and our greatest activators are names; abstractions are the poor man's equivalent of the name. For the name is

---

3.  Rosenzweig, *The Star of Redemption*, 294.
4.  Franz Rosenzweig, 'The New Thinking', in *Franz Rosenzweig, Philosophical and Theological Writings*, translated, edited, notes and commentary by Paul Franks and Michael Morgan (Indianapolis: Hackett, 2000), 138.

a response to a truth impressed upon people in a heightened moment of intensity. The durability of that truth, that is, the real significance of the experience lays in the circulatory continuity of the name, in its power to inform further action. A name, in other words, persists only as long as it is still (potentially) vital within a community. On the other hand, a philosophical abstraction is the submission of a name to a particular process of analysis in which only the universal is allowed to persist. It is a means of delimiting and ultimately of devitalising. For Rosenzweig, death is rigidity and petrification and nothing is more rigid than the philosopher's universal. Philosophy, then, has generally been parasitic on existence.

Rosenzweig argues that instead of the philosopher's All, humankind has generally grasped existence in terms of three irreducibles: the divine, the world, and 'man.' Creation itself, the grounding sphere of experience, had up until, and way after and outside of philosophy, found itself ever explained in terms of these three groundings. They are, in this sense, 'the common sense' bases of our understanding of life. For Rosenzweig, then, philosophy suffers from two fundamental deficiencies. The first is that it does not grasp human existence in as rich and complex a manner as the myths and experiences of peoples do. It has a truncated understanding of 'creation' (creation, he says, is understood by philosophers simply as generation). Further, and as a direct consequence, it has no genuine grasp of revelation and redemption. At best it can follow art and ingest that into its work. What Rosenzweig has really accomplished in his critique of philosophy, then, is a recovery of the revealed truths of the Bible, as well as the creative potencies of the pagan world. On the other hand, philosophy itself is partly redeemed by Rosenzweig once it takes God, man and world, and creation, revelation and redemption as the two ineradicably overlapping triads that form the *Star,* that eternal basis out of which human experience of reality emanates.

If, then, philosophy was a deficient form of enlightenment due to the unreality of the abstractions it sought to build with, it is also the case that it was a reaction to a world that is often experienced as unbearably tumultuous, tormented and fractured. To this world of chaos, philosophy offered the pseudo-redemption of a false sense of control, and a false triumph of life over death, as taught, for example, in the doctrine of the immortality of the soul, or the purity of the moral self□ that is, inventing an abstract dualism that has no connection with life, except as a 'rational' means of escape from real life and death into their pseudo forms.

The experience that gives birth to philosophy, the original condition of humanity, is designated by Rosenzweig as the pagan. The pagan is a term that thus includes the tribes and ancient empires as well as the polis. It is the world of the Vedas, Confucius and the tragic poets. It is the ground of all art and politics. The pagan is the response to life 'in its elemental, invisible, un-revealed form'.[5] Unlike philosophy, paganism is a true response to the world, a response that has grasped creation through the three irreducibles, and left everything splintered. In an allusion to Goethe, he neatly encapsulates it as a 'classic Witches' Sabbath with a chromatic dance of the Spirits'.[6]

But the pagan world is deficient in that it is unable to ingest adequately the revelatory power that transposes creation outside of its own ground. The pagan world is an eternal return, an endless cycle of the same akin to the life and death cycles of nature. Indeed the realm of truth inhabited by the pagan is the natural realm. Nothing less but also nothing more. The commandment to love which forms the basis of redemption is itself based upon the revelation that love triumphs over nature by triumphing over death. Conversely, to live outside of revelation is to live outside an understanding of death as more than just petrification or simply life continuing as life, albeit in some ethically enhanced or even purified form. Hence, Rosenzweig says, the limitation of paganism is really the limitation of death. 'The pagan knows nothing of death. As he knows nothing of sin.'[7]

This does not mean that there is no sense of revelation and redemption within the pagan, just that they find themselves forced into and constrained by the sphere of creation. For the pagan, art, rather than life, is the zenith of its revelatory and redemptive process, and the state the highest form for solving problems stemming from our nature. But, in the pagan world, art is a means of private redemption and the redemption of the state is only ever partial, both in the range of powers it can activate and who it includes.

---

5. Rosenzweig, 'The New Thinking', 120.

6. Rosenzweig, *The Star of Redemption*, 87.

7. Franz Rosenzweig, *'Paralipomena'*, in *Zweistromland: Kleinere Schriften zur Religion und Philosophie* (Berlin: Philo, 1926), 96. All translations from *Zweistromland* are mine.

In sum, the pagan leaves a potency within us unfulfilled and thus it is a diminished form of existence. The traditions of revelation have taken their point of departure from awareness of this deficiency. Of the three ostensible revealed traditions, one, Islam, is, according to Rosenzweig, merely a 'parody' of revealed religions,[8] 'a monistic paganism . . . God himself competes with God himself at every moment, as if it were the colourful, warring heaven of the gods of polytheism'.[9] Being too reliant on *a* Book and *a* prophet, Islam does not partake of the truth of the Book that is God's word, which infuses all of Judaism and gives to Christianity what truth Christianity has. Islam preaches mercy but, according to Rosenzweig, does not grasp the full plenitude of God's love 'Islam knows of a loving God as little as of a beloved soul'.[10] And, just as philosophical idealism had exaggerated the intellect's role in life, and thereby is bereft of the genuinely revelatory role of God, Mohammed 'took over the concept of revelation externally, [and] he necessarily remained attached to heathendom in the basic concept of creation. For he did not recognise the interconnection which ties revelation to creation.'[11]

Rosenzweig also makes a distinction that cuts to the heart of the matter of what separates the revealed God of the Jews and Christians from the creator God of monistic pagans (of Platonists, Aristotelians, as well as the neo-variants, and Muslims): 'Revelation knows of no "all-loving father,"' he says starkly. Love 'is no attribute of God'; rather, God's love is an event, an event that is never directed at the All. God's love is 'ever wholly of the moment and to the point at which it is directed, and only in the infinity of time does it reach one point after another, step by step, and inform the All.'[12] He 'loves everything, only not yet. His love roams the world with an ever-fresh drive'.[13] The pagan fails to grasp revelation in its true depth because there is no second tier, nothing different in *kind* from creation. Revelation, however, is about reversal and renewal in and through death.[14] For that to occur the death that is the universal experience must also be capable of being conquered in each and every individuation not as a

---

8.  Rosenzweig, 'The New Thinking', 131.
9.  Rosenzweig, *The Star of Redemption*, 123.
10. Rosenzweig, *The Star of Redemption*, 172.
11. Rosenzweig, *The Star of Redemption*, 117.
12. Rosenzweig, *The Star of Redemption*, 164.
13. Rosenzweig, *The Star of Redemption*, 164.
14. Rosenzweig, 'The New Thinking', 129.

universal rule, but as an event. For Rosenzweig it is precisely in the particularity of the particular that such a triumph is possible. The 'this here and now' receives its revelation in the unique how and where of its love. There is no such thing as abstract love, just as there is no love that is general. The fulfilment of the command to love the neighbour only occurs through the unique act, being dependent on the specificities of both the lover, the neighbour, and the uniqueness of their relationship. Everything about revelation, then, from the God revealing, to the one to whom the revelation is made, to the content of what is revealed is indicative of particularity in its experience of the more encompassing universal of creation. 'Revelation', as he says in 'The *Urzelle*', 'pushes itself into the world as a wedge; the this struggles against the This'.[15]

Revelation, then, as the means by which the petrification of the universal is overcome, is what makes redemption possible, that renewal of the soul that is the surrender to God. The soul's triumph over death comes from its hunger to fulfil God's movement of next to next, to entreat and prepare the way for the coming of the kingdom of God. To be redeemed is to be open to revelation, and hence to be aware of the presence of the revealer, of the 'I am here' that is ever here, the eternal middle point that at any moment can refashion, reform, and, to repeat, 'renew and reverse' creation.

Redemption, the fulfilment of the revelation that love is stronger than death, is the eternal hope of the Jews. The Jews have conquered the problem of death through genuinely living under it and loving beyond it. Their love beyond it is a practice of the requirement of redemption, the love of the next, to wit, love of the next generation. It is a love that is the birth right of the Jew, that belongs in the blood. Judaism is not a religion of conversion, like Christianity or Islam. Its overcoming of death is not mere metaphysical speculation although the Jew too speaks of personal immortality, but not of a one-sided immortality of the soul. Redemption of one's own soul is part of redemption, but redemption, won step by step, is of creation itself, of the entire world.

The overcoming of death is experienced by the Jews collectively as a people who live in eternity and thereby forego what defines other peoples: their own soil, language, and extrinsic laws and modes of

---

15. Franz Rosenzweig, 'The *Urzelle*', in Franks and Morgan, *Franz Rosenzweig, Philosophical and Theological Writings*, 65.

governance. These people, forever strangers, 'must deny itself active and full participation in the life of this world'.[16] His eyes are ever on the ultimate community, an eternal community here and in the future, not simply a living worldly community whose survival and perpetuity, due to its naturalness, require the state. Hence Rosenzweig's teaching is only compatible with a form of Zionism that makes no pretence to being the definitive form of Judaism. The Jews are stronger than death, stronger than all those mighty empires, nations and tongues that have come and gone. The Jews are the ineradicable, a thought the irony and profundity of which seems almost immeasurable given the time and place in which it is so powerfully argued and the savage trial in which they would be put to the test. As ineradicable, and hence eternal, the Jew is the elect.

Perhaps, after the experience of the twentieth century, there are few ideas that are more fraught with terror and sheer evil than that of being God's elect. Yet this is precisely the thought at the root of Rosenzweig's entire thinking. But this thought is not carried through in the way of the murderer or warmonger. On the contrary, for the Jew alone, says Rosenzweig, the holy war (a Jewish discovery)[17] no longer has meaning. And in a formulation that is uncompromisingly anti-Zionist, the Jew 'knows nothing of war' because he 'has left its holy war behind in mythical antiquity'.[18]

In Christendom, on the other hand, war is still an essential component of life, as it is for the modern soul which is, according to Rosenzweig, a hybrid of Christian and pagan energies that cannot be disentangled. The Jew is elect because s/he is not enmeshed in creation and the spatial and temporal limitations which engulf other peoples. S/he alone truly transcends the pagan by living completely with the reality of redemption. The Jews do not exist only for themselves, but for all mankind. Their role in redemption, in entreating it, in *living* it, in their ever anticipation of the messiah, in their rites and rituals, feast-days and festivals is to help make it possible for all humanity to be redeemed.[19] The Israelites are not only blessed by their God, the One God who is not just the God of creation, but the God who is revealer and redeemer, who with all his love wishes to redeem all of creation.

---

16. Rosenzweig, *The Star of Redemption*, 332.
17. Rosenzweig, *The Star of Redemption*, 330.
18. Rosenzweig, *The Star of Redemption*, 331.
19. Rosenzweig, *The Star of Redemption*, 308.

The Jews are nothing less than God's blessing to the world,[20] a blessing that resides in living in the truth of the love of the neighbour. But the neighbour will not necessarily love the Jew back; on the contrary, the calling of the Jew, for Rosenzweig, is to love in the face of the neighbour's hatred; that eternal hatred, which Rosenzweig, claims is at the essence of the Christian attitude to the Jew.

Resting God's law on love of God and love of neighbour even in the face of hatred, that is, loving one's enemies would not seem to be anything unique to the Jews. Indeed, has not Rosenzweig simply identified the Christian essence of revelation and redemption and re-appropriated it for the Jews? It is clear that the difference between Christians and Jews ultimately is not about the supremacy of the commandment of love. Both religions claim this. But, according to Rosenzweig, the Christians, by rejecting the law and creating a tension between love and the law show they do not grasp it. The law,

> in its multiplicity, and strength ordering everything, comprising everything 'external', that is all the life of this world, everything that any worldly jurisdiction may conceivably comprise, this law makes this world and the world to come indistinguishable. God himself, according to Rabbinic legend, 'studies' in the law.[21]

As well as the dispute about the law there is also the irreconcilable issue of the messiah. Bluntly, the Christian worships a false messiah. Concomitantly, for the Jew the messiah is always to come, while for the Christian he has been, although he will come again. According to Rosenzweig, the sin of idolatry in Christianity is compounded by complacency: each Christian knows who the messiah is, and it is not he or herself, whereas 'no Jew knows whether he himself may not be the messiah'.[22]

Rosenzweig does not deny the possibility of great acts of love by individual Christians. On the contrary, the saint is an essential Christian type.[23] But the momentary irruption of love is not alien to the pagan either. What Rosenzweig unequivocally denies is that the

---

20. Rosenzweig, *The Star of Redemption*, 308.
21. Rosenzweig, *The Star of Redemption*, 405–6.
22. Rosenzweig, *'Paralipomena'*, 103.
23. Rosenzweig, *The Star of Redemption*, 399–400.

Christian deficiencies, unlike the Jewish dangers or temptations of denial, disdain and mortification of the world due to the inwardness demanded by God[24] are surmountable. The Christian dangers are: 'that the Spirit leads onto all ways, and not God; that the Son of man be the truth, and not God; that God would become All-in-All and not One above all'.[25] Christianity is in its essence, according to Rosenzweig, riven. Its faith, love and hope pull in different directions, as do its 'spiritualization of God, apotheosis of man, [and] pantheification of the world'.[26] At any given moment the Christian is drawn into one of these poles, while the others disappear. But this rivenness is precisely what characterises the natural and its prototype, the pagan. What, then, Rosenzweig is saying is that Christianity never overleaps the pagan half of its origin; it never truly grasps the unity of creation, revelation and redemption, and God, man and world that All, which is reality (as opposed to the abstract All of idealist philosophers) and which forms the basis of the life of every religious Jew. The Christian too lives in the same fractured, that is, diminished manner as the pagan.

That pagan half of Christianity is immediately evident, to Rosenzweig, in the fact that for the Christian everyone is born a pagan and then receives Christ in baptism, while the Jew is born a Jew.[27] Of course, the Christian believes that he overleaps this half. But this belief, for Rosenzweig is always *just belief*; while the Jew *knows* s/he is no pagan and s/he can always rely on the pagan and Christian to remind them, if they forget, that they do not belong.

The pagan side of the Christian is also evident historically. For Christianity emerges on pagan soil, in the Roman empire and absorbs and perfects administrative techniques which enable its mission of conquest to far surpass that achieved by the secular Roman empire. But just at the historical moment Christianity thinks it has conquered the pagan (the Middle Ages), its pagan memories flood back in and repossess the external body that is Christendom. Thus, for Rosenzweig, the Protestant elevation of the individual conscience is ushering in a return to the pagan world of multiple and sundered energies.[28]

---

24.  Rosenzweig, *The Star of Redemption*, 407.
25.  Rosenzweig, *The Star of Redemption*, 402.
26.  Rosenzweig, *The Star of Redemption*, 402.
27.  Rosenzweig, *The Star of Redemption*, 407.
28.  Rosenzweig, *The Star of Redemption*, 278–82.

This hybrid of Christian and pagan is the modern age. It is essential for understanding Rosenzweig to emphasise that the modern age has indeed been formed directly by Christianity, and hence by its Old Testament, which is also to say (perversely, due to its truncation, and hence indirectly) by Judaism. The pagan as such, the pagan unsullied by Christianity and Judaism, then, no longer exists in the West. Hence, as Rosenzweig says in 'The New Thinking', its creations belong in museums.[29] Even the great modern pagan philosophers such as Schopenhauer and Nietzsche are said by Rosenzweig to be Christians, but they are so ignorant of Christian tradition that they don't realise that concepts such as 'conversion, overcoming, change of will, the holy, rebirth, compassion, hardness' are not pagan.[30] Yet, as I have also said, if the pagan has been Christianised, it is equally the case that the Christian has been paganised.

The first man who grasped and expressed this, observes Rosenzweig, was Goethe, whose youthful prayer[] 'Labor of my hands that I/finish, grant, oh Fortune high'[31][] is the formulation of the new man. This prayer, says Rosenzweig, is a prayer of 'unbelief,' 'which is at the same time a wholly believing prayer, namely believing in creaturely fashion'.[32] It is also the prayer now prayed by all Christians. That is, within Christendom, each *hopes* that their will is to be blessed; it is the old pagan love of fate. Not 'thy will be done,' but would that my will be divinised. Such a prayer, though, is bound to fail. For it is a false entreatment, one that Rosenzweig says:

> borders directly on [that of] the prayer of the sinner, who presumes himself free to entreat everything, and of the fanatic, who thinks that, for the sake of the distant One which the moment of the prayer indicates as essential to him, everything other than this One, everything nighest, must be forbidden to him.[33]

---

29. Rosenzweig, 'The New Thinking', 130.
30. *Franz Rosenzweig, Der Mensch und sein Werk*, edited by Rachel Rosenzweig, *et al* (Hagg, 1979). See letter to Rudolf Ehrenberg, 1.12.1917, 486. My translation.
31. Rosenzweig, *The Star of Redemption*, 275.
32. Rosenzweig, *The Star of Redemption*, 283.
33. Rosenzweig, *The Star of Redemption*, 286.

That is to say, the prostration of one before God, the act that is undertaken in the knowledge of our deficiency, of our dependency upon powers outside of our control, of our wish to work with what is higher has been replaced by an act of hubris. The supplicant might want everything now (the sinner)□ this is in opposition to the righteous who waits for the proper time to receive the gifts that they will be ready to appreciate□ and is so sure of how to get it (the fanatic) that they brush aside the nearest to get to their goal. This new supplication, then, creates sinners and fanatics. Or to express it in more secular terms, Rosenzweig is saying that modern men and women are simultaneously driven by their own selfishness *and* a fanatical ruthlessness to bring about a better future. Nietzsche's Zarathustra is the prototype: a sinner and fanatic in one, 'an immoralist who smashes all the old tablets, and a tyrant who overpowers his neighbour as well as himself for the sake of the next-but-one, his friend for the sake of new friends'.[34]

The revolutionary fervour of the age in which Rosenzweig lived is, then, seen as the result of the false messianism which is at the root of Christianity and which, through its falseness, is not only incapable of preventing, but has accelerated and facilitated, the diabolical outbreak of sinners and fanatics. This is the antithesis of the messianic politics that the stateless Jew embodies. The fanatical pursuit of false redemption delays the redemption that is the object of messianic politics. What Rosenzweig calls 'the entreatment of the kingdom' is, amongst the moderns, a sickness. And, for Rosenzweig, the utopianisms of Rousseau, Tolstoy, and Bolshevism are symptoms of the modern cultural sickness. But the doctrines of such utopians cannot provide the cure, as is evident in the failure of each to live his utopia.[35]

The messianic age, on the other hand, comes from the work done on the daily basis, on the love given to 'anybody' who is the neighbour. The Jews know how to wait in preparation of the messiah, and they must be ever prepared. In a letter to Gertrude Oppenheim, Rosenzweig wrote, 'Every act must be done as if the fate of eternity

---

34.  Rosenzweig, *The Star of Redemption*, 286.
35.  Rosenzweig, *Zweistromland*, 588.

were to hinge on it. Because one never knows whether it weren't to hang on it.'[36]

Near the conclusion of the *Star* Rosenzweig argues that before God both Jews and Christians labour at the same task, in enmity with each other, yet 'most intimately bound with each other'.[37] The Jews are the truth of eternity: they look directly upon the eternal star itself (that overlaying triad of God, man, world, on the one hand, creation, revelation, redemption, on the other) while Christians build and prepare the world for his coming. For the Christian, 'the advent of the kingdom becomes a matter of secular and ecclesiastical history'.[38] Pursuing the truth in temporality, the Christian ever follows the rays of the star. The whole truth, Rosenzweig insists, is in both Jew and Christian. In this sense, then, the Christian as world maker is necessary for God's plan, but s/he is further making the world that the Jew will redeem.

Christianity remains a religion based on a fundamental untruth, a 'world conquering fiction,' as he writes in a letter to Rosenstock.[39] And, as he also says in a letter to Rosenstock, the Jews were right to crucify the impostor and, they would be right to do so again and again. While Christians teach that they have inherited the Old Testament, that Judaism is merely a preparation for Christ, Rosenzweig teaches the reverse:

> Christianity is like a power that fills the world. According to the saying of one of the two scholastics, Yehuda ha-Levi: it is the tree that grows from the seed of Judaism and casts its shadows over the earth; but its fruits must contain the seed again. The seed that nobody who saw the tree noticed.[40]

---

36.  *Franz Rosenzweig, Der Mensch und sein Werk*, edited by Rachel Rosenzweig, *et al.* See letter to Gertrude Oppenheim, 5.2.1917, 344–5. My translation.
37.  Rosenzweig, *The Star of Redemption*, 415.
38.  Rosenzweig, *The Star of Redemption*, 368.
39.  *Judaism Despite Christianity: The 'Letters on Christianity and Judaism' between Eugen Rosenstock-Huessy and Franz* Rosenzweig, edited by Eugen Rosenstock-Huessy (New York: Schocken Books, 1971), 112–13.
40.  *Judaism Despite Christianity*, 112.

In other words, the Christian is the unwitting servant, thinking s/he is doing one thing while really doing another. S/he thinks s/he is the world. But the Jew is, and is always, the elect.

In conclusion, the *Star* is an attempt to identify the Jew and a call for Jews to live in a blazing truth, a truth unprotected by the pagan potencies and shelters of art and the state, which the rest of us take as 'ours,' and which conspired murderously against the Jews. What makes the *Star* particularly profound is the historical moment of its construction. Rosenzweig sensed the ominous proportions of the surrounding anti-Semitism, the failures of philosophies and theologies, and he taught the Jews to love their God, to love who they were and to love their neighbour, whose face, as he describes with such poetic power toward the end of the *Star*, is the mirror of the divine countenance.

*The Star of Redemption's* concluding paragraph points to an unknown tomorrow with the question: 'whither, /then, do the wings of/the gate open? Thou/ knowest it not?' Rosenzweig's answer is 'INTO LIFE'. When he wrote this he did not know that the gate for him would open into a terrible sickness in his own life and, after his death, for his people, into the holocaust.

His solution 'to walk humbly with thy God' is the solution of one who, not knowing where life will lead, is prepared to be a witness. It is a solution whose brilliance never loses its radiance. That it would be the blood line that made the Jews martyrs, and that such martyrdom would be the consequence of the fusion of pagan and Christian false revelations, false redemptions and false messiahs venting ancient hatreds, makes it one of the most profoundly prophetic works in the history of philosophy.

# 17

# The Power of the Present: Tillich on Messianism, Apocalypse and Redemption

## Phillip Tolliday

By any reckoning Paul Tillich (1886–1963) was one of the most influential Protestant (Lutheran) theologians of the twentieth century.[1] Serving in World War I as a chaplain, Tillich, in common with many in his generation, underwent a fundamental change. He wrote to his family in 1916 that: 'We are experiencing the most terrible catastrophes, the end of the world order . . . [which] is coming to an end, and this end is accompanied by deepest pain'.[2] The awareness and the pain caused by the endless individual deaths around him appeared to parallel the death of civilisation itself. He wrote, 'I have become purely an eschatologist in that what I, along with others, am experiencing is the actual end of the world of this time'.[3] According to one biographer this time spent on the Western Front would mark *the* turning point in Tillich's life. 'The traditional monarchist had become a religious socialist, the Christian believer a cultural pessimist, and repressed puritanical boy a "wild man".'[4]

Returning to Berlin in 1919 Tillich threw himself into teaching and 'sought the company of esoteric intellectual groups which shared his own interests: politics, religious socialism, painting, economics, the theatre, and later depth psychology'.[5] It is worth noting that during this period from 1919 until the Nazi rise to power in 1933, Tillich's

1. See, for example: Wilhelm Pauck and Marion Pauck, *Paul Tillich: His Life & Thought, Volume 1: Life* (London: Collins, 1977).
2. Pauck, *Paul Tillich*, quoting a letter from Paul Tillich to his father Johannes, 10 December 1916, 51.
3. Robert P Scharlemann, 'Paul Tillich', in *The Oxford Companion to Christian Thought*, edited by Adrian Hastings (Oxford: Oxford University Press, 2000).
4. Pauck, *Paul Tillich*, 41.
5. Pauck, *Paul Tillich*, 58.

teaching appointments were not to theological faculties but to religious studies or philosophy departments.[6] In later life Tillich would refer to these experiences as having been 'on the boundary'. It would seem that he enjoyed being 'at the point of intersection between a religious tradition and major movements in secular culture'.[7] It would be a position that he would continue to hold and which would provide the motivation for developing a mediating theology that would 'exhibit a correlation between religion and culture'.[8] This mediating theology would be developed in his three-volume *Systematic Theology* (1951–63) written in the United States, after fleeing the Nazis in 1933, and completed just before his death.

The themes of messianism, apocalypse and redemption run through Tillich's theology because they are the very concerns that form the core the existential questions that mark one aspect of his mediating theology. That Tillich figures them with an emphasis on the power of the present is the argument that I wish to develop here. In order to show this I need outline the extent to which I think Tillich's theology can be characterised correctly as 'existentialist'. Secondly, I need to develop at least a summary understanding of his distinction between 'essence' and 'existence' and 'actuality', since it is the disjunction between 'essence' and 'existence' which is 'actuality' that produces the situation of estrangement into which messianism brings the New Being. Third, these points cannot really be dissociated from a brief look at his ontology from the perspective of the correlation between questions generated by ontology and existential concerns and correlated with theological answers in the form of symbols. Fourth, messianism, symbolised by the Christ who brings the new being, effects salvation or redemption in the form of healing. Such redemptive moments are simply that—*moments*. They are fragmentary and are always given in the midst of the actuality of life, which is ambiguous, yet, says Tillich, they provide us with a glimpse of a life that is (could be?) unambiguous. Fifth, this leads to a discussion of actual life as it is lived in history and from there the question is raised as to whether history has any meaning. Sixth the question of the

*momentary redemption*

---

6.    Pauck, *Paul Tillich*, 114. His four years at Frankfurt, 1929–33 turned out to be 'the richest and most successful of his German career'.

7.    David H Kelsey, 'Paul Tillich', in *The Modern Theologians: An Introduction to Christian Theology in the Twentieth Century*, Volume 1, edited by David F Ford (Oxford: Basil Blackwell, 1989), 135.

8.    Kelsey, 'Paul Tillich', 136.

meaning of history is addressed by the symbol of the kingdom of God, a realm which has both an inner-historical and a transhistorical aspect. This takes us close to that unambiguous realm and raises the tantalizing question of whether such a state might be permanent and supranatural in the sense of being beyond the world. Tillich presses Schelling for the latter's use of the word 'essentialization' though he feels free to change its meaning. However we shall suggest that even here the eternal future not only gains its power from the present but also is constituted by it.

There can be little doubt that existentialism has had a profound influence on Tillich's thought. We can note for example the influence that Heidegger had upon him.[9] Moreover when Tillich talks about the distorting power of existence that results in estrangement he speaks of the 'universal experience of anxiety, so distinctive a feature of existential philosophy'.[10] Indeed it is this very experience of anxiety that becomes Tillich's 'justification for bothering with ontology at all'.[11] Tillich's existentialism, insofar as it is present, and here we ought to note that it is present only as 'an important element' in an otherwise 'highly eclectic ontology' and is not determinative of the whole,[12] serves an apologetic purpose. Indeed for him existentialism necessarily attended to the social, political, economic and technological trends of the times.[13] It is the present situation, the social-political environment, that throws up, as it were, the existential questions that provoke theological answers. Indeed it because of this very background that Tillich so pain-stakingly explores the ambiguities of human existence in the world, particularly in history. He knew intimately that millenarian expectations were bound to disappoint.

Tillich aims to produce a mediating theology by exhibiting a correlation between religion and culture, or as he puts it, between message and situation.[14] It is an attempt to interpret Christian symbols as providing answers to ontological questions generated in turn by

---

9.   Paul Tillich, *On The Boundary* (London: Collins, 1967), 48, 56.

10.  Adrian Thatcher, *The Ontology of Paul Tillich* (Oxford: Oxford University Press, 1978), 97.

11.  Thatcher, *The Ontology of Paul Tillich*, 97.

12.  Thatcher, *The Ontology of Paul Tillich*, 24.

13.  Paul Tillich, *The Spiritual Situation in Our Technical Society* (Georgia: Mercer University Press, 1983).

14.  Paul Tillich, *Systematic Theology*, Volume 1 (London: SCM Press, 1978), 1–6.

existential concerns. This interpretation was effected through what Tillich called his 'method of correlation' by which he showed how the question of the meaning of being (the ontological question) was correlated with the symbol of God as its answer (the theological answer). Implicit here is Tillich's working assumption that 'philosophy and religion cannot be reduced to each other, neither can the one be derived from the other'.[15] In his theology it is always possible to correlate religion and culture because they are always a single whole of which 'the form of religion is culture and the substance of culture is religion'.[16] He claimed that:

> Philosophy cannot answer ultimate or existential questions *qua* philosophy. If the philosopher tries to answer them (and all creative philosophers have tried to do so), he becomes a theologian. And, conversely, theology cannot answer those questions without accepting their presuppositions and implications. Question and answer determine each other; if they are separated, the traditional answers become unintelligible, and the actual questions remain unanswered.[17]

Tillich's systematic theology consists of five parts, in each of which a correlation is made between a major biblical symbol and a major human question, as expressed in modern culture:[18]

> Part I (Reason & Revelation) correlates the symbol 'Logos' with modern culture's form of the sceptical question: How can we know with certainty any human truth? Part II (Being & God) correlates the symbol 'God as Creator' with modern culture's expressions of the question of finitude: How can we withstand the destructive forces that threaten to disintegrate our lives? Part III (Existence & The Christ) correlates the symbol 'Jesus as the Christ' with modern culture's

---

15. Scharlemann, 'Paul Tillich'.
16. Kelsey, 'Paul Tillich', 136.
17. Paul Tillich, *The Protestant Era* (London: Nisbet & Co, 1951), xlii.
18. Kelsey, 'Paul Tillich', 136.

secular expressions of the question of estrange-ment: How can we heal the alienation we experience from ourselves and from our neighbours? Part IV (Life & the Spirit) correlates the symbol 'Spirit' with modern culture's expressions of the question of ambiguity: How can our lives be authentic when our morality, religious practices and cultural self-expressions are so thoroughly ambiguous? And Part V (History & the Kingdom of God) correlates the symbol 'Kingdom of God' with the question: Has history any meaning?[19]

This formal overview of Tillich's system permits us to see the range of his questions, however it does not, by itself, provide us with a sense of just how the correlation between question and answer takes place. Tillich's distinction between 'essential nature', 'existence' or existential disruption, and 'actuality' explores how life is actually lived and it is in answer to the way the human being is in the world that the themes of messianism, apocalypse and redemption provide a response.

## 1. Essence, existence and actuality

For Tillich essence is 'what Plato called *eidos* or Idea'.[20] Elsewhere he claims that essence is 'that which makes a thing *what* it is, and what it *is* is its *ousia*'.[21] The essential belongs with the term potentiality and it conveys the sense of 'that kind of being which has the power, the dynamic, to become actual (for example, the potentiality of every tree is treehood)'.[22] It exists in the form of a concept and is available to us,

---

19.   Kelsey, 'Paul Tillich', 136–7.
20.   Paul Tillich, *My Search For Absolutes* (New York: Simon & Schuster, 1967), 72–3.
21.   Tillich, *Systematic Theology*, Volume 1, 203.
22.   Tillich, *Systematic Theology*, Volume 3, 12. The way Tillich defines essence is problematic. See, for example: 'When Tillich speaks of the *ousia* of a thing, he contrasts what he calls the 'really real' with the 'seemingly real'. The imagery is Platonic. When he speaks of potentiality, he contrasts the actual with the non-actual. Here the imagery is Aristotelian . . . For Plato it is the realm of essence which is 'real'; for Aristotle it is actuality. Tillich however, is happy to equate essence with potentiality and potentiality with essence. He does not use either with much precision . . . [making] the meaning of his

if at all, only through intuition, for it is intuition that 'penetrates through the bounds of thought and therefore furnishes us with knowledge of a pre-critical or pre-conceptual type'.[23]

Our experience concerns the result of the transition from essence to existence. For Tillich 'existence' and 'existential' convey the sense of being estranged from essence.[24] Estranged from essence we find ourselves likewise estranged from being; we are unable to hold the twin polarities of 'individualization and participation, dynamics and form, destiny and freedom in balance in our transactions with the world'.[25] Consequently our world becomes more chaotic and this sense of chaos provokes a universal existential anxiety within us as we become aware of our estrangement from being. Moreover our relations with ourselves are disrupted and become progressively more disintegrated. Out of this sense of disintegration or estrangement is generated the quest for overcoming or healing this alienation. Where can we find the power of new being for such overcoming? The Christian symbol for this 'where?' is the Messiah[26] or the messianic —specifically Jesus the Christ as the power of the New Being.

The third sub-division, 'actuality' refers to the way life is lived precisely in its *concrete* uniting of essence and existence.[27] Since life is the 'actuality of being'[28] born out of the uniting of essence and existence, it follows that life is a process: the process of 'actualising potentiality or essential nature'.[29] Actuality is aligned with Part's IV and V of the system and involves the three functions of self-integration, self-creation and self-transcendence. Here it is important to recall that Parts IV and V have to do with life, history and the kingdom of God and thus these three functions are considered in their concrete actuality. Moreover, as we experience each of these functions we are alerted to the inherent ambiguity of life and history. Tillich claims that:

---

philosophical terms extremely difficult', in Adrian Thatcher, *The Ontology of Paul Tillich* (Oxford: Oxford University Press, 1978), 106.

23. Thatcher, *The Ontology of Paul Tillich*, 116.
24. Tillich, *Systematic Theology*, Volume 3, 29–39.
25. Kelsey, 'Paul Tillich', 142.
26. Kelsey, 'Paul Tillich', 143.
27. Tillich, *Systematic Theology*, Volume 3, 11.
28. Tillich, *Systematic Theology*, Volume 3, 11.
29. Kelsey, 'Paul Tillich', 144.

Every life process has the ambiguity that the positive
and negative elements are mixed in such a way that a
definite separation of the negative from the positive is
impossible: life at every moment is ambiguous. It is my
intention to discuss the particular functions of life, not
in their essential nature, separate from their existential
distortion, but in the way they appear within the
ambiguities of their actualisation, for life is neither
essential nor existential but ambiguous.[30]

It is this ambiguity that then drives us toward a quest for the
unambiguous: a quest satisfied, albeit in a fragmentary way, by the
power of the New Being that is manifested in the present. Life as it
exists in its actuality can be described as not simply *asking* the question,
but *being* the 'question which finds its answer in the presence of the
divine Spirit.'[31] And this sense of 'being the question' is generated by
the three functions of self-integration, self-creation and self-
transcendence.

Self-integration, with regard to human life, refers to the moral
life.[32] It is human actions that render us morally accountable and the
more we develop this accountability the more integrated we become.
However all moral acts are ambiguous and so even in those situations
where we have acted as well as we could there is always the reality
that either we may have done better by choosing other acts, or our
good acts may have unintentionally diminished someone else. Tillich
argues that these considerations, which are always present, drive us to
ask whether there is any way to fulfil our inherent drive to self-
integration through unambiguous morality.

Self-creation refers to the way we participate meaningfully in
culture.[33] Engaged in culture we are immured in symbols and styles
of art and behaviour. Culture, says Tillich, is 'that which takes care of
something, keeps it alive, and makes it grow'.[34] Yet culture is
composed of many artefacts and symbols some of which nurture life
while others oppress new life. 'Because our lives inherently drive

---

30. Tillich, *Systematic Theology*, Volume 3, 32.
31. Christoph Schwöbel, 'Paul Tillich', in *The Blackwell Encyclopedia of Modern Christian Thought* (Oxford: Basil Blackwell, 1993).
32. Tillich, *Systematic Theology*, Volume 3, 38–50.
33. Tillich, *Systematic Theology*, Volume 3, 57–86.
34. Tillich, *Systematic Theology*, Volume 3, 57.

toward self-creation, we ask whether there is any way to achieve it through an unambiguous culture.'[35]

Self-transcendence refers to the situation in which human beings engage in religious activity.[36] It is always morally integrated and culturally creative lives that self-transcend. Thus Tillich draws the consequence that there is a religious dimension to and in all cultural and moral activity.[37] However ambiguity is no less present in religion than anywhere else. The institutional structures in which religion is expressed are inherently ambiguous. Since they are finite structures, 'functioning religiously to express the unconditioned, that toward which one 'transcends' oneself . . . they invite for themselves the ultimate concern appropriate only to the unconditioned. Thereby they become "demonic".'[38]

'Religion is *not* the answer to the quest for unambiguous life',[39] says Tillich, yet this poses a question for us. Because our lives inherently drive toward self-transcendence, is there any way to achieve it through unambiguous religion? To anticipate, the answer is yes and this takes us into a discussion of messianism and the New Being which constitutes the 'restorative principle overcoming the cleavage between essential and existential being'.[40]

## 2. Messianism and the New Being

The symbol 'Christ' or 'Messiah' means the one who brings the new state of things, the New Being.[41] This new being appears in a 'personal life', the life of Jesus of Nazareth.[42] When applied to Jesus as the Christ, the concept of the new being points to 'the power in him which conquers existential estrangement or, negatively expressed, to the power of resisting the forces of estrangement'.[43] Thus it is the task of

---

35. Kelsey, 'Paul Tillich', 145.
36. Tillich, *Systematic Theology*, Volume 3, 86–106.
37. Tillich, *Systematic Theology*, Volume 3, 94–8.
38. Kelsey, 'Paul Tillich', 145–6.
39. Tillich, *Systematic Theology*, Volume 3, 106.
40. Tillich, *Systematic Theology*, Volume 2, 119.
41. Tillich, *Systematic Theology*, Volume 2, 97.
42. Tillich, *Systematic Theology*, Volume 2, 120.
43. Tillich, *Systematic Theology*, Volume 2, 125.

the messiah to 'overcome the structures of evil and to establish a new reality from which they are excluded'.[44]

There is both an historical and transhistorical meaning to the symbol of 'messiah'. Beginning from an historical and political background the notion of the messianic expanded over time. As it did so the once immediate political meaning was transcended and the figure of the messiah itself became more symbolic. However this did not mean that the messianic became disconnected from history. 'The Messiah does not save individuals in a path leading out of historical existence; he is to transform historical existence.'[45] Thus Christian theology has attempted to argue that the 'historical type of the expectation of the New Being could include the non-historical type',[46] although this did not work in the opposite direction. The non-historical was unable to embrace the historical.

This trajectory from the historical through to the inclusion of the non-historical can be traced in four steps. Firstly, there is the messianic figure through whom God will establish God's people in 'Israel and, through Israel, in the whole world'.[47] Here we need to distinguish between the prophetic period during which the historical emphasis of the messianic symbol prevailed, and the apocalyptic period in which the transhistorical aspect was dominant. Secondly, during the period of late Judaism the apocalyptic literature of the time brings the human situation of injustice and misery into sharp relief:

> The present eon in its totality, including individuals, society, and nature, is perverted. A new eon, a new state of things in the universe, must be asked for. It is the Messiah who will bring it with divine power.[48]

Thirdly, comes the advent of Christianity and a consequent 'reception and transformation of this set of symbols'.[49] Conditioned by

---

44. Tillich, *Systematic Theology*, Volume 2, 27. See also, 'the messiah is to transform historical existence' [88], and 'in messianic thought, the New Being does not demand the sacrifice of finite being; instead, it fulfils all finite being by conquering its estrangement' [88].
45. Tillich, *Systematic Theology*, Volume 2, 88.
46. Tillich, *Systematic Theology*, Volume 2, 89.
47. Tillich, *Systematic Theology*, Volume 2, 110.
48. Tillich, *Systematic Theology*, Volume 2, 111.
49. Tillich, *Systematic Theology*, Volume 2, 111.

previous historical and transhistorical expectation of the messianic symbol the people expect that Jesus will sweep away the power of the old eon in a miraculous demonstration of divine power. In the event the opposite happens and 'the Messiah who is supposed to bring the new eon is defeated by the powers of the old eon'.[50] For Judaism such a cataclysmic event spells a disproof of Jesus' messianic pretensions. For Christianity 'the defeat of the Messiah on the Cross is the most radical transformation of the symbol of the Messiah'[51] and, we can add, the messianic.

Finally, according to Tillich, comes the 'literalistic distortion of the messianic paradox'.[52] Here the word 'Christ' meaning 'messiah' and thus denoting a function, has been turned into a proper name. Jesus the Christ, Tillich's preferred designation becomes instead Jesus Christ. Moreover this figure now had become an 'individual with supranatural powers who, through a voluntary sacrifice, made it possible for God to save those who believe in him'.[53]

The explanation of the person of Christ is to be found in his work; that is, 'soteriology gives direction to the christological answer'.[54] Jesus the Christ as the power of the New Being comes to save us. Playing on the etymological meaning of the word *salvus* Tillich interprets salvation/redemption as healing. He observes that 'healing means reuniting that which is estranged, giving a center to what is split, overcoming the split between God and man, man and his world, man and himself'.[55] Salvation and revelation name two aspects of the same reality. Salvation can be likened to a type of insight, in this case insight in which 'one experiences one's unity with the depth of reason . . . that is the ground of being and meaning'.[56] This is because the power of meaning that is given through Jesus as Logos is, of course, none other than the power of being. It can also be likened to the 'moment of therapeutic insight in psychoanalysis, in that insight one is healed of one's ontological disintegratedness'.[57] Indeed this is quite an

50.  Tillich, *Systematic Theology*, Volume 2, 111.
51.  Tillich, *Systematic Theology*, Volume 2, 111.
52.  Tillich, *Systematic Theology*, Volume 2, 111.
53.  Tillich, *Systematic Theology*, Volume 2, 111.
54.  Tillich, *Systematic Theology*, Volume 2, 150.
55.  Tillich, *Systematic Theology*, Volume 2, 166.
56.  Kelsey, 'Paul Tillich', 143.
57.  Kelsey, 'Paul Tillich', 143.

apt comparison since lack of integration is one of the marks of ambiguity inherent in our actual moral life.

However it is important to recognise that this redemption or healing to which Tillich refers does not eliminate the situation of existential distortion. The power of New Being is mediated and it is redemptive or healing but it always takes place 'in the midst of continuing estrangement'.[58] Whenever the event happens it is genuine, but it is never complete. It always needs to be repeated. Such redemptive moments are always fragmentary and ambiguous. This leads to the question of an analysis of the context in which these fragmentary and ambiguous moments happen, and that moves us into a discussion of history. History itself, with all its ambiguities, is correlated with the kingdom of God. The kingdom is entirely without ambiguity and there is some sense in which the 'eternal kingdom of God can already be experienced in fragmentary form and so provides meaning in the vacuum of meaninglessness'.[59]

### 3. History and its ambiguities

We have seen that 'essence' and 'existence' are abstractions for Tillich, only 'actuality' conveys the situation of life as it is lived. It is from the actual situation that ambiguities in morality, culture and religion are experienced; it is within the context of life that they are addressed and fragmentary unambiguous perspectives are glimpsed. These glimpses of unambiguous life ensure that there is a quest in the life of every creature for an unambiguous fulfilment of its essential potentialities.

'Religious symbolism' says Tillich, has 'produced three main symbols for unambiguous life: the Spirit of God, the Kingdom of God and Eternal Life'.[60] These three symbols 'mutually include one another'.[61] Yet they do have differing shades of meaning. Thus:

> Spiritual Presence for the conquest of the ambiguities
> of life under the dimension of the spirit, Kingdom of
> God for the conquest of the ambiguities of life under

---

58.   Kelsey, 'Paul Tillich', 143.
59.   Schwöbel, 'Paul Tillich'.
60.   Tillich, *Systematic Theology*, Volume 3, 107.
61.   Tillich, *Systematic Theology*, Volume 3, 109.

the dimension of history, and Eternal Life, for the
conquest of the ambiguities of life beyond history.[62]

That which makes the quest possible is Tillich's conviction that all
life has the character of self-transcendence. There is a quest for 'an
unambiguous morality and an unambiguous culture reunited with an
unambiguous religion'.[63] The answer to this quest is, as we have
already noted, the 'experience of revelation and salvation'.[64] In
abstraction as it were, they seem to constitute 'religion above religion',
however once they are received or apprehended 'they become
religion'.[65] But since all religions are embroiled in history and thus in
existence (in Tillich's terms) it follows that under such conditions of
existence 'even the absolutely great—the divine self-manifestation
—becomes not only great but also small, not only divine but also
demonic'.[66]

A further motivation that generates Tillich's quest for the kingdom
of God is an analysis of various interpretations of history, many of
which he finds to be deficient. Tillich classifies history into two general
groups: the non-historical 'negative answers to the question of the
meaning of history' and the historical, or what he prefers to designate
the 'positive but inadequate answers to the question of the meaning of
history'.

Under the non-historical interpretation are to be found the tragic,
the mystical and the mechanistic. The tragic interpretation of history
moves in a circle back to its beginning. Periods of time exist but all is
ruled by fate and 'there is no hope, no expectation of an immanent or
transcendent fulfilment of history'. It is nothing more than a 'tragic
circle of genesis and decay'.[67] According to Tillich, the mystical
interpretation of history is similarly non-historical. He claims that this
view of history can neither create the new nor be truly real'.[68]
Without these characteristics it could not qualify as historical. He
argues that mystical versions of history 'contain no impulse to
transform the direction of universal humanity and justice' nor does

62.  Tillich, *Systematic Theology*, Volume 3, 109.
63.  Tillich, *Systematic Theology*, Volume 3, 109.
64.  Tillich, *Systematic Theology*, Volume 3, 109.
65.  Tillich, *Systematic Theology*, Volume 3, 109.
66.  Tillich, *Systematic Theology*, Volume 3, 110.
67.  Tillich, *Systematic Theology*, Volume 3, 351.
68.  Tillich, *Systematic Theology*, Volume 3, 351.

history appear to have 'any aim, either in time or in eternity'.[69] Here the ambiguities of existence are not fated as they were in the tragic interpretation of history; however they are to be transcended rather than engaged and transformed. Finally, there is the mechanistic view of history which owes its genesis to the modern scientific interpretation of the world. According to this perspective, history has become a 'series of happenings in the physical universe'.[70] Since it is based around the technical control of the environment there is a sense, says Tillich, in which it can be classed as progressive. However such progress is generally conceived in an instrumentalist sense and thus it remains true for the mechanistic view of history that it does not share the point of view 'of an inner-historical or transhistorical aim toward which history is supposed to run'.[71]

Under the heading of the positive views of history can be found the progressive, the utopian and the transcendental. The progressive view of history does mark an advance on the previous categories inasmuch as it attends to historical time running toward an aim. However Tillich faults the progressivist understanding of history because it 'posits an infinite process [and progress] without an end'.[72] This view, which is indebted to Kant and Hegel and carried on through the work of Comte and Spencer in the nineteenth century, was found to be wanting by the manifest tragedies of the twentieth century. Tillich marvels that so great and sudden was the demise of the notion of history as progress that 'many (including this writer) who twenty years ago fought against the progressivistic ideology now feel driven to defend the justified elements in this concept'.[73]

The utopian understanding of history bears some resemblance to the idea of history as progress, with the exception that here the end is actually attained. 'Utopianism is progressivism with a definite aim: arrival at that stage of history in which the ambiguities of life are conquered.'[74] In theories of utopia there is an assumption that present action, usually revolutionary, will bring about a transformation of reality, a reality that will not carry any of the ambiguities associated

---

69. Tillich, *Systematic Theology*, Volume 3, 352.
70. Tillich, *Systematic Theology*, Volume 3, 352.
71. Tillich, *Systematic Theology*, Volume 3, 352.
72. Tillich, *Systematic Theology*, Volume 3, 353.
73. Tillich, *Systematic Theology*, Volume 3, 354.
74. Tillich, *Systematic Theology*, Volume 3, 354.

with historical existence. Moreover the utopia (literally, *no place*) will become the universal place. As with progressivism so also with utopianism, though even more radically. The march of history subjects such views to critical scrutiny and finds them wanting. Thus, the fatal flaw with utopianism is demonisation, which confuses the uncond-itioned with the conditioned:

> Utopianism, taken literally, is idolatrous. It gives the quality of ultimacy to something preliminary. It makes unconditional what is conditioned (a future historical situation) and at the same time disregards the always present existential estrangement and the ambiguities of life and history. This makes the utopian interpretation of history inadequate and dangerous.[75]

The third form of historical interpretation is the transcendental. This view of history is 'implicit in the eschatological mood of the New Testament and the early church up to Augustine. It was brought to its radical form in orthodox Lutheranism'.[76] Briefly, it is the view that once saving revelation appears in history, nothing new can be expected in the world. Salvation is restricted to what happens to the individual when he or she dies. 'There is no relationship between the justice of the Kingdom of God and the justice of power structures.'[77] This is because there exist two worlds: the historical world and the transcendent world, but neither seems to have any influence on the other. It typically 'contrasts the salvation of the individual with the transformation of the historical group . . . thus separating the one from the other'.[78] And finally, it interprets the 'symbol of the Kingdom of God as a static supernatural order into which individuals enter after their death' and thus dismisses the understanding of it as 'a dynamic power on earth'.[79] Consequently religion becomes privatised and both nature and culture are excluded from God's salvific activity.

It was as a consequence of the inadequacies of these views of history that Tillich decided to explore the symbol of the Kingdom of God from a double perspective. He argued that Kingdom of God 'has

---

75. Tillich, *Systematic Theology*, Volume 3, 355.
76. Tillich, *Systematic Theology*, Volume 3, 355.
77. Tillich, *Systematic Theology*, Volume 3, 355.
78. Tillich, *Systematic Theology*, Volume 3, 355.
79. Tillich, *Systematic Theology*, Volume 3, 356.

an inner-historical and a transhistorical side'.[80] Having an inner-historical aspect, it participates in the dynamics and ambiguities of history; while having a transhistorical character, it answers the questions implied in the ambiguities of the dynamics of history.[81] Yet from both perspectives the symbol seeks to address those drives of self-integration, self-creation and self-transcendence that we have encountered previously. Fundamentally, the symbol of the kingdom of God seeks to express a Christian response to the question about the possibility of unambiguous life in its historical rather than social dimensions: 'how is an answer to the question of the meaning of history possible?'[82] An inquiry into such meaning provides an entry into the way that Tillich addresses the motifs of apocalypse, messianism and redemption.

### 4. The kingdom of God and its relationship to history

Tillich claims that there are four elements that are characteristic of the symbol of the kingdom of God and which make it a viable symbol for the aim or *telos* of history. It is political; it is social; it is personal; and it is universal. Moreover, these characteristics disclose that the Kingdom of God is both immanent and transcendent, that is to say, both in history and above history.

As 'political', the kingdom of God corresponds to the political character of history-bearing groups. In the Old Testament the symbol of the kingdom of God can be identical with 'Mount Zion, Israel, the nations or the universe'.[83] In the writings of the New Testament the symbol has become identified with a new heaven and a new earth. There is the notion of a new creation and thus the kingdom of God as a 'political symbol is transformed into a cosmic symbol, [but] without losing its political connotation'.[84]

As 'social', the kingdom of God 'includes the ideas of justice and peace—not in contrast to the political quality and, therefore, not in contrast to power'.[85] But the denominator 'kingdom' is acutely qualified by what Robert Scharlemann calls the *alienator* 'of God' and

---

80.   Tillich, *Systematic Theology*, Volume 3, 357.
81.   Tillich, *Systematic Theology*, Volume 3, 357.
82.   Tillich, *Systematic Theology*, Volume 3, 349.
83.   Tillich, *Systematic Theology*, Volume 3, 358.
84.   Tillich, *Systematic Theology*, Volume 3, 358.
85.   Tillich, *Systematic Theology*, Volume 3, 358.

this effectively breaks any utopian expectation. The addition of the words 'of God' indicates the 'impossibility of an earthly fulfilment is implicitly acknowledged'.[86]

As 'personal', the kingdom of God symbolises that the individual does not find him or herself merged into some sort of cosmic whole. No individual is obliterated by identity with the Ultimate, but humanity is fulfilled in every particular human life. This is because 'the transhistorical aim toward which history runs is not the extinction but the fulfilment of humanity in every human individual'.[87]

As 'universal', the kingdom of God embraces all of creation. It is not restricted to human beings, but 'involves the fulfilment of life under all its dimensions'.[88] Embracing all of life, the kingdom of God moves beyond any anthropocentric vision of human destiny. Instead the human being is set among a redeemed creation in which 'the individual-social element is transcended, though not denied'.[89]

It is clear that the symbol of the kingdom of God is not simply an otherworldly event. Instead it is both in history and above it. The appearance of the kingdom of God is a process that connects with the dynamism that is the irreversible current of history. The appearance of the kingdom of God within history must, according to Tillich, be considered in relation to the 'appearance of Jesus as the Christ as the center of history.'[90] By using the word 'centre' Tillich makes it clear that he intends this in a qualitative rather than a quantitative sense. Thus it constitutes a critique of relativism and 'dares to assert its dependence on that event which is the criterion of all revelatory events'.[91]

This 'historical event in which history becomes aware of itself and its meaning'[92] in turn makes way for the appearance of the kingdom of God in history and constitutes a moment of breakthrough which

---

86. Tillich, *Systematic Theology*, Volume 3, 358.
87. Tillich, *Systematic Theology*, Volume 3, 358.
88. Tillich, *Systematic Theology*, Volume 3, 359.
89. Tillich, *Systematic Theology*, Volume 3, 359.
90. Tillich, *Systematic Theology*, Volume 3, 364.
91. Tillich, *Systematic Theology*, Volume 3, 364.
92. Tillich, *Systematic Theology*, Volume 3, 369.

Tillich calls the '*kairos*'.[93] In order to recognise the *kairos*—the opportune time—one must be able to discern the signs of the times.

Although the original appearance of Jesus marks the great *kairos,* the manifestation is expressed again and again in moments of conversion. When this happens it is as if the 'appearance of the center of history is . . . re-experienced through relative *kairoi,* in which the kingdom of God manifests itself in a particular breakthrough'.[94] When, from time to time, these *kairoi,* or special signs, take place there is always the question of just how they are to be interpreted. As a formal condition it is necessary that the cross of Christ proclaimed in the great *kairos* be the constant criterion of the lesser *kairoi.* However while the principle may not be contested the application often is.

Awareness of a *kairos* is 'a matter of vision' not of 'detached observation but on involved experience'.[95] Recalling his experience in Europe after World War I, he observes how both nationalists and religious socialists appropriated the term *kairos,* and raises two cautions. Firstly, the *kairoi* may be 'demonically distorted',[96] as they were, for example, in the case of Nazism. Secondly, they can be erroneous. The knowledge that we have of such epochal moments is not an object of analysis or calculation; it precludes foresight in any technical sense. Thus:

> No date foretold in the experience of a *kairos* was ever
> correct; no situation envisaged as the result of a *kairos*
> ever came into being. But something happened to some
> people through the power of the kingdom of God as it
> became manifest in history, and history has been
> changed ever since.[97]

Indeed, rare though these decisive turns in history are, they provide sufficient illumination in Tillich's view to convince us of the constant presence of the kingdom of God in history even though the experience of its presence may be seldom evident. The reason for this is

93.  Tillich, *Systematic Theology,* Volume 3, 369. Tillich notes that '*kairos*' is used by both John the Baptist and Jesus when they announce the fulfilment of time with respect to the kingdom of God which is 'at hand'.

94.  Tillich, *Systematic Theology,* Volume 3, 370.

95.  Tillich, *Systematic Theology,* Volume 3, 370–1.

96.  Tillich, *Systematic Theology,* Volume 3, 371.

97.  Tillich, *Systematic Theology,* Volume 3, 371.

that '*kairoi* are rare and the great *kairos* is unique, but together they determine the dynamics of history in its self-transcendence'.[98] Fragmentary moments though they undoubtedly are, they give us some glimpse of a 'trans-historical actualisation of unambiguous historical life'.[99] This leads us to the second aspect of the kingdom of God: together with its questions of personal immortality, is there any permanent value to history (as opposed to transitory value and meaning)?

Under the transhistorical aspect of the kingdom of God, Tillich argues that there is a real sense in which history is always ending and with that ending comes the opportunity for the 'elevation of the temporal into eternity'.[100] So for Tillich it is not the case that there exists some supranatural realm into which we are inserted. For if this were the case there would be questions about 'whether and in what way' we could enter such a realm. But more critically, 'history would be valuated merely as an important element in . . . earthly life . . . but irrelevant for the kingdom of God'.[101] Instead, the transhistorical dimension of the kingdom of God *is* (and he intends this as present reality just as much as future hope) constituted by the temporal: 'the ever present end of history elevates the positive content of history into eternity at the same time that it excludes the negative from participation in it'.[102]

The symbol of 'Eternal Life' indicates a transhistorical realm constituted by what Tillich calls 'essentialization'. It is a term he borrows from Schelling though he gives it a somewhat different meaning. For Tillich, 'essentialization' 'amounts to an unambiguous and permanent participation of finite life in the very life of Divine Spirit'.[103] In a vein that seems to be much indebted to the process philosophical speculations from Whitehead and Hartshorne, and that would have been current at the time when Tillich was completing this volume, he writes:

> Participation in the eternal life depends on a creative
> synthesis of a being's essential nature with what it has

---

98.   Tillich, *Systematic Theology*, Volume 3, 372.
99.   Kelsey, 'Paul Tillich', 147.
100.  Tillich, *Systematic Theology*, Volume 3, 396.
101.  Tillich, *Systematic Theology*, Volume 3, 397.
102.  Tillich, *Systematic Theology*, Volume 3, 397.
103.  Kelsey, 'Paul Tillich', 148.

made of it in its temporal existence. In so far as the
negative has maintained possession of it, it is exposed
in its negativity and excluded from eternal memory.[104]

His final vision is one where all that is negative is sloughed off
while that which is positive is held in the divine memory.

## 5. Conclusion

Tillich aims, I believe, to consider messianism, apocalypse and
redemption against the background of the ambiguities and contradic-
toriness of existence. Conditioned to some extent by Heidegger's
existentialist philosophy, his understanding of the future is firmly tied
to the power of the present. Indeed the power of the present is a
constant, though largely underlying, theme of Tillich's thought. The
themes of existential estrangement, of life in its concrete actuality, of
the ambiguities of historical and social existence—as exemplified by
our inherent drive toward self-integration, self-creativity and self-
transcendence—all witness to this power of the present.

Though our power to make (or at least, to *have made*) decisions
seems to be a controlling factor in Tillich's notion of 'essentialization'
and the destiny of Eternal Life, his warnings about ambiguity and
demonic distortions of the *kairoi*, alert us to the reality that our
decision-making is in truth crimped at every turn. Yet whether these
are decisions that we make or in which we find ourselves being made,
they are undeniably part of our social and historical being and as such
they make up the power of the present that is the cauldron from which
the tropes of messianism, redemption and apocalypse are figured.

---

104. Tillich, *Systematic Theology*, Volume 3, 401.

# 18

# Gnostic Messianism and Catastrophe of the Twentieth Century in Eric Voegelin's Political Thought

## Rodney Fopp

### 1. Introduction

Eric Voegelin is perhaps most widely recognised as a political philosopher, though his work also spans history, theology and anthropology. His work sought to expose what he regarded as the inadequacies of Western culture and, particularly, the dominant positivist political and social sciences that denied it was possible to meaningfully discuss the good society or the best political regime.

Born in Cologne in 1901, Voegelin completed his doctoral studies in the Law Faculty of the University of Vienna in 1922 under the jurist Hans Kelson. After studying abroad, he returned to teach there in 1928. As a consequence of his publications on the authoritarian State, and race and the State in the 1930s,[1] he was dismissed from his position by the Nazis and, only just escaping the Gestapo, fled to the Unites States. He taught in several universities before moving to the Louisiana State University where he remained for 16 years until he accepted the Chair of Political Science at the University of Munich. He retired in 1966 and returned to reside in California. He died in 1985.

---

1.  The publications deemed inimical by the Nazis would have included: *Der Authoritaere Staat* (Vienna: Vienna, 1933); *Rasse und Staat* (Tuebingen: JCB Mohr, 1933); *Die Rassenidee in der Geistesgeschichte von Ry bis Crus* (Berlin: Junker und Duennhaupt, 1936); and *Die politischen religion Vienna* (Vienna: Bermann-Fischer, 1936). For a number of intriguing details on these publications, including their rationale and circulation being stopped by the Nazis, see Eric Voegelin, *Auto-biographical Reflections,* 50–3.

Undoubtedly, from the time of the writing of his books on the authoritarian state and anti-Semitism in the 1930s, his work was largely an attempt to explain and understand the upheaval in Europe which he experienced personally as Nazism, but which extended to the communism of the Soviet Union. Initially, he explored the antecedents of this disorder in a mammoth project on the history of ideas, which he abandoned to write the first of six volumes on *Order and History*. Later, he wrote that by 1943 he had reached 'a dead-end' in his attempts to find a theory commensurate with the task of providing an 'adequate interpretation of his chosen field of studies.' He continued: 'The analysis of the movements of Communism, Fascism, National Socialism and racism, of constitutional liberalism, and authoritarianism had made it clear beyond doubt that the centre of a philosophy of politics had to be a theory of consciousness.' However, 'the academic instruments of the Western world . . . did not offer the intellectual instruments that would make the political events and movements intelligible'.[2] It was in the endeavour to provide the necessary intellectual instruments that Voegelin explored many concepts, including those of apocalypse, messianism and redemption. These central terms, to which he gave particular meanings, became the vehicle for his denunciation of those who arrogated to themselves revealed knowledge which, in messianic hands, would save the world. In analysing the links forged between the positions of theorists—such as Hegel, Comte and Marx—and the great tyrants of the twentieth century, this article concludes with Voegelin's view of the Apostle Paul.

## 2. Apocalypse

'Apocalypse' usually means to reveal, to disclose or uncover some arcane or secret truth. In the Judeo-Christian apocalypse literature of, for example, *Daniel* in the *Tanakah* and *Revelation* in the Christian Bible, such revelations or disclosures from a transcendent source tend to occur in a time of crisis such as, for example, being in captivity or during persecutions and pogroms. For Voegelin, 'apocalyptic' knowledge from a specific divine revelation is used by those who have received the revelation to judge crises, to point to the passing of the current age and to the inauguration of a redeeming new era.

---

2. Eric Voegelin, *Anamnesis* (Notre Dame: University of Notre Dame Press, 1972), 3–4.

Integral to apocalypse is a dramatic contrast between the present and the future, diagnosis and prescription, crisis and salvation, lament and promise, the retrograde present and the redeemed future. But there is not only contrast; there is, in every contrast, the defeat of the former and the emergence of the latter. As Klaus Vondung notes, for Voegelin: 'The ancient apocalyptic conception of history . . . presupposes the concept of salvation history as a foil.'[3] Such a view can be readily identified in Voegelin's analysis of the revelation to Daniel in the *Tanakh* which related to Palestinian captivity during the Seleucid Empire. For the prophet Daniel, Voegelin comments:

> The succession of empires is senseless; there is no hope of pragmatic victory over the imperial enemy or of a spiritual transformation of mankind. Since the present structure of reality is without meaning, a divine intervention has to change the structure itself, if divine order is to be re-introduced. The consciousness of the divine ordering has contracted into the visions of the apocalyptic thinker. The stage has been set for the divine messengers who abandon created reality altogether and concentrate on the Gnosis of the redeemptive exodus from the cosmos.[4]

Devoid of meaning, and in the context of the discrepancy between the people's hopes and persecution in captivity, the prophet anticipated the ending of the age of the current disorder in the new age of the divine reign. Whether Voegelin is justified in attributing such a 'contraction' of knowledge to the prophet is beyond the scope of this paper. However, it was in the prophets of Judaism and in the teaching of early Christianity that he undoubtedly saw the antecedents of what he regarded as the modern political messiahs' privileged knowledge.[5]

---

3. Klaus Vondung, 'Eric Voegelin, the Crisis of Western Civilization, and the Apocalypse', in *International and Interdisciplinary Perspectives on Eric Voegelin*, edited by Stephen A Knight and Geoffrey L Price (Columbia: University of Missouri Press, 1997), 124.

4. Eric Voegelin, *Order and History*, Volume 4, *The Ecumenic Age* (Baton Rouge: Louisiana State University Press, 1974), 26.

5. Compare: 'Though Gnosticism is not a Jewish but a multicivilizational movement in an ecumenic empire, its peculiar fervour and secular momentum are hardly intelligible without the prophetic and apocalyptic

Voegelin also used 'apocalypse' in another non-Biblical sense. In this second meaning the source of the revelation, rather than being divine or transcendent, is mundane, immanent and secular. After his point above about salvation being the foil for the apocalyptic conception of history, Vondung continues by claiming: 'The same is true for modernity. In the modern form the concept of salvation history is replaced by concepts of history that differ in content, but are similar in structure, namely, by concepts of history as a systematic process of progress.'[6]

However, while Voegelin can descry the traces of modern apocalyptic thinking in the centuries before the Common Era, there is a radical difference between the apocalypse of Daniel and the modern apocalyptic. In the latter period, perhaps beginning in the Middle Ages, continuing in the Enlightenment, and culminating with figures such as Comte and Marx, the apocalyptic language is immanent and secular. Thus in 1952 Voegelin wrote:

> However fatuous the surface arguments may be, the widespread belief that modern civilization is Civilization in a pre-eminent sense is experientially justified; the endowment with the meaning of salvation has made the rise of the West, indeed, an *apocalypse of civilization.* On the *apocalyptic spectacle,* however, falls a shadow; for the brilliant expansion is accompanied by a danger that grows apace with progress.[7]

Here Voegelin is advancing the view that, largely through techno-logical progress, there may be some justification in regarding the West as the apogee of civilization. However, the flaunted 'apocalypse of civilization' has its darker side. On another occasion he used the phrase 'apocalyptic founders' and 'contemporary apocalyptic figures'[8] which, as we will see, refers to the messiah figures he believed were so

---

history, culminating in the epiphany of Christ, as an important genetic factor,' in Voegelin, *Order and History*, Volume 4, 27.

6. Vordung, 'Eric Voegelin, the Crisis of Western Civilization, and the Apocalypse', 124.
7. Eric Voegelin, *The New Science of Politics* (Chicago: University of Chicago Press, 1952), 130.
8. Eric Voegelin, *From Enlightenment to Revolution,* edited by John H Hallowell (Durham, North Caroline: Duke University Press, 1975), 159.

dangerous. An exemplar was Auguste Comte (1798–1857) of whom Voegelin wrote:

> there can be no doubt even now that Comte belongs, with Marx, Lenin and Hitler, to a series of men who would save mankind by divinising their particular existence and imposing its law as the new order of society. The satanic Apocalypse of Man begins with Comte and has become the signature of the Western crisis.[9]

Here we can see what is a *leitmotif* in Voegelin's thought, namely, that the revelation of a certain form of knowledge by self-appointed saviours would redeem the past and inaugurate a new and more perfect reign. The symbol Voegelin used to analyse this much vaunted knowledge was 'gnosticism'.

## 2. Messianism and gnosis

Although 'gnosticism' has many nuances, the common thread Voegelin focused upon was the belief that the deities were unconcerned about worldly existence and that an inferior demiurge created the world in such a way that it is vulnerable to the malign forces of ignorance and dread. The gnostics believed that the spiritual part of human beings was separate from earthly human existence and that, with their specially acquired knowledge and understanding, they could be delivered or saved from it.[10] This ancient gnosticism is differenttiated from its more modern variants, which he called 'secular gnosticism'.

Voegelin adapted the religious form of *gnosticism* to analyse modernity and particularly the diabolical political regimes of twentieth century totalitarianism. On one occasion he wrote that it was important to recognise the 'essence of modernity as the growth of gnosticism'.[11] However, secular gnosticism had a long lineage. Voegelin began his analysis of it in the work of the Cistercian abbot and mystic, Joachim of Flora (1232–1202). According to Voegelin,

---

9. Voeglin, *From Enlightenment to Revolution*, 159.
10. See Hans Jonas, 'Gnosticism and Modern Nihilism', in *Social Research*, 19/4 (September 1976): 107–32.
11. Voegelin, *The New Science of Politics*, 126.

Joachim provided the 'first clear and comprehensive expression of the idea'.[12]

Firstly, Joachim applied the Christian symbol of the Holy Trinity to the sequence of history. Thus, in his schema there were epochs of the Father, Son and Holy Spirit. Just as later Comte believed that the theological, metaphysical and scientific ages would result in stages of ever increasing enlightenment, so Joachim's progression would correspond to increasing degrees of spiritual enlightenment.[13] According to Voegelin, 'in the trinitarian eschatology Joachim created the aggregate of symbols which govern the self-interpretation of modern political society to this day'.[14] Of particular interest to Voegelin was the idea of the three stages with the final consummation in the third stage.[15]

A second symbol that Voegelin found in Joachim was that of 'leader', while a third characteristic of Joachim's schema was the unique knowledge the leader possessed 'either through a direct revelation or speculative gnosis'. Such knowledge would herald and introduce Joachim's third and final stage. A fourth symbol introduced by Joachim was the 'brotherhood of autonomous persons', perhaps epitomised by what Voegelin dubbed the 'Marxian mysticism of freedom and the withering-away of the state'.[16]

Voegelin discerned the symbols used by Joachim in the work of a long line of thinkers from Boussuet, Voltaire, Helvetius, Turgot, Comte and Saint-Simon and Marx, and then in the authoritarian regimes of Lenin, Hitler and Stalin. This is not the place to analyse the developments Voegelin emphasised which are detailed and are now outlined in many volumes.[17] However, it is noteworthy that Voegelin saw in Hegel, Comte and Marx the burgeoning 'social Satanism' and 'social immanentism' which he located in a religious form in Joachim and in a more secular form in the early Helvetius.[18]

---

12. Voegelin, *The New Science of Politics*, 110.
13. Voegelin, *The New Science of Politics*, 111.
14. Voegelin, *The New Science of Politics*, 111.
15. The following paragraph is based Voegelin, *The New Science of Politics*, 111–12.
16. Voegelin, *The New Science of Politics*, 112–13.
17. See the eight volumes of the *History of Political Ideas*, part of Voegelin's *Collected Works* published by Louisiana State University Press.
18. Voegelin, *From Enlightenment to Revolution*, 71.

Voegelin was concerned that this immanentism totally usurped the transcendent which resulted in some human beings acting like God and, to varying degrees, believing they were God. This process Voegelin call 'secularization'[19] and was epitomised by Feuerbach and Marx who,

> interpreted the transcendent God as the projection of what is best in man into a hypostatic beyond; for them the great turning point of history, therefore, would come when man draws his projection back into himself, when he becomes conscious that he himself is God, when as a consequence man is transfigured into superman.[20]

On another occasion Voegelin explained that in secular gnosticism 'what actually takes places is the externalization of the processes of the soul and their enactment on the stage of society'.[21] This is consistent with Voegelin's view that the perversions of aggrandising gnostic thought can be identified in the social and political realm; 'the life of the soul has become perverted and the religious symbols which express the perversion dominate the scene'.[22]

According to Voegelin, in claiming a revealed and privileged knowledge the secular gnostics were self-proclaimed messiahs. Thus, in a part of his early *History of Ideas* project,[23] Voegelin has a heading called 'The Messiah' in the chapter entitled 'The Apocalypse of Man: Comte'.[24] The subsequent analysis refers to an essay by Comte concerning the scientific prerequisites for the re-organisation of society. Voegelin is forthright: 'In this essay Comte appears as the messiah who announces the gospel of the new age, if not yet to mankind, at least to

---

19. Voegelin, *The New Science of Politics*, 119.
20. Voegelin, *The New Science of Politics*, 125.
21. Voegelin, *From Enlightenment to Revolution*, 71.
22. Voegelin, *From Enlightenment to Revolution*, 71.
23. Omitted in the edited selection, *From Enlightenment to Revolution*, by John H Hallowell but published in 1999 in its entirety. See Footnotes 9 and 24.
24. Eric Voegelin, *Collected Works*, Volume 26 (*The History of Political Ideas*, Volume 8, *Crisis and the Apocalypse of Man*), edited by David Walsh (Columbia: University of Missouri Press, 1999), 241.

the Occident.'[25] Of particular concern for Voegelin is the role of the scientist in this new age:

> The scientists will inevitably be the new spiritual power of society because (1) they have the capacity and intellectual culture that makes them competent for this type of work, because (2) in fact even now they are the bearers of the new spirit, because (3) they alone in modern society possess the moral authority that will compel the people to accept the new organic doctrine, and because (4) of all the existing social forces only that of the scientists is European in character.[26]

In subsequent work Voegelin used the phrase the 'new Christs'[27] or the 'new God-man, the new Messiah'[28] to describe Comte, Marx and Hegel who were followed, 'at the distance of a century, by the practitioners of transfiguration into the millennium by mass murder and concentration camps, by Hitlers and Stalins'.[29]

### 3. The apocalyptic messiahs and valid knowledge

Thus far we have emphasised that, for Voegelin, secular gnosticism was the apocalyptic medium by which the messianism he detected in the modern period was to deliver the new age or era. But if secular gnosticism was Voegelin's general label for the revealed knowledge of the modern political saviours, then science was an influential modern example. Even in political science, it was 'the science' that determined the 'political'. That was Voegelin's diagnosis and complaint.

---

25.  Voegelin, *Crisis and the Apocalypse of Man*, 241.
26.  Voegelin, *Crisis and the Apocalypse of Man*, 243.
27.  See Voegelin, *Order and History, Volume 4, The Ecumenic Age* (Louisiana: Louisiana State University Press, 1974), 254, 259, 269 and Eric Voegelin, 'The Gospel and Culture' in *Jesus and Man's Hope*, edited by DG Miller and D Hadidian (Pittsburgh: Pittsburgh Theological Seminary, 1971), 89–90.
28.  Voegelin, *The Ecumenic Age*, 255.
29.  Voegelin, *The Ecumenic Age*, 254.

Accordingly, 'the prodigious advancement of science since the seventeenth century' became 'the symbolic vehicle of Gnostic truth'.[30] Voegelin called this 'scientism', and lamented that it 'remained to this day one of the strongest gnostic movements in Western society.' He continued: 'The immanentist pride is so strong that even the special sciences have each left a distinguishable sediment in the variants of salvation through physics, economics, sociology, biology and psychology.'

Voegelin argued that the 'scientistic creed' possessed three 'dogmas'.[31] The first emphasised the unity of science; the second dogma was that the epistemology and methodology of the natural and physical sciences should be used exclusively to examine all aspects and facets of human experience; the third, which relied on the previous 'dogmas' and was the most important, emphasised that if any part of human experience was beyond the limit of 'mathematized' science, or was not amenable or open to scrutiny by scientism, then it was 'either irrelevant or, in the more radical form of the dogma, illusory'.[32]

The net result of this dogma is that 'the methods of the natural sciences become the criterion for the validity of all knowledge claims.' This 'was the real source of danger' and the reason for the 'positivistic destructiveness'.[33] According to Voegelin, scientism 'subordinates theoretical relevance to method and thereby perverts the meaning of science'.[34]

Voegelin understood science to be the 'search for truth concerning the nature of the various realms of being'.[35] With this the positivist might agree. But because only the natural and physical realms are open and accessible to the dominant scientific method, other realms (such as, for example, knowledge about what might constitute the best political regimes) cannot be so examined. Further, other realms cannot be the source of exact or valid knowledge. That possibility is excluded, having been defined out of existence by the criterion used. The result

---

30. For the citations in this paragraph, see Voegelin, *The New Science of Politics*, 127.

31. Eric Voegelin, 'The Origins of Scientism', in *Social Research*, 15/4 (December 1948): 462. See also: Voegelin, *The New Science of Politics*, 3–6.

32. Voegelin, 'The Origins of Scientism', 462.

33. Voegelin, 'The Origins of Scientism', 462.

34. Voegelin, 'The Origins of Scientism', 462.

35. Voegelin, 'The Origins of Scientism', 462.

was not only the scientistic privileging of knowledge gained from the natural and physical world, but that all claims about all other realms were consigned to matters of taste and were merely subjective. They were ideologies between which it is impossible to arbitrate.

Voegelin insisted that 'different objects require different methods'.[36] But 'the positivistic conceit',[37] that the one scientistic creed should be used to explore all objects of human research, meant that the 'knowledge' from other realms are not amenable to this privileged and excluding method. The *a priori* exclusion of some realms of being from the very possibility of yielding valid knowledge, results in 'a morass of relativism'.[38] This was particularly true, Voegelin claimed, in such areas as ethics, politics and values, with the consequence that rational debate is largely impossible.

However, it is important to realise that Voegelin is not referring to a *descriptive* or *sociological* relativism which emphasises the obvious diversity and multiplicity of cultures and values. He is not referring to the normative claim that we should treat all values, or study other cultures, as if they were equal. Voegelin is referring to an epistemological claim which states that it is impossible to arbitrate between values: 'the method of value relation and value relativism . . . as ideology, has had as much world wide success as Marxism, positivism and psychoanalysis.'[39] The combination to which Voegelin refers may surprise but there can be little doubt about the prevalence of epistemological value relativism. Furthermore, the morass of relativism becomes the quagmire of competing ideologies for, in a 'society undermined and infested with ideology, the result is as many definitions of the subject as their ideological value posits'.[40]

### 4. The apocalypse and liberalism

It is clear from the previous analysis that, according to Voegelin, Comte and Marx devised systems which were characterised by the privileged knowledge of secular gnosticism and its deformities. Of course it is one thing to devise systems of thought, as Comte and Marx,

---

36.  Voegelin, *The New Science of Politics*, 5.
37.  Voegelin, *The New Science of Politics*, 11.
38.  Voegelin, *The New Science of Politics*, 13.
39.  Eric Voegelin, 'Liberalism and Its History', in *The Review of Politics*, 63/4 (October 1974): 518.
40.  Voegelin, 'Liberalism and Its History', 518.

for example, surely did. Yet it is quite another to usurp power, as did Hitler, Lenin and Stalin, and impose centralised authoritarian power over citizens. Comte and Marx may have been the intellectual messiahs but there is a gulf between making a claim to exclusive revelatory knowledge, on the one hand, and actually developing and maintaining the oppressive instruments of state in a totalitarian regime, on the other.

Nonetheless, the modern deliverers and saviours flaunted a special knowledge which they believed would redeem the times. Thus, for Voegelin, the 'true dividing line' in the early years of the Cold War did 'not run between liberals and totalitarians but between the religious and philosophical transcendentalists on the one side, and the liberal and totalitarian sectarians on the other side'.[41] When it came to the dividing line which most concerned Voegelin, liberalism was on the same side as totalitarian.

This does not necessarily mean that Voegelin blurred distinctions others believed were significant; it does not mean that he belittled or discounted the nefarious influence of Nazism from which he fled to the United States. From personal experience he realised the differences between liberalism and tyranny. However, on the issue which preoccupied him, namely, the understanding of the political disorder and the pre-requisites for a proper examination of the good society, he maintained that the similarities between liberal and totalitarians sectarians were more significant than their differences.

This is epitomised in his discussion regarding revolution and reform. He seems to have accepted that liberalism involved peaceful change but believed the changes were so constant as to be revolutionary. Thus, he wrote that:

> the idea of peaceful change, a policy of timely adaptation to the social institution which, in the age of industrial revolution, changes very quickly, has become a constant in all shades of liberalism. From this point of view liberalism becomes a method for carrying on the revolution with other, less destructive, means.[42]

41. Eric Voegelin, 'The Origins of Totalitarianism', in *Social Research*, 15/1 (January 1953): 75.
42. Eric Voegelin, 'Liberalism and Its History', in *The Review of Politics*, 36/4 (October, 1974): 509.

Moreover, as with the problem with state communism, liberalism is also based on the attempt to transform human nature by asserting that by political means human beings can be content, that the perfect state and perfect humanity can be realised. In reformist liberalism even pluralism and debate are impossible because, as indicated, immanent reason in the social sciences leads to the value relativism which makes all views merely ideologies.[43]

## 5. Voegelin's prescription

Voegelin argued that there were certain verities about human existence which did not change. One was that from human experiences symbols arise. These include rites, myth and theory and reflect that experience. By illuminating experience, symbols allow humans to discern that they are a part of a much larger realm, which Voegelin came to refer to as the 'divine beyond'.[44] As humans participate in this divine reality they become aware that they are able to sense something of it.

The human being 'discovers the something in his humanity that is the site and sensorium of divine presence.' Furthermore, human beings 'find such words [as] *psyche*, or *pneuma*, or *nous*, to symbolise the something'.[45] When humans participate in this 'theophanic event', they become aware or conscious of their relationship to the gods of the transcendent order 'whose moving presence in the soul evokes the movement of response'.[46]

So, for Voegelin, 'history is not a stream of human beings and their actions in time, but the process of man's participation in a flux of divine presence that has eschatological direction'.[47] This participation occurs in between the poles of humanity and the divine which Voegelin called the 'In-Between or Metaxy'.[48]

Another way of expressing this for Voegelin was in terms of the divine reality known in the 'Beyond and the Beginning'. The Beyond is the experience of the divine in the soul; the Beginning comes into consciousness through the experience of the intelligible ordering of the

---

43.  Voegelin, 'Liberalism and Its History', 518.
44.  Voegelin, *The Ecumenic Age*, 11.
45.  Voegelin, *The Ecumenic Age*, 8.
46.  Voegelin, *The Ecumenic Age*, 8.
47.  Voegelin, *The Ecumenic Age*, 6.
48.  Voegelin, *The Ecumenic Age*, 11.

cosmos.[49] Each is expressed in different language. The language of Beyond is articulated in terms of seeking and questioning; the language of the Beginning concerns a 'divine force which creates, sustains and preserves the order of things'.[50]

In such experience there is the arcane and the inscrutable, the mysterious. But this does not deter Voegelin. The meaning of human existence is derived by exploring the mysteries between the poles between an awareness of the Beginning order which attests to a creative force, on the one hand, and the searching and seeking for the divine Beyond, on the other. There is a critical balance between both poles.

If one end was the Beginning and the other the Beyond, we have an (albeit inadequate) image of Voegelin's 'philosophical anthropology', as he once described his position.[51] Voegelin argues that human existence is in the space and time between the symbols of Beyond and Beginning. As long as humans move in the order between the two, recognising both, they are acting in accordance with the given order between the divine and the human.[52] But when, via their apocalypse, the messiahs of secular gnosticism attempt to redeem the past, they arrogate to themselves the symbols of the Beyond which degenerate into an immanentist secular Beginning.[53] In contracting the movement between the human and divine the sham messiahs, with their bogus apocalypse, bring hell on earth.

### 6. Voegelin on the Apostle Paul

Voegelin advocated what he believed was the essence of the classical philosophy of Plato and Aristotle, namely, the restoration of 'the life of reason'.[54] This life of reason in the metaxy of divine-human relations was also exemplified for Voegelin by Christianity and, particularly, the writing of the Apostle Paul. For him:

> Plato and Paul agree that meaning in history is inseparable from the directional movement in reality.

---

49. Voegelin, *The Ecumenic Age*, 17.
50. Voegelin, *The Ecumenic Age*, 16–17.
51. Voegelin, *The New Science of Politics*, 12, 17.
52. Voegelin, 'The Gospel and Culture', 63.
53. Voegelin, *The Ecumenic Age*, 19.
54. Voegelin, 'The Gospel and Culture, 101. See also 54.

'History' is the area of reality where the directional movement of the cosmos achieves luminosity of consciousness. They furthermore agree that history is not an empty time dimension in which things happen at random but rather a process whose meaning is constituted in theophanic events. And finally they agree that the reality of history is metaleptic; it is the In-Between where man responds to the divine presence and the divine presence evokes the response in man.[55]

While the 'Pauline Vision of the Resurrected' contains for Voegelin the prerequisites for the life of the soul it also convinced the Apostle that 'man is destined to rise to immortality if he opens himself to the divine *pneuma* as Jesus did'.[56] Paul's vision of the risen Christ convinced him that the new age was at hand and would be fulfilled in the *parousia* or 'Second Coming'.[57] Yet despite Paul's confidence that the meaning of history was disclosed and the end was near, the *parousia* did not eventuate as was anticipated.

But the problem Voegelin diagnosed was that in the Christian empire the *eidos* and *telos* expected in the coming (*parousia*) of the new age, the 'transfiguration' as Voegelin described it, was to be earth bound. Paul's vision became a paradigm for the modern 'new Christs' who were 'bent on achieving the state of transfiguration in "history" that has been denied to Paul in spite of his vision, and to everyman since, because he [Paul] died before the Second Coming.' Voegelin continued, 'to this purpose they [the new Christs] try to force the Parousia into history in their own person'.[58]

The other side of this concern with the secular gnostics can be identified in Voegelin's discussion of 1 Corinthians 15: 19 (as Voegelin translates): 'If we have no more than hope in Christ in this life, then we are of all men the most pitiful.' Voegelin comments:

This sentence is the *key* to the understanding of Paul's experience of reality—or so at least it appears to me. Hope in this life, in our existence in the Metaxy, not

---

55.   Voegelin, *The Ecumenic Age*, 242.
56.   Voegelin, *The Ecumenic Age*, 242.
57.   Voegelin, *The Ecumenic Age*, 268.
58.   Voegelin, *The Ecumenic Age*, 262.

only is not enough, it is worse than nothing, unless this
hope is embedded in the assurance that derives from
the vision.[59]

There are other interpretations of Paul's claim. But for Voegelin,
Paul's view was that hope is misplaced if it is based on earthly
existence. The hope of transfiguration, the new age, redemption, the
*eidos* and *telos* of history, which is known about on earth, is in vain and
futile if it is not regarded as completed and fulfilled in the life beyond.
This means that for Voegelin redemption occurs *after* this life, not
during it. As he wrote on another occasion: 'Christian thinkers had to
explain that the Gospel was no social gospel, redemption no social
remedy, and Christianity in general no insurance for individual or
collective prosperity.'[60]

## 7. Conclusion

For Voegelin the intellectual precursors or messiahs of the political
regimes of the twentieth century were apocalyptic in claiming a unique
knowledge which would bring redemption. But their panacea
exemplified the metastasis against which Voegelin critically analysed.
This metastasis asserted that 'through an act of faith—or any other
act—human nature will cease to be what it is and, one way or another,
will be replaced by a new transfigured nature, a new society and a new
transfigured history'.[61] It was the eclipse of the metaxy in modernity,
and its displacement by metastatic faith, that inspired Eric Voegelin.

---

59.   Voegelin, *The Ecumenic Age*, 248, (emphasis added).
60.   Eric Voegelin, *Order and History*, Volume 1: *Israel and Revelation*
      (Baton Rouge: Louisiana State University Press, 1956), 183.
61.   This quotation comes from an exchange organised by Raymond Aron
      under the title 'The Decline of Messianism?', in *World Technology and
      Human Destiny*, edited by Raymond Aron (Ann Arbor: University of
      Michigan Press, 1963), 170.

# 19

# Gerhard von Rad: Heilsgeschichte and Apocalypse

## Erich Renner

'There was a stillness within him which emanated from a deep listening.'[1]

Gerhard von Rad was amongst the most productive and 'charismatic' German Protestant Old Testament scholars of the twentieth century. By his unqualified acceptance of the Old Testament and its kerygmatic content, von Rad influenced many of his contemporaries in German universities and elsewhere to see it, in spite of its so called 'Jewishness', as a vital source for understanding the second part, the New Testament, of the Christian canon. This view went beyond the narrow academic liberal scholarship of nineteenth century Protestant theology and was in direct opposition to that taken by the National Socialist Party.

Gerard von Rad (1901–71) was a private lecturer in his early career at Leipzig University, already famous for its Old Testament historian and scholar Albrecht Alt, and became professor at Jena University in 1934. In 1930 Alfred Rosenberg had published *The Myth of the 20th Century*, an attempt to be an exegesis of the Nazi ideology built on the idea that the Germanic races were superior to all others. It tried to argue that the development of European culture came through the influence and creativity of the Germanic tribes. Christ was hailed as an

---

1. Hans-Georg Gadamer speaking of von Rad in 2001. A tribute to von Rad, in extraordinary circumstances, was a three-day symposium (18–21 October 2001) at the University of Heidelberg, Germany, on the hundredth anniversary of his birthday. The diversity and richness of papers, presentations and discussions is evidenced in the collation *Das Alte Testament und die Kultur der Moderne* (Lit Verlag Münster, 2004).

Aryan in this ideology, which became the 'philosophical' and 'spiritual' basis of the Nazis. Despite the intensely anti-Semitic climate of this time, von Rad became a source for those seeking to understand the significance and relevance of the Old Testament. In the summer of 1944 he was called up for war duties, which ended with his difficult, yet formative, experience as a prisoner in a camp near Bad Kreuznach under the Americans.

In 1945 he accepted an appointment to the University of Göttingen as an Old Testament professor where large numbers came to hear his lectures, filled with scholarly and church-oriented material that had been suppressed under the Nazis. In 1949 he moved to the University of Heidelberg, where he completed his long and highly influential career as a professor of theology, and to the nearby *Peters Kirche*, where he continued as a magnetic preacher.

Von Rad re-examined much of the literature of the Hebrew Scriptures and found not just a recorded history of the people but an openness and promise of the future for humanity, especially with reference to 'the word'. This introduced the kaleidoscopic concept of time in Hebrew, connecting those listening to the word with the events and actions of the past, present and future. He highlighted redemptive messianism with is hidden and paradoxical evolution throughout the history of the Israelite community which then led into the era of the New Testament. He also analysed the apocalyptic literature of the Old Testament and compared and contrasted it with the Messianic message of the times. It was these aspects of Old Testament under-standing that von Rad redeemed for the Protestant church community of firstly Germany and then the world beyond.

It is generally agreed among scholars of the Old Testament that von Rad was deeply interested in the Israelite traditions, as evidenced in his two volumes of *Old Testament Theology*: *The Theology of Israel's Historical Traditions* (Volume 1) and *The Theology of the Prophetical Traditions of Israel* (Volume 2).[2] Von Rad means by 'tradition' both the pre-literary, oral traditions and the written records (*Überlieferungen*). His Genesis commentary shows that form-critical analysis, where genres of the writings of the Old Testament are highlighted within their historical contexts, was of great importance to him. He gave full

---

2.    Gerhard von Rad, *Old Testament Theology*, Volumes 1 and 2, translated by DMG Stalker (Edinburgh and London: Oliver and Boyd, 1962).

consideration to the theologically complex and multi-tiered traditions of Israel in an attempt to answer the salient question concerning the *Sitz im Leben* (situation and context in life) in which these traditions emanated and developed. His deep love of the Hebrew language and his 'listening' to the traditions developed a dialogue between the modern reader and the past.

To understand von Rad's notion of apocalypse attention will be focussed on his *Old Testament Theology*. It is important to remember that while his work was certainly always academic, von Rad was, at the same time, conscious of the pastoral dimensions of theology and that meant for him that he saw the texts of the Old Testament (after exegetical study had been done) finding their full expression in the pulpit.

> Does not everything presented in the Old Testament have a characteristic openness toward the future? And the future in the Bible always means a future which God will give from his own hands. With creation the horizon of history already opens up, and the attention of the reader is accordingly directed forward. The stories of the patriarchs, too, are told with reference to the future, namely the people, which is to come and the fulfilment of the promises . . . Is it any wonder that the early church began to read this Old Testament which was so thoroughly open to the future with a new understanding? The church saw everything in the Old Testament in the light of the appearance of Christ, and in this light the possibility of a new interpretation was indicated . . . the Christ-event became an aid to understanding the Old Testament.[3]

Von Rad then, like others before him, saw in the Old Testament an embryonic prefiguring of the New Testament. As a member of the Confessing Church, with Karl Barth and Dietrich Bonhoeffer, he defended the significance of the Old Testament against the *Deutsche Christen*, the arm of the German Protestant Church that was

---

3.   Gerhard von Rad, 'Ancient Word and Living Word', *Interpretation: A Journal of Bible and Theology*, 15 (1961): 10f.

established by the National Socialists in order to attempt to entice the Evangelical Church into racism and anti-Semitism.

The major thrust that comes through most of his works was the importance of the *Heilsgeschich* translated as 'redemptive history' or 'salvation history'. In this context it can be emphasised that he found great importance in the employment of the *debar Jahweh* (word of God) in messianism and redemptive history. He was influenced partly by Lutheran and Barthian word theology. For von Rad the word of *Jahweh* in the Old Testament was always an efficacious action-producing word. The *debar Jahweh* became *dabar*; that is, the *debar Jahweh* became that which is spoken—*debar* has a double meaning in the Old Testament, meaning both the spoken word and the activity brought into effect by its utterance. Thorlief Boman's *Hebrew Thought Compared with Greek* states categorically that *dabar* is dynamic: 'both objectively and linguistically . . . *dabar* means not only word but also deed'.[4] This allowed von Rad, I believe, to see the whole of redemptive history, from the exodus through to its culmination, as a result of the word of God, which had come to his word-chosen and word-directed people:

> The Old Testament portrays a history brought to pass by God's Word from creation to the Son of Man . . . We see how the ancestors of Israel were called by the divine Word and how in obedience to further divine words they wandered thither and yon; we see the promise of great prosperity come to fulfilment and Israel become a people. Then we see this people wandering at God's direction, and we see offices and institutions coming into being within it founded by God's Word. In other words, we see the people continually driven, moved about, shaped, reshaped, destroyed and resurrected through the divine Word that ever again came to it.[5]

---

4.   Thorlief Boman, *Hebrew Thought Compared with Greek* (London: SCM Press, 1960) 58ff.

5.   See Claus Westermann, *Essays on Old Testament Hermeneutics* (Virginia: John Knox Press, 1963).

The origin of redemptive history is then to be traced back to the miraculously powerful word of God, who, *ex nihilo*, created and rescued his people through the word, so that it might become a blessing for all nations on the earth (the starting point of the Abrahamic tradition of Genesis 12). That means, to put it perhaps too simply, that Israel's writers of the Old Testament saw their release from Egypt and the gift of the laws as cut adrift from any neighbouring mythologies—and especially from those of the Canaanites, with their Baal-Astarte religion and cult—and founded it in *Jahweh's* promissory *dabar* alone.

Von Rad considered that the worship of Israel in tabernacle and temple was word-centric and that meant also that the creative-redemptive word had come to them first in their history before they were able to answer it with festivals, with worship and sacrifices, with obedience to the law given to Moses on Mt Sinai. But the full fulfilment of the salvific word of their God was not at any time experienced in their history. How could it be when they were attacked within and without their land or when they found themselves imprisoned in the Babylonian captivity? It was then that the prophetical, charismatic elements in Israel and in Babylon, on the basis of the traditions that they preserved and employed, pointed to a future liberation which would last forever (See, for example, Jeremiah 31:31ff). In addition, there were the spiritualising attempts of the cultic officers, priests and Levites that buoyed the *zaddikim* (the faithful righteous) in faith and hope in Jahweh, who would indeed fulfil his promises beyond the comprehension of human beings.

Von Rad is most aware of the significance and understanding of 'time' in Israel, which he saw as mainly connected with event and action.[6] He cites a number of sections from Kohelet (3:1 ff) and Psalms (31:16). His comments on the latter show how to him the psalmist meant these words, where the plural 'times' is employed, implying that life is made up of events. Then, too, in the cultic festivals the redemptive actions of the past were celebrated and in doing this they were made ever again present. So von Rad sees redemptive history in the Old Testament not only as a horizontal chain of events of the past—Israel certainly confessed this too—but as that which was also

---

6.  See von Rad, *Old Testament Theology*, Volume 2, for a full treatment of Israel's understanding of history and time, 112ff.

still within the present. Thus its worship was re-presentation, *Vergegenwärtigung* activity; the Israel of today was the Israel of the past and vice versa.

It is of significance for von Rad that redemptive history in the Old Testament is perceived as coming from that God who is righteous, slow to anger and plenteous in *rachamim* (love; in Hebrew it has the connotation of mother's love for an unborn child). At the same time he is beyond the comprehension of the limited, sinful human beings. He is a God who, whilst revealing himself to his people in many tangible ways, nevertheless hides himself (Isaiah 45:15). Scholars of the Old Testament had often overlooked this mysterious, inscrutable element of God. In his hiddenness, his seeming weakness and at times tormenting silence (as in the lament psalms), he does his redemptive work. His anointed ones, especially the kings of Israel, were certainly capable of ruling their people, even leading them in the worship in the tabernacle (as David is portrayed by the Chronicler). Yet they were people of clay-feet, who fell into adultery, idolatry, syncreticisms and disobedient alliances with foreigners on whom they placed their reliance in wars and battles. In spite of their malfeance, God nevertheless used them, punished them and saved them. It can be seen that redemptive history and the messianism within it, is not some straight evolutionary line but is filled with contradictions, discrepancies and paradoxes.

As for messianism in the Old Testament, von Rad claimed that it grew out of the promise to David (Samuel 2, chapter 7), the prophecy that set the enduring David tradition in motion and that had its culmination and fulfilment in the New Testament. There was no doubt in von Rad's mind that whilst the Noah, Abraham and Sinaitic covenants were of significance for maintaining the people in those days as the chosen of Jahweh, it was especially the David covenant which strongly helped to set Israel up as a kingdom whose grandeur, wisdom and power reached its heights in David's and Solomon's day. That is why von Rad made so much of the David throne succession account.[7] As stated earlier, many of the kings that succeeded these two famous and highly efficient leaders were of a dubious nature, leading Judah and Israel into nefarious and anti-traditional paths. As a result, *nebiism* (prophetical work and movement) arose as a corrective and

---

7.    See von Rad, *Old Testament Theology*, Volume 2.

also as condemnation of kings on behalf of Jahweh, who had called them into his 'council'. In this history of redemptive message both grace and judgment were deeply incorporated. Von Rad states:

> According to the Deuteronomic presentation, Jahweh's word is active in the history of Judah creating history and that in a double capacity: [firstly] as law, judging and destroying [and secondly] as gospel, that is in the David tradition, which was constantly being fulfilled—saving and forgiving.[8]

In briefly rehearsing the messianic tradition in respect to the future we have reached von Rad's understanding of eschatology and apocalypticism. In his section on '*Apokalyptic*'[9] in his *Old Testament Theology* he gives no clear definition of either. However, he makes a distinction between the two showing that eschatology is essentially orientated to the future of Israel's history in their land while apocalypticism includes the history of nations and the cosmos; that is it includes heavenly dimensions, the separation of good and evil, and the resurrection of the dead. He rejects the notion that apocalypticism has its roots in prophecy and propounded the thesis that it was fathered by wisdom circles in Israel. In his view it could be called a science of eschatology.

Von Rad highlights certain phenomena of apocalypticism. He maintains that it sharply distinguishes between the two aeons; that is, between the evil *haolam* (aeon), which is of this world, and the blessed one, which is beyond this life in another world. He sees this apocalypticism as strongly transcendental and, therefore, anti-secular and pessimistic concerning this life. It holds that the *eschata* (last things) are already laid in the *prota* (first things). Protology is interested in creation and the universe, so too its eschatology is not focussed on Israel only, but on the whole world. However, only certain people, especially chosen by God, are given the power to unlock the mysteries of the last times and the events contained in them. (The word *raz* is employed as a loan word from the Persians and means 'mystery'. It appears in the Dead Sea Scrolls numbers of times). These chosen ones

---

8. See von Rad, *Old Testament Theology*, Volume 1, 89.
9. See von Rad, *Old Testament Theology*, Volume 2, 314ff.

are given dreams and visions to explore and see the *eschata*. This apocalypticism propounds a pre-deterministic theology. The *telos* of the coming aeon has been fixed in the counsel of God prior to this world.

It claims that the 'Son of Man' will not come from Israel but be 'in the clouds of heaven', thereby emphasizing the universality of the work of redemption.

In assessing von Rad's theological contribution to the academic and ecclesiastical scene it can be safely asserted that this theologian broke through the liberal and stagnant approaches to the Old Testament of his time which had its roots in the historical-critical schools of the nineteenth century, as exemplified by Wellhausen and Graf with their source analysis of the Pentateuch and their evolutionistic hypotheses in determining the history of Israel. His experience in a USA prison camp at Bad Kreuznach Germany in the forties had a profound effect on his exegetical work. It was there (in his 'desert' experience) that his famous Genesis commentary, probably the most widely read and influential commentary on Genesis, had its roots. It was there too that not only the historical-critical, form-critical method but also the empirical-critical method of exegesis, which later characterised his commentary writing, was developed. Using the work of Karl Barth, who had broken the liberal influence with his commentary on Romans, and, to a certain extent, that of Rudolph Bultmann of demythologizing fame, he deliberately set out to elevate the status and kerygmatic content of the Old Testament. Galvanised by the Gunkelian form-critical method in hermeneutics he breathed fresh life into the biblical fields of study. Walter Bruegemann assessed his contribution in this way: 'Subsequent work is inescapably an effort at revision and submission not departing too far or too quickly from these governing versions of the discipline'.[10]

It is widely recognised by readers of his works that though his homiletical treatment of the Old Testament texts many pastors were strongly encouraged to preach the Old Testament, to see that the truths contained therein could be present-tensed. His contribution in this respect can be strongly acknowledged when assessing his value to twentieth century thought and influences. Stylistically, they were

---

10.   Gerhard von Rad, *Old Testament Theology*, with a new introduction by Walter Brueggemann (Westminster: John Knox Press, 2001), xv.

always of the highest aesthetic order reflecting his deep knowledge of classical German literature especially the works of Goethe. While his sermons were text-based, with the historical, social and context of the Old Testament passage sermons being presented, he never became slavishly exegetical but moved quickly to its evaluation and application for his listeners. Following his approach to the Old Testament, he preached God's unending and contra-rational love in Christ, who was the Messiah *par excellence* for him. Eschatological hope can be found in his addresses but only in the Messiah of the New Testament. It might be called tangential eschatology.

In all his work both as exegete and as mentor it is patent that he set an example of a humble and self-critical theologian who, even in his latter days, came back to his works and revised them as was the case with the new edition of his Genesis commentary—he is reported on one occasion in respect to revision work to have quoted Proverbs 26, verse11: 'as a dog returns to his vomit, is a fool who returns to his folly'. In this he clearly demonstrates how he could modify and even abandon some of his earlier findings as he did with, for example, the 'historical creed', which he thought he had discovered in Deuteronomy 6. With his academic sensitivity he sought what in German is called the *Wahrheitsanspruch* of the text (the claim made by the truth).

Von Rad was one who tried successfully to overcome the divide between church and academia. He was concerned that every attempt should be made to demonstrate that the Old Testament, with its redemptive *kerygma*, should be owned by and addressed to the community of the church. He was resistant to all attempts to straightjacket the Old Testament with dogmatic formularies and an enemy of what he called *Geschwätz* (empty talk) carried on by some Old Testament scholars who led students into all manner of words rather than 'the word' of promise and hope as found in the Old Testament's messianic promises. It was the word of messianic redemption and hope that von Rad listened to and then enabled others to hear during times of false hopes and false messiahs, in otherwise hopeless circumstances before, during and after the Third Reich.

# Contributors

*Lisa Marie Anderson* is the Postdoctoral Lecturing Fellow in the Department of Germanic Languages and Literature at Duke University in North Carolina. She has also taught as Assistant Professor of German at Lock Haven University in Pennsylvania. She has specialised in the early twentieth century Germanic literature and the intersections between literature and theology. She is currently working on a translation of GWF Hegel's review of JG Hamann.

*Wendy Baker* has been a teacher within all levels of education. She is now retired and sometimes works as a research assistant in Adelaide. Her interests and concerns are in contemporary European philosophy, psycho-analysis and theology.

*Paul Bishop* is Professor of German and Head of German at the University of Glasgow. His publications include studies of Nietzsche, Jung, Goethe, Thomas Mann and Ludwig Klages. His most recent book is *Nietzsche and Antiquity: His Reaction and Response to the Classical Tradition* (Camden House, 2004) which he edited.

*Wes Campbell* is an ordained Minister of the Word of the Uniting Church in Australia (1975). He studied in Germany under Jürgen Moltmann and was awarded the degree of Doctor of Theology by the Melbourne College of Divinity (1996). His work has been in church congregations, social justice policy and advocacy with occasional tertiary teaching of theology. He is an oil painter who has exhibited in solo and group shows. His most recent publications include 'Art, Sin and Salvation' in *Sin and Salvation: Task of Theology Today III*, edited by Duncan Reid and Mark Worthing (Adelaide: ATF Press, 2003) and 'Aesthetics of the Vision: Meditation on "The Apocalypse"', in: *Hope: Challenging the Culture of Despair* edited by Christiaan Mostert, (Adelaide: ATF Press, 2004).

*Max Champion* is a Uniting Church minister at St John's, Mt Waverley in Victoria. His doctoral studies were in Systematic Theology and Christian Ethics and his thesis was on the knowledge of God in Bonhoeffer. He has chaired a number of groups, within and beyond the Church. Committed to the Church's engagement with contemporary society he has conducted many courses and written many articles and reviews on the themes of 'Gospel and Culture' such as post-modernity, human rights, guilt, consensus, bio-ethics and spirituality. He has contributed to books on worship and mission, the Basis of Union (UCA), reconciliation, social justice and multi-culturalism. He is presently the national chairperson of the Reforming Alliance within the UCA.

*Wayne Cristaudo*, recently of University of Adelaide's Centre for European Studies, is an Associate Professor and Co-ordinator of the European Studies Programme at the University of Hong Kong. He has published articles in international journals and chapters in books on Kant, Hegel, Heidegger, Marx, Ernst Cassirer, Eric Voegelin, Rosenstock-Huessy and Rosenzweig as well as thematic pieces on damage and the negative theology of rock music. His most recent publication is *Great Ideas in the Western Literary Canon* (University of America Press, 2003) with Peter Poiana. He has just completed the manuscript of *Power: Love and Evil*.

*Frances Daly* is currently writing a book on the twentieth century German philosopher, Ernst Bloch. Her research interests are in modern and contemporary European philosophy, aesthetics and cultural theory. She is Humanities Fellow in the Department of Philosophy, School of Humanities at the Australian National University.

*Denis Edwards* is a senior lecturer in the School of Theology of Flinders University and at the Catholic Theological College within the Adelaide College of Divinity. Recent publications include *Breathe of Life: A Theology of the Creator Spirit* (Maryknoll, New York: Orbis Books, 2004), *The God of Evolution: A Trinitarian Theology* (New York: Paulist Press, 1999). Edited volumes are *Earth Revealing Earth Healing: Ecology and Christian Theology* (Collegeville: Liturgical Press, 2001) and with Mark Worthing, *Biodiversity and Ecology: An Interdisciplinary Challenge* (Adelaide: ATF Press, 2004).

*Rodney Fopp* is a senior lecturer in Sociology at the University of South Australia. His PhD concerned the contribution of pre World War 11 German émigré intellectuals to the debate in the English-speaking world between relativist and absolutist justifications for democracy. His main research and teaching interests are in the areas of political philosophy and social theory.

*Robert W Jenson* joined the Centre of Theological Inquiry in 1998 as a Senior Scholar for Research after a long career teaching theology at St Olaf College (Minnesota), the Lutheran Theological Seminary (Pennsylvania) and Oxford University. Amongst his many initiatives is the founding of the Centre for Catholic and Evangelical Theology. He is the author of a large number of publications, culminating in the two volumes of his *Systematic Theology*, published by Oxford University Press in 1998 and 1999.

*David Kaufmann* is a graduate of Princeton and Yale Universities and was for six years the Chair of Philosophy and Religious Studies at George Mason University where he is now an Associative Professor of English. He is the author of *The Business of Common Life: Novels and Classical Economics Between Revolution and Reform* (1995) as well as numerous articles on Critical Theory (Adorno, Benjamin, Scholem and Bloch), contemporary literature and modern art.

*Bram Mertens* studied English, German and Philosophy at the Universities of Leuven, Keele and Nottingham. He is the author of several articles on Walter Benjamin, Gershom Scholem and Franz Joseph Molitor and currently teaches German, Dutch and Jewish studies in the German Department at the University of Nottingham.

*Christiaan Mostert* is Professor of Systematic Theology in the Theological Hall of the Uniting Church in Melbourne and teaches in the United Faculty of Theology, Parkville. He has written *God and the Future: Wolfhart Pannenberg's Eschatological Doctrine of God* (2002) and edited *Hope: Challenging the Culture of Despair* (2004) and, with Peter Matheson, *Fresh Words and Deeds: The McCaughey Papers* (2004).

*Erich Renner (Rev Dr JTE)* is a pastor of the Lutheran Church of Australia and emeritus lecturer at Luther Seminary (Adelaide, Australia) where he has taught for three decades after completing his doctoral studies in Heidelberg, Germany, studying under von Rad. He has published many articles and has written five commentaries on the Old Testament.

*Cecil Schmalkuche* is a parish pastor of the Lutheran Church of Australia, with an interest in Hebrew and the work of Martin Buber. He is currently serving in Footscray, Melbourne.

*Geoff Thompson* is Director of Studies in Systematic Theology at Trinity Theological College, a member school of the Brisbane School of Theology, and a Visiting Fellow of the School of Theology at Griffith University. He co-edited, with Christiaan Mostart, *Karl Barth: A Future for Postmodern Theology?* (2000).

*Phillip Tolliday* lectures in Systematic Theology at the Adelaide College of Divinity and the Flinders School of Theology where he is Associate Head. His interests include pneumatology, eschatology, holocaust studies and the ethical philosophy of Emmanuel Levinas. He is a priest in the Anglican diocese of Adelaide.

*Martin Travers* is Associate Professor in Literary Studies at Griffith University. Recent publications include *From Romanticism to Post-modernism: An Introduction to Modern European Literature* (London: Macmillan, 1998) and *Critics of Modernity: The Literature of Conservative Revolution in Germany* (New York: Peter Lang, 2001). He has completed the manuscript for *The Poetry of Gottfried Benn: Text and Selfhood.*

*Luke Vieceli* is a postgraduate student at the University of Adelaide. He is currently working on a dissertation contrasting George Bataille and Gilles Deleuze's conceptions of Franz Kafka's works.

*Koral Ward* is completing her PhD at Murdoch on the development of the concept of *Augenblick*, or the decisive moment, in nineteenth and twentieth century philosophy. She has written poems and an essay on 'the moment' for two photographic books. She has almost twenty years experience in writing, recording and performing in a partnership called 'Poets of the Machine'.

*Engelhard Weigl* studied German Literature and Philosophy in Hamburg and Bochum, completing his PhD on the work of Jean Paul. He has worked at the Max Planck Institute for Human Development in Berlin and taught at the University of Japan. He is currently a Lecturer in German at Adelaide University. His most recent publication is *Schauplätze der deutschen Aufklärung. Ein Städterundgang. Reinbeck bei Hamburg* (1997).

# Index

323